THE SOUTHWARK
FIRE COURT

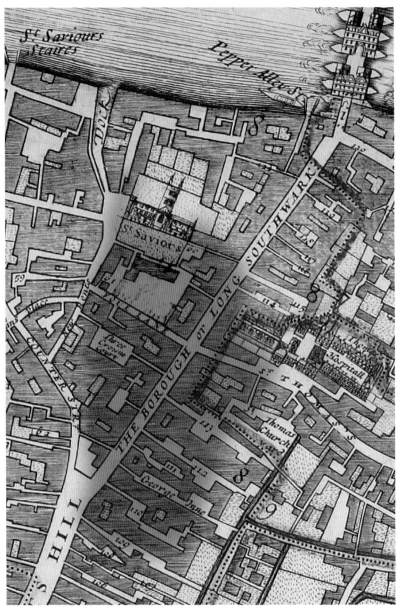

William Morgan, *London &c. Actually Survey'd*, 1682, detail marked to show the approximate extent of the fire in 1676 and of buildings destroyed in order to prevent its spread. The key to the map identifies the following sites mentioned in the Decrees: 60, Chain Gate; 61, Angel Yard; 109, Queen's Head Inn; 110, Talbot Inn; 111, Three Crown Court; 112, White Hart Inn; 113, King's Head Inn. The dotted line indicates parish boundaries: to west, St Saviour's, to east, St Olave's and St Thomas's.

THE SOUTHWARK
FIRE COURT

by

Jay Tidmarsh

Judge James J. Clynes, Jr., Professor of Law
Notre Dame Law School

LONDON TOPOGRAPHICAL SOCIETY
Publication No. 188
2024

For Wes Ward

Edited by Sheila O'Connell
©
LONDON TOPOGRAPHICAL SOCIETY
312 Russell Court
Woburn Place
London WC1H 0NG

2024

ISBN
978-0-902087-75-0

PRODUCED IN GREAT BRITAIN BY
SCORPION CREATIVE

CONTENTS

ACKNOWLEDGEMENTS

I could never have written this book without the love and support of Jan Pilarski, who has indulged my fascination with fire courts by holding everything down at home during my research trips to England. I am also grateful to my deans, Nell Newton and Marcus Cole, as well as associate dean Randy Kozel, who have provided the necessary financial and administrative support for my research.

I also acknowledge the kindness of Sheila O'Connell and the patience of the London Topographical Society in waiting for a manuscript that we had begun discussing well before anyone had heard of Covid-19. Sheila's editorial suggestions for the manuscript were invaluable, as were her dogged detective skills in tracking down some of the original images reproduced in this book.

Ian Doolittle, whose work on the court established after the Great Fire of London inspires me, generously read the manuscript and provided important ideas that shaped the final draft.

Andrew Wareham's guidance on the hearth-tax records was both gracious and deeply enlightening.

Two research assistants, Stephen Cord and Raymond Cordova, helped me to organize and analyse the records of the Southwark fire court. Another assistant, Chase Opperman, read the manuscript and provided suggestions. I am grateful to each of them.

Linda Fisher proved to be a wonderful and patient copy editor. Steve Hartley's design of the book was exceptional.

Whether on the subject of fire courts or other matters, my conversations with His Honour Donald Cryan, former Treasurer and Master of the Silver of the Inner Temple and now President of the Selden Society, always enlighten and enliven me.

Finally, I thank the following archivists and staff for answering questions and finding resources: Dr Mari Takayanagi and Annie Pinder at the Parliamentary Archives; Chris Scales at the Southwark Archives; Guy Baker at the London Metropolitan Archives; Phil Oakman at the Northamptonshire Archives and Heritage Service; Melanie Strong at the Guildhall Library; Fiona Davis, Samuel Sales and Vanessa Wright at the Bodleian Libraries; Laurence Spring at the Surrey History Centre;

and the staffs at the National Archives and the British Library. At each of these archives, generations of records keepers and staff, whose names I do not know, have curated and preserved documents through the centuries. Without their considerable efforts, historical projects such as this one would be impossible. Thank you.

ABBREVIATIONS

CSPD   *Calendar of State Papers, Domestic Series — Charles II, 1676–77*, ed. by F. H. Blackburne Daniell (London, 1909)

HC Jour.   *Journal of the House of Commons* (available at British History Online)

HL Jour.   *Journal of the House of Lords* (available at British History Online)

LMA   London Metropolitan Archives

Rep.   *The Repertories of the Court of Aldermen* (LMA COL/CA/01/01)

TNA   The National Archives

GLOSSARY

The following glossary defines terms, many of them legal, used in the decrees of the Southwark fire court. The definitions provide the meaning of the words as used in the seventeenth century, not their modern meaning.

Action at Law — A lawsuit commenced in one of the three royal courts: King's Bench, Common Pleas or Court of the Exchequer.

Ancient Rent — A rent that had been established for a property before the present lease (or sublease) was made; often the ancient rent was established in a prior lease of a property that was now being subleased for a portion of the original lease term.

Appear (or Appearance) — To be present in court; with respect to lawyers, to be present in court to represent a client.

Bond — A formal written agreement to pay a sum of money if a person fails to perform an obligation or duty.

Chancery — The office of the Chancellor, in which suits in equity (but not actions at law) were commenced; suits in equity provided, in some instances, remedies unavailable in actions at law and also enforced obligations (like trusts) that the common-law judges did not enforce.

Counterpart — A copy of a lease. After the tenant had met all of the lease's obligations, the lessor surrendered the counterpart to the tenant for cancellation: a lessor could not commence an action or suit on a cancelled lease.

Covenant — A formal agreement or promise, enforceable at law; typically, covenants were made under seal, which distinguished them from ordinary contractual promises.

Coverture — The legal status of a married woman, who was regarded as being under the authority and protection of her husband. Typically, the status rendered married women unable to enter contracts or own property in their own right.

Demise — To transfer an interest in property, typically by lease (but also potentially through a will). See also Devise.

Determination (or Determinable) — The termination or cessation of an interest in property.

Devise — To make a gift of an interest in real property through a will. See also Demise.

Dowager — A widow who held property, typically for her lifetime, by virtue of her marriage. The word was used mostly to describe widows with aristocratic titles.

Dower — The portion of a deceased husband's estate held by a dowager. See Dowager.

Estate — An interest in property. See Interest.

Fee Simple — The absolute and permanent ownership of an interest in land, which allows the owner to dispose of the land without limitation; a freehold. See also Seised (in Fee).

Fee Tail (Male) — An interest in property under which the owner of the interest was required to pass that interest to one or more children, who must then do likewise with their own children. Typically, in the seventeenth century the interest would be 'fee tail male', which passed the property to the eldest son (and to that son's eldest son, and so on).

Feme Covert — A married woman whose legal existence was merged with that of her husband under the concept of coverture (see Coverture).

Fine — A sum of money, paid by a tenant to a lessor at the outset of the lease, that typically reduced the annual rent for the property. See also Rack Rent.

Ground Rent — The rent that is paid for a piece of land that has no buildings on it; the rental value of the land itself.

Indefeasible — Not capable of being lost; granted without any conditions on ownership.

Indenture — A legal contract, often used for apprenticeships and other labour but also used for leases and real-estate transactions. An indenture was written in duplicate and cut into two pieces along a jagged line, with each party retaining one half. The pieces could then be fit back together to assure authenticity. See also Counterpart.

Infancy (or Infant) — A state of legal disability until the age of twenty-one; the status that made underage persons unable to enter contracts or own property in their own rights.

Inheritance — In the context of the decrees, the legal interest in a property at the conclusion of another person's interest in the property. Typically, the lessor 'inherited' the property from the tenant when the lease expired.

Interest — The rights of a person with respect to ownership, possession and use of property. Different persons might hold different interests in the same property: for instance, a tenant might hold the interest of immediate possession, while a widow lessor might hold, during her lifetime, the interest of possession at the end of the lease, and the lessor's eldest son might hold the interest of possession after his mother died (thus ending her life estate) and the lease expired (thus ending the tenant's interest in the possession).

Life Estate (or Life Interest) — An interest in property that ended when the holder of the interest died; often, widows held a life estate in their deceased husband's property, with the property interest then falling to one or more children on the widow's death.

Moiety — One of two parts into which something is divided; typically in law, two equal parts.

Penthouse — A structure with a sloping roof that extended from the side of a building.

Peppercorn — Quite literally, a peppercorn. The law required that, in order for a contract to be enforceable, each party provide something of value to the other. There was no requirement that the exchange be of equal value. Hence, a promise to pay a peppercorn (something of virtually no value) in return for something valuable made the parties' agreement mutually enforceable.

Petition — The formal complaint of a plaintiff, filed with a court, that requests relief from the court.

Privity — A relationship between two persons that the law recognizes as relevant in establishing obligations.

Purpresture — An encroachment on public or common land.

Rack Rent —Assuming no fine, the rental value of a property on the open market. See also Fine.

Reversion (or Reversionary Interest) — A future interest in property at the conclusion of another person's interest. More than one person might hold reversionary interests. In the example given under Interest, the widow lessor and eldest son both held reversionary interests in the leased premises. See also Inheritance.

Seised (or Seised in Fee) — To have title to property either through outright ownership or through a very long-term leasehold interest (e.g., one thousand years).

Serve (or Service) — To present a summons to a defendant as a means of compelling that person's attendance in court.

Situs — The place where property is deemed to be situated for purposes of determining legal jurisdiction.

Summons — A formal document issued by a court commanding a defendant to provide the court with an answer to a plaintiff's complaint or petition.

Toft — The site of a dwelling and outbuildings; the entire holding of land.

Trust — A right, enforceable through a suit in equity, of one person (the beneficiary) to the beneficial enjoyment or use of property to which another person (the trustee) owns legal title.

Use — The right to use or profit from property owned by another; typically, a trust. Although technically abolished by the Statute of Uses in 1536, uses in effect continued when equity developed the law of trusts. See Trust.

Vested — Having an absolute right of possession or title to property.

INTRODUCTION

By this you may see the people of this Nation is very Unstable.[1]

Not to be outdone by its neighbour across the Thames, Southwark has had not one, but two 'great fires'. The Great Fire of Southwark in 1212 may have been one of the world's most devastating urban fires, as hundreds (possibly thousands) of people who were trapped on London Bridge burned or drowned as the fire blazed toward the middle from both ends.[2]

This book concerns the second Great Fire. On 26 May 1676, a fire broke out in an oil shop on St Margaret's Hill. Before it died out twenty hours later, the fire had destroyed much of the High Street, as well as hundreds of shops, houses and tenements west of the High Street and north toward the river. Though badly damaged, St Saviour's Church (Fig. 1; now Southwark Cathedral) avoided the fate of St Paul's Cathedral, which had crumbled in the Great Fire of London ten years earlier. The Borough compter (located on St Margaret's Hill), the meal market (located in the High Street) and St Saviour's free grammar school (located in St Saviour's churchyard) were not so lucky.

After the fire, Parliament erected a special court designed to spur the swift rebuilding of Southwark. Parliament had first established such a 'fire court' after the Great Fire of London in 1666.[3] It again created a

1 Letter, Holden to Williamson, TNA, SP 29/382/243 (26 June 1676).

2 The usually cited number — 3,000 dead — is likely an exaggeration. The first written account of the fire appeared in 1274. The figure of 3,000 fatalities is generally attributed to John Stow, who wrote centuries later. See John Stow, *A Survay of London* (London, 1598), pp. 21–22 (available on EEBO and many later editions); Stephen Inwood, *A History of London* (London, 1998), p. 121. Even the year of the fire is in doubt. See Christopher N. L. Brooke, *London 800–1216* (Berkeley, 1975), p. 53 (citing one medieval source, possibly in error, that put the fire in 1211); William Rendle, *Old Southwark and Its People* (Southwark, 1878), p. 17 (giving the year as 1213). Manning and Bray, who also gave the year as 1213, may have been Rendle's source. Owen Manning and William Bray, *The History and Antiquities of the County of Surrey*, III (London, 1814), p. 548.

3 The initial act for the London fire court was 18 and 19 Car. II, c. 7 (1667), reprinted in *The Statutes of the Realm printed by Command of His Majesty King George the Third in Pursuance of an Address of the House of Commons of Great Britain*, V, p. 601. Although originally intending the court to go out of existence after two years, ibid., § 5, Parliament extended the court's life and expanded its jurisdiction on three

Fig. 1.   Wenceslaus Hollar, *St Saviour's Church, Southwark*, 1661, from William Dugdale's *Monasticon Anglicanum*. Although the church had been re-named 'St Saviour' at the Reformation, its earlier name 'St Mary Overie' was often used. The coat-of-arms of Ralph Sheldon on the right indicates that he sponsored the illustration.

© Trustees of the British Museum, G,1.304

fire court to respond to a devastating fire in Northampton in 1675.[4] The Southwark court, held at the Guildhall, was the third fire court erected in a decade.[5] It was also an end to the first generation of fire courts. Despite a number of urban fires in the interim,[6] Parliament would not establish another fire court for nearly two decades.[7]

subsequent occasions. 22 Car. 2, c. 11 (1670), reprinted in *Statutes of the Realm*, v, p. 665; 22 and 23 Car. 2, c. 14 (1671), reprinted in *Statutes of the Realm*, v, p. 724; 25 Car. 2, c. 10 (1673), reprinted in *Statutes of the Realm*, v, p. 795

4   27 Car. II (1675), reprinted in *Statutes of the Realm*, v, p. 798. The Northampton statute has no chapter number because it was the only act passed before Charles II prorogued that session of Parliament.

5   29 Car. II, c. 4 (1677), reprinted in *Statutes of the Realm*, v, p. 842.

6   For instance, a 1677 fire in Wem destroyed the principal church, the market house and 140 dwellings, and a 1689 fire in Southwark's St George's parish destroyed or damaged forty-one houses. For the charitable Brief describing the Wem fire, see Shropshire Archives 484/240; for the sufferers in Southwark and their itemized damages, see LMA CLA/040/02/007.

7   This court concerned a fire in Warwick. See 6 and 7 Wm & Mary c. 1 (1694).

At Parliament's command, the decrees of the fire courts were bound into books and lodged with local officials or in local records offices. These decrees have proven useful for numerous purposes, including genealogy, documenting property ownership and development,[8] determining the prevalence of legal forms for holding property,[9] understanding the ways in which gender and gender-laden legal rules (such as fee tail, dower and feme covert) interacted,[10] and providing detailed insights into the economic, social and political histories of localities touched by fire. By far, the greatest use has been made of the decrees of the court for the Great Fire of London — although work is ongoing, as the decrees of the London court have yet to be fully calendared and analysed.[11] The records of the Southwark fire court have seen far less use. Amateur social historians and professional political historians have mined the details of a decree or two.[12] Until now, however, the Southwark decrees have never been calendared or systematically analysed. My hope is that the ensuing calendar will aid further research.

Although no introduction can surface all salient features of interest, I will highlight a few ways in which the fire and the decrees shed light on social, economic, political and legal conditions in seventeenth-century London and England. I begin with the fire itself.

Parliament also created courts to respond to three fires in the eighteenth century and one in the early nineteenth century. 5 Geo II, c. 14 (1731) (Tiverton); 5 Geo II, c. 16 (1731) (Blandford Forum); 3 Geo III c. 54 (1762) (Wareham); 48 Geo III, c. 89 (1808) (Chudleigh).

8 See Ian Doolittle, 'Who Owned London in 1667?', in *London Topographical Record*, XXXII (2021), pp. 235–67.

9 See Ian Doolittle, 'Property Law and Practice in Seventeenth-Century London', *Urban History*, XCII (2015), pp. 208–12.

10 Ibid., pp. 212–16.

11 The London fire court produced nine volumes of engrossed records. Philip Jones calendared the first four volumes more than fifty years ago. Philip E. Jones, *The Fire Court*, I (London, 1966); Philip E. Jones, *The Fire Court*, II (London, 1970). Relying both on Jones's draft and on his own research, Ian Doolittle has calendared the next two volumes. Ian Doolittle and the late Philip Jones, *The Fire Court*, III (London, 2020).

12 Principal in the camp of amateurs is William Rendle, a physician and Southwark enthusiast. See Rendle, *Old Southwark*; William Rendle and Philip Norman, *The Inns of Old Southwark and Their Associations* (London, 1888). David Johnson's masterful effort to lay bare the centuries-long legal and political entanglements of Southwark and London is an example of a professional historian's use of the decrees, although Johnson focused mostly on one decree that exposed tensions between the City and the bailiff of Southwark. David J. Johnson, *Southwark and the City* (London, 1969),

I. THE SOUTHWARK FIRE OF 1676

Nearly all that we reliably know about the Southwark fire comes from six contemporary sources: Robert Hooke's diary,[13] a short blurb in the *London Gazette*,[14] a royal Brief that solicited charitable contributions for sufferers from the fire (Fig. 2),[15] two pamphlets (the *Account*[16] and the *Narrative*[17]; Fig. 3) attributable to Roger L'Estrange, journalist and royal censor,[18] and two eyewitness accounts that I will come to

p. 197 (discussing *Eyre v. Mayor of London* (Decree 32)).

13 *The Diary of Robert Hooke*, ed. by Henry W. Robinson and Walter Adams (London, 1935), p. 234 (entry for 26 May 1676). The entirety of the entry concerning the Southwark fire read:
Friday, May 26th.— […] With Grace [his niece] at Column [the Monument] to see the great fire in Southrick which burned 8 or 900 houses. It stayd about 8 *p.p.* [*post prandium*, i.e., after dinner] At St Mary Overy church and St Thomas's Hospitall.
Because he was involved in the rebuilding of Southwark and served as a witness in two cases (Decrees 44 and 46), Hooke's diary is also a helpful source for later events. See notes 184–86, 238, 272, 275, 311 and accompanying text.

14 *London Gazette* No. 1098, p. 2 (25–29 May 1676). The full story ran as follows:
London, May 27. Yesterday about four in the morning broke out a most lamentable Fire, in the Burrough of *Southwark*, and continued with much violence all that day, and part of the night following, notwithstanding all the care and endeavors that were used by his Grace the Duke of *Monmouth*, the Earl of *Craven*, and the Lord Mayor to quench the same, as well as by blowing up of houses as otherways. His Majesty accompanied with his Royal Highness, in a tender sense of this sad calamity, being pleased himself to go done [*sic*] to the Bridge foot in his Barge, to give such orders as his Majesty found fit for putting a stop to it, which through the mercy of God was finally effected, after that about 600 houses had been burnt and blown up.

15 *Brief for the Southwark Fire*, University of Oxford, Bodleian Library, Gough Maps, 19, fol. 64 (14 August 1676). The Brief acknowledged as the source of its information several petitions that Charles had received from Southwark residents and the Justices of the Peace for Surrey. Those documents do not appear to have survived.

16 Roger L'Estrange, *A faithful account of the late dreadful fire in Southwark* (29 May 1676), available at https://ota.bodleian.ox.ac.uk/repository/ (hereafter L'Estrange, *Account*). The *Account*, licensed by L'Estrange, was five pages in length. Its tone has an immediacy suggesting that L'Estrange arrived on the scene while the fire was yet fiercely burning, but that sense could be an artifice of writing.

17 Roger L'Estrange, *A True Narrative of the Great and Terrible Fire in Southwark on Fryday the 26th of May, 1676*, British Library, 10803.aa.16 (10) (undated) (hereafter L'Estrange, *Narrative*). The *Narrative*, published with L'Estrange's permission, ran for eight pages. The undated *Narrative* provides, for the most part, a more detailed account of the fire and is also better constructed — suggesting that it was written later than the *Account*. The *Account* may have been rushed to press to take advantage of the immediate clamour for news about the Southwark fire.

18 L'Estrange was a journalist, as well as a censor and polemicist for the Stuarts. (See, for instance his *Account of the Growth of Knavery Under the Pretended Fears of Arbitrary Government and Popery*, a Tory broadside against Andrew Marvell's

shortly.[19] A seventh source — two sermons that Richard Martin preached on the first two weekends after the fire — contains a few bits of information, although they are mostly confirmatory of other sources.[20] Works that proved valuable in understanding the Great Fire of London provide no insight on the Southwark fire.[21]

In describing why the Southwark fire exploded so ferociously, L'Estrange's *Account* recited the exact conditions that had made the Great Fire of London destructive: tightly packed buildings, dried timber, a fresh southerly wind and meddling gawkers who frustrated efforts to combat the fire.[22]

TIME AND DURATION

The sources contain inconsequential disagreements about the time and duration of the fire. L'Estrange's *Account* stated that the fire began at three in the morning, the *Gazette* said four and L'Estrange's *Narrative* split the difference, relating that the fire broke out 'between three and four of the clock'.[23] Beginning near St Margaret's Hill, the fire spread rapidly up the High Street. By noon, the northern edge had reached St Thomas's Hospital (Fig. 4), the Borough's meal market and St Saviour's.[24]

The *Gazette* did not mention when the fire was brought under control. From the distance and elevation of the Monument, Hooke thought that the fire had died down at eight o'clock in the evening. Martin's sermon stated that the fire lasted eighteen hours,[25] as did the charitable

Whiggish tract discussed in note 74.) He was a controversial figure at the time, often the subject of booksellers' complaints due to his alleged heavy-handedness, favouritism toward the rich and openness to bribery. See *CSPD*, XVIII, pp. 143 (3 June 1677), 492–93 (3 January 1678). He earned much of his income by selling his own pamphlets, so the Southwark fire was for him a monetary opportunity. While we must therefore treat his account of the fire carefully, his descriptions appear credible. See pp. 39–40.

19 Notes 96–97 and accompanying text.

20 Sermons of Richard Martin Preached at St Michael's Wood Street and St Saviour, 1675–89, University of Oxford, Bodleian Library, MS Eng. Th. E. 168, pp. 11ᵛ–29ᵛ.

21 Samuel Pepys's diary stopped in 1669, and John Evelyn's diary, while continuing until 1706, made no mention of the Southwark fire — and in fact contained few entries for 1676 and 1677. *The Diary of John Evelyn, Esq.*, ed. by William Bray (London, 1818), pp. 484–97.

22 L'Estrange, *Account*, pp. 2–3. L'Estrange's *Narrative* gave a slightly different characterization to the wind, which became 'indifferent calm' before noon and shifted slightly afterwards. The *Narrative* credited the shift in the wind with saving St Thomas's Hospital from ruin. L'Estrange, *Narrative*, p. 6.

23 L'Estrange, *Narrative*, p. 3.

24 L'Estrange, *Account*, p. 3.

25 *Sermons*, p. 16ᵛ.

Fig. 2.   *Brief for the Southwark Fire issued by Charles II, 1676.*
The Bodleian Libraries, University of Oxford, Gough Maps, 19, fol. 64

Parifhes, Chappelries, Villages, Hamlets, and all other places whatsoever, ... the faid Free-School
for and towards the fupport and relief of the faid poor Sufferers, and reparation of the faid Parifh Church, and Re-building of the faid Free-School, fhall come or repair to any your Churches,
and command you, and every of you, that at fuch time and times, as the Deputy and Deputies, and the Bearer and Bearers hereof, fhall come or repair to any your Churches,
Chappels, Congregations, or other places, to afk and receive the Alms and charitable Benevolence of Our faid loving Subjects, quietly to permit and fuffer them fo to do,
without any manner your letts or contradictions, but to be aiding and affifting to them therein: And you the faid Parfons, Vicars, and Curates, upon fome Lords-day,
within a Month or fix Weeks at the fartheft after that thefe Our Letters Patents fhall be produced, and the true Copies thereof tendred unto you, or the faid Church-wardens
or Chappel wardens respectively, and before the expiration of thefe Prefents, deliberately and affectionately to publifh and declare the tenor of thefe Our Letters Patents,
unto Our faid loving Subjects, and earneftly to exhort, perfwade, and ftir them up, to extend their liberal Contributions in this behalf: And you the faid Church-wardens,
Chappel-wardens, Collectors for the Poor, and their Overfeers, to Collect the Alms of Our faid loving Subjects: And for the better and more effectual collecting thereof,
you the faid Church-wardens, Chappel-wardens, Collector for the Poor and their Overfeers, aflifted by the respective Minifters within the Cities of *London* and *Weftminfter*, within our
and the Weekly Bills of Mortality, and in all other Cities, Corporations, Market-Towns, Parifhes, Villages, Hamlets, and all other places whatfoever, within our
Kingdom of *England*, Dominion of *Wales*, and Town of *Berwick upon Tweed*, are to go from houfe to houfe upon the Week-days next following after the publication of
thefe Prefents, to collect the Alms of Our faid loving Subjects, and the fum and fums of money fo respectively collected by virtue of thefe Prefents, to endorfe upon thefe
Our Letters Patents, or the faid Copies, in words at length and not in figures, together alfo with the names of the Counties, Cities, Towns, Parifhes, and Chappelries
respectively, wherein and the time when fuch fums are gathered; as alfo in another Writing to be figned as aforefaid, to exprefs the feveral Names and Qualities of the
respective Givers, Donors, and Benefactors, within the faid feveral Cities, Univerfities, Towns, Parifhes, Chappelries, and Priviledged places, and the fums by them
respectively given: And you the faid Church-wardens, Chappel-wardens, Collectors, and Overfeers for the Poor, within Our faid Cities of *London* and *Weftminfter*, and
and *Weftminfter*, and the Weekly Bills of Mortality, are hereby required to deliver fuch Briefs fo endorfed, and fuch Catalogue of Benefactors fo had and taken, within Our faid Cities of *London*
the Weekly Bills of Mortality, together with the Money which fhall be collected by virtue hereof, unto Our Trufty and Well-beloved Sir *Jofeph Sheldon*,
Knight, Lord Mayor of the City of *London*, and the Lord Mayor of *London* for the time being, Sir *Thomas Gould*, and Sir *John Shorter*, Knights, Sheriffs of Our faid City,
and the Sheriffs of Our faid City for the time being, or any two or more of them, whom We do hereby appoint to be Receivers of all fuch Moneys, as fhall be fo collected
by virtue hereof, as aforefaid, in truft, to be difpofed as is herein after exprefled, and whole Acquittance or Acquittances fhall be your fufficient difcharge for fo doing:
And you the faid Church-wardens, Chappel-wardens, Collectors for the Poor, and their Overfeers, in all other Our Cities, Towns, Villages, Hamlets, and places
whatfoever, within Our Kingdom of *England*, Dominion of *Wales*, and Town of *Berwick upon Tweed*, not herein before otherwife appointed, are hereby required to deliver
fuch Briefs fo endorfed, and fuch fums of Money, with all fuch Copies and Writings as fhall be respectively by you made, gathered, and collected to the respective Mayors,
High Constables, or other Head Officers, in whofe Division you are, which faid Mayor, High Conftable, or other Head Officer, unto whom the fame fhall be delivered,
as aforefaid, are hereby required fafely to pay and deliver the fame Moneys and Papers unto the Bearer and Bearers hereof, (authorifed as herein is appointed) whenfoever you
and Town of *Berwick upon Tweed*, are hereby required upon receipt of the faid Monies, forthwith to pay the fame, and deliver all the faid Copies and
fhall be by them or any of them thereunto required, whole receiving thereof, together with their or any of their Acquittance or Acquittances fhall be your fufficient difcharge:
Which faid Bearer and Bearers hereof, are hereby willed and required, upon receipt of the faid Monies, forthwith to pay the fame, and deliver all the faid Copies and
Writings unto Our Trufty and Well-beloved *John Appleby*, Efquire, *James Reading*, *Richard How*, *John Freeman*, *Peter Rich*, *William Caftle*, Efquires, Juftices of Peace for Our faid
County, and *Jofeph Day*, Gentleman, or any two or more of them, whom We do hereby appoint Receivers of fuch Moneys as fhall be fo collected by the faid Bearers hereof,
which faid receivers for *London* and *Weftminfter*, and the Weekly Bills of Mortality, as alfo the receivers for all other places, within Our Kingdom of *England*, Dominion of *Wales*,
and Town of *Berwick upon Tweed*, are hereby required upon receipt of the faid Monies forthwith to pay the fame, and deliver all the faid Copies and Writings unto Our Trufty
and Well-beloved Coufin and Councellor *William Earl of Craven*; Our right Trufty and Well-beloved *George* Lord *Barkley*; and to Our Trufty and Well-beloved Sir *Adam*
Browne, Baronet; Sir *Thomas Bloodworth*, Knight; Sir *Edmund Bowyer*, Knight; whom together with the faid Lord Mayor and Sheriffs of *London*, and alfo the faid *James Reading*,
Richard How, *John Freeman*, *Peter Rich*, *William Caftle*, *John Appleby*, and *Jofeph Day*, Receivers as aforefaid, or any three or more of them, We do hereby appoint to be Treafurers
and Difpofers of the faid Moneys fo Collected by virtue hereof, of which number We will that you the faid *James Reading*, *Richard How*, *John Freeman*, and *Jofeph Day*, fhall
always be one: And that the faid Treafurers and Difpofers, or any three or more of them, as aforefaid, fhall (taking to their Affiftance, the Minifters and Church-wardens of the
aforefaid Parifhes) diftribute all the faid Moneys, which fhall be fo Collected by virtue hereof, amongft the faid poor Sufferers, and towards the repair of the faid Church, and
Re-building of the faid Free-School, and School-houfe, as to them fhall feem juft and equal. **And laftly**, Our Will and Pleafure is, that no perfon or perfons whatfoever, fhall
collect or receive the faid Moneys, of or from the faid Mayor, High Conftable, or other Head Officers, or any of them, but fuch only, as fhall be authorifed and appointed fo to do,
by Deputation in Writing, under the Hands and Seals of the faid Truftees and Difpofers, or any three or more of them, as aforefaid: Any Law, Statute, Ordinance, or Provifion,
heretofore made to the contrary notwithftanding. **In witnefs** whereof, We have caufed thefe Our Letters to be made Patents, and to continue from the date hereof, until the
Feaft of St. *Michael* the *Archangel*, which fhall be in the Year of Our Lord God One Thoufand Six Hundred Seventy and Seven, and no Longer. **Witnefs** Our felf at *Weftminfter*,
the Fourteenth day of *Auguft*, in the Eight and Twentieth Year of Our Reign.

Smith.

GOD SAVE THE KING.

LONDON, Printed by *WILLIAM GODBID*, Dwelling in *Little-Britain*, 1676.

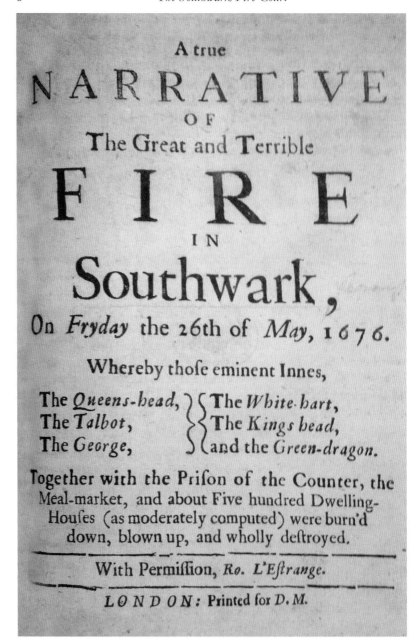

A true

NARRATIVE

OF

The Great and Terrible

FIRE

IN

Southwark,

On *Fryday* the 26th of *May*, 1676.

Whereby thofe eminent Innes,

The *Queens-head,* } { The *White-hart,*
The *Talbot,*   }   { The *Kings head,*
The *George,*   }   { and the *Green-dragon.*

Together with the Prifon of the Counter, the Meal-market, and about Five hundred Dwelling-Houfes (as moderately computed) were burn'd down, blown up, and wholly deftroyed.

With Permiffion, *Ro. L'Eftrange.*

LONDON: Printed for *D. M.*

Fig. 3.   Roger L'Estrange, *A true Narrative of The Great and Terrible Fire in Southwark*, 1676, title page.

Fig. 4.   William Henry Toms, *St Thomas's Hospital, Southwark*, 1720, from John Strype's edition of Stow's *Survey of London*. The illustration shows the Hospital as it would have appeared in the late seventeenth century before alterations to the courtyard.

Brief.[26] L'Estrange's *Account* noted that the fire had been brought into a narrower compass by four or five in the afternoon, but it was not mastered until eleven o'clock that night.[27] His *Narrative* provided a possible explanation for the slight discrepancies in the sources: the fire in fact had died had down around 'seven or eight at night', but it 'strangely' reignited near St Saviour's at ten o'clock. Blowing up the house on fire contained the threat, and the fire was finally conquered.[28]

FIREFIGHTING RESPONSE

L'Estrange's pamphlets suggest that the Great Fire of London had taught valuable lessons. Fire engines procured after the London fire were swiftly brought into Southwark, where they worked to arrest the progress of the fire along the east side of the High Street at St Thomas's Hospital.[29] Although L'Estrange complained that onlookers got in the way and slowed the response, the fire engineers did not hesitate during the early hours of the fire to blow up buildings to create fire breaks that limited the fire's spread.[30] The initial hesitation to do the same during the London fire had been a major factor in the fire's spread, and the eventual use of sailors and gunpowder to demolish houses was a principal factor in its abatement.[31]

Gunpowder, more than fire engines, may have prevented the utter ruin of Southwark. To fight the fire, the Mint in Southwark supplied sixteen barrels of gunpowder.[32] The decrees of the Southwark fire

26 *Brief,* line 12.

27 L'Estrange, *Account*, p. 3.

28 L'Estrange, *Narrative*, p. 8.

29 L'Estrange's *Account* stated that 'Engines' had been brought with 'imaginable expedition' to fight the fire, although 'the Engines [were] overpowered and able to do but little good'. L'Estrange, *Account*, p. 2. His *Narrative* mentioned 'Several Engines […] brought with all imaginable speed'. L'Estrange, *Narrative*, p. 5. A bill of expenses, dated 29 May 1676, requested reimbursement of £1 that had been paid for labourers 'to helpe bring home the two great Engines'; it also requested 7s. 6d. for money paid to take other engines back to Greenyard. LMA CLA/040/02/005. See Figure 5.

30 L'Estrange, *Account*, at p. 2; L'Estrange, *Narrative*, p. 3. The *Narrative* stated that gunpowder was employed to blow up the Compter, thus saving houses west of Compter Lane, as well as to blow up houses around St Saviour's, thus saving the church from utter destruction. L'Estrange, *Narrative*, pp. 6–7.

31 See *The Diary of Samuel Pepys*, VII, ed. by Robert Latham and William Matthews (Berkeley, 1974) (entry for 4 September 1666); Walter George Bell, *The Great Fire of London in 1666* (London, 1920), pp. 115–16.

32 TNA, SP 29/382/183. According to a petition from the Justices of the Peace for Southwark, Charles had ordered gunpowder to be supplied to stop the fire, but the barrels were late in coming. The firefighters instead obtained sixteen barrels

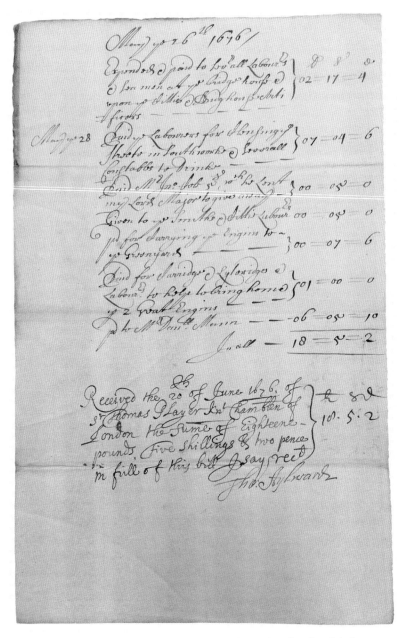

Fig. 5.   Receipted bill to the Chamberlain of London for fire-fighting expenses totalling £18 5s. 2d.

court made occasional reference to properties blown up or defaced by explosion,[33] and a report in the court records of St Thomas's Hospital suggested that numerous houses south of the hospital were blown up. In particular, Thomas Hollier's High Street messuage, located at the gate of the hospital, was blown up before the fire reached it. The hospital's Jonah's Ward lay under Hollier's back yard, and its timber construction was seen as the weak link where the fire could have penetrated into the hospital itself.[34] Had the fire spread into St Thomas's Hospital, the entire east side of the High Street up to London Bridge might also have burned.[35]

The *London Gazette* noted that firefighting efforts were led by the Duke of Monmouth[36] and the Earl of Craven, as well as by the Lord Mayor of London (John Sheldon), whose response might be favourably contrasted with the infamous ineffectiveness of Thomas Bludworth, Lord Mayor during the Great Fire of London. In addition, Charles II

from the Mint in Southwark. The petition requested that Charles replenish the Mint with a like quantity of powder, as Josias Deweye of the Mint was demanding payment. TNA, SP 29/382/309 (undated). The Minutes of the Committee on Trade show that the petition was submitted on 29 June 1676. *Minutes of Committee of Trade*, TNA, SP 29/382/307 (29 June 1676).

33 See *Waggorne v. Beacon* (Decree 3); *Marshall v. Overman* (Decree 38); *Young v. Bradway* (Decree 42); *Rous v. Kellett* (Decree 43).

34 In return for payment of a fine of £20 and an agreement to build a new brick messuage of the third rate, the Governors of St Thomas's Hospital extended Hollier's existing lease by roughly twenty-seven years, for a total term of forty-one years. Included in the new lease was the portion of Jonah's Ward under Hollier's yard. The lease required Hollier to build a brick party wall between his property and the hospital to prevent the spread of future fires. Atypically for the Governors when they negotiated new leases for their tenants burned out in the fire, they reduced Hollier's rent (from £5 to £4). See *Minute Books of General Court of Governors of St Thomas's Hospital, 1619–77*, LMA H01/ST/A/001/005, fol. 174ᵛ (20 September 1676).

A report written by the Governors to the Court of Aldermen five and a half years after the fire recounted that another danger point was Jonadab Ballam's house, which lay on the south side of the hospital gate and shared 'Timber Walls' with the hospital. Ballam's house burned down. *Minute Books of General Court of Governors of St Thomas Hospital, 1677–1735*, LMA H01/ST/A/001/006, fol. 21ᵛ (11 November 1681).

35 A board placed over the courtroom door in the old St Thomas's Hospital recorded how the fire touched but stopped at the hospital, 'by which stop in all probability all this [east] side of the Borough was preserved'. LMA, H01/ST/Y/45/011; Rendle, *Old Southwark*, p. 47. The board was mounted on an outside wall of one of the buildings of Guy's Hospital until its recent removal to the London Metropolitan Archives. See Figure 6.

36 The eldest illegitimate son of Charles II.

Fig. 6. Board from a wall of St Thomas's Hospital, Southwark, recording the extent of the fire 'in the 28th Year of the Reign of […] King Charles the Second'. Note that at some time the date was mistakenly altered to 1616.
© London Metropolitan Archives H01/ST/Y/45/011

and James Duke of York (both of whose personal efforts had helped to contain the London fire ten years earlier) came by royal barge to view the fire.

The *Gazette*, which was the Crown's newspaper, credited Charles's leadership in suppressing the fire — although it said nothing about what Charles did.[37] L'Estrange's *Account* described 'persons of Eminence' who helped to bring the fire under control by 'undertaking to give the Engineers instructions, and encouragement by Rewards, and their

37 In the Brief, Charles acknowledged that he was 'Our self in person a sorrowful Spectator of that dreadful Fire, and saw the best of means used to prevent the spreading thereof'. The Brief made no mention of any aid he gave.

own personal hazards'.[38] L'Estrange's *Narrative* described 'the vigilant Magistrates of the City' who gave orders to blow up buildings; it also noted that 'divers persons of Quality' stayed the day and 'omitted no care or personal pains to succour the distressed inhabitants and by their own example, as well as power, obliged thousands to contribute their helping hands'.[39]

Persons of eminence were not alone in providing support. Shortly after the fire, the City of London reimbursed two bills. The first bill, for £1 4s. 10d., was submitted by William Smith at the Bear Tavern, located at Bridge Foot, and sought reimbursement for bread and wine.[40] The second, for £18 5s. 2d., was from Thomas Aylwards, who sought reimbursement for payments made to seamen and labourers to fight the fire, payments to labourers to cleanse the streets and bring home the fire engines, and several other items. One such item was 5s. that Aylward had loaned to the Lord Mayor 'to give away' (presumably to those fighting the fire). Another item was £6 5s. 10d. that Aylwards had paid to Daniell Mann, whose own bill in that amount (for expenditures at the Swan Tavern in Fish Street and other costs incurred) still survives.[41]

In addition, the Governors of St Thomas's Hospital reimbursed John Nelson, a victualler whose restaurant was called the Crispiano, for 'Beere Ale Brandy Bread Cheese and other necessaryes'. Nelson valued his contribution at £25; the Governors reimbursed him £12.[42]

SCOPE

Devastation was complete. L'Estrange saw only a single house in the path of the fire still standing.[43] Otherwise, all the houses and shops on

38 See L'Estrange, *Account*, p. 3.

39 See L'Estrange, *Narrative*, pp. 5–6.

40 On the bills, Aylwards and Smith also acknowledged receipt of payment. See LMA, CLA/040/02/005. The Bear escaped damage, with the fire stopping about thirty houses short. L'Estrange, *Narrative*, p. 7. For a history of the Bear, a tavern likely frequented by Shakespeare and definitely by Pepys, see Rendle and Norman, *Southwark Inns*, pp. 302–15.

41 LMA, CLA/040/02/005.

42 *Minute Books 1619–77*, fol. 174 (20 September 1676). The Governors also approved the rewards paid by James Hayes, the Hospital's treasurer, to those employed in fighting the fire, and further permitted Hayes to reward others who 'took pains' to preserve the hospital and its estate. Ibid., fol. 172ᵛ (16 June 1676). The Governors also awarded Richard Finch, servant to the Hospital's clerk, 40s. for his efforts in saving the hospital's 'writings and other attendances'. Ibid., fol. 174 (20 September 1676).

43 This paragraph blends the descriptions in L'Estrange's *Account* and *Narrative*. The two descriptions essentially agree, but each provides a few details missing in

the east side of the High Street had burned from St Margaret's Hill to the southern walls of St Thomas's Hospital. On the west side of the High Street, the houses and shops from St Margaret's Hill to the Chain Gate in St Saviour's churchyard were gone, as were houses and shops in side streets like Angel Court, Three Crown Court, Fowl Lane and Compter Lane (or Street). There was no trace left of the Southwark meal market. St Thomas's Hospital was badly defaced, its porch ruined, and its windows shattered. St Saviour's caught fire two or three times. Its chancel was saved with difficulty: the chapel on the east side was pulled down and lay in ruins.[44]

L'Estrange also listed some of the well-known Southwark inns that burned down:

> the Cock and Hart yard neer the Spur-Inn, down to St Thomas's Hospital, Viz. The Talbot, the George, the White-Hart, the Kings-head, the Queens-head, Inns; Together with their Back-houses, Stables, Barns, and Warehouses.[45]

St Saviour's free grammar school also went up in flames.[46]

The exact number of buildings destroyed in the Southwark fire is unknown. Hooke's guess was 800 to 900 buildings. While it is usually a bad bet to question the assessment of Hooke — one of the surveyors of the City of London, who possessed vast experience in plotting the City after the Great Fire — his vantage point was far from the

the other. L'Estrange, *Account*, pp. 3–4; L'Estrange, *Narrative*, pp. 7–8.

44 The Brief noted that St Saviour had suffered 'great Breaches and Damages', but did not provide details.

45 See L'Estrange, *Account*, pp. 3–4. L'Estrange's *Narrative* added to this list 'The Green Dragon in Foul Lane'. L'Estrange, *Narrative*, p. 6. The Green Dragon was an ancient inn, existing since at least 1309. It lay on the south side of St Saviour's churchyard and sat on the land purchased by St Saviour to construct its free grammar school. Rendle and Norman, *Southwark Inns*, pp. 7, 295–96.

Work undertaken during the Thameslink project, which included limited excavations in the area of the present Borough Market, unfortunately revealed 'no conclusive archaeological evidence for the Southwark fire of 1676'. Amelia Fairman et al., *Bridging the Past: Life in Medieval and Post-Medieval Southwark*, ii (Oxford, 2020), p. 323.

46 The charitable Brief stated that both the 'Free-school and School-house' had been lost. We can also infer the grammar school's fate from the destruction of the Green Dragon, which lay adjacent to the school. See note 45. Writing nearly 140 years later, Manning and Bray also noted the grammar school's destruction. The school was rebuilt after the fire: an inscription on a stone tablet on the school's south gate listed on one side the date of the school's initial founding and on the other side the school's governors on 26 May 1676. Manning and Bray, *Surrey*, pp. 583–84. Four of the school's six governors (John Appleby, John Freeman, Jonadab Ballam (misspelled as 'Ballant') and Josiah Nicolson) were judges or parties in the Southwark fire court.

fire. In his *Account*, L'Estrange reported a general consensus among those at the fire that 1,000 buildings had burned or been blown up. But L'Estrange, who measured the length and breadth of the burned ground, was more circumspect: he thought it likelier that the number lay between 500 and 600.[47] His *Narrative* relayed that 'inhabitants and most intelligent persons computed it to be about 500'.[48] The *Gazette* estimated 600. Richard Martin's sermon and the charitable Brief both estimated the number to be above 500.[49]

Beyond the buildings were the lost wares of High Street shops, as well as household goods, furniture, clothing and the like.[50]

L'Estrange's *Narrative* refused to estimate the damage from the fire,[51] but the Brief had no such inhibition. Relying on the petition of the Justices of the Peace for Surrey, which in turn relied on the sworn testimony of two bricklayers (William Mason and Samuel Bridges) and two carpenters (William Gray and Thomas Kentish), the Brief set the damage at a very precise £84,375 13s.: £58,375 for demolished and defaced houses and £26,000 13s. for 'Goods, Wares, and Houshold-Stuff'. The Brief also acknowledged (but did not attempt to calculate) the loss of fines that tenants had paid on leasing their premises and other losses suffered by residents.

The Brief's estimate seems low. For instance, three days after the fire, Oliver Gregory, the landlord of the Talbot Inn, wrote to Sir Joseph Williamson, the principal Secretary of State to Charles II, that he had suffered a £2,300 loss in the fire.[52] As another example, Edmund Geary, owner of the White Hart Inn, spent £2,400 rebuilding his inn after the

---

47 L'Estrange, *Account*, pp. 4–5.
48 L'Estrange, *Narrative*, p. 6.
49 Two hundred and fifty years later, without explaining how he calculated the figure, another author declared the destruction of precisely 624 houses, plus the Compter. Arthur Hardwick, *Memorable Fires in London Past and Present* (London, 1926), p. 1. That number has been employed subsequently. See Michael Turner, 'The Nature of Urban Renewal After Fires in Seven English Provincial Towns, Circa 1675–1810' (doctoral dissertation, University of Exeter, 1985), p. 86, table 2.1.
50 L'Estrange made brief reference to the loss of goods, noting that the ruined part of the Borough was home to 'Wholesale men and great dealers'. L'Estrange, *Narrative*, at p. 6. The decrees of the Southwark fire court sometimes made reference to a party's significant loss of goods or wares. See *Waggorne v. Beacon* (Decree 3); *Marshall v. Peryn* (Decree 17); *Weyland v. Sayer* (Decree 22); *Gale v. Wight* (Decree 23); *Sledd v. Oliver* (Decree 30).
51 Except to say that the loss was 'a mighty and exceeding Sum'. L'Estrange, *Narrative*, at p. 8.
52 TNA, SP 29/381/270 (29 May 1676). The letter does not say why Gregory had lost so much money, but *Sledd v. Gregory* (Decree 30) supplies the missing

fire.[53] Putting anecdotes aside, if we assume that 500 houses had been destroyed and we accept the Brief's figure of £58,375 in damage to real estate, the average pre-fire house in Southwark would have been worth £116. But a number of the Southwark fire-court decrees referenced the cost of rebuilding, with figures in the range of £300 or more.[54] Even granting that the new houses were better built and more valuable than the old, the Brief seemed to underestimate significantly the losses in the fire.[55]

information: Gregory had purchased the landlord's interest in the Talbot shortly before the fire. Gregory had previously lent Charles II a substantial amount of money, for which Charles had assigned to him £3,951 payable out of the hearth tax and other duties. When Charles instituted the stop on the Exchequer in 1672, however, the loan effectively became unrecoverable. On receipt of Gregory's letter, Williamson petitioned Charles to pay Gregory the amounts due to him. TNA, SP 29/381/272 (undated).

53 *Taynton v. Collett* (Decree 27).

54 *Sledd v. Gregory* (Decree 30) (noting that the petitioner's husband had built a messuage before the fire for £300 and ordering the petitioner to spend at least £250 in rebuilding); *Cannon v. Cannon* (Decree 40) (noting that it cost £300 to rebuild); *Williams v. Browker* (Decree 30) (noting that the petitioner had spent £600 rebuilding his messuage, but could have done so adequately for £300). A report submitted to the governors of St Thomas's Hospital noted that two new brick tenements, 18 feet across and 18 feet deep, could be built on the High Street for £300. *Minute Books 1677–1735*, fol. 19 (8 July 1681).

55 In view of the number of churches, public buildings, livery halls, and great mansions lost in the Great Fire of London, an apples-to-apples comparison between the Great Fires in London and Southwark is impossible. Nonetheless, the usually recited loss from the Great Fire is £10 million. Bell, *The Great Fire*, pp. 223–24; Stephen Porter, *The Great Fire of London* (Stroud, 1996), pp. 55–56. The usually recited number of lost buildings is 13,200. Bell, *The Great Fire*, pp. 174, 210, 223–24; T. F. Reddaway, *The Rebuilding of London After the Great Fire* (London, 1941), p. 26. On those numbers, the average loss per household in the London fire was £758. Ian Doolittle, who has made a more precise count of buildings in London, has concluded that there were 24,260 houses in the City. See Ian Doolittle, 'Who Owned the City of London in 1666?'. Using the standard estimate that 80 per cent of the City burned down, the Great Fire may therefore have destroyed 19,400 houses, or an average loss per household of £515. This number is more than three times the Brief's estimate of losses per household in the Southwark fire (£168). A different way to view the problem is to compare the Southwark fire of 1676 to the fire in St George's parish in 1689, for which a precise accounting of damages exists. The St George's fire destroyed or defaced forty-one houses. The loss of real property was calculated at £4,304 and the loss of goods at £5,634. See LMA CLA/040/02/007. The real-estate loss in 1689 (an average of £104) matches up well with the Brief's estimate of real-estate losses in the 1676 fire (£116). But the estimate of lost goods and wares does not. Under the Brief's estimate of lost goods and wares, losses averaged £52 per household for the Southwark fire, while the 1689 accounting reflected lost goods and wares of £137 per household.

Whatever the exact tally, no one would dispute L'Estrange's grim assessment that the fire 'impoverish'd some hundreds of families, who had all their substance swept away in a moment'.[56]

Less is known about injuries or deaths. The *Gazette* made no mention of them. L'Estrange's *Account* noted injuries to people who recklessly tried to rescue goods or obstruct firefighting efforts. It also stated, without proof, that others might have 'burned in their beds, to a number not yet to be computed'.[57] In contrast, while the *Narrative* made no mention of people dying in their beds, it claimed that 'several unwary people' were killed in the explosions that blew up buildings, and others were 'sorely wounded'. Somewhat sensationally, it even repeated hearsay of a significant death toll, noting that 'some say twenty or more' people had been killed in explosions. Parish records, however, challenge the *Narrative*'s description: they suggest no great loss of life, if any at all.[58]

Similarly, Richard Martin, the minister at both St Saviour's and St Michael Wood Street, preached sermons on the two Sundays after the fire. The first, at St Michael Wood Street, was a fire-and-brimstone affair, calling the Southwark fire God's rod of judgment and linking the fire to Southwark residents' unrepentant wickedness despite the warnings of the 1665 plague and 1666 fire in London. The second sermon, at St Saviour's, was more comforting. Although they highlighted the loss of houses and goods, neither sermon mentioned loss of life or serious injury — even though such losses would have played directly into the sermons' themes.

Later renditions of the Southwark fire sometimes asserted a significant loss of life from the fire — indeed, a far greater loss than that of the Great Fire of London.[59] The source of this assertion was likely L'Estrange's *Narrative*. Silence on the loss of life in less trustworthy

---

56 L'Estrange, *Account*, at p. 5.

57 L'Estrange, *Account*, at p. 2.

58 Burial records for St Saviour's parish showed no rise in deaths after 26 May 1676. In the two weeks following the fire, twenty burials were recorded. By way of comparison, in the two weeks before the fire, twenty-three burials were recorded. Two burials, on 1 June and 2 June, were of seamen. Given the role of sailors in setting gunpowder charges to halt the London fire, this fact is suggestive; but on further examination, the parish records often noted the burial of seamen, with one seaman and the daughter of another seaman buried in the week before the fire. As an aside, one burial was recorded on 26 May. The service must have taken place as the fire blazed toward the church. See *St Saviour Parish Records, 1673–1705*, pp. 366–67, available at www.ancestrylibrary.co.uk.

59 See, e.g., Rendle, *Old Southwark*, p. 46.

contemporary accounts,[60] which had every reason to play up a large death toll, also calls into doubt the *Narrative*'s reliability, at least on this matter.

ORIGIN AND CAUSE

As for the origin of the fire, the *London Gazette* was silent. L'Estrange's *Account* was clear about where the fire started: 'at an Oyl-shop over-against the *Counter*, upon St *Margarets-hill*'.[61] His *Narrative* added considerable detail. Herb sellers making their way to the Borough market noticed a tiny fire in the basement of 'the house of a Colour man, or Oyl shop' lying on the east side of the High Street between the George and the Talbot, but the sellers passed by without raising a hue and cry. By the time that letter-carriers working for the Post Office happened upon the shop, the fire was casting a light through the basement window. The flames were still small enough that a few pails of water might have extinguished them, had the letter-carriers been able to get inside. But the door proved too stout, and the owner of the shop and his family were gone to the country. Only one son (described as 'sober, temperate, and careful') and a maid remained behind. By the time that the son and maid were roused, the fire had started to feed on oil in the shop. Flames prevented the son and maid from coming down the stairs to open the front door; they were fortunate to escape through a window or back door into the Talbot. The fire then spread to the George and the Talbot and leapt to the west side of the High Street, due to the narrowness of the High Street at that point and 'the unhappie situation of an old rotten timber house jutting over exactly opposite'.[62]

As for who or what caused the flames to kindle in the oil shop, L'Estrange's *Narrative* noted the carefulness of the son and the owner's (unsurprisingly self-serving) claim that no fire had been lit in the house for several days. L'Estrange commented that many people might ascribe the fire 'to that common cause of such disasters, *viz.*, neglect and carelessness, [while] others may have other Conjectures'. L'Estrange himself did not rise to the bait of speculation: the cause of the fire was 'yet unknown'. Assertions about the origin were 'the meer results of [...] active and suspicious Imaginations'.[63] L'Estange *Account* was equally cautious about ascribing a cause:

60 See notes 127, 143 and accompanying text.
61 L'Estrange, *Account*, at p. 5. An oil shop sold paints and a range of oils.
62 L'Estrange, *Narrative*, pp. 4–5.
63 Ibid.

how it began remains as yet doubtful; the very next neighbours knowing nothing of it, and though the Reader may expect to have his curiosity satisfied in this particular, I shall not attempt to traduce one man to pleasure another [...].[64]

This curious phrasing requires some context.

* * *

As I have said, most of what we *reliably* know about the Southwark fire comes from the *London Gazette*, L'Estrange and a few other sources. But we also have unreliable sources. To appreciate their untrustworthiness, we must take a step back. First, the enduring reality of seventeenth-century England was an uncompromising anti-Catholicism.[65] Second, especially after the Great Fire of London, Londoners had a morbid fascination with urban fire.[66] Their fear had plenty of fuel. Although the Great Fire was the largest, London suffered numerous catastrophic fires in the 1660s and 1670s.[67]

Unfortunately, these two mindsets cross-pollinated. Many people came to believe that papists — and in particular Jesuits — had designs to burn down all of England, thus weakening the kingdom and making way for an Irish or Spanish army (reinforced by England's remaining Catholics) to conquer England, restore Catholicism and impose despotic rule. Even before the Southwark fire, widely distributed pamphlets laid blame for fires, including the Great Fire of London, at the doorstep of papists.[68] Like conspiracy theories that blossom in the politics of

64 L'Estrange, *Account*, p. 5.
65 *See* John Kenyon, *The Popish Plot* (New York, 1972), p. 1.
66 Ibid., pp. 239–40 (discussing Londoners' 'obsession' with fire).
67 In statutes re-authorizing and extending the life of the London fire court, Parliament gave the court jurisdiction over other fires as well: first, over any fires that had occurred in London during the three years preceding the Great Fire, see 22 Car. 2, c. 11, § 31 (1670), in *Statutes of the Realm*, v, p. 671; second, over fires that had occurred in London and Southwark between 1 October 1666 and 1 October 1670, see 22 and 23 Car. 2, c. 14, §1 (1671), in *Statutes of the Realm*, v, p. 724; and finally, over houses that had recently burned down in Seething Lane, see 25 Car. 2, c. 10, § 5 (1673), in *Statutes of the Realm*, v, p. 796. For a description of other fires in and about London, see William Bedloe, *A narrative and impartial discovery of the horrid Popish plot, carried on for the burning and destroying of the cities of London and Westminster, &c.* (1679), pp. 15–25, available at EEBO. For reasons that will soon be apparent, however, events related by Bedloe are particularly suspect.
68 See, e.g., *Londons flames discovered by informations taken before the Committee Appointed to Enquire after the Burning of the City of London and after the insolency of the papists, &c.* (1667), available at EEBO. The House of Commons' investigation into

our own day, a spurious seed lay at the centre: Robert Hubert, a French Catholic, had confessed to starting the Great Fire. Of course, even the judge who sentenced Hubert to hang (and hang he did, on 29 October 1666) did not believe Hubert, who was mentally unwell.[69] Later research has shown that Hubert arrived in England only after the fire began; he was also Protestant (a Huguenot). As with modern conspiracy theories, however, reality could not penetrate the belief system: 'the Great Fire at once took its place in the mythology of ultra-Protestantism'.[70]

Some members of Parliament and others with political or religious influence — for instance, the Earl of Shaftesbury and his allies — cultivated this misconception for political ends. To an extent, they sought to shift the government's focus away from Protestant dissenters, who were less than loyal to Charles II.[71] To a greater extent, they sought to undercut an increasingly unpopular Charles and his heir apparent, James Duke of York, who were seen as overly tolerant of Catholics (and relatedly of France), as well as overly attracted to an absolutist rule that had no need of Parliament.[72]

Anti-Catholicism, and particularly the view of Catholics as treasonous arsonists, were more an undercurrent than a main feature of English social and political life at the time of the Great Fire of London.[73] But the generally tolerant attitude toward Catholics began to shift in the early 1670s, first when Charles allied Britain with the Catholic French against the Protestant Dutch and then when James's conversion to Catholicism became known. Charles had adjourned Parliament in November 1675, and by the time he reconvened it in February 1677, he found an even more fractious body — one seething with concern for 'popery'.[74] This Parliament had much on its plate and, to its credit,

the Great Fire of London produced a report that, although almost entirely hearsay, strongly implicated papists in the Great Fire. Although all remaining copies of the report were ordered burned in October 1667, some remained in circulation. See Kenyon, *Popish Plot*, p. 12.

69 For Hubert's indictment, see Bell, *The Great Fire*, pp. 353–54. For the authorities' disbelief of Hubert's confession, see ibid., pp. 191–95, 200–08.

70 Kenyon, *Popish Plot*, p. 13.

71 See Peter Hinds, *'The Horrid Popish Plot'* (Oxford, 2010), p. 366.

72 On Shaftesbury's opposition to the ministry of Charles II and general attitudes toward Catholicism after the Restoration, see Victor Stater, *Hoax* (New Haven, 2022), pp. 17–32, 48; see also ibid., p. xi ('The Whigs had no qualms whatever about inflating the public's fear of Catholicism').

73 For a summary of the generally tolerant climate toward Catholics, see ibid., pp. 22–32; see also Kenyon, *Popish Plot*, pp. 13–19.

74 Perhaps the most notable expression of this anger, which conflated Catholicism with despotic rule, was Andrew Marvell's *An Account of the Growth of*

it registered a number of accomplishments. Most notably, it supplied Charles with funding to strengthen the British navy, but it also enacted useful domestic legislation, including creating the first Statute of Frauds and erecting the Southwark fire court. But popery was always front and centre: the Journals of both Houses overflowed with debates about whether to exclude Catholics from the Houses of Parliament and how best to suppress popery.[75]

The Southwark fire had played a role in these shifting attitudes. Put simply, the fire panicked England. Intelligence reports poured into Secretary of State Williamson from around the country. The first report, on 3 June 1676, relayed that three people (two of them French) had been apprehended while trying to fire Chipnam (or Chippenham), twelve miles from Bristol. Two perpetrators had already confessed, claiming that the French had employed one hundred agents to fire towns around the country.[76] In Falmouth, there were rumours that Dover, Bristol and Portsmouth had all burned and that the French king had sent fifty to sixty persons to burn other seaport towns.[77] A later report passed on the confession of an arsonist in Hoddesdon who put the figure at

Popery and Arbitrary Government, published near the end of 1677. Highly critical of the government of Charles II, the pamphlet was published anonymously. In his capacity as censor, Roger L'Estrange energetically hunted for the pamphlet's author, while at the same time writing pro-government tracts to staunch the bleeding. See note 18. Today Marvell is generally acknowledged as the writer, although Marvell denied L'Estrange the satisfaction of exposing his identity by dying in August 1678 — failing by a month to witness the political conflagration that his *Growth of Popery* had kindled. See Stater, *Hoax*, pp. 9–15.

75 One of the first matters that the House of Commons took up in the session was whether to expel Thomas Strickland from membership after his conviction for being a Popish Recusant. *HC Jour.*, IX, p. 384 (16 February 1677); ibid., p. 385 (19 February 1677). The House did so. Ibid., p. 393 (6 March 1677). The House also moved quickly to consider bills to suppress popery, eventually focusing on two bills sent from the House of Lords: one to prevent papists from sitting in either House of Parliament and another to make more effectual the prosecution and conviction of popish recusants. *HC Jour.*, IX, p. 384 (21 February 1677); ibid., p. 389 (26 February 1677); ibid., p. 395 (8 March 1677); ibid., p. 401 (17 March 1677); ibid., p. 402 (19 March 1677); ibid., p. 407 (27 March 1677); ibid., p. 409 (30 March 1677); ibid., p. 414 (4 April 1677). In the end, no popery bill passed both Houses during the session.

76 Letter, Bathorn to [unknown], TNA, SP 29/381/349 (3 June 1676). This report may be the one that Anthony Gylby, another correspondent with Williamson, later ridiculed. Gylby reported that the supposed arrest of three French arsonists in Bristol was in fact the mere questioning of two Englishmen and a French tutor. Letter, Gylby to Williamson, *CSPD*, XVIII, p. 161 (14 June 1676).

77 Letter, Holden to Williamson, TNA, SP 29/382/243 (26 June 1676).

precisely sixty-two evildoers.[78] Bristol's mayor heard rumours of efforts to burn down Worcester with fireballs.[79]

More rumours of fires constantly emerged.[80] Some people construed every fire, however innocently (or in some instances, intentionally) caused, to be part of this nefarious design. A correspondent from London reported 'very much murmuring about the many fires that happen, which some say are not mere casualties'.[81] The towns of Bristol, Hull and York were especially on edge.[82] Another letter to Williamson ended ominously: 'By this you may see the people of this Nation is very Unstable.'[83]

As one sign of how serious the matter was becoming, Charles appointed the Committee on Trade and Plantations — which included, among others, the Lord Privy Seal, the Lord Vice Chamberlain, the Earl of Craven and Williamson — to investigate.[84] The Committee leaned hard on the Lord Mayor of London and the Justices of the Peace for Surrey to bring them evidence — and quickly. The information collected concerned the great Southwark fire of 1676, as well as other fires in Southwark and around the country.[85] Most of the information was hearsay. Several witnesses reported that they had heard someone else say that Southwark was burning even before the fire occurred: the implication was that this foreknowledge proved a plot to burn down

---

78 In early June, the Mayor of Bristol asked Rolfe Baylye, the town clerk of Marlborough, to account for reports of persons who had been arrested and had confessed to plans to burn down Bristol, Marlborough, and Chippenham. Letter, Cann to Williamson, TNA, SP 29/383/3 (1 July 1676). Baylye replied that several persons who had been apprehended in setting a fire at Blandford claimed that there were sixty-two others planning to burn down Salisbury, Marlborough, Bristol and other places. But Baylye did not find 'any truth of any such hellish horride intentions'. Certificate of Rolfe Baylye, TNA, SP 29/383/5 (3 June 1676).

79 Cann Letter, note 78.

80 Letter, Gylby to Williamson, TNA, SP 29/382/225 (25 June 1676) ('there is scarce a day there does not come newes of The burning of one grate towne or other'). Gylby thought them 'silly, but yet malicious reports'.

81 Letter, T. B. to [unknown], TNA, SP 29/382/307 (23 June 1676). The *Calendar of State Papers Domestic* identified T. B. as Thomas Barnes. *CSPD*, XVIII, p. 180.

82 See note 99 and accompanying text.

83 See note 1.

84 Charles's role in ordering the Committee to investigate was mentioned in several documents, including Letter, Committee to Mayor of Hull, TNA, SP 29/382/231 (undated).

85 Examination of James Gardiner, TNA, SP 29/382/129 (17 June 1676) (fire in Southwark on 16 June); Information of Joseph Wight, TNA, SP 29/382/298 (20 June 1676) (fire in Southwark on 10 June); Informations of Andrew Anderson and others, TNA, SP 29/382/214 (24 June 1676) (fire in East Smithfield on 21 June).

the borough.[86] Of these statements, the most significant was that of Elizabeth Browne, a maid. After hearing about a fire on St Margaret's Hill on the evening before the great fire started, Browne went to Mrs Welsh's house, located next to the Talbot Inn, and asked Mrs Welsh's maid about the report. The maid replied that there was no fire.[87] As it turned out, Welsh's shop was where the Southwark fire started later that night.[88]

In the end, Browne's statement and most of the other claims of prior knowledge of the Southwark fire were explainable. Anne Symmes, a widow living on St Margaret's Hill, reported that she had suffered a chimney fire at eight o'clock on the evening before the great fire started. She said that her fire had raised a report among people of a fire on St Margaret's Hill.[89]

Other information that the Committee received also pointed toward an intentional origin. The problem, however, was not a lack of suspects, but too many. First, there were the hundred French arsonists. Second, a man named James Peirce stepped forward and claimed that he was in service to a Captain Morgan, the leader of a troop of horse at Somerset House.[90] Peirce said that he had crossed the Thames with Morgan, who set fire to a house in Southwark. Peirce later accompanied a man named Dowse, a coal heaver, who gave Peirce a stick filled with gunpowder and ordered him to fire more Southwark houses.[91]

---

86 See Information of Richard Taylor, SP 29/382/233 (26 June 1676); Information of Jeremiah Johnson, TNA, SP 29/382/261 (27 June 1676). In one instance, a London merchant reported hearing that Southwark was burning on the day of the fire, but, as he was one hundred miles from London, no such reports could have reached him in due course. Information of Thomas Demycke, TNA, SP 29/382/266 (27 June 1676).

87 Information of Elizabeth Browne, TNA, SP 29/382/264 (27 June 1676). William Hester, a soap boiler whose mother was Browne's mistress, confirmed what Browne said but knew nothing himself. Information of William Hester, TNA, SP 29/382/263 (27 June 1676).

88 See note 97 and accompanying text.

89 Information of Anne Symmes, TNA, SP 29/382/298 (undated). Although undated, the information of Symmes (or Syms — both spellings were used) was written at the bottom of Joseph Wight's information, see note 85, which was dated 20 June 1676. James Reading, one of the justices of the peace for Southwark, likewise told the Committee that reports of a fire on St Margaret's Hill concerned a chimney fire. *Minutes of the Committee of Trade and Plantations*, TNA, SP 29/382/175 (23 June 1676).

90 The reference to Somerset House was lost on no one at the time. It was a residence of Catherine of Braganza, Charles's queen and a Catholic.

91 Examination of James Peirce, TNA, SP 29/382/183 (23 June 1676). Peirce said that he threw Dowse's stick into the Thames, where it exploded with a noise like a cannon.

Third, a man named Norris Finch, who was caught setting fire to a barn in Hoddesdon, claimed that two unsavoury characters, Richard Hilliard and Robert Norris, had paid him 30s. to do so. Hilliard and Norris wished to 'have the advantage of plundering' in the chaos of the ensuing fire. According to Finch, Hilliard and Norris said that they were the ones who had set fire to the Talbot, also 'upon the Act of plunder', and that they had received £5 from a person unknown to Finch to do so.[92]

All these stories fizzled out. The one hundred French arsonists never materialized. As for Peirce, the justices of the peace ordered the beadle of St Saviour's and the keeper of the House of Correction in Southwark to take Peirce to Somerset House. No one there had heard of Captain Morgan or recognized Peirce; and when Peirce was asked to show where Captain Morgan lived, he went first to the Queen's chapel and then to a long-unoccupied house. When Peirce was taken to the place where Dowse supposedly lived, no one of that name could be found. Peirce's mother then told the beadle and the keeper that Peirce was not capable of service and that she had never heard of anyone named Captain Morgan or Dowse.[93] It was evident that Peirce was delusional, perhaps not unlike Robert Hubert.

Similarly, nothing came of Finch's allegations. The Committee left the Finch investigation to the Lord Mayor of London to prosecute — a fact suggesting that the Committee saw nothing in the accusation.[94]

The Committee of Trade and Plantations, which restyled itself as a Committee for Enquiring after the Fire, convened at least five times (23, 26, 27 and 29 June, and 6 July). The first meeting was the most decisive. Several justices of the peace and constables provided information on the various reports of fires.[95] So did several witnesses, including

92 See Letter, Monson to Sheldon, TNA, SP 29/382/196 (23 June 1676); Examination of Norris Finch, TNA, SP 29/382/198 (22 June 1676). Sir John Monson and Henry Monson of Broxborn forwarded Finch's examination to the Lord Mayor of London, Joseph Sheldon, so that Sheldon might apprehend Hilliard and Norris.

93 Examination of John Moth, TNA, SP 29/382/247 (27 June 1676); Examination of William Dagger, TNA, SP 29/381/248 (27 June 1676). Peirce contradicted his mother by claiming that she had often entertained Morgan and Dowse in her home. Examination of James Peirce, TNA, SP 29/382/246 (27 June 1676).

94 *Minutes of the Committee for Enquiring after the Fire*, TNA, SP 29/382/229ᵛ (27 June 1676). The State Papers included no further information from the Lord Mayor on the matter. Likewise, the *Repertories* made no mention of Hilliard or Norris. Given that the *Repertories* almost never mentioned criminal investigations, however, no conclusions can be drawn from that fact.

95 *Minutes of the Committee of Trade and Plantations*. Among the justices to attend were James Reading, John Freeman and Richard How, all of whom would serve as judges on the Southwark fire court.

the last credible sources of information on the Southwark fire: two eyewitnesses.[96]

Mr Hart, next-door neighbour to the oil shop where the fire began, testified that a servant had been seen smoking a pipe on the porch around midnight. While Hart could not say how the fire began, he believed 'noe malice to be in it, but mere accident by ye young servants taking tobacco'. Next, the smoker, a young man named Welsh, testified that he did not know how the fire started. When he heard shouts of fire, he ran to the top of the house and saw the chimneys ablaze. When he got to the street, people were breaking the windows of the shop, which was the only house on fire.[97]

Although Williamson's notes of the meeting are crabbed, fading and replete with abbreviations difficult to decipher, one line is clearly readable: 'The great fire happened merely by accident.'[98]

The Committee continued to meet and receive information into July, but nothing changed the view that the Committee had evidently reached on 23 June. In letters to the Mayors of Bristol and Hull and to the Lord Mayor of York soon after 23 June, the Committee chastised all three for letting rumours of malicious fires spread through their cities. They were ordered to tamp down the chatter immediately, for, as the Lord Mayor of York and the Mayor of Bristol were told, the Southwark fire resulted not from 'malice or contrivance to effect ye same, but rather much negligence and want of care in the persons who should be more concerned'.[99]

---

96 For other reliable sources, see notes 13–17 and accompanying text.

97 *Minutes of the Committee of Trade and Plantations*. Although Hart referred to 'servants', Welsh had the same name as the shop owner. See note 87 and accompanying text. L'Estrange's *Narrative* also stated that the son (as well as a maid) was present on the night of the fire. See note 62 and accompanying text. The *Minutes* identified Welsh as 'ye young man which smoaked'.

98 Williamson Notes, TNA, SP 29/382/177 (23 June 1676). Nothing indicates that these notes belonged to Williamson; I relied on the *Calendar of State Papers* for identification. *CSPD*, XVIII, p. 174.

99 Letter, Committee of Enquiry to Lord Mayor of York, TNA SP 29/382/256ᵛ–257 (undated). A notation at the top of this letter indicated that the Mayor of Bristol received the same letter. There were two drafts of the letter to the Mayor of Hull, and they varied slightly from each other and from the letters to the other mayors. Again, the Committee's conclusion was clear: 'we can find nothing of Malice or Contrivance therein, But a great want of care in the Partys concern'd and the common accidents that follow thereupon'. Letter, Committee of Enquiry to Mayor of Hull, TNA SP 29/382/253 (27 June 1676); see ibid., TNA SP 29/382/253 (undated). The mayors' letters in response, which varied in their levels of obsequiousness and righteousness, indicated that the Committee's message and

The Committee's actions generally calmed nerves, one correspondent wrote, but 'at Yorke I hear they are still in greatt feares'.[100] Later in July, Williamson heard from another intelligencer that '[t]here is a flying report all over the Country of severall fiers in severall parts of the Country as well as London'.[101]

Beliefs have a persistence that official government conclusions cannot suppress. The persistent belief of a nefarious origin to the Southwark fire is one example. This persistence was also likely the reason that L'Estange wrote two pamphlets about the fire. L'Estrange earned much of his income from the sale of his pamphlets, and the Southwark fire was what people wanted to read about.

His entrepreneurial instincts may also explain L'Estrange's reluctance to assign a cause to the Southwark fire. L'Estrange was a Stuart supporter, and he knew that some people would lay blame for the Southwark fire at the feet of the Jesuits. That narrative was not in the interest of Charles's government. As Kenyon noted, even in 1673 Parliament was 'in a ferocious mood' regarding the government's tolerance toward Catholics.[102] L'Estrange was not going to feed that anger, but he was also not going to alienate a paying audience. Both the *Account* and the *Narrative* implicitly acknowledged that some would attribute the fire to Catholics. The *Narrative* related facts suggesting arson: the son's soberness, the lack of fire in the oil shop for days and the origin just inside a reachable basement window. At the same time, L'Estrange refused to put that theory directly in print. Rather, he subtly put a thumb on the scale in favour of an accidental origin, calling accidents 'the common cause' of fire.[103]

In the case of the Southwark fire, the persistent belief that Catholics started the fire had far-ranging effects, playing an underappreciated role in one of the cataclysmic events in seventeenth-century English politics. It was during this political upheaval that several untrustworthy accounts of the Southwark fire emerged.

Appearing in various forms, both oral and written, the two most noteworthy such accounts belonged to Titus Oates and William Bedloe.[104] Oates is the more familiar name. He and Bedloe were the

criticism had been received. Letter, Shires to Williamson, TNA SP 29/382/314 (27 June 1676) (Hull); Cann Letter, note 78 (Bristol); Letter, Horner to Coventry, TNA SP 29/383/14 (3 July 1676) (York).

100 Letter, Gylby to Williamson, TNA, SP 29/383/7 (1 July 1676).

101 Letter, Aslaby to Williamson, TNA, SP 29/383/105 (10 July 1676).

102 See Kenyon, *Popish Plot*, p. 15.

103 L'Estrange, *Narrative*, p. 4.

104 Other accounts, like that of John Ward or the hearsay declarations of

leading interlocutors in the 'Popish Plot', an utter fiction that cost the lives of more than twenty Catholics and cemented the two-party system that has dominated political life in Britain and elsewhere ever since.[105] The lie at the heart of the Popish Plot was the claim that Jesuits, with the aid of the Pope, had concocted a plot to assassinate Charles II in order to bring the Catholic James to the throne and thus return the country to despotic Romish rule.

Oates fell in with Israel Tonge, a paranoid crackpot who lost the living of St Mary Staining when it burned down in the Great Fire of London. Tonge saw Catholic conspiracies everywhere. Tonge appeared to many as unhinged, but Oates was glib and clever — as well as something that Tonge was not: an alleged eyewitness to the Catholic conspiracies. Oates claimed that he briefly spent time with Jesuits in Spain and France, which was true enough. But Oates took that bit of truth and built upon it a monstrous lie: that he had attended, or knew of, nefarious meetings of Catholics both overseas and in England, to plot England's downfall. Oates crafted forty-three articles, or depositions, the sum of which was to allege a Catholic conspiracy to kill the King. None of the articles mentioned the Southwark fire.

In August 1678, Tonge — long a believer in such a plot but now armed with Oates's 'evidence' — obtained audiences with senior government officials, who directed Tonge and Oates to Sir Edmund Berry Godfrey, a Justice of the Peace for Westminster. In September 1678, Godfrey reluctantly took depositions from Tonge and Oates.[106] Although claims of royal assassination always received scrutiny, Godfrey, like other officials, was sceptical of the tale and was ready to dismiss Tonge and Oates outright. Oates, however, had begun to embellish the story, adding more articles and claiming to Godfrey that Jesuits — in particular, a lay brother named John Grove — had set the Southwark fire.[107]

William Johnson and Joseph Wright, deserve less attention. See notes 143–44 and accompanying text.

105　For the enduring political influence of the Popish Plot, see Stater, *Hoax*, pp. xi–xii. Even the names of the parties that came to dominate British politics for centuries — the Tories and the Whigs — were first employed during the Popish Plot. Ibid., p. xi.

106　See Notes of Israel Tonge, TNA, SP 29/409, fols 59, 70, 109–09A. One of Godfrey's later depositions of Oates, taken on 27 September 1678 after Oates had fully fleshed out his story, still survives. Examination of Titus Oates, TNA SP 29/409, fols 14–36. Historians have relied on Tonge's notes, which were intended as an introduction to a book, to flesh out the events in the earliest days of the plot. Over the next two paragraphs, I do the same — albeit with reluctance in view of Tonge's unreliability.

107　Tonge Notes, fols 59, 109–109A.

Strictly, that claim had nothing to do with the assassination plot, but it piqued Godfrey's curiosity. Oates had also named Grove as one of two people who were tasked with carrying out the original assassination plan: shooting Charles with a silver bullet as he strolled in St James's Park. Godfrey was not unfriendly to Catholics, and he doubted in the extreme the claim that Grove set the fire; Godfrey recollected seeing Grove at the fire labouring mightily to put it out.[108] It is a testament to the blind spot that even elite Londoners had about Catholics and fires that Godfrey entertained Oates's claim of Catholic involvement in the Southwark fire.[109] Without the Southwark fire, Oates, and the entire Popish Plot, might have disappeared in history.

Instead, Tonge and Oates forged ahead, ultimately receiving an audience before Charles and the Privy Council. Charles thought Tonge mad, and left before the more persuasive Oates testified. By this time, Oates's articles had expanded to eighty-one, of which the Southwark fire was number 49.[110] The Council was ambivalent, although it ordered the arrests of the plotters that Oates named. The matter might again have ended there, but for an event that, quite literally, changed the course of history: Godfrey's strangled and stabbed body was found on Primrose Hill on 17 October 1678, roughly five days after it was estimated that he had died.

Godfrey's death remains a mystery even today. It might have been a suicide — Godfrey had been despondent in the days before his death — that was covered up to look like a murder.[111] At the time, however, it was widely seen as a murder — one perpetrated by Catholics trying to hush up the Popish Plot. The death lent an imprimatur of truth to Oates's claims and thus became the match that set fire to the kindling that years of agitation about popery had built up. The Parliamentary session that began four days after discovery of Godfrey's body immediately called for an examination of the Popish Plot and advanced a proposal

108 Ibid. See also Kenyon, *Popish Plot*, pp. 49–61; Stater, *Hoax*, pp. 47–52. One of the tenants of St Thomas's Hospital was Eliza Grove, whose messuage near the gate of the hospital was demolished in the fire. *Minute Books 1619–77*, fol. 174 (20 September 1676). I have been unable to establish a connection between John and Eliza, but a family relationship provides a benign explanation for John's presence at the fire.

109 Kenyon, *Popish Plot*, pp. 239–40 (noting the accepted belief among London's elite of Catholics' pyromania).

110 Oates Examination, fol. 25.

111 For an account of the death, opting for suicide as the likely explanation, see Alan Marshall, *The Strange Death of Edmund Godfrey* (Stroud, 2000). Kenyon opted for a murder theory, suggesting a number of alternatives but not definitively

to remove all papist recusants to twenty miles from London.[112] The *Journals* of the House of Commons and the House of Lords, as well as sources such as the *Manuscripts of the House of Lords*[113] and Grey's *Debates*,[114] reveal that the Plot sucked up almost all the Parliamentary oxygen for months. Considerable judicial and Parliamentary effort was also expended in trying the alleged conspirators for treason and in convincing Charles to carry out their executions.[115]

Oates would repeat his claim about Catholic involvement in the Southwark fire in numerous forums and publications. The gist of his information never varied, so two recountings will suffice. Appearing before the bar of the House of Lords on 31 October 1678, Oates set out his eighty-one articles. Article 49 read in full:

> That, on the 10th of August, *Old Style*, the Deponent did meet with *John Groves* in *Wild Street*, in the Afternoon; and, as near as the Deponent remembers, it was about Eight of the Clock; and he having made several Promises to the Deponent of giving him an Account of *Southworke* Fire in 1676, the said *Groves* took the Deponent into *Wild House Garden*, and then began: He said, 'That they had certain Fire-works, which were made for that very Purpose; and he, with Three *Irishmen* that were his Assistants, went into *The Burrough*; and, not finding an Opportunity nor fit Place there, went to St *Margret's Hill*, where they found an Oil Shop, which the said *Groves* bragged he fired.' The Deponent asked the said *Groves*, 'How he came acquainted with the said *Irishmen*?' He said, 'His Acquaintance with them was not much; but they were procured by Dr. *Fogarty*, the *Irish* Doctor; for the which, the Society [of Jesus, i.e., the Jesuits] (*Richard Strange* then Provincial) gave him and his Assistants One Thousand Pounds; *videlicet*, Four Hundred Pounds to the said *Groves*, and Two Hundred Pounds apiece to the said *Irishmen*.' And the said *Groves* told

settling on any murderer or motive. Kenyon, *Popish Plot*, pp. 264–70. Neither historian thought that Catholics were the likely killers. L'Estrange, who worked feverishly to disprove the Popish Plot's allegations for years, interviewed numerous people and came to the view that it was a suicide. Ibid., p. 264.

112   *HC Jour.*, IX, pp. 517–18 (21 October 1678). Acting with more haste than wisdom, the House of Commons resolved unanimously that 'there hath been, and still is, a damnable and hellish Plot contrived and carried on by the Popish Recusants, for the Assassinating and Murdering the King'. Ibid., p. 530 (31 October 1678).

113   Hist. Manuscripts Commission, *The Manuscripts of the House of Lords 1678–88* (11th Rpt. App. Part II) (London, 1887).

114   See Anchitell Grey, *Debates of the House of Commons 1667–1694*, VI and VII (London, 1763).

115   See, e.g., T. B. Howell (ed.), *A Complete Collection of State Trials*, VII (London, 1816), fols 1–78, trial of Edward Coleman; fols 79–144, trial of William Ireland, Thomas Pickering and John Grove; fols 159–230, trial of Robert Green, Henry Berry and Lawrence Hill for Godfrey's murder; fols 1294–1576, trial upon impeachment of William, Viscount Stafford. There were numerous other trials as well, see Howell, *State Trials*, VI, fols 1402–98, 'Introduction to the Trials for the Popish Plot'.

the Deponent, 'That the Society got at least Two Thousand Pounds in that Fire;' which was also told the Deponent at another Time by *Richard Strange*.[116]

The second recounting occurred at the trial of Grove and four others for treason in the supposed plot to kill Charles. Conviction for treason required two witnesses. Oates was the first. Most of Oates's testimony regarding Grove concerned the assassination plot. But the Lord Chief Justice, William Scroggs, inquired of the defendants if they knew Oates. Most did not, but Grove admitted that he had once lent Oates eight shillings. Oates seized on this admission to relay that there were other times when he and Grove had met:

> *Oates.* [...] Twice more he drank in my company, at the Red Posts in Wild-street, and once more when he owned to me that he fired Southwark.
>
> *[Lord Chief Justice].* Now by the oath that you have taken, did he own to you that he had fired Southwark?
>
> *Oates.* My lord, he did tell me that he with three Irishmen did fire Southwark, and that they had 1,000*l.* for it, whereof he had 400*l.* and the other 200*l.* a piece.[117]

After eliciting that testimony, Scroggs moved immediately to ask another defendant whether he knew Oates, so Grove had no chance then to deny the accusation. When given the opportunity to present a defence, Grove tried to undermine Oates's credibility by establishing that Oates had never stayed at Grove's house — Oates having testified that he had learned details of the assassination plot while staying with Grove.[118] Because Scroggs gave none of the defendants much ability to produce evidence, Grove never specifically denied that he set the Southwark fire, although he continued to assert his overall innocence all the way to the scaffold (Fig. 7).[119]

116 *See Titus Oates his Narrative*, in *HL Jour.*, XIII, p. 320 (1678). The fact that Oates gave a deposition is noted in the *Journal of the House of Lords* for 31 October. *HL Jour.*, XIII, p. 311 (31 October 1678). Subsequently the Lords took the unusual step of voting to insert Oates's entire deposition into the *Journal* as part of the proceedings for 31 October. *HL Jour.*, XIII, p. 369 (21 November 1678). Five days before appearing before the Lords, Oates (along with Tonge) had 'deliver[ed] his information' to the House of Commons. The exact information that Oates gave to the Commons does not appear in the *Journal for the House of Commons*, but it likely aligned with what he told the Lords a few days later. *HC Jour.*, IX, p. 522 (25 October 1678). Oates appeared again to provide the Commons with further information. *HC Jour.*, IX, p. 522 (28 October 1678).

   Oates's testimony before Godfrey was nearly verbatim the same as that given before the Lords. One small difference: before Godfrey, Oates claimed that he and Grove had met at five o'clock, not eight. Oates Examination, fol. 25. In both testimonies, Oates referred to the man he met as 'John Groves', although his name was John Grove.

117 Howell, *State Trials*, VII, fols 102–03.

118 Ibid., fol. 126.

119 Ibid., fol. 143. Because no other justice was available, the judge who

Fig. 7.　　Francis Barlow, Four playing cards from an anti-Catholic Popish Plot pack, 1679: *Two of Hearts*, Titus Oates informs Sir Edmund Berry Godfrey, JP, of an alleged Roman Catholic conspiracy to kill the King; *King of Hearts*, Oates presents his allegations to the King and Privy Council; *King of Clubs*, William Bedloe testifies to the House of Commons; *Five of Clubs*, The execution of five Jesuit priests — Wiliam Barrow, John Fenwick, John Gavan, Anthony Turner and Thomas Whitebread — falsely accused of conspiring to kill the King.

Grove's trial was largely a morality play and a show: Scroggs constantly belittled the defendants and devastatingly summed up against them. But Scroggs was fair enough in one regard. Because two of Grove's co-defendants, Whitebread and Fenwick, had only Oates to testify against them, Scroggs remanded their cases until a second witness could be found.[120] For Grove and his other two co-defendants, Ireland and Pickering, a second witness was willing to testify to their treason: William Bedloe.

Israel Tonge was an imbalanced zealot, and Titus Oates was a man adrift who stumbled upon fame and (for a time) fortune. For William Bedloe, however, a special place in Hell is reserved. Bedloe had recently returned from Europe, where he lived by petty theft, horse robbery and swindling — sometimes claiming that he was Lord Cornwallis (or Lord Gerard or Lord Newport). In Kenyon's words, he was 'a professional criminal, a robber, highwayman, and a confidence trickster'.[121] Like Oates, Bedloe had been a servant in Catholic households before he left London with the sheriff on his tail. Indeed, he had met Oates briefly when they were both in Europe, relieving Oates of ten pieces of eight in the process.

When word of Oates's Plot and a £500 reward for information about Godfrey's death[122] reached Bristol around 1 November, Bedloe leapt. He smelled money, and he was not going to leave it entirely to Oates

---

pronounced Grove's death sentence was the Recorder of the City of London, Sir George Jeffreys, who played a large role in the proceedings of the Southwark fire court. See notes 291–92 and accompanying text. Later Lord Chief Justice and Lord Chancellor, Jeffreys is best known as the 'Hanging Judge of Bloody Assizes' for the death sentences he imposed after the Duke of Monmouth's rebellion. He also closed the circle on the Popish Plot by presiding at Oates's trial for perjury in 1685. It is difficult to reconcile the Jeffreys who sentenced Grove to death with the Jeffreys who presided over Oates's trial, where Jeffreys decried Oates's 'foul and malicious perjury' and called Oates 'this villainous, perjured wretch'. See Kenyon, *Popish Plot*, p. 256.

120 Howell, *State Trials*, VII, fol. 120. Another witness willing to commit perjury emerged, and Whitebread and Fenwick were subsequently convicted of treason and then hanged, drawn and quartered. Ibid., fols 311–418, 570–90. Richard How, the sheriff of London who presided over their executions, expressed his disbelief of their protestations of innocence. Ibid., fols 499–500. How was both a litigant and a judge in the Southwark fire court. See note 255 and accompanying text.

121 Kenyon, *Popish Plot*, p. 93. For a further description of Bedloe, see Stater, *Hoax*, pp. 85–86. Even Bedloe described himself as a 'great rogue', but he turned that fact to his advantage. '[H]ad I not been soe', he told the Speaker when he came before House of Commons, 'I could not have knowne these things I am now about to tell you.' See *The Autobiography of Sir John Bramston, K.B.* (London, 1845), p. 194. Bramston characterized Bedloe as 'wittie and impudent, and certainly a villain'.

122 Charles issued a proclamation offering the reward on 20 October 1678. See Grey, *Debates*, VI, p. 112 n.*.

to capitalize. By 7 November Bedloe was in London, where he told the Privy Council that he saw Godfrey's body at Somerset House, where it had allegedly been stored after his murder. On 8 November he appeared at the bar in the House of Lords and on 10 November before the House of Commons.[123] Not as skilful a liar as Oates and with less time to hone his lines, Bedloe had issues with consistency.[124] For instance, he sometimes denied knowing Oates.

The inconsistencies in the stories of Oates and Bedloe should have given everyone reason to pause. But they did not: with Bedloe, Shaftesbury and other opponents of the government now had a witness to corroborate Oates, whose own story had started to unravel. One of Bedloe's gifts was to tease out bits of his story over time. Eventually he expanded his testimony beyond Godfrey's death to implicate Grove and others (including the Queen, Catherine of Braganza[125]) in the plot to assassinate Charles — thus his testimony against Grove, Ireland and Pickering at their trial for treason. At the trial, however, Bedloe limited his testimony to the assassination plot; he had nothing to offer regarding Grove's supposed involvement in the Southwark fire.[126]

Bedloe cashed in on his notoriety by authoring numerous pamphlets. Two of them (coincidentally entitled, as were those of L'Estrange, an *Account* and a *Narrative*[127]) discussed the Southwark fire and other fires

123 *HL Jour.*, XIII, p. 342 (8 November 1678); *HC Jour.*, IX, p. 537 (10 November 1678).

124 Stater suggests that Shaftesbury or others worked with Bedloe to assure his conformity with Oates. For instance, Bedloe's testimony to the Privy Council on 7 November said nothing about Oates's plot. When Bedloe testified before the Lords on 8 November, however, he began to confirm some of Oates's evidence. See Stater, *Hoax*, pp. 87–88. Charles believed that someone had 'tampered with' Bedloe overnight. Kenyon, *Popish Plot*, p. 93, n.*.

125 The attempt to rope in Catherine, who was widely popular, was a miscalculation and an overreach by the government's opponents. These accusations never gained traction in either House or with Charles. *See* Stater, *Hoax*, pp. 91–92, 98–105.

126 Howell, *State Trials*, VII, fols 106–14.

127 William Bedlow (sic), *An impartial account of the several fires in London, Westminster, Southwark, and the places adjacent* (1679), available at EEBO (hereafter Bedloe, *Account*); Bedloe, *Narrative*.

Bedloe's career as a pamphleteer, which got off to a prolific start, was cut short when he died in Bristol in August 1680. See Kenyon, *Popish Plot*, p. 200. His death likely saved four lords from a traitor's death, as his testimony would have provided the necessary second witness to corroborate Oates's evidence of these lords' treasonous involvement in the assassination plot. Unfortunately, other witnesses corroborated Oates's evidence against a fifth lord, William, Viscount Stafford, who was tried upon impeachment in the House of Lords in December 1680. Despite

around London — all of which, Bedloe claimed, were the work of Catholics. Unsurprisingly, the pamphlets focused primarily on papist involvement in the Great Fire of London. Equally unsurprisingly, most of Bedloe's evidence was plagiarized.[128]

But the Great Fire of Southwark also featured in Bedloe's screeds. Because Bedloe's *Account* spent little time on the Southwark fire, it is best to begin with his *Narrative*. For the most part, the *Narrative's* description of the Southwark fire blended Oates and L'Estrange. Bedloe repeated Oates's assertion about Grove and three Irishmen setting the fire in return for £1,000, as well as the loot (worth £2,000) being carried off to Wild Street and Somerset House. Otherwise, Bedloe generally parroted L'Estrange: the fire started in the basement of an oil shop on St Margaret's Hill, and it was discovered by letter carriers who were unable to quench the fire while it was small.

Bedloe, however, added a few literary flourishes not found in L'Estrange's *Narrative*: for instance, 'meeting with great store of Oyle, [the fire] instantly set the Shop and Stairs on a Flame, and the people had much ado to get out at a Window into the Talbot Inn to save their Lives'.[129] Bedloe added the name of the shop owner (Welsh)[130] — a small fact, but one suggesting how widely known the story of the Southwark fire was. Following the charitable Brief, Bedloe provided a conservative estimate of 500 buildings burned and a loss of £80,000 to £100,000 from the fire.[131] Contradicting L'Estrange, Bedloe stated that

Stafford's constant and credible protests of innocence, the Lords found Stafford guilty of treason on 7 December 1680 (by a vote of 55–31). He was beheaded on 29 December 1680, although the remorse of his peers in the House of Lords was soon evident. Howell, *State Trials*, VII, fols 1217–1576.

Heneage Finch, Lord High Steward, presided over Stafford's trial. In imposing the death sentence, he made a comment that was utterly irrelevant, except to show how popish conspiracy theories had brainwashed even England's elite: 'Does any man now begin to doubt how London came to be burnt?' Ibid., fol. 1556. Not a word had been uttered at Stafford's trial about the Great Fires of London and Southwark, or about any other fire.

128 Hinds, 'Horrid Plot', p. 377. L'Estrange lit into Bedloe's *Narrative* with a sarcastic wit:

I found the *Narrative part* of it to be taken, *Verbatim* almost, out of two or three *old Seditious Libells* against the *Government,* that were printed by Stealth, some *ten* or *a dozen years agoe,* (before Mr. *Bedloes* time of Action) and scatter'd up and down in most of the Publique Houses upon the great Roads of *England* […].

Roger L'Estrange, *L'Estrange's Narrative of the Plot*, 2nd edn (1680), p. 17.

129 Bedloe, *Narrative*, p. 18. L'Estrange had been less definitive about the path of escape.

130 Ibid.

131 Ibid.

the fire engines were effective in preserving St Thomas's Hospital — the unhappy consequence of which was that the engine's inventor had been 'threatned to have his house Burnt for his pains'.[132]

The *Narrative* linked the Southwark fire to the larger papist conspiracy. Bedloe wrote that he had been at a Benedictine monastery in Paris in June 1676, just a month after the Southwark fire. Due to his knowledge of the city, the priests decided to employ him to set fires around London. He was to conduct this work with Gifford, a Jesuit who had orchestrated the Great Fire of London and who was also involved in the Southwark fire. On returning to London, Bedloe claimed to have gone on a number of missions to reconnoitre sites and collect material to set fires. Having failed to conquer England directly, Bedloe wrote, the priests had hit upon

> another medium of destruction, to ruine Protestants in a more oblique and clandestine way: [...] they resolv'd, and make it their business treacherously to Fire their Houses, to destroy their Goods and Estates, till they might be strong enough to venture on their Persons.[133]

Most of the *Narrative* laid out his proof of this design, which included three details of interest to the Southwark fire. First, after the Great Fire of London, Gifford had set his sights on the suburbs, and especially on Southwark, which was 'a place of eminent Trade, and generally a sober industrious people'.[134] Bedloe described a number of pre-1676 fires in Southwark that he claimed had been failed efforts to burn down the Borough; among them was the burning of the George Inn in 1670.[135] Second, Bedloe stated that the fire reignited at 10 p.m. because the Jesuits rekindled it.[136] Third, Bedloe provided the context for Oates's claim that the Jesuits 'had got at least £2,000 by' the Southwark fire. Knowing the chaos that the fire would cause, the Jesuits sent people to plunder abandoned houses. These looters carried off £2,000 worth of goods to their warehouses in Wild Street and to nearby Somerset House.[137]

---

132 Ibid. It may be this claim that allowed Edward Walford, two hundred years removed from the fire, to credit the deployment of fire engines for stopping the fire at the hospital. Edward Walford, 'Southwark: Old London Bridge', in *Old and New London*, VI (1878), p. 15.

133 Bedloe, *Narrative*, p. 1.

134 Ibid., p. 15.

135 The George's destruction in 1670 became the subject of a decree of the London fire court. *Weyland v. Andrewes*, Fire of London Court of Judicature Decrees, vol. G, fol. 265 (18 July 1671). For the decree detailing the destruction of the George in the Southwark fire, see *Weyland v. Sayer* (Decree 22).

136 Bedloe, *Narrative*, p. 18.

137 Ibid., p.1.

Bedloe's shorter *Account* spent less time on the Southwark fire, and added only one detail: that the London fires, including the Southwark fire, were started by dropping fireballs from the ends of poles into cellars with grated bars.[138] In another regard, the *Account* contradicted the *Narrative*, claiming that looting during the fire profited the Jesuits £4,000 and that all the stolen goods were transported to Somerset House.[139]

It is easy to recognize the basic elements of Oates's and Bedloe's stories: they are a mash-up of Peirce's focus on Somerset House[140] and Finch's claim that people were paid to set the fire for plunder,[141] all re-interpreted through the lens of anti-papist sentiment. However misguided, they represent what a substantial part of the English public believed about the Southwark fire. Indeed, some later accounts of the Southwark fire rely on details found only in Bedloe's pamphlets.[142] I think the better course is to distrust every single 'fact' that Bedloe related.

Two other unreliable accounts require less discussion. The first is the diary of John Ward, a minister in Stratford-upon-Avon. The diary is a rambling and hearsay-riddled affair, filled with musings on matters both historical and contemporary. Some of its descriptions of historical events are provably wrong. In one undated entry, Ward described the Southwark fire.[143] Nothing suggests that Ward observed the fire; like Bedloe, his concern was to trace every bad event, including urban fires, to papists.

Second, on 15 May 1679, the Earl of Clarendon reported to the House of Lords that the Lords' Committee of Examinations, which had been established to gather information about the Popish Plot, had received from Edward Warcupp, a Justice of Middlesex, two sworn declarations. William Johnson, pipemaker, and Joseph Wright, clerk, testified that

138 Bedloe, *Account*, pp. 3–4.
139 Ibid. p. 4.
140 See notes 90, 91, 93 and accompanying text.
141 See notes 92, 94 and accompanying text.
142 See Rendle, *Old Southwark*, pp. 45–46; see also note 132.
143 *Diary of the Rev. John Ward, A.M.*, arr. by Charles Severn (London, 1839). Regarding the Southwark fire, the entirety of Ward's entry read:
> Grover and his Irish ruffians burnt Southwerk, and had 1000 pounds for their pains, said the narrative of Bedloe. Gifford, a Jesuite, had the management of the fire. The 26 of May, 1676, was the dismal fire of Southwark. The fire begunne att one Mr. Walsh, an oil-man, neer St Margaret Hill, betwixt the George and Talbot Innes, as Bedloe, in his narrative, relates.

Ibid., pp. 155–56. Following this description was an entry noting that the great fire in London began in Pudding Lane, in the house of 'Mr. Farmer', a baker. Ward was challenged by names, getting neither 'Grove', 'Welsh' nor 'Farriner' correct.

they shared a room with Jonathan Smith, a papist. Smith stated to them that 'His Majesty was as great a Papist as any was in the Nation; and He, we do think, was One that set the Borough of Southwark on Fire'.[144] If this information was intended as a way to measure the Lords' appetite to go after Charles, it failed. The Lords wisely set the allegation aside without investigation.

Thus did the Southwark fire contribute to a drama of national scope and enduring political significance. The manner in which Oates and Bedloe used the Southwark fire is a testament to the ability of conspiracy theorists to turn every unfortunate event to their purpose and the grip that conspiracy theories can exert over a people. It is also a reminder that contemporary materials describing historical events must always be handled with care.

THE EVIDENCE OF THE SOUTHWARK FIRE COURT DECREES

Bearing that admonition in mind, the decrees of the Southwark fire court add modestly to our understanding of the fire. Unfortunately, on the fascinating question of how the fire started, the decrees provide no information. Likewise, the decrees make no reference to Oates, Bedloe or popish plots — although, in fairness, all but four of the fifty-two decrees were rendered by 28 May 1678, more than three months before anyone had heard of Titus Oates. There was, however, a curious gap in the decrees: after 28 May 1678, the Southwark fire court did not convene again until 2 March 1680 to resolve its final four cases. The national distraction of the Popish Plot may account in part for the delay in completing the fire court's work.

In other regards, the decrees of the Southwark fire court bolster L'Estrange's account. Forty-nine of the court's fifty-two decrees involved properties burned or destroyed in the fire.[145] Of that number, forty-five decrees listed a property location (or at least provided sufficient information from which a location can be inferred). Twenty-four properties were located either on the west side of the High Street or in locations even further west: Fowl Lane, Angel Yard, Three Crown Court, East Chain Gate, West Chain Gate and Montague Close. Thirteen properties were on the east side of the High Street or in the yards of inns located there. Eight additional properties were located on the High Street, although the decrees did not indicate whether they were on the east or west side. No decree involved a property further

---

144 *HL Jour.*, XIII, p. 573 (15 May 1679).

145 The other three involve the widening of the High Street. See notes 271–72 and accompanying text.

east than the yards behind the High Street. Among the properties on the east side of the High Street, none was located further south than the Talbot and none further north than St Thomas Close. These facts match L'Estrange's observation about the limited range of the fire on the eastern side of the Borough.[146]

On the west side of the High Street, the decrees related that the Compter on St Margaret's Hill burned down. No properties south of St Margaret's Hill were mentioned, and one decree suggested that houses along Compter Lane (which lay to the west of the Compter) were defaced but survived.[147] The decrees also showed how the fire danced all around St Saviour: cases arose from East Chaingate (on the south-east corner of the church), West Chaingate (on the south-west corner), and Montague Close (to the west and north of the church). Most of the properties were described as having burned down, but a few were 'demolished' or blown up and a couple were only defaced — clues that further indicated the fire's extent.

These clues align nicely with L'Estrange's rendition of the fire. If we credit L'Estrange's claim that a fresh wind was blowing from the south, the Talbot, as the most southerly property mentioned, must have been the approximate source of the fire. Moreover, the lack of any ruined properties north of St Thomas Close suggests that St Thomas's Hospital indeed acted as a fire wall. Finally, the lanes, alleys and courts mentioned in the fire court's decrees match L'Estrange's list of streets destroyed in the fire.

The Southwark fire court's records also suggest that, roughly at least, L'Estrange correctly estimated the magnitude of the fire. The forty-nine decrees dealing with properties damaged or destroyed concerned forty-seven plots of ground.[148] If we credit L'Estrange's estimate of 500 destroyed premises, the cases amount to a bit over 9 per cent of the total properties affected. By comparison, the London fire court heard roughly 1,560 cases arising from the Great Fire, or about 8 per cent of the total number of properties destroyed.[149] The Great Northampton

---

146 L'Estrange's *Narrative* stated that the eastern side of the Borough suffered damage only along the High Street, with some buildings and stables in the yards of the inns also destroyed. L'Estrange, *Narrative*, p. 7.

147 *Gale v. Wight* (Decree 23).

148 *Debnam v. Body* (Decree 28) and *Chandler v. Body* (Decree 29) involved one property, as did *Cannon v. Cannon* (Decree 40) and *Cannon v. Brace* (Decree 41). In addition, a few decrees involved multiple adjoining properties. See, e.g., *Williams v. Browker* (Decree 50) (ten properties).

149 The London fire court resolved approximately 1,585 cases, about twenty-five of which either were appeals from prior cases or involved fires other than the

Fire of 1675, which is believed to have burned down about 700 houses, yielded seventy-eight decrees, or approximately 11 per cent of the number of properties destroyed.[150] Although variations among the courts make precise comparisons difficult, these numbers suggest that L'Estrange's estimate was in the right range.

One such variable involved the tenants of St Thomas's Hospital. In September 1676, the governors of the Hospital voluntarily set up a committee that, in effect, acted as a fire court and recommended adjustments (or in instances of minor damages, no adjustments) in the leases of twenty-five tenants who had suffered damage in the fire.[151] These cases never came before the Southwark fire court,[152] but had some of them done so, the percentage of cases heard, relative to the total number of properties destroyed, would have ticked up.

In short, although L'Estrange's role as Stuart apologist requires caution before accepting his factual claims, the fire court's records bolster the reliability of L'Estrange, who is the Southwark fire's principal raconteur.

II. CREATING THE FIRE COURT

Seventeenth-century Southwark is often thought of as the situs of bear pits and brothels, of distillers and soap boilers and other noxious trades, and of the evils emanating from that dubious form of entertainment known as the theatre. But Jeremy Boulton's careful research has shown that, by the early to mid-seventeenth century, Southwark was in fact a blend of prosperous merchants, a broad (and reasonably well-off) working class and a small number of inhabitants mired in poverty.[153] Hearth-tax records from the 1660s reflect a significant amount of

Great Fire. To derive the 8 per cent figure in the text, I used the estimate, discussed in note 55, of 19,400 properties burned in the Great Fire.

150 See Decrees of the Northampton Fire Court, Northamptonshire Archives.

151 *Minute Books 1619–77*, fols 172ᵛ–75ᵛ (20 September 1676); ibid., fol. 177 (30 May 1677). In all instances, the governors accepted the committee's recommendations. As a general rule, the governors refused to reduce the rent, instead granting lengthy extensions of the leases (often 41 years, inclusive of the remaining term of the existing lease). Some of the tenants paid a considerable fine for their extensions. See Appendix.

152 Indeed, in the act erecting the Southwark fire court, Parliament specifically refused to give the court authority to determine disputes when the parties had already come to a post-fire agreement on lease terms. 29 Car. II, c. 4, § 15 (1677), reprinted in *Statutes of the Realm*, v, p. 845.

153 See Jeremy Boulton, *Neighbourhood and Society* (Cambridge, 1987). As one measure of wealth and social structure in Southwark, Boulton examined the 1621 subsidy assessment (in rough terms, a wealth tax) from 1621 and the 1621–22 poor-

new construction in St Saviour's parish, as well as many homes with three to ten (and sometimes more) hearths — a fact loosely signalling a degree of wealth and comfort.[154] L'Estrange's *Account* affirmed this view, describing Southwark as 'lately known to be a spacious Burrough, and a place of a great trade, full of Houses and Inhabitants, and those for the most part wealthy'.[155]

There was no doubt, therefore, that Southwark would rebuild after the fire. The only questions were how expeditiously and on what terms. Leases executed at the time almost always contained a covenant requiring the tenant to uphold and repair the premises in the event of damage (including fire). Because properties might then be sublet and even sublet again, a string of obligation, ultimately ending with the tenant in possession, determined who bore the legal responsibility for rebuilding.

Legal responsibility was one thing, but financial and practical responsibility was another. The tenant in possession might not have the wherewithal to rebuild. Even if the tenant could afford to do so, the incentive was often limited. Say, for instance, that a tenant had only another six months on the lease. To expect the tenant willingly to rebuild a ruined premises — likely constructing a better building than the one that had burned down — when the tenant reaped little of the benefit was fanciful. Of course, landlords could bring actions at law for unpaid rent and, at the end of the lease term, for breach of the covenant to repair. But that process might be lengthy. If the tenant died in the meantime, the action would abate and the landlord would bear the full loss. At a minimum, resort to the legal process would retard the rebuilding of Southwark for years.

Precisely the same reality had faced the country when London burned in 1666. There Parliament had crafted an innovative solution: the fire court. The fire-court concept sprang from the reality of how

---

rate assessment. Granting that these assessments were subject to evasion, they reflect that 15.5% of households in Boroughside (roughly, St Saviour's parish) paid a subsidy assessment and 30.7% of households paid a poor-rate assessment. At the same time, 11.4% of households received either a pension or an extraordinary payment due to impoverished circumstances. Ibid., pp. 95, 106–08.

154 See, e.g., TNA, E179/254/8; E179/258/7. This does not mean that everyone lived in comfort. For instance, exemption certificates in 1671 reflect that more than 700 residents in St Saviour parish lived in homes with only one or two hearths and were otherwise too impecunious to pay the tax. TNA, E179/346, fols 28–35.

155 L'Estrange, *Account*, p. 1. To the extent that he can be relied upon, Bedloe was in accord. See note 134 and accompanying text.

seventeenth-century real-estate development was typically financed: the owner (or at least the head landlord, possessed of a long term of years in a property[156]) would lease the land to a person willing to develop the property. The lease would be on terms sufficient to induce the tenant to develop the property: for instance, the landlord might agree to accept just a ground rent for the property for a term of forty years. After developing the property, the tenant would often sublease the property, recouping the cost of construction (plus a profit) over life of the lease.[157] At the end of the initial lease, the lessor (or more likely, the lessor's descendants) then had a valuable property that could be leased out at market rates, with profits henceforth accruing to the lessor.

The idea of the fire court was to insert judges into this process: to identify a willing builder (typically, though not always, the existing tenant) and then to mediate — or when necessary, adjudicate — the dispute between that builder and the lessor. The court's goal was to establish a new lease, usually at a reduced rent with an extended term of years, that gave the builder an incentive to rebuild. To make the new lease effective, the court had the power to override the terms of old leases, order the execution of new leases, and modify or even eliminate interests in the property that conflicted with the terms of the new leases.

The court was not always necessary: a willing lessor and a willing tenant could agree new terms on their own. But sometimes the landlord and the tenant disagreed over who should rebuild, or they could not settle on the length of the lease or the amount of the rent. The case also might require resolution of a boundary dispute.[158] Even if they could agree, other interests (like reversions at the end of a life estate)

---

156 I use the word 'landlord' consciously but advisedly. In rare instances a woman might hold the property of her own and, as landlady, enter into a long-term lease with a developer. One example (more or less, at least) was Mary Browker, whose name appears frequently in the decrees and who converted her fee-simple interest in various properties into a trust that gave her certain rights to develop the properties. See *Cole v. Browker* (Decree 10). In nearly all instances, however, property held for a long term of years was owned either by men or by institutions. To the extent possible, I use the neutral term 'lessor', but for the sake of brevity, I occasionally use 'landlord' rather than the more accurate 'landlord or landlady'.

157 Indeed, in the wake of the London fire, Primatt published a treatise that systematically determined the proper rents for builders to charge based on the return on investment that might be expected for various types of property. Stephen Primatt, *The City & Country Purchaser & Builder* (London, 1667).

158 In the days before party walls, neighbouring properties often interlocked vertically (for instance, the first neighbour might hold the second floor of the second neighbour's property, while the second neighbour might hold the third floor of the first neighbour's property). For examples of such interlocked holdings,

were not bound to respect the agreement, thus threatening the deal. In these situations, a court could cut through the barriers to negotiation and jumpstart rebuilding.[159] In doing so, it redistributed the loss among the lessor, the tenant and the other interested persons, rather than forcing the entire loss to fall on one party.

In 1667, when Parliament erected the London fire court, the concept was radical and risky. The court might have flopped colossally, which is perhaps the reason that Parliament initially legislated the court out of existence at the end of 1668. In reality, though, the court was a huge success: the London fire court was widely regarded as the indispensable institution that spurred the rapid rebuilding of London.[160] Parliament repeatedly reauthorized the London fire court to allow it to complete its work — a feat it finally accomplished on 18 February 1676, just three months before the Southwark fire.[161] Given the success in London, Parliament also authorized a fire court to handle the consequences of the devastating Northampton fire of 1675.[162]

It would therefore seem natural for Parliament to create a fire court to aid in rebuilding Southwark. And it did so, although the path to creating the Southwark court was somewhat more tortured.

A. THE ROUTE TO ENACTMENT

The first difficulty in securing passage of a fire-court statute for Southwark was that Parliament was not in session when the fire occurred. Because of Parliament's hostility, Charles II governed without Parliament as much as possible during the 1670s. When he prorogued Parliament after a five-week session in November 1675 — the only legislation that this Parliament produced was the Northampton fire statute — Parliament remained out of session for fifteen months. This 'Long Prorogation' ended in February 1677 when Charles, desperate to

---

see *Ely v. Mence* (Decree 1); *Young v. Bradway* (Decree 42). For a more run-of-the-mill boundary dispute, see *Taylor v. Smith* (Decree 52).

159 Indeed, in many of the cases that the Southwark fire court heard, rebuilding had already commenced; the parties were looking to the court either to confirm their agreement or to protect their leases against claims by others with reversionary interests.

160 See Bell, *The Great Fire*, p. 248 ('The Fire Judges' Court, by its practice and example, alone made the speedy restoration of London possible'); Reddaway, *The Rebuilding of London*, p. 94 ('[The Fire Court] had the greatest possible success').

161 For the acts reauthorizing the London fire court, see note 3. The London court's final case was *Rookes v. Mayor of London*, Fire of London Court of Judicature Decrees, vol. I, fol. 171 (18 February 1676).

162 For the act creating the Northampton fire court, see note 4.

finance his entry into the Dutch War, was forced to convene Parliament again.

Financing a navy and an army was Charles's principal concern, but Parliament had other ideas, extensively arguing over whether the Long Prorogation had effectively dissolved Parliament (thus requiring new elections that opponents hoped would be less favourable to Charles) and, as discussed, contemplating measures to remove Catholics from Parliament and eliminate popery. The two personal accounts of this session — Grey's *Debates* and Andrew Marvell's anonymously published *Account of the Growth of Popery and Arbitrary Government in England* — suggested that debates focused almost entirely on pressing matters of state: the precarious balance of international affairs, the King's desire for money, and Parliament's reluctance to provide it in view of Charles's controversial alliance with France and perceived papist influence at court. The *Journals* of the House of Commons and the House of Lords reflect the same focus. Parliament had little time for other matters.

Fortunately, some capacity remained. As Marvell noted, Parliament 'had not sat to any effect this four yeares', and members of the Commons did not want to be perceived as 'tak[ing] little care to redresse Greviances, or passe Good Laws, for the People, and that they should not be able to give any account of themselves to the Neighbours in the Country' and were therefore keen to 'passe some necessary Bills for the Kingdome'.[163] Thus, in the two-month session of Parliament that ended in April 1677, Parliament enacted eight public and fourteen private bills, in addition to the two pieces of legislation that provided Charles with funding for the navy.[164]

The historical record does not establish precisely why members of Parliament regarded a statute establishing a fire court for Southwark as one of the domestic matters most worthy of immediate attention. But there are clues, and these clues also help to explain some of the difficulties that the bill encountered prior to passage.

i) The City's Response to the Southwark Fire

To step back, Southwark had a long and fraught legal relationship with the City of London.[165] In a charter granted by Edward VI on 23

---

163 Andrew Marvell, *An Account of the Growth of Popery, and Arbitrary Government in England* (London, 1678), pp. 108–09.

164 *HL Jour.*, IX, pp. 120–21 (16 April 1677).

165 I distil the discussion in this paragraph principally from various chapters of Johnson, *Southwark and the City*, and from entries in the *Repertories of the Court of Aldermen* and the *Journal of the Court of Common Council* between 1670 and 1685.

April 1550, the City finally obtained jurisdiction over the Borough, but precise lines of authority remained blurred. By 1670, some of the City's liberties in the Borough had been seized into the King's hands. Justices of the peace for both the City and the County of Surrey claimed authority over Southwark, much to the chagrin and harassment of local citizens. It was unclear whether military service was owed to the City of London or to the County of Surrey and whether the City or the County had authority to license trades. The significant number of Protestant dissenters in Southwark complicated matters: preferences for City or County rule shifted depending on the religious tolerance shown by City or County officials at the moment. As Johnson describes, 'the [City's] charter justices — the Lord Mayor and aldermen past the chair — were busy men with their own wards to look after and little time to spare for Southwark'.[166] The County's justices of the peace were willing to step into the breach.

This less than benign neglect of Southwark is evident in the records of the Court of Common Council and the Court of Aldermen, whose entries in the years around the Southwark fire rarely mentioned the Borough. Ironically, in the Court of Aldermen's first session after the Southwark fire, the only three entries in the *Repertories of the Court of Aldermen* concerned property issues arising from the Great Fire of London.[167] In the eleven months between the Southwark fire and the passage of the Southwark fire-court statute, a single property in Bishopsgate Street, which encroached a few feet into the road, occupied more of the aldermen's sessions and time than the destruction of 500 houses in Southwark.[168]

That said, the City was not utterly indifferent to the plight of Southwark residents after the fire. On 29 May and again in June, donations were solicited from each parish in London, resulting in a collection of £393

---

166 Johnson, *Southwark and the City*, p. 236.

167 Rep., LXXXI, fols 199–99ᵛ (30 May 1676). The *Journal of the Court of Common Council*, which likewise contained entries in 1676 concerning items of business arising from the Great Fire of London, was similarly silent about the Southwark fire. That silence is not surprising: the Court of Common Council had less day-to-day oversight of the City's affairs.

168 The property belonged to a Mr Drinkwater, whose persistence in resisting efforts to remove the encroachment paid off: after numerous hearings, orders and reconsiderations, the City leased the encroachment to him. For some (though not all) of the proceedings, see Rep., LXXXI, fol. 215ᵛ (15 June 1676); ibid., fols 223–23ᵛ (22 June 1676); Rep., LXXXII, fol. 17ᵛ (21 November 1676); ibid., fols 70–70ᵛ (1 February 1677).

14s. 10¼d.[169] The Court of Aldermen constituted a committee to determine how best to distribute the proceeds.[170] And a month after the fire, the Court of Aldermen granted a petition from John Freeman, guardian of the orphans of Simon Read, to receive £200 of the £1,000 that the City held in trust for the orphans. Freeman wished to use the money to rebuild a tenement which had burned down in the Southwark fire and to which one of the orphans held the inheritance.[171]

More generally, however, only those Southwark-related matters that touched the City's larger interests commanded attention from the City's politicians. One matter was the ongoing tug of war with Surrey's justices over the exercise of jurisdiction in the Borough.[172] Another was the desire to recover from the Crown the liberties of Southwark, the loss of which exposed the City to the claim of the Borough's bailiff, William Eyre, to be reimbursed for revenue that he was due but unable to collect.[173] A third was the meal market.

The placement and operation of the meal market had long been a thorn in the City's side. Although the market spread along the High

---

169 Account Book, LMA, COL/CHD/PR/02/013. The *Repertories* mentioned the same total. Rep., LXXXI, fol. 248ᵛ (13 July 1676).

170 Rep., LXXXI, fols 212–12ᵛ (13 June 1676). The distribution did not occur immediately, for in the following month the Court again referred to the committee the 'forthwith' distribution of the collection and further asked the justices of the peace for Southwark and local ministers to assist in determining those in greatest need. Rep., LXXXI, fols 237ᵛ–38 (3 July 1676). By 13 July, the committee reported that a list of recipients had been developed and that the justices of the peace (Thomas Barker and John Freeman, both of whom would later serve as judges of the Southwark fire court) had received the funds for distribution. Rep., LXXXI, fol. 248ᵛ (13 July 1676). Two weeks later, Barker and Freeman signified to the Court of Aldermen that they had distributed the funds and requested return of the receipt that they had given the chamber for the proceeds. Rep., LXXXI, fols 259ᵛ–60 (27 July 1676). The Court of Aldermen eventually ordered the Chamberlain to deliver up the receipt. Rep., LXXXII, fol. 80ᵛ (8 February 1677). The minute order giving effect to the decree survives. LMA CLA/040/02/005.

171 Freeman offered to forego receipt of interest on the £1,000, which he had used for the maintenance and education of the orphans, until the £200 had been paid back into the City's Chamber. The Court of Aldermen ordered the payment. Rep., LXXXI, fols 227–27ᵛ (27 June 1676). Freeman may have been the justice of the peace for Surrey (and future judge on the Southwark fire court) referred to in note 170.

172 See, e.g., 47 *Journal of Court of Common Council* [unpaginated] (20 October 1676); Rep., LXXXI, fols 305ᵛ–06 (3 October 1676); Rep., LXXXI, fols 322ᵛ–24ᵛ (17 October 1676).

173 The matter was referred to the City committee that had been appointed to consider other matters regarding Southwark. See notes 172, 175 and accompanying text; Rep., LXXXI, fol. 260ᵛ (27 July 1676). Although the Court of Aldermen

Street, its centre was a house located right in the middle of the road at the intersection with St Thomas's Street, just a little south of London Bridge. On market days, the market badly jammed up traffic seeking to enter the City across London Bridge. Although unsuccessful efforts to move the market began in 1624,[174] the market's location became a matter of recurring concern for the Court of Aldermen after the Great Fire of London. In 1669 the aldermen constituted a six-member committee to make the recommendations necessary to reform the market's charter and effect a move.[175] Nothing was done, despite the Court of Aldermen's fitful prodding for the committee find a solution.[176]

This market committee occasioned the *Repertories'* first (albeit oblique) reference to the Southwark fire. In its third session after the fire, on 6 June 1676, the Court of Aldermen sent to the committee on the meal market several reports from the sheriff 'touching the Southwark market and other matters relating to the said Burrow and to Prosecute them as they shall see cause and to report their proceedings and opinions'.[177] With the fire having destroyed the market house and the shops of most of the vendors along the High Street, the aldermen recognized that the time to act was at hand — and that they could kill two birds with one stone. The Compter had also burned down in the fire, and the City had no desire to rebuild it for its prior purposes as town hall and gaol. On 16 June 1676, responding to a motion from a person named Carter, the aldermen gave the committee another charge: to consider what to do with the 'late Compter and other buildings in the Burrough of Southwark'.[178]

The apparent idea was to move the market from the High Street to the Compter property on St Margaret's Hill. Moving the market

---

eventually concluded that the City owed Eyre £650 for this lost revenue, see Rep., LXXXII, fol. 80[v] (8 February 1677); Rep., LXXXII, fols 291–91[v] (25 October 1677), I found no record indicating that the amount was paid. See also Johnson, *Southwark and the City*, pp. 196–97. The City's reluctance may have resulted from its dim view of Eyre's discharge of his duties and his litigiousness in the Southwark fire court. See note 228; *Eyre v. Mayor of London* (Decree 32).

174 Rep., XXXIX, fol. 19 (11 November 1624).

175 Rep., LXXV, fol. 19[v] (23 November 1669).

176 Rep., LXXV, fols 265[v]–66 (7 July 1670); Rep., LXXVII, fols 183[v]–84 (18 June 1672); Rep., LXXIX, fols 238–38[v] (2 June 1674). This last entry included complaints about stalls, which were set up in front of the houses along the High Street, narrowing the passage along the street.

177 Rep., LXXXI, fol. 207 (6 June 1676).

178 Rep., LXXXI, fol. 214[v] (15 June 1676). The *Repertories* left a blank space before the last name 'Carter', perhaps intending to fill in the first name if it became available.

quickly gained traction among City leaders.[179] The landlords holding the Compter property, as well as adjoining properties that the City wished to acquire to create ample space, were Sir William Twisden, Baronet, and Thomas Cartwright, Grocer.[180] On 23 November 1676, the market committee reported back to the Court of Aldermen that the ground on which the Compter and adjoining tenements had stood was 'very fitt and convenient for a market place'. The committee had already undertaken negotiations with Twisden and Cartwright for the purchase of their interests, and sought direction from the Court of Aldermen. The Court of Aldermen unanimously empowered the committee to finalize the purchase for the City on 'the best and easiest termes they can'.[181]

The owner of the meal market balked at moving and challenged the City's authority to force the change in venue. At a special court on 5 March 1677, the Court of Aldermen requested the market committee to consider whether the charter under which the City was granted the Borough of Southwark contained defects and to recommend the most fitting course of action to remedy any defects and settle the market in its intended location.[182] This date is significant, for Parliament had on 1 March 1677 allowed a bill to establish a fire court in Southwark to be introduced; and the bill was introduced one week later, on 8 March.[183]

The City also drew Robert Hooke, one of the City's surveyors, into discussion about the future of Southwark. On 24 February 1677,

---

179 Regulation of the City's markets was a frequent source of discussion in the Court of Aldermen. On 26 September 1676, for instance, the Court authorized the City solicitor to sue to prevent the operation of a market in Ratcliff Street and also to repair to the Lord Chancellor in an attempt to prevent the issuance of a patent for a new market in Salisbury Court. Rep., LXXXI, fols 298–98ᵛ (26 September 1676).

180 Rep., LXXXII, fol. 7ᵛ (9 November 1676); ibid., fol. 19ᵛ (23 November 1676). Cartwright apparently held the property on which the Compter itself had been located: on 9 November 1676, the Bridgemasters of London Bridge were ordered to use Bridge House funds to pay Cartwright all arrears of rent due him for the Compter and the adjacent houses burned down in the Southwark fire. Ibid., fol. 7ᵛ (9 November 1676). The *Repertories* made no mention of Cartwright's first name or of the occupations of either Twisden or Cartwright. I derived those details from fire-court decrees. See *Hall v. Crosse* (Decree 5); *Nicholls v. Crosse* (Decree 6); *Hudson v. Mayor of London* (Decree 33).

181 Rep., LXXXII, fols 19ᵛ–20 (23 November 1676).

182 Rep., LXXXII, fol. 109 (5 March 1677). Added to the Committee's membership were the Recorder of London (William Dolben), the steward of Southwark ((Edward Smyth) and Thomas Barker. Smyth and Barker would be active judges on the Southwark fire court.

183 See notes 195–96 and accompanying text.

Hooke called on Sir Thomas Player, Lord Chamberlain of London, and the two agreed to meet two days later at the Whale tavern in order to 'view [...] Southwick'.[184] Unfortunately, Hooke became violently ill the following day, and he sent someone else to meet with Player.[185] He later met Player in a coffee house on 27 February, but the diary unfortunately did not relate their conversation.[186]

By this time, Parliament had come back into session, and the story of the meal market's fate — as well as the rebuilding of Southwark more generally — largely shifted to Westminster. Three entries in the *Repertories* shed light on what was occurring in Parliament. First, on 13 March 1677, the Lord Mayor, Thomas Davies, informed the Court of Aldermen of 'divers bills pending in Parliament which may nearly concerne the State of the Citty'. A group of aldermen was delegated responsibility to consider the bills and 'what is required to be desired or offered in relation thereto on behalf of the City'.[187] The *Repertories* make no reference to which bills were under consideration, but the bill to establish the fire court must have been among them, as the bill had received its first reading in the Commons on 8 March.[188]

Second, on 20 March 1677, the Court of Aldermen ordered the city surveyors, Robert Hooke and John Oliver, to attend the Lord Mayor at Bridgefoot and to provide their views on the best way to enlarge the public passage onto London Bridge — including the possible removal of one or more houses. They were to proceed expeditiously, so that their views could be conveyed to the committee established to promote

184 See *Diary*, p. 275 (entry for 24 February 1677).

185 See *Diary*, p. 275–76 (entry for 25 February 1677) ('I sent Scarborough to Sir Th. Player found at the Whale in Southerick'). Likely due to his illness, Hooke's 25 February entry related events of both 25 and 26 February.

186 See *Diary*, p. 276 (entry for 27 February 1677) ('Saw Sir Th. Player in Mans coffee house').

187 Rep., LXXXII, f 113ᵛ (13 March 1677). The committee comprised the Recorder of London (William Dolben), Thomas Allen, William Turner, Richard Ford, Joseph Sheldon, Francis Chaplin, Robert Clayton, Nathaniel Herne and John Shorter. Ford, Chaplin and Clayton were also on the market committee. The 13 March entry in the *Repertories* could be read to infer that the City was unaware of the Southwark fire-court bill before its introduction on 8 March, but that would be only one inference among several that could be constructed from rather non-specific language. On the question of the bill's authorship, see pp. 63–65.

188 *HC Jour.*, IX, p. 394 (8 March 1677). While a number of other bills pending in Parliament touched generally on London's interests, the only bill other than the fire-court bill that specifically affected London was a bill to erect a Court of Conscience (a small-claims court to collect minor debts) in Southwark. *HC Jour.*, IX, p. 397 (12 March 1677).

the City's concerns in Parliament — and specifically with an eye toward obtaining a proviso in the fire-court legislation that would allow the enlargement of the public passage.[189] Hooke's diary noted that he met '[a]t Guildhall with Committee for the Parliament' on 26 March 1677. Unfortunately, with characteristic terseness, the diary reported none of the discussion.[190]

The *Repertories* also noted the Lord Mayor's desire for the insertion of another proviso in the fire-court bill: one that required the City to remove the Southwark market out of the street and onto more convenient space on St Margaret's Hill.[191] Here again, Hooke's diary provides confirming evidence. On 29 March 1677, Hooke went '[t]o Westminster hall with Southerick men at the Baccus and at the Leg about removing Southerick Market'.[192]

Third, on 3 April 1677, as the fire-court legislation neared passage in the House of Commons, the Court of Aldermen specifically asked three members of the parliamentary delegation (Bludworth, Ford and Clayton) to provide advice at its next session about 'prosecuting the agreement recently made' to purchase the land on St Margaret's Hill.[193] The records of the Aldermen's next session, on 5 April, made no mention of an appearance by Bludworth, Ford or Clayton.[194]

---

189 Rep., LXXXII, fols 120–120ᵛ (20 March 1677). A further aspect of the desired proviso was to permit the City to pay out of the coal duty that it had been receiving since the Great Fire for any ground taken. Ibid., fol. 120ᵛ. This proviso did not make it into the final fire-court legislation.

190 *Diary*, p. 281 (entry for 26 March 1677). Hooke's diary also noted that, on the following day, he went '[t]o Parliament at Westminster about opening southwick by water'. Ibid. (entry for 27 March 1677). The diary contained nothing to give this phrase meaning, but it seems unlikely that the meeting related to the fire-court legislation.

191 Rep., LXXXII, fols 120–120ᵛ (20 March 1677). The hoped-for proviso was also to contain language permitting the City to use the coal duty to pay the proprietors of the ground for their interest. Ibid.

192 *Diary*, p. 282.

193 Rep., LXXXII, fol. 139 (3 April 1677).

194 Rep., LXXXII, fol. 142ᵛ (5 April 1677). One reason could be that the agenda for the Court's session on 5 April was already packed. In addition, Clayton, who was an alderman and who almost always attended the Court's sessions, was not in attendance on that day. After 5 April, the Easter holiday kept the Court of Aldermen out of session until 24 April — by which time Parliament had passed the fire-court legislation and largely mooted the need for advice. The next session that mentioned the purchase of the property on St Margaret's Hill was 24 July. Rep., LXXXII, fols 226ᵛ–27 (24 July 1677).

ii) Ushering the Bill through Parliament

Although the legislation to create the Southwark fire court moved through Parliament quickly — from the House of Commons' initial agreement on 1 March 1677 to entertain the bill to the House of Lords' passage of the bill on 14 April 1677 and the King's assent on 16 April 1677 — there were bumps on the road to enactment of the fire-court bill. Matters began smoothly enough. On 1 March 1677, the House of Commons gave leave to bring in a bill establishing the Southwark fire court.[195] There was no registered dissent — a fact suggesting widespread acceptance of the general principle that a fire court to aid Southwark's rebuilding was proper.

The bill was presented in the Commons and had its first reading on 8 March 1677.[196] Its second reading was on 17 March 1677. The bill was then sent to a committee composed of forty-seven named members of the House, as well as other members of the House — those serving for the City of Westminster and the County of Surrey — mentioned by office.[197] The first-listed member of the committee was Sir Thomas Clarges, a staunch Royalist who served as the elected member for Southwark from 1666 until 1679.[198]

On 31 March 1677, Clarges reported back to the House that the committee had agreed several amendments to the fire-court bill and further recommended the addition of a quorum proviso. The amendments were read twice, and all of the amendments — except for one listing the persons who could serve as judges — were accepted. The matter of court membership was quickly cleared up: the House gave leave to the knights who served for Surrey to present additional names of persons eligible to serve. This being done and the list having been read twice, the court's membership was agreed.[199]

The quorum proviso, which would have required one of the common-law judges to be a member of the court for every session, fared less well. To put the proviso in context, only the common-law judges had been authorized to sit on the London fire court.[200] In contrast, for the

---

195 *HC Jour.*, IX, p. 390 (1 March 1677).

196 *HC Jour.*, IX, p. 394 (8 March 1677). On the previous day, the House ordered that the bill should be read the following day. *HC Jour.*, IX, p. 393 (7 March 1677).

197 *HC Jour.*, IX, p. 401 (17 March 1677).

198 See M. W. Helms and Leonard Naylor, 'Clarges, Thomas', in *The History of Parliament: The House of Commons 1660–1690*, ed. by Basil Duke Henning (London, 1983), available at www.historyofparliamentonline.org/ [accessed 2 January 2024].

199 *HC Jour.*, IX, p. 410 (31 March 1677).

200 See 18 and 19 Car. II, c. 7, § 1 (1667), reprinted *in Statutes of the Realm*, V, p. 601.

Northampton fire court, the common-law judges were permitted to serve on the court, but Parliament added local dignitaries and officials as potential members.[201] The act did not require that a common-law judge sit at any session.[202] The Southwark fire court followed the Northampton model, allowing but not requiring common-law judges to sit alongside notable citizens. The point of the quorum proviso was to pull the Southwark fire court back in the direction of the London fire court and to place the process more firmly under judicial control.

The proviso failed to carry.[203] It may, however, have had a practical effect: at least one common-law judge sat on every case that the Southwark fire court decided.[204]

With Surrey members added and the quorum proviso defeated, the bill was engrossed.[205] On 11 April 1677, the bill was then read the third time. At this point, a final controversy — the fate of the meal market — nearly scuttled the bill's passage. When the bill was read, someone (there is no record of who) tendered a proviso designed to keep the market in its pre-fire location. The proviso was read twice.[206] After briefly attending to other business, the House returned to the matter. On the question whether the proviso should be read a third time, the House divided — a rare event in seventeenth-century Parliaments that valued consensus.

By a vote of 74–72, the House permitted a third reading of the proviso.[207] The proviso then came up for a vote, where the House again divided. Here the vote was even closer: 78 in favour and 78 against.

201 See 27 Car. II § 1 (1675), reprinted in *Statutes of the Realm*, v, p. 798.

202 Indeed, no common-law judge sat for any of the seventy-eight cases of the Northampton fire court. See Northampton Decrees, note 150.

203 The *Journal of the House of Commons* did not record ayes and nays, a fact suggesting that the vote was not close enough for the House to divide.

204 See note 285 and accompanying text.

205 *HC Jour.*, IX, p. 410 (31 March 1677).

206 *HC Jour.*, IX, p. 418 (11 April 1677). The proviso is the last section of the act. See 29 Car. II, c. 4, § 20 (1677), in *Statutes of the Realm*, v, p. 846 (providing that the Southwark market 'shall continue and be kept in the same place and at the same times where it hath been auntiently and is at this present kept, and that the said Market shall not be kept in or removed to any other place or held at any other time whatsoever').

207 *HC Jour.*, IX, p. 418 (11 April 1677). The tellers for the ayes were Sir Gilbert Talbot and Sir Robert Howard; the tellers for the nays were Sir Thomas Littleton and 'Mr. Hopkins' (likely Richard Hopkins II of Coventry). Hopkins was among the most active anti-papists and was opposed to granting Charles a supply for the navy. See A. M. Mimardière, 'Hopkins, Richard II', in *The History of Parliament*, available at www.historyofparliamentonline.org/ [accessed 2 January 2024].

Perhaps a fan of urban congestion, the Speaker, Edward Seymour, resolved the tie by voting in favour of keeping the market in its present location.[208] With that issue resolved, the House of Commons passed the Southwark fire-court bill and directed Sir Adam Browne to carry up the bill to the House of Lords.[209]

The bill would pass the House of Lords without alteration but not without controversy. The Lords took up the bill almost immediately. It was read on 12 April 1677, and it was sent to a committee of fifty-one lords, any five or more of whom were to meet 'at Eight of the Clock, in the Prince's Lodgings' on Saturday, 14 April.[210] Minutes and other evidence of the meeting survive, and they reflect that the only concern was the City's fervent effort to remove the market proviso. The Lord Mayor and Aldermen sent a petition (undated but received on 14 April) to the Lords, requesting that they not pass the fire-court bill until the petitioners had been heard (Fig. 8).

The petition recited the gist of the market clause, asserting that it was added at the third reading of the bill in the Commons, when 'the house was very thinne'.[211] This proviso, the petition boldly asserted, stripped the City of its undoubted right by charter, which had been confirmed by act of Parliament, to remove the market to elsewhere in the Borough. The proviso had been inserted into the bill by some inhabitants of Southwark 'for their own private interests', despite the 'publique hurt of the greater part of the Burrough and likewise of the whole Citty and suburbs'. Finally, the petition asserted that, if the market were removed through legal process (a writ *ad quod damnum*), a

---

208 A member for Hindon, Seymour was a strong Tory, a skilled politician, and at the time Treasurer of the Navy. See John P. Ferris, 'Seymour, Edward', in *The History of Parliament*, available at www.historyofparliamentonline.org/ [accessed 3 January 2024]. While I jest about Seymour's motivation for his tie-breaking vote, there were reasonable arguments, which emerged during the proceedings in the House of Lords, to maintain the market in its pre-fire location. See note 214 and accompanying text. Whether Seymour found those arguments meritorious or whether his vote was part of a larger political calculus is uncertain.

In 1677, there were more than 500 members of the House of Commons. With fewer than 160 members voting on the meal-market proviso, attendance at the 11 April session must have been light — a fact that the City seized upon when it sought further to oppose the proviso. See note 211 and accompanying text.

209 *HC Jour.*, IX, p. 418 (11 April 1677). A member for Surrey, Browne was one of the persons listed as eligible to serve as a judge on the Southwark fire court. He ultimately sat as a judge on ten cases.

210 *HL Jour.*, XIII, p. 112 (12 April 1677).

211 Petition to the Lords, in *House of Lords Papers 10 April 1677 to 16 July 1677*, Parliamentary Archives, HL/PO/JO/10/1/369/420.

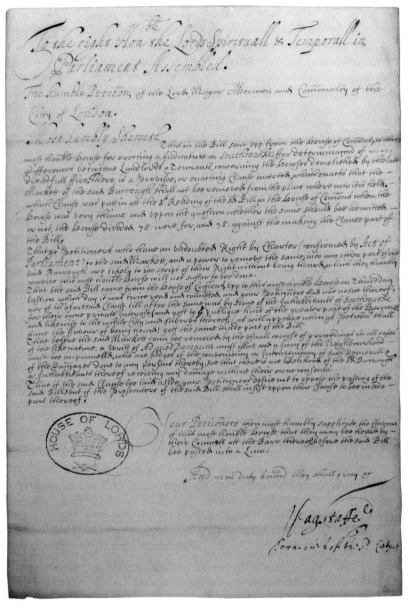

Fig. 8. The Petition of the Lord Mayor, Aldermen and Commonalty of the City of London to the House of Lords objecting to the proviso added to the Southwark fire court bill whereby the borough market was not to be moved, April 1677.

© Parliamentary Archives, London HL/PO/JO/10/1/369/420

jury would be impanelled to determine any damage due to inhabitants, so that they would suffer no unrecompensed loss. The petition closed by stating that, aside from the market proviso, the City and Aldermen did not oppose the bill, but that, if the prosecutors of the bill insisted on the proviso, the City should be allowed to appear at the bar of the House of Lords and to be heard.

The *Minutes of the Committees* then take up the story.[212] A marginal note indicates that one member of the committee — the Earl of Dorset (Richard Sackville) — attended the 14 April meeting, but no other attendees were listed. The bill was read in its entirety, at which point George Jeffreys, then the Common Serjeant of London and the City's counsel,[213] was called in. Jeffreys made two initial observations: first, that the City was lord of the manor of Southwark, and second, that the City had first heard of the proviso's insertion at nine o'clock on the previous evening (13 April). The proviso, he asserted, took away the City's inheritance.

At this point, Mr Offley spoke up,[214] replying that the market proviso should have been no surprise to the City, for the Commons had heard the Recorder of London (William Dolben) several times. Jeffreys responded that he had nothing to say against the bill as it related to the establishment of the fire court. The minutes then stated that 'they withdraw'. It is not clear whether 'they' included Offley, for the next line noted that Offley offered to supply witnesses who would testify that the sheriff of London, Sir John Shorter, had made a bargain with the inhabitants of Southwark: in return for the inhabitants' agreement to allow the widening of the High Street, the City would forbear moving the market. The committee ordered that these witnesses should be sworn at the bar in the morning and attend the afternoon session — along with Shorter, who was to bring the agreement allegedly made. The committee then adjourned.

---

212 Minutes of House of Lords Committees 1672–86, pp. 205–06, Parliamentary Archives, HL/PO/CO/1/3.

213 On Jeffreys' later role as advocate before the Southwark fire court and beyond, see note 119.

214 The tenor of the minutes suggests that Offley (with no first name given in the minutes) was a lawyer representing the interests that inserted the proviso. At least two Offleys were members of the inns of court during the latter seventeenth century. A lawyer (or lawyers) named 'Offley' or 'Ofley' (also no first name given) occasionally appeared as counsel in cases before the London fire court. See, e.g., *Best v. Gerrard*, Fire of London Court of Judicature Decrees, vol. C, fol. 73 (18 February 1668); *Weyland v. Andrewes*, ibid., vol. G, fol. 265 (18 July 1671).

The minutes described no further proceedings in the afternoon session, when a different committee considered another bill. Just before the note indicating that the committee adjourned to the afternoon and the formal order to the witnesses and to Shorter, however, two lines of committee notes appeared. The first indicated that the committee had read the bill paragraph by paragraph. The second line read: 'Agreed to the Provisoe in the Bill'.

The committee apparently came to this agreement before the adjournment, for events quickly switched back to the House of Lords. The Lords had been in session during the morning of 14 April, when the committee met. The fire-court bill was the first matter the Lords took up in the afternoon session.[215] The Bishop of Salisbury reported the committee's view that the bill pass as it was. The petition from the Lord Mayor of London to be heard — likely the petition described above — was then read to the House. The Lords rejected the petition because 'the City of *London* had been heard before the Lords Committee by Counsel, and for other Reasons'.[216]

The *Journal of the House of Lords* did not say what those 'other reasons' might be, but the *State Papers* shed some light. When Parliament was in session, Williamson received an update of each day's session for both Houses. The updates typically said nothing more than the *Journals* of the respective Houses — and often much less. But the update for 14 April stated that the Lord Mayor's petition was 'layd aside', with the Lords 'finding therein some reflections Upon ye House of Commons'.[217] The City had overplayed its hand with the boldness of its petition.

After a third reading, the bill passed the Lords, with only Lord Stafford dissenting.[218]

Two days later, on 16 April 1677, the Lords acquiesced in the Commons' version of the supply bill that Charles so desperately sought. Charles appeared almost immediately in the House of Lords to assent to the supply bill, as well as to eight public bills and fourteen private bills that had passed both Houses.[219] The seventh of the public bills established the Southwark fire court.

---

215 *HL Jour.*, XIII, p.117 (14 April 1677).
216 Ibid., p. 117.
217 TNA, SP 29/393/111 (14 April 1677).
218 *HL Jour.*, XIII, pp. 116, 117 (14 April 1677). The *Journal of the House of Lords* noted no grounds for Stafford's dissent. Three years later, Stafford would become the only lord to lose his head as a result of the Popish Plot. See note 127.
219 *HL Jour.*, XIII, p. 120 (16 April 1677). Charles also assented to a bill — a tax on ale and liquor for three years — designed to pay for the supply, ibid., and withheld

iii) The Market and the Compter: Knock-on Effects of the Legislation

Parliament's decision to leave the meal market in place was not the end of the matter. The market continued to cause congestion at the foot of London Bridge, and the City continued to try, without apparent success, to regulate the congestion.[220] It took another eighty years and several acts of Parliament to get it right, but the market in the High Street was ultimately abolished and then re-established more or less in the location of the present Borough Market.[221]

Having been thwarted in its initial effort to redevelop the Compter and surrounding land on St Margaret's Hill into the market, the City struggled to find a proper use for the land. Initially it forged ahead. On 24 July 1677, the Court of Aldermen authorized the purchase of the land on St Margaret's Hill from Cartwright, the land's owner, for £820.[222] But that purchase, intended for the now-forbidden move of the meal market, left open the question of what to do with the land.

---

assent from one private bill, ibid., p. 121. While the distinction between public and private bills is not especially significant, the Southwark fire-court legislation was the last time that a bill establishing a fire court was treated as a public act. Beginning with the Warwick fire court in 1694, Parliament treated fire-court legislation as private bills.

220 See, e.g., Rep., LXXXIV, fol. 209 (28 September 1679) (requesting that the Bailiff take steps to limit the market to the permitted three days per week).

221 28 Geo. II c. 9 (1755), in *The Statutes at Large*, XXI, ed. by Danby Pickering (Cambridge, 1766), p. 227; 28 Geo. II c. 23 (1755), in *The Statutes at Large*, XXI, p. 310; 30 Geo. II c. 31 (1757), in *The Statutes at Large*, XXII, p. 182. The first of these acts both acknowledged the role of the 1677 Southwark fire-court legislation in fixing the place of the market and described the great obstruction that the market created. It abolished the High Street market. The second act allowed the churchwardens of St Saviour to hold a market in Southwark as long as it did not interfere with the High Street. The third act clarified the terms of the second.

222 In *Hudson v. Mayor of London* (Decree 33), the City's counsel described this price as being twenty years' purchase, based on rental values before the fire: in other words, the properties purchased had rented for £41 per year. The Court of Aldermen ordered the committee to examine Cartwright's title, after which the Bridgemaster was to pay Cartwright £820 from funds advanced by the City Chamberlain. Rep., LXXXII, fols 224ᵛ, 226ᵛ–27 (24 July 1677). That order was later altered, with the money paid directly by the Chamberlain and the property to be improved for the benefit of the Chamber. The trustees who took possession of the land for the City were also ordered to work with Mr Lane, the comptroller of the Chamber, to defend the City's interests in the property before the Southwark fire court. Rep., LXXXII, fol. 261ᵛ (27 September 1677). Subsequently, the Court of Aldermen retained Sir George Jeffreys and Lane to appear as counsel for the City with regard to a petition filed by tenants of the ground on St Margaret's Hill that the City had just purchased. Rep., LXXXII, fols 285ᵛ, 286ᵛ (23 October 1677). The case

Because the City did not want to rebuild a town hall and compter,[223] it approached William Eyre, the Borough's bailiff who held the lease on the Compter (and who paid the rent out of fees extracted from prisoners at the Compter). The City suggested that Eyre develop the property into private residences, with the City offering favourable lease terms as an inducement.[224] But relations between Eyre and the City were strained. The loss to the Crown of some of Southwark's liberties took a bite out of Eyre's income — a fact that, by the City's own admission, required it to compensate Eyre £650. But the City, strapped for cash, was unable to pay Eyre.[225] Undoubtedly, the City hoped to cancel its debt by giving Eyre good terms to develop the land.[226]

For his part, Eyre was uninterested in becoming a developer — perhaps because he was unwilling to allow the City to use the lease as a way to wiggle out of its £650 obligation. Instead, he wanted the City to rebuild the Compter and apparently he continued to operate some sort of compter in a rented property near London Bridge.[227] The mutual recalcitrance of the parties led to one of the Southwark fire court's notable cases, in which Eyre sued the City. The court discharged Eyre

the *Repertories* referred to was *Hudson*. In a shocking move (by modern standards), the Aldermen also asked Edward Smyth and Thomas Barker, both of whom were judges on the fire court, to attend them to discuss the case. The *Repertories* contain no indication that either Barker or Smyth ever attended the Court of Aldermen on this matter. Barker sat as a judge on the case; Smyth did not.

223 Indeed, the second reference in the *Repertories* to the Southwark fire occurred when the Court of Aldermen charged the committee considering the fate of the Southwark meal market with the new task of reporting what to do with the Compter. Rep., LXXXI, fol. 214ᵛ (15 June 1676).

224 See *Eyre v. Mayor of London* (Decree 32).

225 On the loss of the City's liberties (and the loss of Eyre's profits derived therefrom), see notes 166, 173 and accompanying text. The woeful state of the City's finances was a constant theme in the *Repertories* during the latter half of 1677, when Eyre's petition for compensation was pending.

226 After hearing a report from the committee established to consider Eyre's petition and the committee's view that Eyre was owed £650, the Court of Aldermen asked the committee to treat with Eyre about the Compter and to see if something might be worked out without incurring any charges against the City's depleted Chamber. Rep., LXXXII, fols 291–91ᵛ (25 October 1677).

227 On 22 June 1676, just four weeks after the fire, the Court of Aldermen heard the petition of Margaret Barton, a widow, that Eyre had contracted with her to rent a tenement near Bridge House. Eyre then converted the house into a prison, to Barton's great prejudice and to the annoyance and endangerment of the neighbourhood. The Court ordered Eyre to appear on 27 June, Rep., LXXXI, fol. 222ᵛ–23 (22 June 1676), but the *Repertories* provide no indication that Eyre did so, either on that day or any other.

from the £50 per annum lease on the Compter and left the City free to develop the property as it wished.[228]

 But that result left open the question of what to do with the land. The issue continued to percolate before the Court of Aldermen for years,[229] until the City finally determined to build a new courthouse. Construction was completed in 1686 (Figs 9, 10, 11).[230]

228 See Decree 32. The *Repertories* reflect some of the City's legal manoeuvring once the City became aware of Eyre's petition before the Southwark fire court. Rep., LXXXIII, fol. 31 (4 December 1677); ibid., pp. 51ᵛ–52 (8 January 1678). The City may have realized that it was on thin ice; the day before the fire court's hearings, the Court of Aldermen requested Jeffreys and Lane to appear as counsel for the City in Eyre's case and in the related case of other tenants on St Margaret's Hill (see note 221) and to 'make the best defence they can'. The City also retained John Oliver to measure and value the ground, so that Jeffreys could make a better defence. Rep., LXXXIII, fols 51ᵛ–52 (8 January 1678). The *Eyre* decree itself oozes with the animosity between the City and Eyre; the City argued that Eyre had been withholding rent from the City and requested the court to remove Eyre from his position as bailiff as part of the discharge of Eyre's lease. Cf. Johnson, *Southwark and the City*, p. 250 (describing other incidents of Eyre's inadequate performance in office). Removing Eyre from office would have stretched the jurisdictional power of the fire court beyond its breaking point, and the court wisely ignored the request in its decree. As bailiff, Eyre continued to make mischief for the City for years to come. For instance, the Aldermen learned that Eyre was renting out encroachments on St Margaret's Hill (likely on the site of the old Compter). Rep., LXXXVII, fol. 107 (23 February 1682). See also Johnson, *Southwark and the City*, pp. 197–200.

229 Immediately after the Southwark's fire court's decree transferring the Compter lease back to the City, the Court of Aldermen asked the committee that purchased the St Margaret's Hill properties to provide its opinion on what to do with the Compter ground. Rep., LXXXIII, fols 63ᵛ–64 (15 January 1678). The *Repertories* do not contain that opinion, but the best use of the ground continued to come before the aldermen for years. See, e.g., Rep., LXXXVI, fol. 142 (9 June 1681) (requesting the opinion of the Committee for the Bridgehouse to advise on the best use of the void ground on St Margaret's Hill); ibid., p. 151 (23 June 1681) (appointing a committee to investigate a petition to rebuild the courthouse and compter on St Margaret's Hill, which, according to the petition, the City was obligated to do); Rep., LXXXVII, fols 152–52ᵛ (11 May 1682) (describing a similar petition).

230 The courthouse's construction was underway in October 1685, when the Court of Aldermen ordered that a statue of the recently deceased Charles II be placed in front of the building. Rep., XC, fol. 141ᵛ (8 October 1685). Construction had finished by 1686, when the *Repertories* noted that churchwardens of St Saviour were claiming the ownership of the ground on which the courthouse stood. Rep., XCI, fol. 156 (31 August 1686); ibid., fols 176–76ᵛ (5 October 1686). This courthouse eventually fell into ruin and was taken down in 1793, when another courthouse was erected. The statue of Charles was removed to a perch atop a watchbox in Three Crown Court. See Manning and Bray, *Surrey*, p. 550.

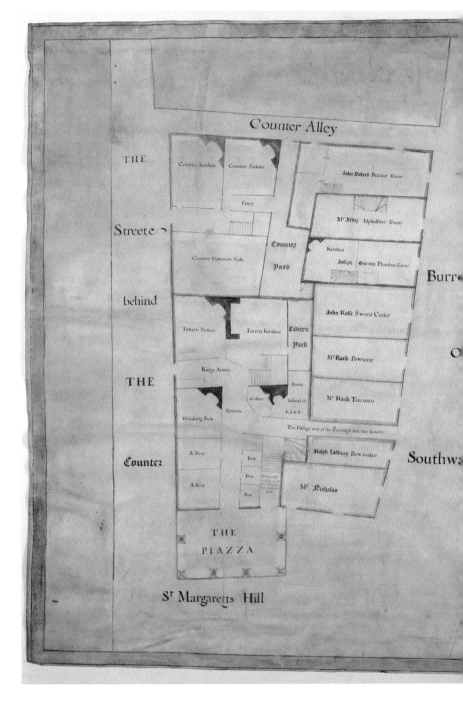

Counter Alley

THE

Counter Kitchen · Counter Parlour

John Ballard Brazier Tenant

Entry

Mr Alde; Upholsterer Tenant

Streete

Counter
Yard

Kitchen

Joseph Garrett Plumber Tenant

Counter Common Side

Burr

behind

John Rolfe Sword Cutler

Tavern Parlour · Tavern Kitchen

Tavern
Yard

Mr Rack Pewterer

Kings Armes

O

THE

Roome

Mr Rack Tin-man

the Store

behind the
BARR

Drinking Box

Tavern

The Passage out of the Borrough into the Tavern

Counter

A Box

Box

Ralph Ledbury Box maker

Southw

A Box

Box

Mr Nicholas

Box

THE
PIAZZA

Sᵗ Margaretts Hill

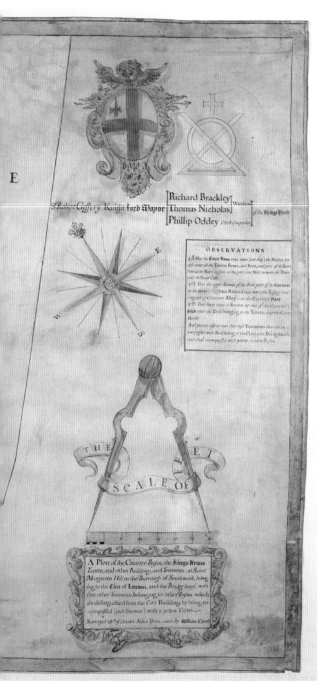

Fig. 9. William Cavell, *Plan of buildings at St Margaret's Hill*, 1686.

OBSERVATIONS on the right of the plan read:

1st That the Court Room runs over (not only) the Piazza, but also over all the Tavern Boxes, and Barr, and part of the Room behind the Barr, as farr as the partition Wall between the Barr and the Stair Case

2dly. That the upper Roomes of the Back part of the Tenement in the occupation of John Ballard run over the Passage leading out of Counter Alley into the Counter Yard

3dly. That there runs a Staires up out of the Counter Yard over the Yard belonging to the Tavern into the Court House

And you are also to note that those Tenements that are encompassed with Red belong to the Citie, and Bridgehouse and those encompassed with yellow to other Persons.

© London Metropolitan Archives COL/CCS/PL/01/049/A

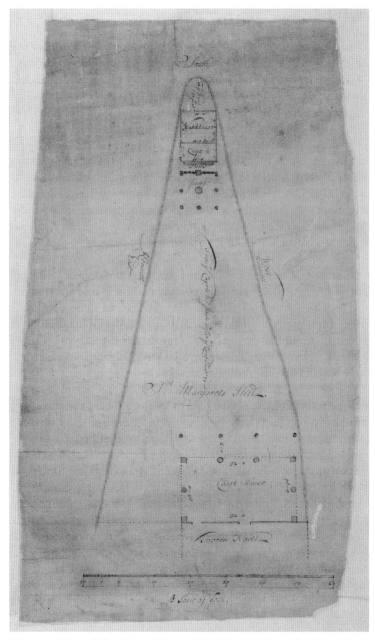

Fig. 10. Plan of the Court House, Watchhouse, Cage, Stocks and Pump at St Margarets Hill. N.B. South is at the top.

© London Metropolitan Archives COL/PL/02/R/003/d

VIEW OF THE TOWN-HALL S? MARGARETS HILL SOUTHWARK .
PREVIOUS TO THE PRESENT ERECTION BY THE CORPORATION OF LONDON IN 1793 .

Fig. 11.   Thomas Dale after Ravenhill, The Town Hall, Southwark, before its demolition in 1793, from Robert Wilkinson's *Londina Illustrata*, 1825.
© Trustees of the British Museum 1880,1113.5226

iv) A Final Question: Who Wrote the Southwark Fire Court Act?

As for the authorship of the Southwark fire-court act, little can be said definitively. In significant measure, the act was copied — sometimes word-for-word, sometimes with comparable phrasing — from the acts establishing the London and Northampton fire courts.[231] Matthew Hale, the great common-law judge of the mid-seventeenth century, is often credited as the inspiration for, if not the wordsmith of, the London act. Unfortunately, the fire that destroyed the records of the House of Commons in 1834 eliminated much of the evidence from which the authorship of the London, Northampton and Southwark acts might have been gleaned.

Michael Turner has asserted that the author of the Southwark act was Thomas Clarges.[232] Given Clarges's role in shepherding the bill through

231 The Northampton act was itself largely derivative of the London act, albeit with changes. See pp. 65–70.
232 Turner, 'Urban Renewal', p. 130.

the Commons,[233] Turner's claims is plausible. Nonetheless, I found no clear evidence to support it. Clarges possessed neither the legal training that would have been helpful in drafting the provisions that deviated from the London and Northampton acts nor the cleverness of mind.[234] Turner also made a broader assertion: that 'the initiative behind the act certainly did not come from the Corporation of London which was apparently ignorant of the bill's contents'.[235] This claim too is unsupported; Turner unfairly extended the City's ignorance of the market proviso to an ignorance of the bill as a whole.[236] To the contrary, the Aldermen were aware of the fire-court legislation no later than 20 March 1677.[237]

At the same time, the historical record does not clearly prove the contrary proposition: that the City drafted the legislation.[238] It seems likely that the City — possibly through Wynne, the City solicitor, Dolben, the Recorder of London, and Jeffreys, then Common Serjeant — had a hand in crafting the language. The Lord Mayor of London's wish list for provisions in the fire-court legislation,[239] including a request for enlarging the High Street that ultimately made its way into the act,[240] suggests as much.[241] So does the original bill's inclusion of London dignitaries (but no Surrey dignitaries) as judges eligible to serve on the court.[242] If true, Offley's comment before the House of Lords committee — that the Commons had heard Dolben several times concerning the legislation — also reveals the City's guiding hand.[243] Of course, the market proviso was certainly drafted by someone else — perhaps Offley.[244]

---

233 See notes 198–99 and accompanying text.

234 Some contemporaries did not hold Clarges's intellect in high regard. See *The Diary of Samuel Pepys*, I, p. 129, entry for 6 May 1660 (recalling the Earl of Sandwich's description of Clarges as 'a man of small *entendimiento* [understanding]').

235 See Turner, 'Urban Renewal', p. 130.

236 On the market proviso, see notes 206–17 and accompanying text.

237 See notes 189–92 and accompanying text.

238 An intriguing line in Robert Hooke's diary related that, on 10 January 1677, he met 'with Sir Chr. Wren at Lord Mayors about passing bills'. *Diary*, p. 267. When Hooke used the word 'bill', he usually meant requests for money, although that meaning makes less sense in this context. In any event, no other diary entries shed light on whether 'bills' here referred to 'legislation' or, if it did, what legislation was under discussion.

239 See note 191 and accompanying text.

240 See notes 270–72 and accompanying text.

241 For other clues suggesting the City's involvement, see notes 182–87 and accompanying text.

242 See note 199 and accompanying text.

243 See note 214 and accompanying text.

244 Ibid.

Otherwise, the people who conceived and drafted the Southwark fire-court act are lost to history.

B. THE PROVISIONS OF THE SOUTHWARK FIRE COURT ACT

The heart of the work for all fire courts, including the Southwark court, was to adjust the terms of leases to share the loss in a fashion that encouraged speedy rebuilding. In this respect, the Southwark fire court was no different from the London and Northampton courts that preceded it, or the five fire courts that succeeded it. Recognizing that 'noe certaine generall Rule can be prescribed',[245] Parliament gave the Southwark fire court the authority to extend the terms of leases, slash the rent, force unwilling parties to contribute or alter the reversionary interests of widows, infants and others[246] — whatever was needed to get the Borough rebuilt.

The work of the court was accomplished with a minimum of procedural baggage. Like the London and Northampton courts before it, the Southwark fire court was to proceed 'summarily and without the Formalityes of Proceedings used in Courts of Law or Equity'.[247] In a time when proceedings at law and in equity were often encrusted with technicalities and traps that frustrated the resolution of cases on their merits, this provision contributed significantly to the speed and success of the fire courts.

In a number of regards, however, the Northampton and Southwark acts were evolutionary: they varied from the London fire-court act in ways suggesting that Parliament had learned from the London fire court's experience. First, the enabling legislation for the London fire court contained a sunset provision that ended the Court after roughly two years. That period of time proved insufficient to hear the crush of petitions; and Parliament needed to re-constitute the London fire court three times so that the court could finish its work.[248] Because Parliament

---

245 29 Car. II, c. 4, § 1 (1677), in *Statutes of the Realm*, v, p. 842. For the essentially identical language of the London act, see 18 and 19 Car. II, c. 7, § 1 (1667), in *Statutes of the Realm*, v, p. 601 ('noe certaine generall rule can be prescribed').

246 29 Car. II, c. 4, § 2 (1667), in *Statutes of the Realm*, v, p. 843. The court could not, however, adjudicate disputes concerning any arrears of rent due before the date of the fire. Ibid., § 1. For one case involving this jurisdictional limit, see *Whaley v. Mercy* (Decree 25).

247 29 Car. II, c. 4, § 1 in *Statutes of the Realm*, v, p. 843. The language closely tracked that used for the London fire court. See 18 and 19 Car. II, c. 7, § 1 (1667), in *Statutes of the Realm*, v, p. 602 (stating that the court should proceed 'summarily and sine forma et figura judicij and without the formalities of proceedings in Courts of Law or Equity').

248 See note 3.

was often prorogued during the late 1660s and early 1670s, the London fire court sat in limbo for years, thus slowing the rebuilding of London. The Northampton fire court was given ten years to conclude its work,[249] the Southwark fire court nearly three years.[250]

Second, the initial enabling legislation significantly constrained the London fire court's power to increase the term of a lease or reduce the rent. For lease terms, the court could create no estate or lease exceeding forty years (inclusive of any unexpired term of the lease on the date of the Great Fire).[251] That limit proved a hindrance to the court's flexibility in spreading the loss, and the first re-authorization expanded the power to create leases (inclusive of the remaining term of the present lease) up to sixty years.[252] In contrast, neither the Northampton nor the Southwark statutes contained any limit on their respective courts' powers to extend a lease term. In the case of the Southwark fire court, extensions of sixty or even seventy years (inclusive of the present term) were common, and a few extensions of ninety-nine years were granted with the landlord's acquiescence.[253] For rents, Parliament prohibited the London court from diminishing rents beneath their ancient and customary level.[254] Perhaps reflecting the reality that little Southwark property was held under such arrangements, the Southwark fire court contained no comparable restriction.[255] It did, however, have one restriction on its power not found with the London court: it could not alter the terms of any agreement that landlords and tenants had made since the fire.[256]

---

249 27 Car. II § 8 (1675), in *Statutes of the Realm*, V, p. 801.

250 29 Car. II, c. 4, § 8 (1677), in *Statutes of the Realm*, V, p. 844. The three years commenced on 25 March 1677. Given that the statute became effective on 16 April 1677, the court's term was slightly more than two years and eleven months. The Southwark court rendered its last decrees on 2 March 1680, just within the allotted period.

251 See 18 and 19 Car. II, c. 7, § 2 (1667), in *Statutes of the Realm*, V, p. 602.

252 22 Car. 2, c. 11, § 8 (1670 in *Statutes of the Realm*, V, p. 669.

253 See notes 373, 378, 379 and accompanying text.

254 See 18 and 19 Car. II, c. 7, § 2 (1667), in *Statutes of the Realm*, V, p. 602 (forbidding the court from setting a rent 'where the Lawes of this Realme doe forbid the Diminishing of auntient and accustomable Rents'). Ancient rents were typically ground rents payable to a head landlord who leased undeveloped land for a lengthy period; many of these head landlords were institutions like the Corporation of London, churches, livery companies and colleges. For further discussion of the ownership of London and Southwark, see note 307 and accompanying text.

255 The issue of ancient rents arose indirectly in a few of the Southwark fire court's cases because a trust at issue restricted a person presently enjoying the beneficial use of the trust from entering into leases that diminished the ancient rents. See, e.g., *Cole v. Browker* (Decree 10); *Bennett v. Browker* (Decree 12).

256 29 Car. II, c. 4, § 15 (1677), in *Statutes of the Realm*, V, p. 845. The Southwark

Third, the composition of the Northampton and Southwark fire courts was different from that of the London fire court. The London court comprised the twelve common-law judges. The judges, who received no fees for their work, are often celebrated for their civic-mindedness. But it would have been unrealistic to expect the common-law judges to travel to Northampton to hear petitions. Thus, as we saw, the enabling act for the Northampton fire court expanded the people eligible to serve on the court to include the county's justices of the peace and judges of the assize, the Mayor of Northampton and eleven baronets, knights and other local dignitaries specifically named.[257] Moreover, unlike the London fire court, for which three common-law judges constituted a panel, the Northampton court required five judges.

As we also saw, the Southwark fire court followed the Northampton model, rejecting a compromise approach that would have required at least one common-law judge to hear every case.[258] As with the Northampton court, the common-law judges were again eligible to sit, but they could be joined on the court by the Lord Mayor of London, the Recorder of London, aldermen who had been Lord Mayor, the steward of Southwark and twenty-one baronets, knights and local dignitaries named in the statute. Five members were again required to constitute the court. Because some of these men had property interests in Southwark, Parliament added a requirement, not found in the London legislation, that no judge vote or sit on a case in which he was interested.[259] Unlike the London fire court, the Southwark

court took a broad view of its powers under this restriction. Immediately after the fire, lessors and tenants could not be certain that a fire-court statute would be enacted. Nonetheless, some leases contained a proviso that, should a fire court be erected, the parties were agreeable to changing lease terms that they were otherwise powerless to change. When presented with these agreements, the Southwark court amended the leases according to the parties' agreement. See Co*le v. Browker* (Decree 10); *Kendall v. Penn* (Decree 35). In two other cases, the court construed a post-fire lease between the parties narrowly either to protect a tenant's investment in rebuilding, see *Ferris v. Cressett* (Decree 36), or to protect a tenant from unduly harsh terms, see *Taynton v. Collett* (Decree 27).

257 See notes 201–02 and accompanying text.

258 See notes 203–05 and accompanying text.

259 29 Car. II, c. 4, § 16 (1677), in *Statutes of the Realm*, V, p. 845. Richard How appeared as a judge in twenty-six cases, but he was also a litigant in six cases. For each of the six cases, he stepped off the bench. In two cases decided on 9 January 1678 (*May v. How* (Decree 34) and *Kendall v. Penn* (Decree 35)), How served as a judge both before and after the cases in which he was a defendant. The judges who skated closest to the line that Parliament drew were John Appleby and John Freeman, who served as two of the six governors of the St Saviour Free Grammar School. See Manning and Bray, *Surrey*, p. 584. One suit required the Southwark fire

legislation contained no prohibition against the court's officers charging fees.[260]

This different composition of the court also altered the manner of appeal. Because appeals could drag out the process and slow down rebuilding, Parliament imposed certain roadblocks to appeal. For the London fire court, a decision rendered by less than seven common-law judges could be appealed within seven days to a larger panel of seven judges but then no further; moreover, no appeal lay from a decree initially decided by seven judges.[261] The Southwark statute similarly exempted from appeal decrees rendered by panels of seven or more judges. For cases decided by fewer than seven judges, an exception could be taken within thirty days to any common-law judge. If the judge found 'probable cause', the appeal was then to be heard before a panel of seven (or more) fire-court judges. Perhaps recognizing the immunity from appeal that seven judges provided, the Southwark fire court decided forty-four of its fifty-two cases with seven or more judges — including eighteen with exactly seven.[262] For the remaining eight cases, no appeals were filed.

Finally, and perhaps most notably, the Northampton and Southwark fire courts received powers more of an administrative nature, thus beginning a metamorphosis of the fire court from a judicial body

court to determine whether, and how much, to reduce payments to two charities (the poor of Southwark and the grammar school) that were payable out of rents that the court had reduced to aid rebuilding. Rather than proportionally reducing the amounts payable to each charity, the court decided that the entire reduction should be borne by the charity supporting the poor of Southwark; it ordered the amount due to the grammar school to be paid in full. Appleby and Freeman were two of the six judges who sat on this decree. *Nicolson v. Browker* (Decree 8).

260 See 29 Car. II, c. 4, § 12 (1677), in *Statutes of the Realm*, V, p. 845. I found no record of any schedule of fees that the court established, but the court almost surely did so. When the executor of the registrar for the Southwark court presented the engrossed decrees to the Court of Aldermen, he asked the City to pay for certain decrees according to the 'settled rate' for the other decrees of the court. Rep., LXXXVI, fol. 161 (9 June 1681).

261 See 18 and 19 Car. II, c. 7, § 6 (1667), in *Statutes of the Realm*, V, p. 603. The lack of a right to appeal to the House of Lords had been the only significant sticking point in the passage of the act establishing the London fire court, with twenty-nine Lords registering their dissent when a clause permitting appeals from the London fire court to the House of Lords was rejected. *HL Jour.*, XII, p. 87 (23 January 1667). Perhaps now comfortable with the quality of the fire courts' work, the Lords voiced no similar objection with respect to the Southwark act.

262 For the London fire court, panels of three judges were typical, so most cases were subject to appeal. Nonetheless, only eight appeals were ever taken, and none resulted in a different outcome. See Jay Tidmarsh, 'The English Fire Courts and the American Right to Civil Jury Trial', in *University of Chicago Law Review*, LXXXIII, (2016), p. 1917 n. 90.

into an institution that responded more broadly to public-safety and urban-planning concerns. This evolution had begun with the London fire court; in its initial re-authorization, the London court had been granted powers to determine the best disposition of land too small to build on (due to the widening of London's streets) and to assure the fair compensation of owners.[263] But most administrative matters for the London Fire were spelled out in the Act for the Rebuilding of the City of London, companion legislation to Fire of London Disputes Act (which established the London fire court).[264] The Rebuilding Act was among the world's first comprehensive building and zoning codes: among other things, it provided the City's Lord Mayor, Common Council and aldermen with the authority to lay out the streets in new-built London and it specified the types of houses that could be built on various streets, the height and look of those houses, and their construction materials. The separate pieces of legislation — the Rebuilding Act and Fire of London Disputes Act — symbolically separated the administrative task of setting the strictures within which rebuilding occurred from the judicial task of reforming lessor-tenant relationships to accomplish the rebuilding itself.

One of the striking features of the Northampton and Southwark fire-court acts, in comparison to the Fire of London Disputes Act, is their length. The Disputes Act runs to about one-and-one-half pages in the *Statutes of the Realm*, while the Northampton and Southwark acts both run to about three-and-one-half pages. Some of the additional bulk is 'language creep': using more words to codify practices or clarify powers that had emerged organically as the London fire court implemented the Disputes Act. But much of the new language described new functions of the latter courts.

This fact is most notable in the Northampton legislation, in which the fire court was given powers akin to those in the Rebuilding Act. Parliament established some boundaries: for example, it limited the Northampton fire court's authority to widen certain streets, and it required that the roofs of new houses be made of lead, slate, or tile.[265] For the most part, however, Parliament delegated to the Northampton fire court the

> power and authority to make and appoint from time to time such Rules and Directions in the Formes and Orders of Building to bee observed in the

263 22 Car. 2, c. 11, § 32 (1670), in *Statutes of the Realm*, V, p. 672.
264 18 and 19 Car. II, c. 8 (1667), in *Statutes of the Realm*, V, p. 603.
265 27 Car. II, §§ 5–6 (1675), in *Statutes of the Realm*, V, pp. 799–800.

rebuilding of such Houses […] as they shall thinke fitt and convenient for the better Securitie and Ornament of the said Towne.[266]

If an owner did not rebuild within three years, the court could grant the land to someone willing to do so.[267] Exercising responsibilities that Parliament had given the Lord Mayor, the Common Council and the Court of Aldermen after the London fire, the Northampton fire court also had the power to enlarge or alter the streets and to add land to (or take land away) from a particular estate to encourage rebuilding.[268] The Northampton fire court was a de facto urban-planning commission.

The Southwark fire court enjoyed less of this power. As a London borough, Southwark was already subject to the Rebuilding Act. But Parliament gave the Southwark fire court other administrative responsibility. For instance, like the Northampton court, the Southwark court had the authority to dispose of any property on which no one had rebuilt within two years and to provide it to someone willing to rebuild.[269] Most significantly, however, the Southwark fire court received a power to 'regulate[ ] reduce[ ] and reform[ ]' encroachments on the High Street from London Bridge to St Margaret's Hill.[270] Before the fire, owners of shops and houses along both sides of the High Street had pushed out their buildings and stalls beyond their ancient foundations, effectively claiming a portion of the public way as their own and adding to the High Street's congestion.

The Southwark fire court accepted the task of eliminating encroachments with relish. Over the course of three decrees, the court ordered eighty-nine shopkeepers and house dwellers — a number of whom were parties in other petitions before the Court — to remove encroaching stalls, posts, or structures, typically within a month.[271] On average, the City surveyors found that the buildings encroached

266 Ibid., § 3, in *Statutes of the Realm*, v, p. 799.

267 Ibid., § 5, in *Statutes of the Realm*, v, p. 800. A jury was to be impaneled to determine the value of the taken ground.

268 *Id.* If ground were taken away from an owner, a jury was to be impanelled to determine the value of the land.

269 29 Car. II, c. 4, § 4 (1677), in *Statutes of the Realm*, v, pp. 843–44. The decrees of the Southwark fire court do not reflect that this authority was ever exercised.

270 Ibid., § 10, in *Statutes of the Realm*, v, p. 845. The statute allowed shopkeepers open for business to drop their stall boards into the street 'one Foote and noe more for the Conveniencies of their Shops'.

271 Decrees 44–46. Decree 44, involving only John Gerrard, was heard on 17 July 1677. Decree 45 then determined the next eighty-seven cases *en masse* on 17 October 1677. Decree 46, involving only Evan Evans, was heard on 8 May 1678.

between two and three feet,[272] so the court's decrees effectively widened the High Street by about five feet.

The City zealously enforced these orders. When John Gerrard, a hosier and tenant of a property at Bridge Foot, refused to tear down his encroachment as the Southwark court had ordered,[273] the Court of Aldermen directed William Lightfoote, the newly appointed City Solicitor, to prefer a prosecution for nuisance at the next Borough quarter session.[274] The case resulted in a 20s. fine for Gerrard, with commitment to prison until payment.[275] Two more encroaching parties, Charles Hutchest and Evan Evans, found themselves convicted in the following quarter session; Hutchest was fined 5s. and Evans 6s. 8d., both with commitment until payment. Much to the chagrin of St Thomas's Hospital, five encroachers who were its tenants refused all reasonable inducements from the Hospital to remove their encroachments;[276] the last of them did not tear down their encroachments until late in 1681, just before their trials before the quarter session were to commence.[277]

272 According to Decrees 44 and 45, the surveyors, Robert Hooke and John Oliver, viewed the properties on 13 July 1677, along with a carpenter, William Gray, and two members of the court, Thomas Barker and Peter Rich. They then created a report detailing their findings. Hooke's *Diary* provides some confirmation. On 13 July, Hooke was '[a]t Lord Mayors for Directions about Southwick' and then 'made a view of encroachments in Southwick'. *Diary*, p. 301 (entry for 13 July 1677). On 17 July, he went '[t]o Guildhall signed report to Southwick. Judges attended there all the morning'. Ibid., p. 302 (entry for 17 July 1677). Decree 44 noted Hooke's testimony at the hearing that day. For the hearing on 17 October, Hooke again noted that he '[a]ttended on Judges at Guildhall about Southwark proprietors'. *Diary*, p. 301 (entry for 17 October 1677). Decree 45 indicated that Oliver and Gray testified at the hearing, but it made no mention of testimony from Hooke.

273 Decree 44.

274 Rep., LXXXIII, fol. 147ᵛ (19 March 1678).

275 This is the best sense that I can make of the quarter-session records, which contain abbreviations best known to the writer. Southwark Quarter Session Records, LMA CLA/046/01/003. The case was filed on 28 March 1678. Gerrard was bailed on a recognizance of £40 on 26 June 1678, and his case adjudicated, with Gerrard protesting, on 4 October 1678. Whether Gerrard was in fact imprisoned is uncertain; the notation in the records may have been merely the formal language of judgment rather than a reflection of what occurred. I am indebted to my colleague David Waddilove, whose expert knowledge of seventeenth-century court records, secretary hand and Latin notation helped me to decipher Gerrard's legal fate.

Hooke's *Diary* contains an intriguing reference, noting that, on 28 May 1678, he was 'at Guildhall about the corner house in Southerick'. *Diary*, p. 360 (entry for 28 May 1678). Decree 44 stated that Gerrard's house sat 'at the very corner of the street at the Bridge Foot'. I might speculate that Hooke was referring to Gerrard's house, but the diary does not indicate the reason that Hooke was consulted.

276 *Minute Books, 1677–1735*, fol. 16 (20 April 1681); ibid., fols 18–19 (8 July 1681).

277 Report to the President of St Thomas's Hospital, in *Minute Books, 1677–1735*,

C. THE OPERATION OF THE SOUTHWARK FIRE COURT

The Southwark fire court heard a total of fifty-two petitions.[278] As described, three cases involved the removal of encroachments along the High Street.[279] Four could be characterized primarily as disputes between neighbours.[280] The remaining forty-five petitions concerned disputes over the rights of tenancy.[281]

Sessions

The court conducted its proceedings at the Guildhall. In total, there were nine sessions: six in 1677 (8 June, 17 July, 5 October, 17 October, 5 December and 19 December), two in 1678 (9 January and 28 May) and one in 1680 (2 March). The court had concluded most of its work by 1678; it heard only four cases, including one holdover from 1678, in 1680.[282] Its busiest day was 5 October 1677, when it resolved fifteen cases.[283]

In almost every instance, the court decided the petition on the same day as its hearing. In only two instances did the court carry the case over to a second day.[284]

Judges

The number of judges who sat for each case varied. As might be expected, the greatest number of judges — fourteen in total — sat for the two petitions heard at the court's first session (8 June 1677). The smallest number of judges to preside — the statutory minimum of five — heard six cases on 17 October 1677.

---

fol. 20–20ᵛ (11 November 1681).

278 Three cases involved cross-petitions. *Austen v. Beacon* (Decree 3); *Bayley v. Browker* (Decree 12); *Gregory v. Sledd* (Decree 30). Because the fire court resolved these cross-petitions with the main petitions, I do not count them as separate cases.

279 Decrees 44–46.

280 *Lane v. Mayor of Shrewsbury* (Decree 26); *Cannon v. Brace* (Decree 41); *Young v. Bradway* (Decree 42); *Taylor v. Smith* (Decree 52).

281 Nearly all involved lessors and tenants. But *Cannon v. Cannon* (Decree 40) involved a 'dispute' between a mother and her elder son, who was still a minor: the mother held a life estate in a home devised to her by her husband's will, with the reversion held by her elder son. The widow was willing to rebuild, but only if she obtained a greater term for herself than her life interest. Thus, the petition did not involve a landlady and a tenant, but rather the present owner and the reversionary owner.

282 There is no indication why the court took nearly a two-year hiatus before tidying up its remaining cases.

283 It also heard a sixteenth case, but it deferred final decision until 17 October. See *Bennett v. Browker* (Decree 12).

284 *Bennett v. Browker* (Decree 12); *Cannon v. Brace* (Decree 41).

The participation of common-law judges varied. At least one common-law judge sat to hear each petition. Of the thirteen common-law judges eligible to sit on the Southwark fire court between 1677 and 1680, however, only seven heard a case. Lord Chief Justice Francis North of the Court of Common Pleas and Lord Chief Justice Richard Raynsford of King's Bench heard the two cases on the first day of the fire court and then disappeared from view. Baron Edward Thurland heard three petitions and Chief Baron of the Exchequer William Montagu four. Justice Hugh Wyndham of Common Pleas attended sixteen hearings. As the second most active judge, Justice Thomas Jones of King's Bench attended thirty-six hearings. The most active common-law judge was Baron Timothy Littleton, who sat for forty-five cases.[285]

The same unequal distribution of workload applied to the non-judicial commissioners of the Southwark court.[286] The sitting Lord Mayor of London heard eight cases. Former Lord Mayor Thomas Bludworth (of Great Fire of London infamy) heard nine petitions; and several other former Lord Mayors chipped in on occasion. The Steward of Southwark,

---

285 Littleton died in 1679. Thus, he sat on forty-five of the forty-eight cases heard during his lifetime.

For Littleton, North, Raynsford, Thurland and Wyndham, sitting on the Southwark fire court was *déjà vu*. All had sat on the London fire court. See, e.g., *Lucy v. Lucy*, Fire of London Court of Judicature Decrees, vol. 1, fol. 3ᵛ (27 June 1673) (heard before Littleton and Wyndham, in addition to Lord Chief Justice Vaughn); *Jacobsen v. Jacobsen*, ibid., fol. 11 (31 October 1673) (heard before Raynsford, Wyndham and Thurland); *Cockery v. Dean and Chapter of St Paul*, ibid., fol. 158ᵛ (17 January 1676) (heard before Raynsford, Littleton and Wyndham); *Adkinson v. Parson and Churchwardens of St Peter in Westcheape*, ibid., fol. 160 (18 February 1676) (heard before North, Raynsford and Wyndham). Indeed, on 18 February 1676, North, Raynsford and Wyndham presided over the final group of cases pending before London court.

Raynsford might be excused his light attendance on the Southwark fire court. He had been a workhorse on the London fire court from its inception, hearing 251 cases during the first two years of the court (see Jones, *Fire Court*, I, p. 298; Jones, *Fire Court*, II, p. 390) and continuing at a strong pace thereafter. Hugh Wyndham's brother, Wadham, had also been a leading judge on the London court before his death in 1668. As for Hugh Wyndham, he too gave notable service to the London fire court after his reappointment as a judge in 1670 — in addition to being involved in one of the London fire court cases as a tenant of a capital messuage whose fifty-year lease passed by assignment through several hands before coming to the petitioner. *Herring v. Churchwardens of St Mary Aldermanbury* Fire of London Court of Judicature Decrees, vol. 1, fol. 357 (12 November 1667). Hugh Wyndham's portrait, commissioned by the Corporation of London to commemorate his service, is one of the surviving portraits of the twenty-two common law judges who served on the London fire court. It is held by the Guildhall Art Gallery.

286 The decrees referred to the court's non-judicial members as 'commissioners' rather than judges. See, e.g., *Sledd v. Gregory* (Decree 30).

Edward Smyth, sat for sixteen cases. Of the twenty-one dignitaries that
Parliament appointed to the court, thirteen never showed at all. Along
with Baron Littleton, six Southwark citizens — John Appleby, Thomas
Barker, John Freeman, Richard How, James Reading and Peter Rich —
carried the court on their shoulders. Freeman heard fifty cases, Appleby
forty-eight, Rich forty-five, Barker forty-two and How twenty-six. The
prize for unflagging devotion to civic duty, however, went to Reading,
who sat for all fifty-two cases.

Lawyers

The simplicity of the proceedings before the fire courts dispensed with
the necessity of employing a lawyer. Indeed, many parties represented
themselves before the London fire court, especially in its early years.
Eventually, however, the London court was well served by the rise of a
professional bar that helped the court to mediate and resolve disputes.[287]
That bar sprang back into existence for the Southwark fire court. Although
some new names surfaced, most of the barristers appearing before the
Southwark court had prior experience before the London court.

   In only four of the forty-nine non-encroachment cases did all parties
appear pro se,[288] and in all of these cases the parties either sought a
decree to corroborate an agreed deal or were amenable to mediation.
In another twenty cases, at least one party appeared with counsel while
other parties went unrepresented. Five of these cases involved agreed
deals, and another twelve involved a common factual circumstance
in which the most critically interested (and disputatious) parties were
usually represented. In twenty-five cases, counsel represented all parties
— sometimes even when the parties had agreed the lease.[289]

   In all, sixteen counsel appeared before the court.[290] The labouring oar
fell to Mr Jenner,[291] who appeared in forty-four of the forty-five non-

---

287 Jones, *Fire Court*, I, pp. xiii–xiv.
288 *Hyland v. How* (Decree 19); *Hawkes v. How* (Decree 20); *Rushley v. How* (Decree
21); *Weyland v. Sayer* (Decree 22).
289 In contrast, of the eighty-nine tenants ordered to remove encroachments
in the three encroachment cases, only one tenant, Evan Evans, appeared through
counsel (the ubiquitous Mr Jenner). Evans' petition was also one of only a few
to raise a substantial legal issue, with Jenner arguing that the fire court lacked
jurisdiction over the property.
290 In a couple of instances, parties were represented by someone described as
an agent or by a co-defendant. See, e.g., *Lane v. Mayor of Shrewsbury* (Decree 26). In
numerous instances, infants were represented by their parents or guardians. See,
e.g., *Nicolson v. Browker* (Decree 8).
291 Unfortunately, the decrees do not provide Christian names for the barristers.

encroachment cases in which at least one party was represented. Other attorneys who appeared frequently included Mr Bowes and Sir George Jeffreys. The bar seems to have been tightly knit: for instance, Bowes and Jeffreys would sometimes appear as co-counsel with Jenner, but the three would then appear opposite each other in other cases — indeed, sometimes in other cases heard on the same day.[292]

Methods of Dispute Resolution

One dynamic that emerged over the course of the London fire court's tenure was the court's evolution from an adjudicatory body to a dispute-resolution body, in which the court's principal functions were to place a judicial imprimatur on a previously agreed lease or to mediate between the parties, who resolved their dispute amicably with the court's encouragement. Disputes where the parties could not agree — thus requiring the London fire court to set the lease terms — became rarer and rarer.

Settlement and mediation were in evidence with the Southwark fire court, but less so. All four of the disputes involving neighbours required the Court to adjudicate the parties' ferocious and often very unneighbourly disagreements. Among the forty-five landlord-tenant cases, insofar as brief decrees can give a flavour of what happened at Guildhall nearly three hundred and fifty years ago, eleven cases involved situations in which the parties had agreed a deal in advance; in these cases, the parties typically looked to the court for a confirming decree that would bind an infant, a feme covert or others with reversionary interests in the property.[293] The court also successfully mediated two

---

292 Compare, e.g., *Waggorne v. Beacon* (Decree 3) (Jenner and Lane representing the petitioner, with Jeffreys and Bowes representing defendants) with *Houghton v. Mayor of Shrewsbury* (Decree 4) (Bowes and Jenner representing the petitioner with Jeffreys, Ward and Jones representing defendants) and *Hudson v. Browker* (Decree 48) (Jeffreys, Bowes and Jenner representing the petitioner, with Ward and Pettit representing some of the defendants).

Legal ethics in the seventeenth century were not what they are today, but Jeffreys engaged in one practice sure to raise an eyebrow. He served as counsel for the petitioner in *Cannon v. Brace* (Decree 41) when it was first heard on 28 May 1678. The second hearing did not occur until 2 March 1680, when Jeffreys, having since been appointed Recorder of London, sat as a judge in the case (with Jenner and Ward having replaced him as petitioner's counsel).

293 See Decrees 7, 10, 19–22, 29, 31, 34, 35 and 37. I include among these eleven cases five involving Richard How (Decrees 19, 20, 21, 34 and 35) and one involving Thomas Browker. In the How cases, How, as landlord, had previously agreed a lease with the tenants, but there was some uncertainty about the length of the term How had granted; hence the tenants filed their petitions. How's magnanimity in court — readily giving the tenants the extended terms they desired — led me to characterize the cases as agreed rather than mediated. The same is true of Decree

cases, dissipating the parties' disagreement by the end of the hearing.[294] In three other cases, the court gave either the landlord or the tenant a free choice of two options: for instance, between rebuilding with an extended lease or occupying the premises for the remaining term of the lease after the landlord rebuilt.[295]

The remainder of the landlord-tenant cases were disputed. A few of the disputes could be described as friendly; the court used its powers cut through a legal obstacle that lay beyond the parties' ability to resolve.[296] In other cases, only some of the parties to the petition were locked in disagreement, while other parties were indifferent to the outcome.[297] Nonetheless, the number of cases in which true friction and disagreement existed among the parties was high — at least in relation to the experience of the London fire court.

To resolve disputes, the Southwark fire court occasionally took evidence from witnesses,[298] but most typically resolved the dispute after

---

10, one of twelve cases involving lands owned by Thomas Browker's descendants. See note 320 and accompanying text (listing all of the Browker cases). Unlike most of the Browker cases, the parties in this case had agreed terms, but were unable to set the length of the lease due to the nature and limitations of the Browker trust. In court, all parties were amenable to the length of the term that the petitioner desired and the court decreed.

In addition, a twelfth decree (Decree 12) involved an agreement between lessor and tenant, but the cross-petition of two other persons claiming a reversionary interest in the premises required adjudication. A thirteenth decree (Decree 9) required the court to adjudicate a dispute between the lessors and the tenant; after the court did so, the lessors agreed to sell their interest in the property to the tenant.

294 See *Ely v. Mence* (Decree 1); *Waggorne v. Beacon* (Decree 3). In addition, in *Sledd v. Gregory* (Decree 30), the court resolved the dispute in general terms and then deputized two of the judges to work with the parties so that the rebuilding of the parties' adjoining properties was accomplished with convenience to both. The decree does not report whether the judges' post-hearing mediation was successful, but the lack of further report suggests that it was.

295 See *Lane v. Sledd* (Decree 18) (giving the tenant the option to rebuild on certain terms or to allow the landlord to rebuild and then occupy the premises at the existing rent for the remaining term of the lease; ordering the landlord to rebuild when the tenant chose the latter option); *Marshall v. Overman* (Decree 38) (giving the landlord the option to purchase the tenant's interest in the property or to submit to a new lease; ordering the landlord to complete the purchase when he accepted the first option); *Butcher v. Taynton* (Decree 39) (giving the landlord the option to purchase the tenant's interest in the property or to submit to a new lease; on the landlord's refusal to buy out the tenant's lease, ordering a new lease to the tenant).

296 See, e.g., *Bankes v. Wight* (Decree 2).

297 For instance, this characterization applies to most of the petitions involving the Browker properties. See note 320 and accompanying text.

298 See, e.g., *Gale v. Wight* (Decree 23); *Debnam v. Body* (Decree 28).

hearing the parties, or more often their lawyers, present their side of the argument.

Results

While the court on occasion adopted one side's argument in full, its decrees often split the difference. The London fire court had developed a reputation as a tenant's court: the court operated with a presumption favouring the tenant as the rebuilder,[299] and it gave generous terms to rebuild.[300] As a rule, the same was true of the Southwark fire court. Characterization of decrees is perhaps in the eye of the beholder, but in my assessment, thirteen decrees in disputed cases were clear victories for tenants. Another nine cases, although a compromise of interests, generally favoured tenants. Five decrees clearly favoured landlords, with another two decrees best seen as a compromise that leaned in the direction of the landlords.

Preparation of the Decrees

Most of what we know about the conduct of the Southwark fire court appears from the fifty-two engrossed decrees calendared in this book. To prepare these decrees, the Southwark fire court appears to have followed the pattern used for the London fire court. For the London court, a draft folio of each case was prepared. Pursuant to Parliament's command that a permanent record be made of the London court's decrees,[301] the folios were then copied onto parchment and bound into nine volumes. The court's registrar, Stephen Mundy, his son James, and his assistant, Richard Antrobus, prepared the engrossed decrees, with Antrobus's signature appearing at the foot of many.[302]

299 See Jones, *Fire Court*, I, p. xv. For a brief reference to this presumption, and the argument that it should extend to the work of the Southwark fire court, see *Sledd v. Gregory* (Decree 30).

300 Perhaps because of Londoners' experience of the London fire court, a number of the litigants in the Southwark fire court conceded that the court would prefer the tenant to be the rebuilder. See, e.g., *Hall v. Crosse* (Decree 5); *Nicholls v. Crosse* (Decree 6).

301 18 and 19 Car. II, c. 7, § 4 (1667), in *Statutes of the Realm*, V, p. 601.

302 A complete set of the draft folios is available at the British Library (Add. MSS 5063-5103); additional copies of some folios can also be found in other archives. The nine volumes of engrossed degrees are available for viewing at the London Metropolitan Archives (LMA CLA/039/01). The nine volumes were presented to the Court of Aldermen on 20 March 1677, about one year after the conclusion of the London court's work. By this time, Stephen Mundy had died, and his son James, who helped complete the books, presented the volumes. The Court of Aldermen awarded the Mundys £100 for their efforts and Antrobus £20. Rep., LXXXII, fols 121ᵛ–22 (20 March 1676).

For the Southwark court, I have found three such draft folios still in existence: *Eyre v. Mayor of London*,[303] *Bankes v. Wight*[304] and *Gale v. Wight*.[305] Antrobus assumed the role of registrar for the Southwark court: he signed the *Eyre* and *Bankes* folios at the foot, giving his title as registrar.[306] These draft folios are identical to the engrossed decrees, making it likely that Antrobus used folios to create the fifty-two engrossed decrees. These decrees were then bound into a single volume, which is still available at the London Metropolitan Archives.[307]

III. INITIAL LESSONS FROM THE SOUTHWARK DECREES

Readers will likely mine these calendared decrees for different information, much of which I cannot anticipate. This section lays out a few highlights that the decrees provide about the nature of property holdings in seventeenth-century Southwark.

A. WHO OWNED SOUTHWARK?

The records of the London fire court have aided historians in evaluating numerous issues of property ownership in the City at the time of the

303 Decree 32. For the folio, see LMA CLA/040/02/005.

304 Decree 1. There are actually two folios of this decree. They vary slightly in length due to the vagaries of handwriting, but they otherwise appear identical, TNA, C 6/80/43. Further records concerning the lease between Bankes and Wight can be found as exhibits in Chancery pleadings that indirectly involved the scope of Wight's property holdings, TNA, C 108/129.

305 Decree 23. For the folio, see TNA, C 108/129/29.

306 The Southwark decrees made no specific reference to the identity of the registrar. Nonetheless, like the London decrees (where Antrobus's signature commonly appeared), Antrobus's signature appeared at the foot of the engrossed Southwark decrees. The *Repertories* confirm Antrobus's role as registrar. On 9 June 1681, Henry Antrobus, executor of the estate of Richard Antrobus, presented the Court of Aldermen with the volume of engrossed decrees of the Southwark fire court. The *Repertories* noted Richard Antrobus's role as registrar of the court. Henry Antrobus requested the Court of Aldermen to award him £18 3s. for the work in engrossing 'several publicke decrees' (in other words, the encroachment decrees). The request noted that this amount was calculated according to the settled value of other decrees — implying that the parties themselves were charged for the rendering of their decrees. The Court of Aldermen constituted a committee of six (including three who had sat as judges on the Southwark fire court) to report whether Antrobus should be paid and, if so, from which account. Rep., LXXXVI, fol. 142ᵛ (9 June 1681). After receiving the committee's report, the Court of Aldermen awarded Henry Antrobus £10 payable out of Bridge House funds. Ibid., fol. 161 (12 July 1681).

Richard Antrobus was no stranger to the aldermen. Among his other duties, he had been appointed as City Solicitor in 1678. Rep., LXXXIII, fol. 179 (30 April 1678).

307 LMA CLA/040/02/006.

Great Fire.[308] For instance, the London fire court's records confirm that a large percentage of the City was owned by institutions: most of all, by the City itself, but also by other towns and by churches, livery companies and the colleges of Oxford and Cambridge.

The decrees of the Southwark fire court can provide similar guidance for understanding issues of property holding in Southwark. Because not every landlord or tenant sued, reliance on the records requires acute attention to issues of selection bias. That caution is especially true because nearly a quarter of the court's non-encroachment petitions (twelve out of forty-nine) involved a single family's property holdings.[309] With these caveats in mind, we can turn to the records of the Southwark fire court.

Institutions

Jeremy Boulton's work on early seventeenth-century Southwark has shown that institutional landlords were far less common in Southwark than in the City of London.[310] The fire-court decrees extend Boulton's observations into the mid- to late seventeenth century. Of the forty-nine cases involving fire-related disputes, only four involved institutional landlords: two disputes involved the town of Shrewsbury, which owned property in Three Crown Court,[311] and two involved the City of London.[312] In addition, one of the encroachment cases showed that St Thomas's Hospital owned a number of parcels along the High Street.[313]

---

308 See Doolittle, 'Property Law' and sources cited therein.

309 See note 320 and accompanying text.

310 Boulton, *Neighbourhood and Society*, p. 204 (stating that, in the first part of the seventeenth century, 'institutional landlords holding property direct were unusual in the Boroughside').

311 *Houghton v. Mayor of Shrewsbury* (Decree 4); *Lane v. Mayor of Shrewsbury* (Decree 26). *Houghton* suggested that the Town of Shrewsbury held many of the properties in Three Crown Court. See also *Ferris v. Cressett* (Decree 36) (making the same suggestion). Hooke's diary noted that he went to '[v]iew […] Shrewsbury houses in Southwick'. *Diary*, p. 305 (entry for 6 August 1677). When Hooke described a 'view' of a property, he typically meant that he staked out the boundaries of the property for rebuilding. The plural 'houses' supports the idea of Shrewsbury's significant ownership interests in Southwark.

312 Of these two, one concerned the lease of the Compter and the continued tenure of the bailiff of Southwark, William Eyre, rather than a more typical lessor-tenant dispute. *Eyre v. Mayor of London* (Decree 32), discussed in notes 223–28 and accompanying text. The other case was *Hudson v. Mayor of London* (Decree 33), which concerned the property adjacent to the Compter that the City had purchased in the failed attempt to develop St Margaret's Hill into the market. See note 218 and accompanying text.

313 One of the encroachment decrees, Decree 45, listed seven tenants of St Thomas's properties.

With these exceptions, the fire court resolved disputes between human landlords and human tenants.

Small and Large Landlords

Although institutional landlords were uncommon, private landlords with large holdings were not. Boulton demonstrated that, in the early seventeenth century, property ownership along the High Street was fragmented into small holdings. On the other hand, for alleys, yards and courts off the High Street, ownership was concentrated in the hands of fifteen or so private landlords (including Thomas Browker, Thomas Collett and Thomas Overman).[314] That arrangement seems to have held all the way to 1676. Of the forty-nine non-encroachment cases, at least twenty-five decrees involved properties on the High Street.[315] For the most part, these properties were held in different hands; no landlord owned more than a couple.[316]

In contrast, sixteen decrees located the property in dispute in an alley, yard or court off the High Street. Here the family names of Boulton's large landlords were more commonly seen; for instance, Thomas Overman's widow had apparently sold most of her interests in Three Crown Court to the Town of Shrewsbury,[317] but the Overmans still owned numerous properties in Montague Close.[318] Occasionally, a decree recited the lineage of a property all the way back to Browker, Collett or Overman. More commonly, the decrees mentioned their widows or descendants — either as litigants before the fire court or as parties who had demised their interests to others who appeared before the court.

314 Boulton, *Neighbourhood and Society*, pp. 198–200.

315 Although most of the decrees mention the location of the property in dispute, some decrees do not state the location or provide sufficient information from which a location can be inferred. Among the properties for which no location was provided, some decrees mentioned the sign that hung over the shop. See, e.g., *Waggorne v. Beacon* (Decree 3) (sign of the Rose and Crown). Given that many taverns and shops with signs were likely to have been located on the High Street, the number of High Street properties may be as high as thirty.

316 In addition, the three encroachment cases (Decrees 44–46) involved nearly ninety High Street properties. For the most part, however, these decrees are of little help in discerning ownership. The party sued was the tenant in possession, who was responsible for removing the encroachment. Aside from St Thomas's Hospital, the encroachment decrees mention only two landlords by name.

317 See *Lane v. Mayor of Shrewsbury* (Decree 26). Since remarried, Overman's widow still retained an ownership interest in other property in Three Crown Court. See *Ferris v. Cressett* (Decree 36).

318 *Marshall v. Overman* (Decree 38).

Particularly noteworthy were the holdings of Thomas Browker, who died in 1658.[319] Sixteen of the fire court's forty-five landlord-tenant cases involved property originally held by Browker. In twelve of the cases, Browker family members still held an interest (either present or reversionary) in the properties and their rents. For the ten Browker properties where decrees recited the leases' terms, the rents receivable were worth more than £117 per annum in total, with the amounts varying from £40 for a tavern on the High Street to £2 5s. for part of a messuage in Angel Yard.[320]

By reading between the lines of the decrees, a picture emerges of large landlords who were not just holders of property but also developers of seventeenth-century Southwark. A few decrees recite that a landlord had granted a pre-fire lease to a tenant on the understanding that the tenant would erect new buildings or refurbish old buildings on the ground, with the low rent reflecting the tenant's costs and charges in construction.[321]

The decrees also provide some evidence of the changing fortunes of leading Southwark landlords. The Browkers were a family in decline. The founder of the family, Hugh Browker, had been the protonotary of the Court of Common Pleas in Queen Elizabeth's time, and he had become rich enough to buy the manor of Paris Garden, west of the High Street, in 1602.[322] Hugh's interests descended to his son Thomas, who shrewdly expanded the family's holdings in Southwark and London before retiring to a manor in Cheshire.[323] When he died, Thomas devised almost his entire estate in fee to his wife, Mary. Retaining a life estate for herself, Mary then established a trust in fee tail male to benefit the eldest Browker male — first, her son Thomas the elder and, on his death, her grandson Thomas the younger, and then his eldest male issue — with contingent reversions to other male descendants and, failing male issue, various female descendants.

---

319 Executed on 23 September 1656, Browker's will was proven on 10 November 1658. See Will of Thomas Browker, TNA, PROB 11/280/635. There was usually a gap of a month or less between a testator's death and proof of the will.

320 The Browker cases are Decrees 8, 10, 11, 12, 13, 14, 15, 47, 48, 49, 50 and 51.

321 See *Roberts v. Browker* (Decree 11); *Hudson v. Browker* (Decree 49). See also *Marshall v. Overman* (Decree 38) (describing some of the development in Montague Close).

322 Manning and Bray, *Surrey*, p. 531.

323 Hugh's son Thomas was rich enough that, when the piqued James I granted a patent vesting title in Paris Garden in other owners in 1625, Thomas bought the land a second time in 1627. Ibid. Thomas Browker's property holdings at the time of his death were catalogued in his will. See note 319, Will of Thomas Browker.

Thomas the younger apparently dissipated the family fortune, as evidenced by the merchants, grocers and brewers who had come into possession of most of his life interests in the rents.[324] Thomas the younger appeared to have been at liberty as late as December 1676.[325] By July 1677, however, the Browker decrees recite that Thomas the younger was ensconced in the King's Bench Prison, a debtor's prison just south of where the Southwark fire started.[326] While it is uncertain whether and to what extent the Southwark fire contributed to Thomas the younger's ruin, the cessation of rental payments after the fire likely hit Browker hard.

The fire court's decrees did little to help. The reason that the Browker cases comprised such a large proportion of the fire court's docket was that Thomas the younger had no heir, and some of the Browkers who held reversionary interests on his death stubbornly refused to give tenants reasonable encouragement to rebuild. In case after case, however, the Court ruled against the Browker interests and decreed lower rents and longer terms for tenants. In total, the court shrank the £117 annual revenue stream to £81.[327]

At the other end of the spectrum, the decrees reflect the ascendancy of two new landlords, Richard How and John Snell, as well as the continuing good fortunes of the Overman and Collett families.[328] By 1676, Richard How had become a sizeable landlord who, in addition to serving as a judge in twenty-six cases, appeared as a defendant in six. He had purchased two of his properties from Thomas Browker.[329] All of How's cases involved

324 See, e.g., *Nicolson v. Browker* (Decree 8) (indicating that Thomas Browker had devised his interests in a property to Samuel Wight, a brewer, on 24 March 1676). Thomas the younger also took measures to squirrel some of his interests away from creditors and provide for his sisters. See, e.g., *Cole v. Browker* (Decree 10) (noting that Thomas had devised his interests in the property to his uncle by marriage, who held the property in trust for the benefit of Thomas's sisters, Mary and Martha).

325 The *Cole* decree mentions that, in December 1677, Browker and his uncle had made certain agreements with Cole to develop the property at issue in the decree.

326 The Browker cases were adjudicated on 5 July 1677, with one case held over to a second hearing on 17 October 1677. Unfortunately, available records of the King's Bench Prison do not reflect whether Browker was actually incarcerated.

327 Because Thomas the younger had already alienated his life interest in these properties, the loss of income did not affect him; but it did affect the various Browker heirs to whom the rents would be distributed upon his death. Despite efforts to do so, I was unable to determine the ultimate fate of Thomas the younger or the other heirs mentioned in the decrees.

328 On the ownership interests of Thomas Collett and Thomas Overman, see Boulton, *Neighbourhood and Society*, pp. 78–79, 198–202.

329 It is unclear from the decrees *which* Thomas Browker had sold the properties to How. Given that How owned (and sold) the land in fee, it was likely the Thomas

prior agreements that the court needed to confirm, and the generous terms that How granted his tenants revealed a magnanimity that proved either How's prosperity or his foolishness — or perhaps both.

Snell, a Merchant Taylor, seems to have regarded the Southwark fire as a buying opportunity, as he snapped up numerous leaseholds both to build a larger home for himself and to hold as investments. In some cases, Snell bought the remainder of a tenant's lease; in other cases, Snell (who was likely one of Thomas the younger's creditors) obtained Thomas the younger's interest, as landlord, in the rents. Whether as landlord or tenant, most of Snell's purchases involved Browker properties. Snell also sold one of the Browker interests, which he had procured from Thomas the younger for a peppercorn, to another person — likely at a profit.[330]

As for the Overman and Collett families, Thomas Overman and Thomas Collett were long dead, but their interests had passed to a widow or a succeeding generation. The fire court's decrees forced various members of the Overman family to make concessions for rebuilding, but they seemed to emerge relatively unscathed.[331] Before the Southwark fire-court act had been passed, John Collett, who owned the White Hart Inn, had struck a particularly one-sided deal with the tenant innkeeper to rebuild; the Southwark fire court essentially upheld all but the deal's most onerous terms.[332]

Women

Ian Doolittle has analysed one volume of the London fire court's records for a better understanding of property ownership in London. Among other matters, he has shown that, despite restrictive property rules associated with marriage and inheritance in seventeenth-century England, women in London often owned their own property and were active participants in London's property markets.[333]

The Southwark fire court's records extend Doolittle's observations. As a landlady, a tenant or a holder of a reversionary interest in a property,

---

Browker who was the husband of Mary Browker and the grandfather of Thomas Browker the younger.

330 See *Hudson v. Browker* (Decree 49).

331 *Nicolson v. Cressett* (Decree 9); *Ferris v. Cressett* (Decree 36); *Marshall v. Overman* (Decree 38).

332 See *Taynton v. Collett* (Decree 27). In fairness, the Southwark fire court helped the innkeeper as much as it could; Parliament had denied to the court any power to alter leases that had been agreed after the fire. 29 Car. II, c. 4, § 15 (1677), reprinted in *Statutes of the Realm*, v, p. 845.

333 See, e.g., Doolittle, 'Property Law', pp. 212–16.

women appeared as parties in thirty-three of the fifty-two petitions.[334] To begin with women as tenants, the three encroachment decrees listed the tenants for eighty-nine properties along the High Street, where most of the shops were located and where most of the trades were conducted. Here, only five of eighty-nine tenants were women.[335] Among the non-encroachment decrees, however, women as principal tenants were more common. The forty-nine non-encroachment cases concerned forty-seven distinct properties.[336] For twelve properties, women held the tenancy. For one property, a woman had brought the tenancy into the marriage and the rules of feme covert subjected it to the husband's control.[337] For two properties, a husband and a wife entered a lease together as tenants; the women's interests were also likely subject to feme covert, although the decrees did not so say.[338] In nine petitions, a woman either possessed the tenancy outright or held a life interest in the tenancy as relict of a deceased husband.[339]

Even more women held interests as owners and landladies.[340] Women appeared to be outright owners (or co-owners) of two properties,[341] as

334 In addition, women were often mentioned in the decrees as prior tenants, prior landladies, sub-landladies, deceased holders of reversions and the like. As an example, Mary Browker had owned in fee the twelve Browker properties in dispute before she chose to put the land in trust — to herself for life and then for the benefit of the eldest male Browker (with reversions to other family members should male issue fail, as it did).

335 Of course, women could have held the tenancy of some of the eighty-four properties that mentioned male tenants: a woman may have had an interest from a prior marriage in a High Street tenancy, but a new husband assumed control of that interest on remarriage. Unfortunately, unlike the non-encroachment decrees, the encroachment decrees do not sort out the niceties of life estates and feme coverts.

336 Decrees 28 and 29 concerned a single property, as did Decrees 40 and 41.

337 Decree 25.

338 Decrees 10 and 22.

339 See Decrees 1, 3, 5, 6, 11, 26, 30, 31 and 41. Unfortunately, the decrees did not always specify whether a woman owned a tenancy of her own or as a relict with a life estate only. One reason is that the decrees — as Doolittle similarly observed with the London fire court's decrees, see Doolittle, 'Property Law', p. 214 — did not distinguish between a woman's tenancy interest as devisee under her husband's will and her role as the executor of her deceased husband's will.

340 This is a different result from the one Doolittle obtained for London, where female occupiers of premises as tenants were more frequent than female owners. See Doolittle, 'Property Law', p. 214. The difference can be explained, at least in part, by the large percentage of London property owned by institutions. That phenomenon did not pertain to Southwark, where private ownership was more typical. See notes 307–10 and accompanying text.

341 Decrees 17 and 28.

well as relics with a life or dowager interest in seven others.[342] Married women also owned (or co-owned) ten other properties that were subject to their husbands' right of control under feme covert.[343]

Women also appeared as parties in their capacities as owners (or co-owners) of reversionary interests,[344] as guardian of the interests of their infant children[345] and as holder of an annuity against rent charges.[346]

Women proved themselves more than adequate to protect their interests in court. In one case, the landlord and his wife begged the court to order the widowed petitioner to be the rebuilder because she was richer than they were; be that as it may, the widow still drove a hard bargain in court.[347] In another case, which involved the most extensive back-and-forth negotiations reported in the decrees, a widow refused to budge, eventually agreeing to be bought out of her lease for £25 — even though she had been willing before the passage of the fire-court statute to pay £100 to exit the lease.[348] And in one case, a widow with a life estate — with the reversion held by her son, the eldest of her three children — successfully convinced the court to grant her a lease for a term of years as an inducement to rebuild.[349] The effect of her request was to allow her to bequeath something to her two younger children, who otherwise would have held no interest in the property when she died.

Trusts

Doolittle has also used the records of the London fire court to show that simple trusts were a common way for ordinary Londoners — not just the landed wealthy — to hold property.[350] The evidence of the Southwark fire court can provide another lens through which to view such property holdings in seventeenth-century England.

---

342 Decrees 1, 5, 6, 7, 17, 37 and 42. In Decree 17, one woman owned her interest in the property outright, while another held a life interest.

343 Decrees 1, 3, 5, 6, 7, 9, 17, 35, 36 and 42. Decrees 5, 6 and 42 also involved other women as co-owners; as discussed in the prior note, their interest was that of a relict. Among the women who held property subject to feme covert, they had typically inherited the property or held a relict's interest that they brought into the present marriage.

344 Decrees 7, 8, 10, 11, 12, 13, 14, 15, 47, 48, 49, 50 and 51.

345 Decrees 8, 10, 11, 12, 13, 14, 15, 37, 47, 48, 49, 50 and 51.

346 Decree 43.

347 *Ely v. Mence* (Decree 1).

348 *Waggorne v. Beacon* (Decree 3).

349 *Cannon v. Cannon* (Decree 40).

350 See, e.g., Doolittle, 'Property Law', pp. 208–12.

The Southwark records paint a mixed picture about the use of trusts to hold land. I begin with a caveat: the decrees, which reproduce in fair detail the petitions of the parties, often describe only the property interests of relevance to the dispute; thus, if certain reversionary or beneficial interests were not consequential, they may have eluded mention. For example, none of the three encroachment cases mentioned trusts because the court's order to remove the encroachment ran to the tenant in possession; all that mattered was who had the present possessory interest. Of the forty-seven properties involved in the remaining forty-nine petitions, seventeen were held in *inter vivos* trusts.[351] This number is skewed by the large number (twelve) of Browker cases, in which the trust was of recent origin.[352] The other five properties held in *inter vivos* trusts concerned Richard How, who came into fee-simple ownership of various properties and then established a trust with a life estate for himself and a reversion to his son. Testamentary trusts appear to have been established for four properties owned by other successful Southwark citizens, the Overmans and Abraham Bradway;[353] in each case, the husband granted a life estate to his wife, with the inheritance held by one or more children. A similar trust granting a life estate to the wife but then giving the entire inheritance to the eldest son was involved in another case.[354] The decrees suggest that prior ownership of some of the other properties at issue had been held in trust at one point, but little more can be said definitively because those interests were not directly before the court.[355]

In addition, one property was held in fee tail for the eldest male in the Bergavenny barony.[356]

Occupations

Occupations provide another lens through which to understand property ownership and life in seventeenth-century Southwark.

---

351 An *inter vivos* trust is created while the grantor is still alive. On the other hand, a testamentary trust is established in a grantor's will and takes effect upon the grantor's death.

352 See note 320 and accompanying text.

353 Decrees 9 and 36 concern the Overman properties. Decrees 7 and 42 concern the Bradway properties.

354 See *Cannon v. Cannon* (Decree 40), discussed in note 349 and accompanying text.

355 See, e.g., *Debnam v. Body* (Decree 28).

356 *Sicklemore v. Elizabeth Lady Dowager Burgevenny* (Decree 37). The caption misspelled the Bergavenny (or Abergavenny) surname. The Bergavenny barony was created by error.

Whether landlord or tenant, women were always placed into one of four categories — widow, wife, spinster or infant — even when it is evident that they were carrying on a trade.[357] Among male tenants, the range of trades conducted in Southwark is evident. As might be expected of seventeenth-century Southwark, innkeepers, brewers, distillers and a vintner were tenants, as were those in related trades such as victualler and butcher. What is striking about the decrees is the range of other occupations. A few were described either as 'gentlemen' or as 'esquires'; others were members of City livery companies (described as 'Citizen and [name of livery company]') and others appear to be tradesmen in Southwark or Westminster.

Male landlords generally came from the 'better' ways of life. 'Gentlemen' and 'esquires' were by far the most common statuses for landlords. A baron and a baronet also held certain interests.

Ownership of the Inns of Southwark

Finally, Southwark was known for its inns. Five of its great inns (the Queen's Head, the King's Head, the Talbot, the George, and the White Hart) made appearances in fire court's decrees.[358] All of these inns were owned by gentlemen or London Citizens, not by Southwark entrepreneurs. The innkeepers were tenants operating under long-term leases.

B. TERMS OF SOUTHWARK LEASES BEFORE AND AFTER THE FIRE

Reading decrees of the fire courts is like trying to comprehend a three-dimensional object by examining a two-dimensional slice. The courts' decrees almost always focus on the parties in the most immediately relevant legal relationship: the relationship between the willing rebuilder and the rebuilder's landlord (in most cases) or tenant (in others). The Southwark fire court's decrees are no exception. Occasionally the petitions reveal the three-dimensional context of the relationship: who the landlord's landlord was, who the tenant's undertenants were, who had originally built the premises or who the post-fire developer would be.[359] Sometimes it is possible to determine whether the tenant in the

---

357 See, e.g., *Sledd v. Gregory* (Decree 30), where the widow sought lease terms to carry on her husband's trade as ironmonger.

358 The Index of Places identifies the decrees that mention each inn.

359 Cf. Boulton, *Neighbourhood and Society*, p. 197 ('[T]he "multi-layered landlord-tenant relations" commonly found in sixteenth- and seventeenth-century London are notoriously difficult to disentangle').

petition was the occupant of the premises or instead had subleased the premises to others. But often the crumbs that the decrees leave behind are inadequate. Moreover, some of the leases make little economic sense without knowledge of a business context that the decrees fail to provide.

Nonetheless, the leases tell a story about the types of legal relationships into which people in seventeenth-century Southwark entered. Boulton has observed that, in the early seventeenth century, terms of twenty-one years for dwellings were common.[360] As he noted, the terms of leases — especially their length — raise important questions about social mobility and community cohesion in Southwark.

The records of the Southwark fire court add depth to our understanding of this issue. For the forty-five decrees concerning issues of tenancy, four involved large commercial or public properties: the George, the White Hart, the King's Head and the Compter.[361] All of these properties were located along the High Street. Forty-one concerned properties that served either as a private dwelling or as a shop or tavern (likely with living quarters attached), and of these twenty-two decrees concerned twenty-one different properties on the High Street.[362] Eleven decrees concerned properties off the High Street.[363] The location of the remaining eight properties is uncertain.[364]

For reasons related to the variegated nature of the disputes and agreements before the court, only twenty-seven of the forty-five tenancy decrees provided complete information about the amount of rent and the length of the term for both the pre-fire lease and the post-fire lease; the remaining decrees provided information on either the pre-fire lease or the post-fire lease, but not both. Nonetheless, much useful information can be gleaned from these decrees.

To begin, the most recent pre-fire leases for the large inns were, in comparison to other properties, short: ten years for the George, twenty-one for the White Hart and ten and a half for the King's Head.[365] As might be expected, the negotiated pre-fire rents for the inns were also

---

360 Ibid., pp. 204–05.

361 Decrees 22, 27, 31 and 32.

362 Decrees 1, 2, 6, 7, 10, 12, 17, 18, 19, 20, 21, 24, 28, 29, 30, 33, 34, 35, 36, 39, 40 and 47. Decrees 28 and 29 involved different tenancy matters for same property.

363 Decrees 4, 11, 13, 14, 15, 23, 38, 43, 48, 49 and 50.

364 Decrees 3, 5, 8, 9, 16, 25, 37 and 51. A number of these properties were noted to have signs over the shop or had a significant rent, suggesting that they were High Street properties.

365 In 1670, the London fire court had extended the lease on the George by an additional forty years. In addition, the original lease for the King's Head had

the highest of all the properties: £150 per annum for the George, £55 for the White Hart and £66 for the King's Head.[366]

Rentals of other High Street properties proved to be highly variable. For the fifteen properties for which the information is available,[367] the average pre-fire lease term was 26.1 years; the most frequent term was twenty-one years (five leases), and the range was eleven and a half years to sixty-one years. For the sixteen properties for which pre-fire rents are available,[368] the average High Street rent was £19 2s., with the lowest rent being £7 and the highest being £40. In addition, three of the pre-fire leases involved fines (in the amounts of £17 10s., £90 and £100).

Properties off the High Street tended to be leased for longer terms but, as might be expected, much less money. Unlike decrees concerning High Street properties, it was not uncommon for a single decree to encompass multiple properties that had been leased together. Thus, the ten non-High Street decrees for which pre-fire lease terms are available involved fifteen leases.[369] The average term of a lease was 33.9 years, with nearly half (seven leases) being for forty-one years. The longest lease was forty-four years, and the shortest leases (four in total) were twenty-one years. The average rent was £6 8s., with the lowest being £2 and the highest £14. The top lease was also the only property to involve a fine (of £15).

For the eight properties of undetermined location, the length of the pre-fire leases was available for seven properties: the average term was 29.7 years, with the shortest just under five years and the longest fifty-one years.[370] The amount of the pre-fire rent was available for all eight properties: the average was £19 18s., with a range from £4 to £44.[371] In addition, tenants paid fines for three of the eight properties, in the amounts of £20, £28 and (for the £44 lease) £100.

The decrees of the Southwark fire court significantly increased the length of the leases and decreased the annual rents, and no rebuilder

---

been twenty years, with the innkeeper signing the ten-and-a-half-year extension well before that lease's expiration. Thus, the lease on the King's Head had eighteen and a half years to run at the time of the Southwark fire.

366 Decrees 22, 27 and 29. The London fire court had reduced the rent on the George to £80; the £150 rent was the amount that had been negotiated before that reduction. For the King's Head, the rent had been £60, but the landlord increased the annual rent to £66 — and extracted a hefty £144 10s. fine — in return for granting the ten-and-a-half-year extension on the lease.

367 Decrees 1, 6, 17, 18, 19, 20, 21, 24, 28, 30, 33, 35, 36, 39 and 47.

368 Decrees 1, 6, 17, 18, 19, 20, 21, 24, 28, 30, 33, 34, 35, 36, 39 and 47.

369 Decrees 4, 11, 13, 14, 15, 23, 38, 48, 49 and 50.

370 Decrees 3, 5, 8, 9, 16, 37 and 51.

371 Decrees 3, 5, 8, 9, 16, 25, 37 and 51.

was required to pay a fine. To explain, it might be useful to distinguish between the agreed and disputed cases. Ten of the eleven agreed leases involved properties along the High Street; the location of the eleventh property was unclear.[372] In the eleven agreed cases, the average post-fire lease term (including any unexpired portion of a present lease) was 74.6 years, with the shortest lease being 38.25 years and the longest leases (of which there were five) being ninety-nine years. For the seven agreed leases involving existing tenants, the parties extended pre-fire leases by an average of fifty-three years.[373]

In terms of rents for the agreed cases, the average post-fire rent was £25 16s.[374] For eight of the properties, it is possible to compare pre-fire and post-fire rents:[375] pre-fire rents had averaged £30 10s., and post-fire rents averaged £21 8s. If we exclude the George and the King's Head,[376] pre-fire rents for the six agreed cases for which pre- and post-fire information is available averaged £16 8s., while post-fire rents averaged £13 18s. Thus, aside from the George and the White Hart, landlords in the agreed cases were generally successful in negotiating rents close to their pre-fire level — albeit at the cost of granting very generous lease extensions.

When we turn to thirty-four disputed cases, the picture changes somewhat. For the sixteen disputed cases along the High Street,[377] four can be discarded because they involved disputes unrelated to the length or amount of the lease.[378] Of the remaining twelve, the length of the term (inclusive of any remaining term on the existing lease) and the length of the extension can be determined for nine.[379] The fire court ordered an average lease term (inclusive of the remaining term on the existing lease) of 61.3 years; the most common term (five leases) was

---

372 Decrees 7, 10, 19, 20, 21, 22, 29, 31, 34 and 35 involved High Street properties. Decree 37 did not identify the property's location, although the low rent (£5 pre-fire, £6 post-fire) suggests that it was off the High Street.

373 Decrees 19, 20, 21, 22, 34, 35 and 37.

374 This figure includes the rents for the George and the King's Head, which skew the overall average upwards. If we take out those leases, the average agreed rent falls to £21 14s. per annum.

375 Decrees 19, 20, 21, 22, 31, 34, 35 and 37.

376 Decrees 22 and 31.

377 Decrees 1, 2, 6, 12, 17, 18, 24, 27, 28, 30, 32, 33, 36, 39, 40 and 47.

378 Decrees 2, 24, 27 and 32. Decrees 27 and 32 involved, respectively, the White Hart and the Compter.

379 In Decree 18, the tenant chose not to rebuild under an extended lease but to terminate the lease at the conclusion of the existing lease. Decree 28 terminated a present tenant's interest; the tenant was not allowed to extend the lease. Decree 40

sixty years, and the range was fifty-three years to seventy years. This amounted to an average extension of 45.6 years beyond the end of the present lease.

For nine of the High Street decrees, it is also possible to compare the pre-fire rent with the post-fire rent.[380] The average pre-fire rent was £19 12s.[381] The average post-fire rent was £9 18s. — or roughly half of the pre-fire rent.[382]

For properties off the High Street, their generally low rents gave the Southwark fire court very little room to lower rents as an inducement to rebuild, as some prospective builders complained;[383] thus, the court's principal inducement was to provide a longer lease. The eleven non-High Street properties for which the court resolved a dispute involved fifteen leases.[384] For the eight cases (and twelve leases) for which the information is available,[385] the average term that the fire court ordered (inclusive of any remaining term on the existing lease) was 69.2 years, with eleven of the twelve leases being extended to seventy years and the twelfth to sixty years. On average, the court extended existing leases by 48.9 years to achieve this result. As for rents, it is possible to compare pre-fire rents with post-fire rents in seven cases involving eleven leases.[386] The average pre-fire rent was £5 2s., while the average post-fire rent was £3 2s. — roughly a reduction of 40 per cent.

extended the life interest of a relict by 21 years; because it is impossible to know how long the relict would live, the length of the new term cannot be calculated.

380 Decrees 1, 6, 17, 18, 30, 33, 36, 39 and 47. Decrees 2 and 12 reported the post-fire rent, but not the pre-fire rent. Decrees 24, 28 and 32 involved disputes that made it unnecessary to list either the pre-fire or post-fire rents. Decree 27 mentioned both pre-fire and post-fire rents, but because the rents were fixed by agreement and the fire court was powerless to change agreed terms and my concern is how the court exercised its power, see note 329 and accompanying text, I exclude that case as well.

381 Three of the leases also involved payments of significant fines (£17 10s., £90 and £100), which I exclude from this calculation.

382 It was not uncommon for the court to delay the first rent payment by one year (and sometimes longer); it ordered the payment of a peppercorn for the initial period. This delay provided the tenant with a period to rebuild free of rent payments. I did not attempt to amortise or otherwise account for this reduction, although I recognize that the rent-free period was itself a valuable inducement to rebuild. The figure in in the text, both here and with the post-fire average rents I subsequently provide for non-High Street properties and properties of uncertain location, reflects the rent due after this initial period.

383 See, e.g., *Hudson v. Browker* (Decree 48); *Williams v. Browker* (Decree 50).

384 Decrees 4, 11, 13, 14, 15, 23, 38, 43, 48, 49 and 50.

385 Decrees 4, 23 and 38 did not involve the granting of new lease terms to tenants.

386 Decree 43 did not disclose the pre-fire rent.

For the seven properties of uncertain location where the fire court needed to resolve a dispute,[387] three resolved disputes in a fashion that did not result in the court ordering a post-fire lease.[388] For the remaining four, the average new lease (inclusive of the unexpired term of the existing lease) was seventy years (one sixty years, two seventy years and one eighty years). On average, the court needed to extend the existing leases by fifty-one years. As for rents, the average pre-fire rent was £14 16s., and the average post-fire rent that the court established was £9 16s. — or roughly a reduction in rent of one-third.

If we aggregate all thirty-four disputed cases without regard to location, the court ordered an average new term (inclusive of the unexpired term of an existing lease) of 66.5 years, with an extension of seventy years (fourteen leases) being the most common and sixty years (seven leases) the next most common. The average lease extension was 48.1 years. As for the comparison of pre-fire and post-fire rents for the properties for which this information is available, the average pre-fire rent was £12 4s., while the average post-fire rent was £6 16s. Thus, the fire court on average reduced tenants' rents by roughly 45 per cent as a way to aid their rebuilding.

Comparing the figures in disputed cases to those in agreed cases, landlords were considerably more successful in agreed cases in keeping rents closer to pre-fire levels. But they paid for that victory by giving tenants an average of five years longer on their leases.

Finally, if we back out and assess all of the tenancy disputes that the Southwark fire court resolved — both the agreed and disputed cases — we come to a global assessment of the changes that the court made (or at least acquiesced in) to Southwark leases. A tenant enjoyed, on average, a new lease of sixty-nine years.[389] That amounted to, on average, an extension of 49.1 years. For those cases in which pre- and post-fire comparison is possible, tenants saw their rents reduced by 39 per cent, from £16 14s. to £10 10s.

C. THE COST OF BUILDING

A final observation concerns the cost of construction and the prices of new building in Southwark. A number of the decrees mentioned money that had been laid out in building, repairing, or adding additions onto properties before the fire in 1676. Sometimes the cost of this

---

387 Decrees 3, 5, 8, 9, 16, 25 and 51.
388 Decrees 3, 16 and 25.
389 This term includes the unexpired term of existing leases.

building was recited as part of the consideration for the pre-fire lease. Numerous decrees also mentioned the cost that a party had expended after the fire to rebuild the premises or that the party expected to spend. From this information it can be gleaned that the going rate for a building along the High Street was around £300.[390] In one case, the fire court directed a tenant who was given rebuilding rights to spend a minimum sum of £250 in constructing a new building.[391] In another case, a tenant rebuilt a property in a 'bye alley' off the High Street for £600, but the landlord objected to any rent reduction to account for this rebuilding because the property could have been rebuilt for £300; the landlord claimed that the extra cost was mere ornamentation that suited the tenant but did not improve the value of the property. The court agreed — although it also gave the tenant an eighty-year lease to recoup the investment.[392]

The great inns, of course, were more expensive to rebuild. Pity poor Edmund Geary, proprietor of the White Hart Inn and tenant of John Collett. Part of the White Hart had burned down in 1669, and Geary spent £700 in rebuilding. After the White Hart burned to the ground in the Southwark fire, Geary (with the help of his friends) spent £2,400 rebuilding it — only to find Collett unwilling to reduce the rent. To make matters worse, Geary was unable to enjoy the new White Hart for long, dying in 1677.[393] At least Geary's neighbour Mark Weyland, the proprietor of the also twice-unlucky George,[394] got his landlord, John Sayer, to grant significant encouragement by knocking £1,800 off the rent over the course of his revised lease. Presumably this reduction constituted a large chunk of Weyland's cost of rebuilding.

CONCLUSION

By its nature, the Southwark fire court distributed losses from the Great Fire of Southwark between landlords and tenants. In rough terms, the Court reduced rents by nearly 40 per cent and added almost fifty years to tenants' leases. The immediate expense of rebuilding usually fell on the tenant, who had a long period of reduced rent in which to recoup the investment. On the other hand, landlords had to wait a long time

---

390 See note 54.
391 See *Sledd v. Gregory* (Decree 30).
392 See *Williams v. Browker* (Decree 51).
393 *Taynton v. Collett* (Decree 27).
394 The George had burned down in 1670. See note 135.

— likely longer than their own lifetimes — to rent their properties at full value.

Like all the fire courts that operated with the same mechanism, the Southwark fire court was available only to those who had sufficient capital to incur a significant expense and reap a return on the investment over time. The existence of excess wealth among the parties was the sine qua non of the fire-court approach. Spreading loss across broader segments of society when the parties did not have the means to rebuild — say, by insurance — still lay over the horizon.

Nonetheless, with only limited tools available, the fire court aided the reconstruction of Southwark and the widening of the High Street. A critical question is whether the Southwark fire court can be adjudged a success. More work must be done on the economic and social impact of locking landlords and tenants into long-term relationships before we can pronounce the Southwark fire court an unqualified success, but as a mechanism to ensure the speedy rebuilding of Southwark, the Southwark fire court was invaluable.

NOTE ON THE PREPARATION
OF THE CALENDAR

As is true of other seventeenth-century fire-court decrees, digesting the decrees of the Southwark fire court presents certain challenges. The first is length. In their embossed form, fire-court decrees typically comprised four to six folios, with some running longer. The decree was often written as a single run-on sentence that had the additional disadvantage of repeating the same information more than once. The decrees also had a certain affectation or grandiosity that does not exist in modern judicial writing. How much of this 'flavour' to give readers is a difficult editorial choice. Philip Jones, who calendared the first four volumes of the decrees of the fire court established after the Great Fire of London, opted for brevity and modernity: he eliminated nearly all information extraneous to the outcome, cut out flowery language and trimmed the description of the outcome to its bare essentials: who would be the rebuilder, how long the lease would run and what the new rent would be. As a result, he digested most of the London fire-court decrees down to a page or two, and often less.

For the Southwark fire court, I opted for fuller renditions of the cases. One reason is that the decrees of the Southwark court tended to be longer than those of the London fire court — in part because there was a much higher percentage of disputed cases (as opposed to cases in which the parties had agreed terms before coming to court). I also wished to show the welter of property interests at stake in each decree and to give readers a better sense of the Southwark court's deliberations and decisions. While I cut most of the repetition, I left in one bit. The decrees often recited in brief the Southwark court's reasoning and decision (who would rebuild and under what terms) and then spelled out in legalistic detail each term of the judgment. Sometimes nuances emerged between the quick bottom-line decision and the full judgment. Perhaps because I am a lawyer and these details interest me, I included both the short-form of the decision and the full details of the judgment — even though I am not sure that Philip Jones would have approved of my choice to include the latter.

Another challenge is organization. Each decree opened with a recitation of the allegations in the petition that was submitted in that case.

The petitions are long since destroyed, but it appears that the decrees more or less recited the petitions verbatim. Because different lawyers prepared the petitions, the information that the petitions contained — and therefore that the decrees recited — was structured in different ways. In general, I imposed a common structure on the decrees, first describing the parties and the location of the property, then reciting the original terms of the lease, then stating any changes in the parties' interests (for instance, the death of the original tenant or landlord) that brought the property into the hands of the present parties, and finally indicating the fate of the property (whether it had been burned down, blown up or defaced in the fire). In a few instances, that approach did not make sense, and I followed a different structure instead. Once I had established the basic facts of the parties, the property and the lease, I moved to the decision-making process: the issuance of the summons, the names of lawyers who represented the parties, the arguments made (if any), the witnesses called and evidence taken (if any), the court's deliberations and, finally, the court's judgment.

To make the text readable, I inserted numerous paragraph breaks. I also numbered each term of the court's judgment (something that the decrees themselves did not do), and I reorganized the terms of the judgments so they too had a more consistent form. I typically started with the terms of the new lease (rent due and length of the new term) and then moved to other aspects of the court's orders, such as the payment of back rent, the covenants to include, the process to use for executing new leases and the effect of the judgment on reversionary and other future interests.

A third challenge was spelling. In the seventeenth century, spelling was an inventive enterprise, and the same word or name might be spelled in different ways — even, sometimes, by the same speller. In some decrees, the spelling of parties' names would change over the course of the decree. For those who appeared in multiple decrees, such as the court's judges, lawyers and certain repeat parties, spellings of names could vary from decree to decree. For instance, John Appleby, one of the court's judges, had his name rendered four different ways (and never as 'Appleby', which is the conventional modern spelling). It could sometimes be difficult to ascertain whether a party in one case was the same as a party with a similarly spelled name in a different case.

Rightly or wrongly, I developed a convention: I rendered the name of each judge, lawyer and party as that decree rendered it, rather than providing a common spelling across decrees. In footnotes, I often noted variations, particularly when the spelling differed within a single decree. In the Index of Persons, however, I collected all the different spellings of a name under one listing, with cross-references to alternate spellings. The one exception to my convention was Sir George Jeffreys, who also had three different spellings given for his name. Jeffreys, then London's Common Serjeant, became a notable historical figure during the reign of James II; and in light of his notoriety, it made sense to spell his name consistently as 'Jeffreys', as modern historians do.

In all other regards, I modernized spelling, syntax and grammar.

Fourth, I modernized the dates given in the decrees. In the seventeenth century, England still followed the Julian calendar, so that the new year commenced on 25 March, the feast of the Annunciation. Events occurring before 25 March would be designated with the prior year's date. The decrees followed the old style. Historians sometimes signal the difference in dating by designating events occurring before 25 March with numbers like '1676/7', meaning 1676 in the old-style calendar and 1677 in the modern calendar. Jones adopted this approach. For simplicity, however, I adopted the modern calendar throughout, converting all old-style dates to their present equivalent.

In addition, seventeenth-century London rents were usually payable quarterly on four feast days:

- 25 March, the feast of the Annunciation of the Blessed Virgin Mary (Lady Day);
- 24 June, the feast of the Nativity of Saint John the Baptist (Midsummer);
- 29 September, the feast of St Michael the Archangel (Michaelmas); and
- 25 December, the feast of the birth of our Lord (Christmas).

Leases nearly always commenced (and ended) on one of these feasts. Therefore, in describing lease and rent terms, the decrees referenced the relevant feast day(s) rather than the calendar date(s). Because each feast day went by multiple names, different decrees used different names. While I could have substituted calendar dates for feast-day names throughout, I decided to give the reader a stronger sense of how the decrees read and how religious feasts permeated the consciousness of seventeenth-century Londoners. For simplicity, however, I used only the four feast-day names above, rather than reciting the name of the relevant feast as given in each decree.

Fifth, the decrees often provided an occupation for male parties, such as 'John Snell, Citizen and Merchant Taylor of London'; the name of the trade always capitalized. This indicates that the party was a member of a City of London livery company and thus entitled to trade within the City. In the seventeenth century it was still likely that members followed the nominal trade of their livery company, but this was gradually ceasing to be the norm as men, and less often women, became members through patrimony (following their fathers into the company) or by redemption (purchasing membership), as well as the traditional method of apprenticeship to a master in the trade. I have accumulated a bit of information on a few of the parties involved, but at the distance of 350 years, I cannot know how often the stated trade reflected the trade actually followed by the party. In all instances, I recite the trade given in the decree.

Women, on the other hand, were invariably identified by marital status — spinster, wife, widow, dowager — even when it was apparent from the decree that the woman was following the trade of her (often deceased) husband. The decrees are artefacts of the time in which they were rendered, and again I simply recite the status given in the decree, as misleading as that may be.

Next, unlike Jones's calendar, which cross-referenced only the surveys of Oliver and Hooke (when available), I have occasionally added footnotes with additional information about the cases, the parties and the properties. For instance, the wills of some of the parties provided details that added insights into the dispute or the property holdings at issue. Likewise, the hearth-tax records in the 1660s sometimes helped to locate or provide details about a particular property. Given the limits of the historical record (and the patience of the reader), I did not provide details for every decree; rather, my goal was to show how the decrees could be stitched together with genealogical information, probate records and other historical sources to build a more complete picture of life in Southwark at the time of its Great Fire.

Finally, I precisely followed Jones's lead in one regard: I formatted the caption for the decrees as he did. In part because more judges heard each case, the captions of the Southwark decrees tend to be longer than those found in Jones's calendars, but the basic information is the same: number of the decree; the date rendered; the names and titles of the judges who presided, including a designation of which judges signed the decree; the parties' names; and, when given, the parties' occupations and residences. In calendaring the fifth and sixth volumes of the London fire court's decrees, Ian Doolittle adopted the same format. Even though I departed from his model in other ways, I owe a great debt to Philip Jones for creating the template for calendaring fire-court decrees, and I wanted to make the format of the decrees as familiar as possible to those who will work with the decrees of both the London and the Southwark fire courts.

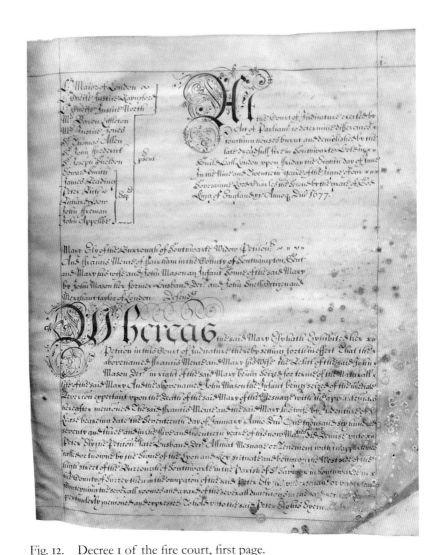

Fig. 12.   Decree 1 of the fire court, first page.
© London Metropolitan Archives CLA/040/02/006

A CALENDAR OF THE RECORDS OF THE COURT OF JUDICATURE ERECTED BY ACT OF PARLIAMENT TO DETERMINE DIFFERENCES TOUCHING HOUSES BURNT AND DEMOLISHED BY THE LATE DREADFULL FIRE IN SOUTHWARK HELD IN GUILDHALL LONDON

Decree 1 (page 1)

8 June 1677.   The Lord Mayor of London [Thomas Davies] (s);[1] Lord Chief Justice Raynsford (s); Lord Chief Justice North (s); Baron Littleton; Justice Jones (s); Sir Thomas Allen (s);[2] Sir John Frederick (s); Sir Joseph Sheldon (s); Edward Smith, Esq. (s);[3] James Reading, Esq. (s); Peter Rich, Esq. (s); Richard How, Esq. (s); John Freeman, Esq. (s); John Appellbe, Esq.

Mary Ely of Southwark, Widow, v. Francis Mence of Fairham in Southampton County, Gentleman; Mary his wife; John Mason, infant son of the said Mary by John Mason, her former husband, deceased; and John Snell, Citizen and Merchant Taylor of London[4]

---

1 '(s)' indicates that the judge signed the decree at its foot. The statute establishing the Southwark fire court required the judges who rendered the decrees to 'subscribe[ ]' the decrees once they had been 'fairely entred into one or more Bookes of parchment'. 29 Car. II, c. 4, § 8 (1677), reprinted in *The Statutes of the Realm printed by Command of His Majesty King George the Third in Pursuance of an Address of the House of Commons of Great Britain* (1810–28), V, p. 844. In some instances, signature proved impossible. For instance, Baron Littleton died in 1679 and John Appleby in 1680 — before the decrees had been embossed onto parchment.

2 In various decrees, the Court's registrar rendered the name as 'Allen' or 'Alleyn'. Allen signed the decrees as 'Aleyn'.

3 The registrar usually rendered the name as 'Smith', although sometimes as 'Smyth'. Smyth, the Steward of Southwark, always signed as 'Smyth'.

4 Snell was a defendant in *Roberts v. Browker* (Decree 11); *Williams v. Browker* (Decree 50); and *Williams v. Browker* (Decree 51). He was the petitioner in *Snell v. Browker* (Decree 13); *Snell v. Browker* (Decree 14); and *Snell v. Browker* (Decree 15). He

Francis Mence and Mary his wife were seised of a messuage with appurtenances. Mary was the relict of John Mason, and she and her husband held the property for Mary's life. Mary's infant son, also named John Mason, held the reversion on Mary's death.

The property was situated on the west side of the High Street in the parish of St Saviour. It contained several rooms and a yard, and was known by the sign of the Lion and Key.

On 17 January 1673, Peter Ely, the late husband of petitioner Mary Ely, leased the messuage. At that time, the property was already in the possession of Peter Ely or his tenants and undertenants. The new lease ran from the feast of the Nativity of St John the Baptist 1675 for fourteen years. The rent was £28 per annum, payable quarterly. In addition, Peter Ely paid a fine of £17 10s. The lease contained various covenants, including one requiring the tenant to repair and uphold the premises.

Peter Ely subsequently died.[5] The petitioner was his relict and sole executrix of his will.

The messuage burned in the fire and was still in ruins. After the petitioner suspended payment of the rent, Francis and Mary Mence brought an action at law for arrears. The petitioner alleged that she was willing to rebuild the messuage on a reasonable abatement of rent and an increased term of years. In the alternative, she was willing to surrender the lease on terms that the Court deemed just and reasonable.

Mary Ely appeared personally in Court, with Mr Bowes and Mr Jenner representing her. Francis Mence appeared personally on behalf of himself, his wife, and her son John Mason (who was less than ten years old). The Court admitted Mence as John Mason's guardian. Mr Ward and Mr Hunt represented the Mences and John Mason.

The petitioner's counsel told the court that the ground was only about ten feet wide in the front. Before the fire, the messuage was intermixed with the house adjoining to the south, whose inheritance belonged to John Snell. One of the rooms of Snell's house to the back, two stairs high, was over the petitioner's house, and one room to the back of petitioner's house plus a garret toward the street was over Snell's house. Because

---

also purchased and then sold an interest in the property at issue in *Hudson v. Browker* (Decree 49).

5 According to parish records, Peter Ely of St Saviour, Grocer, married Mary Smith of St Dunstan's in the West on 1 August 1668. Record of Baptisms, Marriages, and Births 1653–73, St Saviour Parish, fol. 354. He died on 25 November 1675. In his will, made on 10 November 1675 and proved on 30 November 1675, Peter Ely, Citizen and Grocer of London, appointed his wife Mary as executrix. Aside from small legacies to a brother and a cousin, Mary was the only beneficiary of the will. See TNA, PROB 11/349/251.

new-built houses required a party wall of brick, counsel claimed that the ground would be so straightened that the land was not fit to build on, and it would be too inconvenient for the petitioner to rebuild. Counsel suggested that Mary Ely be allowed to surrender the lease gratis, as she had already paid a fine of £17 10s. and had further expended £50 on repairs since taking the lease. This loss was sufficient contribution to satisfy the covenant to repair, especially as Ely was only the executrix of Peter Ely's estate.

Counsel for the defendants told the court that a house could still be built on the ground. A rebuilt house could be made almost as large as the old house by means of exchanging space with Snell's property. Counsel also alleged that the petitioner was rich and able to rebuild, while the defendants were in not as good a condition to do so. If the petitioner refused to rebuild, the defendants required the petitioner to contribute substantially.

The parties made several overtures to settle the dispute. The 'highest rent that either the Petitioner or the said Frances Mence offered to give [was] tenn pounds p annum'.[6] Neither side consented to the other side's offers.

The Court then demanded of John Snell, who was present in Court, whether he was willing to rebuild, a result that was conceived as most commodious in light of the intermingling of the premises. Snell declared that, if Ely consented, he would undertake the rebuilding on reasonable terms. Snell also said that, because the ground was so small, he would build a single house on both properties.

Ely consented to this proposal, and Snell was made a party to the case. Several more demands and offers were made, but none were agreeable. The parties on both sides, however, agreed that the value of the intermixed rooms in the possession of Ely and Snell were of nearly equal value and should be exchanged.

After interposing and moderating between the parties, the Court issued its decree, to which Snell consented.

The Court ordered that:

(1) John Snell was to be the rebuilder.
(2) As encouragement to rebuild, a term of forty-one years was added to the remainder of Ely's term, making the total term of the lease fifty-three years, commencing on feast of the Nativity of St John the Baptist 1677.

---

6 The sense of this quote appears to be that Ely offered no more than £10 per annum, while Mence would take nothing less than £18 per annum (or £10 less than the pre-fire rent).

(3)   Mary Ely was required to pay two-thirds of the rent for Midsummer quarter 1676, because she enjoyed the use of the premises for two months before the fire. She was discharged from paying the final third of the quarterly rent, and was further discharged from paying the annual rent of £28 from the Nativity of St John the Baptist 1676 until the feast of the birth of our Lord 1677.

(4)   The rent was abated from £28 per annum to £12 per annum thereafter.

(5)   Rent payments were to be made to Francis and Mary Mence during Mary's coverture, and then to Mary alone should she survive Francis. On Mary's death, payment was to be made to John Mason or his heirs and assignees.

(6)   On Snell's request, Ely was required to assign the lease to Snell. After assignment, Ely's obligations under the lease's covenants were discharged.

(7)   On Snell's request and upon surrender of the Ely lease, Francis and Mary Mence (and John Mason, when he attained the age of twenty-one) were required to execute a new lease by indenture, prepared at Snell's expense. The new lease should recite the unexpired term of the lease and the annual rent of £12 payable quarterly, and it should contain reasonable covenants usual in new leases made for houses in London.

(8)   By the parties' consent, the rooms lying over the Ely house were exchanged for the rooms lying over the Snell house, and all parties enjoyed the possession of their own ground without regard to the prior intermixture of properties.

(9)   To better set out the dimensions of each property and to preserve the distinct interests of each party upon expiration of the lease, the City Surveyors should, at Snell's expense, view the tofts and make a plot of the ground. The plot was to be affixed to Snell's lease made under this decree.

(10) The two tofts of ground should then be built upright. Snell was required to erect a good and substantial building of brick and to finish the building in good workmanlike manner.

(11) In accordance with the Act of Parliament, Snell might hold the premises for the duration of the lease, notwithstanding the coverture of Mary Mence, the infancy of John Mason or any other estate or interest.[7]

---

7 A gravestone formerly located inside St Saviour's church indicated that Captain John Snell died on 7 September 1681. See Owen Manning and William Bray, *The History and Antiquities of the County of Surrey*, III (London, 1814), p. 574. Snell's

Decree 2 (page 6)

8 June 1677.   The Lord Mayor of London [Thomas Davies] (s); Lord
Chief Justice Raynsford (s); Lord Chief Justice North
(s); Baron Littleton; Justice Jones (s); Sir Thomas
Alleyn (s); Sir John Frederick; Sir Joseph Sheldon (s);
Edward Smith, Esq. (s); James Reading, Esq. (s); Peter
Rich, Esq. (s); Richard How, Esq. (s); John Freeman,
Esq. (s); John Applebee, Esq.[8]

*John Bankes of Southwark, Carpenter, v. Daniel Wight of Southwark,
Distiller*

In January 1677, Daniel Wight[9] affirmed to the petitioner John Bankes
that he was seised of three parcels of ground on which had stood
messuages or tenements burned down in the fire. Paul Foreman, Henry
Young and William Browne had occupied these messuages, which were
situated on the west side of the High Street. They abutted Compter
Lane on the south, a messuage or tenement in the possession of Robert
Gale on the west, and a messuage or tenement in the possession of
Nathaniel Butcher on the north.[10]

will was dated 8 September 1681 and proved on 14 October 1681, with witnesses
testifying that the will had been erroneously dated and that Snell had in fact died
on 7 September. See TNA, PROB 11/368/91. The will devised one property on his
wife Martha for her life, with his daughter Susanna holding the reversion. The will
described the property as a 'mesuage or tenement now in the tenure of John Huck
mealeman […] which I hold by lease and demise of and from the heirs of John
Mason Dyer deceased'. It is almost certainly the property in this decree.

Snell also demised on Martha for her life (with the reversion to his son John) his
own house, as well as the adjoining messuage or tenement to the southward 'now
in the occupation or tenure of Thomas Ely Grocer'. Ibid. The will of Peter Ely
(also a Grocer) did not mention any children, but it mentioned a cousin, Thomas
Ely, who received a £10 bequest.

For other aspects of Snell's will, including more about its misdating, see *Williams
v. Browker* (Decree 51).

8 Unlike the prior caption, the registrar rendered the name as 'Applebee'. Over
the course of the decrees the registrar rendered Appleby's name four different ways
(Appelbe, Appellbe, Appellbee and Applebee). The Act of Parliament erecting
the Southwark fire court spelled the name 'Applebee'. 29 Car. II, c. 4, § 8 (1677),
reprinted in *Statutes of the Realm*, v, p. 843.

9 In reciting the allegations of the petition, the registrar sometimes referred to
Wight as 'Daniell' and sometimes as 'Daniel'. The caption reads 'Daniel'. I follow
the caption's rendering throughout the decree.

10 Wight had purchased the freehold of this land from Susan and Richard
Morrell, the heirs of Gunter Morrell, on 15 January 1668. The indenture stated that
there were three messuages on the property. See TNA, C 108/129/16.

When the three tenants refused to rebuild, Wight took in their interests. Wight and Bankes then entered into a 'treaty' for Bankes to rebuild. They agreed a fifty-year lease from the feast of the Annunciation of the Blessed Virgin Mary 1677. The rent was a peppercorn for the first three years and £40 per annum, payable quarterly, thereafter. The lease was to be drawn up with the usual covenants. They also agreed that Bankes might enter the ground immediately to begin construction.

At the time of the petition, Bankes had nearly finished two messuages and two shops, at a cost of more than £600. Wight nonetheless delayed in executing the lease and finally refused to do so.

Bankes appeared personally and was represented by Mr Bowes and Mr Jenner. Wight appeared personally and was represented by Mr Ward.

Petitioners' counsel prayed the Court to decree that Wight must execute the lease according to the terms of the agreement. Wight's counsel responded that Wight denied neither the agreement nor the stated terms, but indicated that a difference between Bankes and Wight had arisen: whether the lease should contain a covenant restraining Bankes or his tenants from selling beer or ale by licence on the premises. Before the fire, Wight had leased a house in Compter Lane to Gale. In Gale's lease, Wight covenanted to restrain all tenants in the adjoining houses from selling beer or ale. Gale's house had not burned down in the fire but had been defaced. Without a covenant restraining Bankes from selling beer or ale, Wight might be liable to Gale in an action for breach of the covenant.

Petitioners' counsel responded that, when the parties came to agreement in January, no such covenant had been mentioned; nor was it mentioned when the parties later gave instruments to the scrivener to draw up the lease. Counsel asked to be allowed to prove the matter.

At that point, Thomas Hudson, Scrivener, testified under oath that, when Bankes's building was already two storeys high, Bankes and Wight gave him instruments to draw up the lease. Hudson wrote down the heads of the agreement, and read that document to the Court. There was no note of the disputed covenant, nor did the parties mention the covenant to Hudson. About an hour after the parties left, however, Wight returned alone and told Hudson about the covenant with Gale. Wight asked Hudson to insert a covenant prohibiting the sale of beer or ale into the lease.

Petitioners' counsel also informed the Court that the petitioner had already sued Wight in Chancery. In his answer in that proceeding, Wight had confessed that he did not mention any covenant regarding the sale of beer or ale when he made the agreement with Bankes. Rather, when Wight later remembered his covenant with Gale, he insisted that a covenant be put into the lease.

After weighing the matter, the Court thought it most reasonable that Bankes should have his lease according to the agreed terms. It was not reasonable to impose a covenant on Bankes that had not been agreed. To secure Wight from damage for which he might be liable for breach of the Gale covenant, the Court stated that it would itself decree the lease according to the terms of the parties' agreement, with the usual covenants but without a covenant restraining the sale of beer or ale, and then compel Wight to sign the lease.

Wight's counsel then alleged that Bankes's construction was not as substantial as it should have been. Therefore, the Court directed the insertion of a covenant requiring good and substantial building.

The Court ordered that:

(1) Bankes was granted an estate in the three messuages, as well as in the messuages, shops and buildings new built, together with all lights, ways, passages, watercourses, easements, profits, advantages and appurtenances.

(2) The term of the lease was fifty years from the feast of the Annunciation of the Blessed Virgin Mary 1677.

(3) The annual rent was one peppercorn for the first three years, if demanded by Wight, and then £40, payable quarterly on the usual feasts, for the remaining term. The first payment of £10 would be due on the feast of the Nativity of St John the Baptist 1680.

(4) At Bankes's request and expense, Wight was required to execute a good and sufficient lease by indenture, with such covenants and clause of re-entry for non-payment of rent as are usual in leases of houses in London. In addition, the lease should contain a covenant that Bankes well and substantially build and finish the messuages, shops and buildings in good and sufficient workmanlike manner. There was to be no covenant of restraint concerning the sale of beer or ale. Bankes was required to accept this lease, seal it and return the counterpart to Wight.

(5) Bankes might hold the premises notwithstanding any other interests.[11] The authority of the Court shall protect and indemnify Wight for executing the lease.[12]

---

11 Bankes's eagerness to conclude the lease may be explained by the fact that he quickly turned around and assigned the lease to Kenelme Smith for a fine of £540. Part of the premises was used as a tavern, known as The Fleece, while other parts contained messuages or tenements. See TNA, C 108/129/28.

12 Wight was not out of the woods. Gale's loss of the restraining covenant features again in *Wight v. Gale* (Decree 23).

Decree 3 (page 11)

17 July 1677.   The Lord Mayor of London [Thomas Davies] (s);
                   Baron Littleton; Justice Jones (s); Sir Adam Browne,
                   Baronet; Edward Smith, Esq. (s); Thomas Barker (s);
                   James Reading, Esq. (s); Peter Rich, Esq. (s), John
                   Freeman, Esq. (s); John Appelbe, Esq.[13]

*Elizabeth Waggorne of Southwark, Widow, v. Thomas Beacon of London,
Merchant; Anne, his wife; and Thomas Austen of Southwark, Brewer*

Thomas Austen v. Thomas Beacon; Anne, his wife; and Elizabeth Waggorne

Joshua Phynies of the parish of St Andrews, Holborn, London,
Soapmaker, was seised in fee of a messuage. By a lease of indenture
dated 15 October 1662, this property was demised to Thomas Austen
for twenty-one years, commencing on the feast of St Michael the
Archangel 1662. The annual rent was £44, with the usual covenant
requiring the tenant to repair. The property was known as The Rose
and Crown.

On 19 July 1671, in consideration of £100, Austen assigned the lease
to John Waggorne, deceased husband of the petitioner Elizabeth
Waggorne. At that time, John Waggorne entered into a £200 penalty
bond to save Austen harmless from the covenants contained in Austen's
lease with Phynies. Phynies subsequently died without issue, and the
reversion and inheritance of the lease came to his sister Anne Beacon,
who had married Thomas Beacon.

John Waggorne enjoyed the property for not more than five years
when the property was blown up and demolished in the Southwark fire.
John Waggorne had since died, and Elizabeth his relict was executrix
of his will.

The Beacons sued Austen at law for breach of the covenant to repair
contained in the Phynies lease and for arrears of rent since the fire. In
turn, Austen threatened to sue Elizabeth Waggorne on the £200 bond.
Despite her own great losses from the fire, Waggorne was willing to
rebuild the messuage on reasonable encouragement.

Austen then exhibited a petition similarly describing the Phynies lease
and stating that he had laid out more than £140 in repairs and new
building before assigning the lease to John Waggorne. The petition
also recited the £200 bond and other basic facts described Waggorne's
petition. Austen's petition further recited that, after the assignment to

13   This rendering is the registrar's third different spelling of Appleby.

Waggorne, Austen paid the rent to the Beacons until the fire. After the fire, the Beacons brought two actions at law against him: one for breach of the covenant to repair and one for arrears of rent since the fire. Austen had, however, forborne putting the Waggorne bond into suit. He too was willing to be the rebuilder.

Summons were issued on both petitions and all parties appeared personally. Mr Jenner and Mr Lane, comptroller of the City of London, represented Elizabeth Waggorne. Mr Jeffreys, common serjeant of the City of London, represented the Beacons.[14] Mr Bowes represented Thomas Austen.

Waggorne's counsel opened proceedings by offering £15 per annum for a term to sixty years if Waggorne was the rebuilder. Austen's counsel stated that Austen would quit the building to Waggorne if he was discharged from the covenants in his lease and the actions at law. The Beacons' counsel opposed Waggorne as the builder and prayed that Thomas Beacon be the builder, further offering to take in Austen's lease gratis. He also alleged that Waggorne at one point had offered £100 to be discharged of the covenants in the lease.

Waggorne's counsel denied that Waggorne had offered so great a sum, but in any event, any offers were made before the Act of Parliament created the Court and should be disregarded. Waggorne then increased her offer to £20 per annum.

The landlord [Beacon] refused. Beacon's counsel alleged that John Waggorne had never paid the £100 fine to Austen. Beacon nonetheless offered £25 to Elizabeth Waggorne for surrender of her lease. He also offered to discharge Austen from the covenants and actions at law.

Waggorne accepted the offer as long as Beacon and Austen discharged her from all covenants in the leases, Austen delivered up to her the £200 bond, and Austen further acquitted her from all costs and charges from any suit at law.

The Court determined this agreement to be just and reasonable on all sides if Elizabeth Waggorne paid the rent to the landlord for the two months of the quarter in which the fire occurred.

The Court ordered that:

(1)   On the reasonable demand of Elizabeth Waggorne, Thomas Beacon was to pay Waggorne £25, deducting from that amount the two months' rent for the quarter in which the fire occurred.

---

14   George Jeffreys, later Lord Chief Justice and Lord Chancellor, became best known as the Hanging Judge of the Bloody Assizes. He was knighted on 14 September 1677. The decrees after this date referred to him as 'Sir George Jeffreys'.

Waggorne was then to surrender her lease to Beacon, and Beacon was to deliver the counterpart to be cancelled.

(2) Waggorne was discharged from payment of the third month's rent in the quarter in which the fire occurred, discharged from all other rent incurred since the time of the fire, and discharged from all covenants.

(3) Austen was discharged from all rents and covenants. All actions at law against him were to cease.

(4) Austen was required to deliver up the £200 bond to be cancelled. Waggorne was discharged from any costs or charges that might have fallen on her because of the suits at law against Austen.

(5) On Beacon's payment of £25, Waggorne's interest in the premises would cease, and Beacon was entitled to enter and rebuild without interference from Waggorne or any other person claiming an interest in the premises.

Decree 4 (page 15)

17 July 1677.   Baron Littleton; Justice Jones (s); Sir Adam Browne; Sir
                     William Hooker (s); Edward Smith, Esq. (s); Thomas
                     Barker, Esq. (s); James Reading, Esq.; Richard How,
                     Esq. (s); Peter Rich, Esq.;[15] John Freeman, Esq. (s);
                     John Appellbe, Esq.

Marke Houghton of Southwark, Vintner, v. Mayor, Aldermen, and Burgesses of the Town of Shrewsbury and Edward Rice of Southwark, Chirurgeon

By indenture of lease dated 28 September 1657, James Phillips[16] of London, Esquire, demised a messuage to Edward Jones, Citizen and Dyer of London, who already occupied the messuage. The lease ran from the feast of St Michael the Archangel 1657 for twenty-one years at the yearly rent of £8, payable quarterly. The property was located on the south side of Three Crown Court.

---

15 Reading and Rich generally signed the decrees when they sat as judges. For this decree, however, the judge's signatures are cut off at the bottom of the page. Some signatures are fully visible, while only the upper half of Barker's and Freeman's signatures appear. Reading and Rich typically signed the decrees beneath Barker and Freeman, so it is reasonable to surmise that their signatures were lost when the parchment was trimmed to fit into the book of decrees.

16 In reciting the allegations of the petition, the registrar sometimes rendered the name as 'Phillipps' and sometimes as 'Phillips'. I use Phillips throughout.

By another indenture of lease, dated 24 December 1657, Phillips demised to Caesar Willis, Citizen and Carpenter of London, a messuage or tenement in the tenure or occupation of Ellen Baggs, widow. The lease ran from the feast of the birth of our Lord 1657 for twenty-one years at the yearly rent of £8, payable quarterly. This property was in Three Crown Court, adjoining Jones's messuage.

Phillips died and willed the reversion and inheritance of the two messuages to the Town of Shrewsbury. Meanwhile, the petitioner, by good and sufficient assignment and other means, came into possession of the two leases.

The two messuages burned down in the fire. The petitioner was willing to rebuild on reasonable encouragement, but the Town of Shrewsbury had so far refused.

Mr. Bowes and Mr Jenner appeared on behalf of the petitioner,[17] while Mr Jeffreys, Mr Ward and Mr Jones appeared on behalf of the Town of Shrewsbury.

The petitioners' counsel informed the Court that the Town of Shrewsbury had empowered Mr Gibbon as its agent to treat with all its tenants in Three Crown Court. Gibbon had made agreements with other tenants, so that, on surrender of their old leases, the tenants would get new leases for sixty-one years at half their former rents, with the first four years rent-free. The Town of Shrewsbury had since executed leases with all other tenants. It had refused, however, to grant a comparable lease to the petitioner, even though he had begun rebuilding and spent nearly £100 so far. Counsel therefore prayed the Court to grant the petitioner a lease with like terms.

Counsel for the Town of Shrewsbury informed the Court that Edward Rice was the tenant in possession of the messuages in dispute at the time of the fire and that Rice had begun rebuilding himself. The Town would have granted Rice a lease on the same terms as its other tenants, but Rice's interest in the premises had come into the possession of the petitioner, who was a dealer in wines. The petitioner had a house with a large vault, which adjoined Rice's premises at the back. After the petitioner took over Rice's interest, he had broken a doorway through the cellar of Rice's premises into his own vault and removed a stack of chimneys. The purpose of this construction was to allow the petitioner to bring wines through Three Crown Court into the vault. Doing so would be a very great annoyance to the Town's

---

17 The decree does not mention that Houghton appeared personally, but its description of later negotiations makes clear that Houghton was present.

other tenants in Three Crown Court, as well a great detriment to the Town's vaults there. Counsel also insisted that, because the rents that the Town received were for the use of several charities, the petitioner, who became interested in the property only after the fire, should not have a doorway or passage so much to the Town's disadvantage.

Petitioners' counsel then prayed the Court that the petitioner might have the liberty of a doorway out of the first storey over the cellar into his adjoining house.

Upon debate, the Court declared that this request was unreasonable, for the Town had obligated all its tenants to build out their walls entirely on their own ground in order to preserve the Town's own interests. Therefore, unless the petitioner would accept like terms, without the liberty of a doorway, the petition would be dismissed.

The petitioner refused to accept these terms, and his counsel insisted that, because he now held the interest of the tenant in possession at the time of the fire, he ought to have the same privilege of being the rebuilder under the same terms. He also stated that several other tenants had back doors out of their houses. If he was to be denied the same liberty, then he prayed to have satisfaction for the money he had expended thus far in rebuilding.

Counsel for the Town of Shrewsbury replied that none of the other tenants had back doors into adjoining houses, but rather some had back doors into back yards or gardens for their better convenience and accommodation.

At that point, a controversy arose about what the petitioner had paid Rice for his interest and how much had been expended on the rebuilding. During debate, it was alleged that the petitioner paid Rice £50, which reimbursed Rice for the amounts he had paid workmen to rebuild. In addition, the petitioner gave Rice a bond for £40 to be paid when the Town executed a lease to the petitioner.

After further debate and allegations of counsel, the Court thought it most reasonable for the Town of Shrewsbury to pay Rice £20 for his interest in the lease and also to pay the petitioner for the value of the rebuilding thus far, with the Surveyor of the City of London determining the value. In return, the petitioner and Rice would surrender their interests in the premises to the Town.

Rice was present in the Court, and he agreed to accept £20 for surrender of his lease. He also agreed to be made a party to the case.

The Court ordered that:

(1)   By the feast of St Michael the Archangel 1677, the Town of Shrewsbury was to pay Edward Rice £20 in full recompense for

his interest in the premises and in full satisfaction of the bond given by the petitioner.

(2) By the feast of St Michael the Archangel 1677, the Town of Shrewsbury was to pay the petitioner Marke Houghton the amount that the City Surveyor estimated as the value of the new building. The parties were allowed to be present when the Surveyor viewed the premises. The petitioner was ordered to accept this payment in full recompense for the building and for his interest in the premises.

(3) On these payments, Rice and Houghton were to surrender their interests in the premises to the Town of Shrewsbury. If they did not do so, the interests of Rice and Houghton were to cease.

(4) Rice was required to deliver up the £40 bond to Houghton to be cancelled.

(5) Rice and Houghton were discharged from payment of all rent incurred since the time of the fire and from the leases' covenants.

(6) On the payments to Rice and Houghton, the Town of Shrewsbury might hold the premises and proceed to finish the buildings and dispose of them free from any claim of Rice, Houghton or any other person.

Decree 5 (page 19)

17 July 1677.   Baron Littleton; Justice Jones (s); Sir Adam Browne; Sir William Hooker (s); Edward Smith, Esq. (s); Thomas Barker, Esq. (s); James Reading, Esq. (s); Peter Rich, Esq. (s); Richard Howe, Esq. (s);[18] John Freeman, Esq. (s); John Appellbe, Esq.

Judith Hall of Southwark, Widow, v. Frances Crosse, Widow; Sir William Twisden, Baronet;[19] and Dame Frances Twisden, his Wife

By indenture of lease dated 13 July 1652, Thomas Rogers, Gentleman, of Sundrich, Kent, demised to Thomas Hall, the petitioner's late husband,

18   In this decree, the Court's registrar rendered 'How' as 'Howe'. How, who was at various times an alderman of London, sheriff of London, justice for Surrey and member of Parliament for Southwark, invariably signed the decrees as 'How'.

19   Twisden was the grandson of Sir Thomas Twisden, Justice of the Court of King's Bench, who retired from the bench in 1678. Justice Twisden had been one of the workhorses on the London fire court, but made no appearances as a judge on the Southwark fire court.

Frances Crosse and the Twisdens also appeared as defendants in *Nicholls v. Crosse* (Decree 6).

and Elizabeth, his then wife, a messuage or tenement in the tenure or occupation of Thomas Goodhand. The lease ran for thirty-one years from the Nativity of St John the Baptist 1652. The annual rent was £20, payable quarterly, with a covenant requiring the tenant to repair and uphold the premises. The premises were known by the sign of the Three Cupps.

Thomas Rogers since died, and Frances Crosse held the lessor's interest in the property for the term of her life. Sir William Twisden and Dame Frances claimed the reversionary interest upon her death. Thomas Hall, the surviving lessee, was also dead, and the petitioner, his second wife, was the sole executrix of his will.

The property burned in the fire and remained in ruins. The petitioner was willing to rebuild on reasonable encouragement: an increase in the lease term and an abatement of rent. She had thus far been unable to obtain terms.

The petitioner appeared personally. Mr Ward was her counsel. Sir William Twisden also appeared personally, with Mr Jenner serving as counsel for all the defendants.

Petitioner's counsel opened matters by declaring the petitioner's interest in rebuilding. Mr Jenner, on behalf of the reversioners, informed the Court that the leased premises were divided into two messuages and were worth £40 per annum: one had been let at £24 per annum and the second was nearly as good. The ground alone was worth £20 per annum if it were to be let to a new contractor.

Petitioner's counsel responded that, when the premises were let, the premises were only one house, and the tenant afterwards divided it into two tenements. They were very small, and not nearly of the value that the defendants' counsel alleged. The fact that no fine was paid at the time of the lease proved that £20 was the rack rent for the premises. All later improvements to the property were made at the tenants' expense. The ground itself was not worth more than £10 per annum. Therefore, the petitioner needed a considerable abatement of rent and an increase in term to sixty years to rebuild.

Defendants' counsel opposed the abatement and instead offered £40 for the tenants' interest. The petitioner refused. Her counsel pressed the Court to make the petitioner the rebuilder because she was very desirous to return to her ancient place of trade.

Having heard the offers and allegations, the Court thought it most just and reasonable that the petitioner be the rebuilder, that the term be made up to sixty years, and that the rent be set at one peppercorn for the first year and £12 for the remainder of the lease.

The Court ordered that:

(1) Petitioner Judith Hall was to pay Frances Crosse two-thirds of the reserved rent of £20 for Midsummer quarter 1676, since petitioner enjoyed the premises for this time before the fire. She was discharged from paying the final third of the quarterly rent.

(2) Petitioner was discharged from all covenants in the lease.

(3) Petitioner was granted a term of threescore years in the premises from the Annunciation of the Blessed Virgin Mary 1677. The rent was one peppercorn (if demanded) for the first year and £12, payable quarterly at the usual feasts, for the remaining fifty-nine years. Payment was to be made to Frances Crosse during her lifetime and then to Sir William Twisden and Dame Frances and their heirs and assigns.

(4) At her cost and with all convenient speed, the petitioner was to build one or more good and substantial messuages and buildings of brick and finish the building in good workmanlike manner as other front houses in Southwark are generally built.[20]

(5) To avoid difficulties in recovering the annual rent and to ascertain the covenants to be performed, the defendants were required to execute a new lease, prepared at the petitioner's charge, and return it to the petitioner, who was to accept it and return the counterpart.

(6) The petitioner might hold the ground and new building for the term of sixty years, notwithstanding the coverture of Dame Frances or any other interest.

Decree 6 (page 23)

17 July 1677. Baron Littleton; Justice Jones (s); Sir Adam Browne; Sir William Hooker (s); Edward Smith, Esq. (s); Thomas Barker, Esq. (s); James Reading, Esq. (s); Peter Rich, Esq. (s); Richard How, Esq. (s); John Freeman, Esq. (s); John Appellbe, Esq.

Elizabeth Nicholls of Southwark, Widow, v. Frances Crosse, Widow; Sir William Twisden, Baronet; Dame Frances Twisden, his Wife; and Leah Newton, Widow[21]

---

20 Although the decree never specified the location of this property, this condition strongly implies that the property was located along the High Street.

21 Frances Crosse and the Twisdens also appeared as defendants in *Hall v. Crosse* (Decree 5).

By indenture of lease dated 8 February 1671, Leah Newton subleased a messuage or tenement to the petitioner. The messuage had been in the occupation of John Gamage, Tailor, and afterwards in the occupation of Thomas Brockett, Pewterer since deceased, and Leah Newton, then Thomas Brockett's wife. The sublease, given originally to James Nicholls, the petitioner's late husband, ran for eleven and a half years from the feast of the birth of our Lord 1670. The yearly rent was £20, payable quarterly. The sublease contained a covenant on the petitioner's part to uphold the premises. The premises were located at St Margaret's Hill and had now come into the tenure of the petitioner.

Frances Crosse was interested in the property during her lifetime, and Sir William Twisden and Dame Frances his wife claimed the reversion after Crosse's death.[22]

The messuage burned down in the fire. The petitioner was willing to rebuild on reasonable encouragement, but her offer was refused.

The petitioner appeared personally, with Mr Ward as her counsel. Sir William Twisden and Leah Newton appeared personally. Mr Jenner represented Twisden, his wife Dame Frances and Frances Crosse. Mr Richardson represented Leah Newton.

Petitioner's counsel opened the proceedings by affirming the petitioner's willingness to rebuild with encouragement. Counsel for Newton informed the Court that Newton had a short reversionary interest after the end of the petitioner's lease and that Newton was also willing to be the rebuilder; but if the Court thought it fit to make the petitioner the rebuilder because she had been burned out by the fire, then Newton should be compensated for her interest.

Mr Jenner, on behalf of Crosse and the Twisdens, alleged that the petitioner paid Newton £20 per annum in rent, but Newton paid the reversioners only £10 per annum in rent, pocketing the remaining £10 for herself. Therefore, the £10 that Frances Crosse received was only a ground rent, which should not be abated further. He further alleged that there was now a shed on the premises for which petitioner was paying £10 per annum in rent, and the ground was worth £12 to a new contractor who might build.

Petitioner's counsel denied these allegations, stating that the ground was very small and that the building would cost much more than others because it was a corner house. He insisted that the ground was not

---

22 Although the decree does not say so explicitly, the sense of the petition (especially when joined with information in the prior decree) is that Crosse was Newton's landlady, and Newton enjoyed a brief (six-month) reversionary interest in the property once the sublease to Nicholls ended.

worth more than £6, which the petitioner would pay if her term was increased to sixty years.

The Court thought it most reasonable and just that petitioner be the rebuilder, with a term of sixty years at a rent of one peppercorn for the first year and £8 per annum thereafter. Petitioner should also compensate Newton £5 for her interest.

The Court ordered that:

(1) On demand, the petitioner Elizabeth Nicholls was to pay Leah Newton £5 for her residual interest in the property. Newton must then surrender to the petitioner all her interest in the premises. Newton was discharged from paying any rent since the time of the fire and from any covenants in her lease.

(2) Petitioner was discharged from paying all rent incurred since the fire, other than what she has already paid, as well as from all growing rent on the sublease and all covenants in the sublease.

(3) Petitioner was granted a term of threescore years in the premises and new buildings from the Annunciation of the Blessed Virgin Mary 1677. The rent was one peppercorn (if demanded) for the first year and £8, payable quarterly at the usual feasts, for the remaining fifty-nine years. Payment was to be made to Frances Crosse during her lifetime and then to Sir William Twisden and Dame Frances his wife and their heirs and assigns.

(4) At her cost, the petitioner was to build another good and substantial messuage and building of brick, and finish the building in good workmanlike manner as other front houses in Southwark were generally rebuilt.

(5) To avoid difficulties in recovering the annual rent and to ascertain the covenants to be performed, Frances Crosse, Sir William and Dame Frances were to execute a new lease, prepared at the petitioner's charge, and return it to the petitioner, who was to accept it and return the counterpart.

(6) The petitioner might quietly hold the ground and new building for the term of sixty years, notwithstanding the coverture of Dame Frances or any other interest.

Decree 7 (page 27)

17 July 1677.   Baron Littleton; Justice Jones (s); Sir Adam Browne; Sir William Hooker (s); Edward Smith, Esq. (s); Thomas Barker, Esq. (s); James Reading, Esq. (s); Peter Rich, Esq. (s); Richard How, Esq. (s); John Freeman, Esq. (s); John Appellbe, Esq.

Henry Knight of Southwark, Soapmaker, v. Abraham Bradway, Citizen and Weaver of London; Sarah his Wife;[23] *Robert Bedford, Citizen and Haberdasher of London; Sarah his Wife; Rebecca Englebert, Spinster; John Ward, Citizen and Dyer of London; and Elizabeth his Wife*

William Englebert was seised in fee of a messuage or tavern known by the sign of the Three Tonnes.[24] He made a settlement on his wife, Sarah, for the term of her life and, upon her decease, on their issue. William died, leaving three daughters: Sarah, who married Robert Bedford; Rebecca, who was yet unmarried; and Elizabeth, who married John Ward. Their mother, also Sarah, had since remarried Abraham Bradway.

The tavern was burned down and demolished in the fire. The tenant in possession refused to rebuild and surrendered his lease. The defendants therefore built a small house to the front of the street. Not being minded to rebuild on the back part, they came to an agreement under which the petitioner was to have a fifty-year term, commencing on the feast of St Michael the Archangel 1676. The agreement covered the rebuilt front messuage and the remaining ground, except for (a) a watercourse that ran from a yard in the Bradways' dwelling through the premises and (b) the use of a well on the premises to place a pipe underground. The yearly rent was £46, payable to Abraham and Sarah Bradway during Sarah's life, and then to Robert and Sarah Bedford, Rebecca Englebert and John and Elizabeth Ward according to their respective interests. The petitioner and defendants executed a lease.

The petitioner had now built several buildings on the back part of the ground. To further corroborate the agreement and bind the several interests of the feme coverts according to the Act of Parliament establishing the Southwark fire court, the petitioner asked for a decree confirming the lease.

The petitioner appeared personally, and was represented by Mr Hunt. Mr Hunt prayed the Court to confirm the agreement and lease. At that point, Robert Bedford delivered to the Court a writing that described the further agreement regarding the watercourse, the exact language of which was read to the Court.

In effect, the writing stated that the water for both houses was purchased through the Queen's Head Inn, and it ran though the

---

23   Sarah Bradway, Robert Bedford, Rebecca Englebert (spelled Inglebert) and John and Elizabeth Ward also appeared as defendants in *Young v. Bradway* (Decree 42).

24   Later in the decree the property is described as the 'Three Tunns'. I use 'Three Tonnes' throughout.

petitioner's property into the street.[25] One condition of the agreement with the Queen's Head Inn was that, if either the Bradways' house or the leased premises were to be used for the trades of a distiller, butcher or hatmaker, then the watercourse was to be stopped up. If the petitioner were to use the demised premises for one of these trades, the petitioner would be required to provide a new watercourse through his own house for the use of the houses on the demised premises. Conversely, if the Bradways' house were ever let to the trades of a distiller, butcher or hatmaker, then Bradway was required to find a watercourse through his own house for his own water, for as long as the trades continued. On behalf of all the defendants, Bedford asked that that the Court's decree might be in accordance with this agreement.

The petitioner consented, and the Court found it just and reasonable to issue a decree according to the parties' terms.

The Court ordered that:

(1) The petitioner Henry Knight was to have a term of fifty years in the messuage or tavern called the Three Tonnes, except for the use of a well to place a pipe as described in the lease. The term ran from the feast of St Michael the Archangel 1676.

(2) The petitioner was to pay £46 per annum, on the four usual feasts, to Abraham and Sarah Bradway during Sarah's coverture and then to Sarah if she survived Abraham. After Sarah Bradway's death, payment should be made to Robert and Sarah Bedford, Rebecca Englebert and John and Elizabeth Ward according to their respective interests.

(3) The written agreement concerning the watercourse was to be performed by the parties.

(4) The petitioner might hold the ground and buildings (with the exceptions mentioned) for the term of fifty years, notwithstanding the coverture of feme coverts or any other interest.

Decree 8 (page 33)

5 Oct. 1677.   Baron Littleton; Justice Jones (s); James Reading, Esq. (s); Peter Rich, Esq. (s); John Freeman, Esq. (s); John Appellbe, Esq.

Josias Nicolson of Southwark, Brewer, v. Thomas Browker, Esq.; Edward Lloyd, Esq.; Dorothy his Wife; William Kent, Clerke; Jane his Wife;

---

25 The Queen's Head Inn was on the east side of the High Street, which is presumably where the property at issue also lay.

Sir Littleton Osbaldeston, Baronet; Dame Katherine his Wife; Thomas Lowfeild, an Infant; Mary Browker, an Infant; Martha Browker, an Infant; the Churchwardens of the Parish of St Saviour in Southwark; and Samuell Wight, Brewer[26]

Thomas Browker, Esquire, of Upper Peover, in the County of Chester, was seised in fee of a messuage and brewhouse, with appurtenances, known by the sign of the Red Lion. The premises had a yearly rent charge of £10 payable to the churchwardens of the parish of St Saviour in Southwark. Half of this charge was for the use of the poor of the parish and the other half for the maintenance of the parish's free grammar school.

By indenture of lease of 29 November 1656, Browker demised the messuage and brewhouse to Roger Peares, Citizen and Salter of London, who was already in occupation of the premises. The lease ran from the feast of St Michael the Archangel 1656 for forty-one years at the yearly rent of £30, payable quarterly. Subsequently, by good and sufficient lawful means, the petitioner obtained Peares's interest.

In his will, Browker devised the premises (along with divers other messuages and tenements) on Mary Browker, his wife, in fee.[27] Shortly after Thomas Browker died, Mary settled her interests in the premises as follows:

26 Typically, the decrees recited the residence for both the petitioner and the defendant(s). For the Browker decrees, of which this one is the first, the residences of the Browker defendants were omitted, although some residences were given in the body of the decree.

27 Thomas Browker's will was dated 23 September 1655 and proved on 10 November 1658. The will left to 'my loving wife Mary Browker' six houses or messuages in St Saviour's parish that were in the occupation of tenants. Among the tenants mentioned were Andrew Kembe (listed as Browker's tenant in Decrees 21, 34 and 35) and Henry Hawkes (listed as Browker's tenant in Decree 20). The will directed Mary Browker to sell these properties within one year of his death for at least £900. From those proceeds and the rest of his personal property and real estate, his wife was to pay his daughter Elizabeth £2,000. The will further demised to Mary Browker all the other messuages and houses in the High Street, Fowl Lane and Angel Yard, as well as his houses and lands in St George's Field in the parish of St George the Martyr in Surrey; his houses in Christchurch parish in London; his houses in All Hallows parish in London; and his houses, lands and meadows in Lincoln, Cambridge, Warwick and Chester counties. He then demised his other goods, bonds, bills, debts and mortgages on Mary Browker, except for a £20 bequest to his sister, a £10 bequest to his brother, a £50 bequest to a scrivener, a £5 bequest to the poor of St Saviour's parish and a few other minor bequests. See TNA, PROB 11/280/635.

- To her own use for ninety-nine years, should she live so long;
- At the end of this term, to the use of her son, Thomas Browker the elder, for ninety-nine years, should he live so long;
- At the end of this term, to Thomas Browker, son and heir apparent of Thomas Browker the elder, for ninety-nine years, should he live so long;
- After the decease of Mary Browker, Thomas Browker the elder, and Thomas Browker the younger, then:

  ➢ One moiety to the use of the first son of Thomas Browker the younger and the heirs male of the body of this first son; and in default of such issue, to the use of all the other sons of Thomas Browker the younger; and in default of any sons, to the use of the daughters of Thomas Browker the elder and their heirs, to be equally divided; and in default of such issue, to the use of the daughters of Mary Browker and their heirs, to be equally divided; and in default of such issue, to the use of the heirs of Mary Browker; and

  ➢ One moiety, to the use of the first son of Thomas Browker the younger and the heirs male of the first son; and in default of such issue, to all the other sons of Thomas Browker the younger; and in default of any sons, to the use of the daughters of Mary Browker and their heirs, to be divided equally.[28]

---

28   Mary Browker also held significant property apart from her life interest in various properties. Her will, signed on 23 May 1670, recited that she lived in Boscombe, Wiltshire, and that she was of 'sound and perfect memory' but 'weak in body'. Although partially illegible, the will appeared to have been proved on 23 June 1670. The will recited that Mary Browker had more than £400 secured by mortgages and bonds. She made numerous small bequests, such as £4 and a mourning gown to her maid servant, £5 to the maid's mother and 40s. to the poor in whichever parish she should die. She also willed each of her daughters a silver spoon worth 11s. and each son-in-law (for his and his wife's use) a legacy of £15 — with the proviso that the legacy given to Edward and Dorothy Lloyd be reduced by any amount outstanding on £40 in loans Mary Browker had made to them. She also gave £5 apiece to her daughters Jane, Katherine and Elizabeth; her daughter Dorothy apparently was excluded due to the outstanding loan. Thomas Browker the younger, her grandson, received her wedding ring, and his mother (Mary Browker's daughter-in-law, Mary Leighton, who appeared in this case) received £5. Finally, the will allocated £40 apiece to her granddaughters, Mary and Martha Browker, for 'putting [them] to Apprentice in the Exchange or elsewhere' in such trades as her executor thought best. See TNA, PROB 11/333/217. The will made no mention of her son, Thomas Browker the elder, suggesting that he may already have been dead.

Thomas Browker the elder died with no sons other than Thomas Browker the younger. But he also had two daughters, Mary and Martha Browker, who were yet infants. Mary Browker (the grandmother) had also died, leaving four daughters: Dorothy, who married Edward Lloyd; Jane, who married William Kent; Katherine, who married Sir Littleton Osbaldeston; and Elizabeth, who married Robert Lowfeild. Both Robert and Elizabeth Lowfeild had also since died, leaving their child Thomas Lowfeild, an infant.

Thomas Browker the younger had no issue of his body. His interest in the premises vested on the deaths of his grandmother and father. Subsequently, on 24 March 1676, he demised, bargained and sold the lease and its £30 rent to Samuell Wight for a term of eighty years, should Thomas Browker live so long. The term ran from the feast of the birth of our Lord 1675 at the yearly rent of one peppercorn (Fig. 13).

The messuage and brewhouse burned down in the fire. Expecting encouragement through an increase in term and abatement of rent, the petitioner rebuilt and nearly finished the premises at his own expense. But he was unable to obtain terms from the defendants.

Summonses to the defendants were issued. The plaintiff appeared personally, and was represented by Sir George Jeffreys, Mr Bowes and Mr Jenner. Among the defendants, Thomas Lowfeild, Mary Browker and Martha Browker appeared personally. The Court specially admitted Anne Cooke, widow, as Thomas Lowfeild's guardian. The Court also specially admitted Mary Leighton, wife of Charles Leighton, Gentleman, and mother of Mary and Martha Browker, as their guardian; Mr Ward and Mr Petitt[29] were their counsel. The churchwardens also appeared personally, with Mr Richardson as their counsel. Samuell Wight also appeared in person; no counsel appeared on his behalf.

The following defendants did not appear personally or through counsel: Thomas Browker, Edward and Dorothy Lloyd, William and Jane Kent, and Sir Littleton Osbaldeston and Dame Katherine. To satisfy itself regarding the service of summonses on these defendants, the Court took testimony. John Moth of the parish of St Saviour testified under oath that, on 21 September 1677, he went to the King's Bench Prison, where he was informed that Thomas Browker was a prisoner; and he confirmed that fact after he and the clerk searched the prison's files. Moth left the summons and a copy of the petition with the turnkey. Next, Benjamin Colinbine of London, Haberdasher, testified under oath that, on 13 August 1677, he served a summons and copy

---

29 In some later decrees, the name is rendered as 'Pettitt' or 'Pettit'.

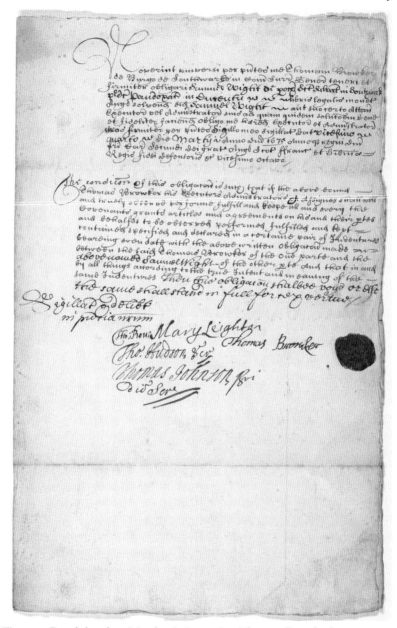

Fig. 13.   Bond dated 24 March 1676 ensuring Thomas Browker's performance of his obligations under the indentures leasing the Red Lion to Samuel Wight.

© London Metropolitan Archives ACC/0262/075/355

of the petition on Katherine Osbaldeston at her home in Woodstocke in Oxfordshire. Colinbine further testified that, on 15 August 1677, he delivered a summons and copy of the petition on Edward Lloyd at his dwelling, called Beth Lloyd, in Montgomery shire. Finally, Colinbine testified that, on 19 September 1677, he served a summons and copy of the petition on Jane Kent at her house near Road in Somersettshire.[30] The Court's registrar collected affidavits in writing to this effect.

The petitioner's counsel then opened matters by noting that the petitioner had already rebuilt the messuage and brewhouse at his cost and therefore prayed for the addition of a considerable term of years to the present lease (which still had nearly twenty years to run) and an abatement of rent. After some debate, the petitioner's counsel offered to give £15 per annum.

The defendants much opposed any rent abatement. They further alleged that the petitioner had purchased several parcels of ground adjoining the property and had made such great alterations in rebuilding that they would not be able to discover which part of the premises belonged to them. Counsel also stated that the petitioner erected the dwelling house and brewhouse on his own ground; the defendants' ground was now chiefly stables.

The petitioner's counsel denied this allegation, stating that the dwelling house and also a great part of the brewhouse were on the defendants' ground. No stables stood on this ground but were rather on other land of the petitioner.

For the Court's satisfaction, Thomas Hudson, Scrivener, testified under oath. Hudson knew the property before the fire. All of the petitioner's dwelling house, which fronted on the High Street, and some part of the brewhouse stood on the defendant's land. The only building on the petitioner's land was a kitchen adjoining the dwelling on the south side of the yard with several rooms above.

Richard Cobett, Bricklayer, then testified under oath. He had built the premises, and he had measured the ground and set out the dimensions of the several interests by means of their deeds. The dwelling house, which fronted the High Street, was a house with a kitchen. Aside from the back kitchen fronting the yard, the entire house stood solely on

---

30 In the decrees involving the Browkers, the registrar consistently spelled 'Montgomery shire' as two words, but 'Oxfordshire' and 'Somersetshire' as one word. In addition, in some other decrees the registrar rendered 'Road'— the modern village of Rode, whose typical spelling in the seventeenth century was 'Road' — as 'Roade'. The registrar also sometimes spelled Somersetshire as 'Somersettshire' or 'Sommersetshire'. I follow the spellings given in each decree.

the defendant's ground. So did a great part of the brewhouse. Further, the building now standing on the defendant's ground had cost the petitioner above £1000.

The petitioner's counsel then offered to make a plot of the defendant's ground for the Court's better knowledge. He again insisted on an abatement of rent to £15 and argued that an addition of years was a matter of small value. The defendants' counsel still opposed an abatement of rent, arguing that £30 was not a rack rent and that the house and buildings which stood on the property at the time of the fire were of much better value.

After hearing the allegations and the offers and demands on both sides, the Court declared it most just and reasonable that the petitioner's term be increased to seventy years from the feast of St Michael the Archangel 1677 at the yearly rent of £20, with the rent being excused from the time of the fire until the feast of the birth of our Lord 1677.

It was then controverted whether the charity payments should be abated in proportion to the overall reduction in the rent. The Court determined that it was not reasonable for the charities to suffer a full one-third abatement; rather, only forty shillings of the £10 annual payment should be abated during the future term of the lease. This abatement should be taken entirely from the £5 payable to the poor, while the £5 payable to the school should continue once rent payments commenced again.

The Court ordered that:

(1) The petitioner Josias Nicolson was to pay Samuel Wight and the churchwardens, proportionally according to their interests, two-thirds of the £30 rent due for Midsummer quarter 1676. The petitioner was discharged from paying rent for the final third of the quarter, and from paying any rent from the feast of the Nativity of St John the Baptist 1676 until the feast of the birth of our Lord 1677.

(2) After that time, the yearly £30 rent should be sunk, abated and reduced to £20 per annum for the remaining term of the lease. The petitioner was discharged of paying the £10 residue of the rent.

(3) The petitioner was to have a term of fifty years added to the present lease. The lease would take effect on the expiration of the present lease on the feast of St Michael the Archangel 1697, and the yearly rent would be £20, payable quarterly.

(4) The petitioner's first payment was due on the feast of the Annunciation of the Blessed Virgin Mary 1678, and further rents

were due at the times established in the present lease. Payment should be made among the several defendants and those to whom the payments may revert according to their interests.

(5) To avoid difficulties in the recovery of the £20 rent and for ascertaining covenants mutually to be performed during the additional term of fifty years, Samuell Wight, Thomas Browker, Edward and Dorothy Lloyd, William and Jane Kent, and Sir Littleton Osbaldeston and Dame Katherine — as well as Thomas Lowfeild, Mary Browker and Martha Browker, when they reached the age of twenty-one — should, at the petitioner's request and charge, sign a lease by indenture under the terms and rent described, with such reasonable covenants as were contained in the original lease. The petitioner must accept this lease and deliver up a counterpart to the defendants.

(6) This lease should have affixed to it a draught or plot setting out the premises demised.

(7) The petitioner might hold the premises notwithstanding the coverture of the feme coverts, the infancy of other defendants or any other interest.

(8) The petitioner must pay the churchwardens two-thirds part of the £10 due for Midsummer quarter 1676. The final third was discharged, and the entire annual rent of £10 was discharged from the feast of the Nativity of St John the Baptist 1676 to the feast of the birth of our Lord 1677.

(9) From 25 December 1677 through the remainder of the present lease and the ensuing fifty-year lease, forty shillings of the annual £10 due to the churchwardens was abated. The remaining £8 per annum was due on the days that the present rent was due.

(10) For the recovery and obtaining of the £8 rent, the churchwardens must pay the full sum of £5 for the maintenance of the free grammar school without any abatement and distribute the remaining £3 to the poor.

(11) On expiration of the present lease and its fifty-year extension, the previous annual rent of £10 due to the churchwardens would revive and be fully paid and distributed according to the original grant, as if neither the fire had happened nor this decree been made.

Decree 9 (page 41)

5 Oct. 1677.　　　Baron Littleton; Justice Jones (s); James Reading, Esq. (s); Peter Rich, Esq. (s); John Freeman, Esq. (s); John Appellbe, Esq.

Josias Nicolson of Southwark, Brewer, v. John Cressett, Gentleman; Elizabeth his Wife; and Edward Keyling, Gentleman[31]

By indenture of lease dated 20 June 1659, Thomas Overman of Southwark demised to Roger Peares, Citizen and Salter of London, a messuage or tenement that had been in the possession of Anne Browne, widow now deceased; then in the possession of Michael Nicholson; and finally in the possession of Peares. The lease ran for thirty-eight and a quarter years from the feast of the Nativity of St John the Baptist 1659 at the yearly rent of £5, payable quarterly. The premises were located between a tenement then in the occupation of John Kenyon on the north-west and the brewhouse of Thomas Browker, Esquire, then in the tenure of Roger Peares, on the south-east.[32]

Thomas Overman has since died. Elizabeth his wife, as relict, had an interest in the reversion of the premises during her life. She had since remarried John Cressett.[33] Edward Keyling claims the reversionary interest in the premises after Elizabeth's death.

By good and sufficient lawful means, the petitioner obtained Peares's interest in the lease. He was also in possession of the adjacent brewhouse, and he used the two properties together until the fire burned them down. At his own expense, he rebuilt on the premises in the hope that the Cressetts and Keyling would abate the rent and increase the term of years, but they had so far refused to give him terms or recompense.

The petitioner appeared personally, with Sir George Jeffreys, Mr Bowes and Mr Jenner as his counsel. The defendants appeared personally. They were represented by Mr Ward and Mr Maudit.

The petitioner's counsel prayed the Court to grant a considerable addition to the remaining twenty years of the lease (from last past feast of St Michael the Archangel), with some abatement of rent in view of the petitioner's great charges in rebuilding. The defendants' counsel

31 The caption of this petition did not recite the defendants' city of residence. The Cressetts and Keyling were also defendants in *Ferris v. Cressett* (Decree 9), and Elizabeth Cressett was likely the Elizabeth Overman mentioned in *Lane v. Mayor of Shrewsbury* (Decree 26).

32 The brewhouse is the subject of the prior decree, *Nicolson v. Browker* (Decree 8).

33 The London Metropolitan Archives contain a document, possibly a draft, granting John Cressett of the Temple, London, Esquire, the office of Steward in Southwark. See LMA COL/SP/02/047 (dated 28 October 1692). The document likely refers to the son of the defendant John Cressett. I do not know the document's purpose. After being restored to the office of Steward in 1690, see Rep., XCV, fol. 107ᵛ (21 February 1690), Edward Smyth did not surrender the office until 1694, see Rep., XCVIII, fol. 351 (21 June 1694).

opposed any rent abatement. Counsel alleged that, at the time of the fire, the premises were an entire messuage of brick, and the lessee was obligated under the lease not only to keep the messuage in repair but also to lay three new floors in the messuage before expiration of the lease. The lessee was also obligated to lay open the passageway that had formerly been on the property. But the lessee had, long before the fire, instead laid the property into his adjoining brewhouse. With his new building, he had done the same, and his building on the ground had been very inconsiderable. Moreover, at the end of the lease the reversioners would not be able to discover what belonged to them and would have no passageway unless one were laid again.

The petitioner's counsel informed the Court that the parcel of ground was very small, and the demised premises were just three small rooms, one over the other. The petitioner had now built on the ground buildings of much better value, as there was now not only part of the brewhouse but also a room to lay malt. This building was much to the better advantage of the reversioners than a small tenement. To avoid the danger of the reversioners not knowing which ground was theirs, counsel offered to attach to a new lease an exact plot or draught of the ground.

Having heard the allegations, the Court propounded as most just and reasonable that the petitioner have fifty years added to his term, for a total term of seventy years from the feast of St Michael the Archangel 1677, at two-thirds of the former rent (that is, £3 6s. 8d.) per annum, with the first payment to be made on the feast of the birth of our Lord 1677. The petitioner was discharged of all rent from the fire until feast of St Michael the Archangel 1677. The new lease must contain the same covenant as the old lease regarding laying open the passageway, and a plot of the ground must be attached to the lease.

The Court ordered that:

(1) On the request of John Cressett, the petitioner Josias Nicolson was to pay two-thirds of the rent due for Midsummer quarter 1676, which was as long as the petitioner enjoyed the premises before the fire. The petitioner was discharged from paying the third part residue of that quarter's rent, and was further discharged of paying the £5 per annum rent from the feast of the Nativity of St John the Baptist 1676 to the feast of St Michael the Archangel 1677.

(2) From that time forward, the rent of £5 per annum was abated to £3 6s. 8d. for the unexpired remainder of the lease. The petitioner was acquitted of paying the £1 13s. 4d. residue of the rent.

(3) The petitioner was to have an additional term of fifty years added to the end of the present lease, to commence immediately on the expiration of the present lease, at the annual rent of £3 6s. 8d., payable quarterly as in the present lease. Payment was to be made to John and Elizabeth Cresset during the coverture between them, and then to Elizabeth (should she survive John) for her life. Payment should then be made to Edward Keyling and his heirs and assigns.

(4) To avoid difficulties in recovering the annual rent and to ascertain the covenants mutually to be performed, the defendants, on the petitioner's reasonable request and at his expense, must execute a new lease by indenture with a fifty-year term, an annual rent of £3 6s. 8d., and reasonable covenants usual in leases made of houses and buildings in London. The lease must also contain a covenant for the laying open of a passageway at the end of the fifty-year term of the lease. A plot of the ground must also be attached to the lease. The petitioner must accept this lease and return a counterpart.

(5) The petitioner might enjoy the ground and that part of the brewhouse and buildings rebuilt on the ground notwithstanding the coverture of Elizabeth Cressett or any other interest.[34]

* * *

After the Court pronounced this decree, the defendants made overtures in Court to the petitioner, asking if the petitioner was interested in purchasing the inheritance of the premises from them. At length it was agreed that petitioner would pay threescore pounds for the defendants' interest.

The Court further ordered that:

(6) If the defendants execute a legally sufficient document that provides an indefeasible estate in the premises to the petitioner, the petitioner must pay the Cressetts and Keyling £60 for their interest. The petitioner might then enjoy the premises notwithstanding the coverture of Elizabeth Cressett or any other interest.

---

34 From this point forward, the decree was written in a different hand. It appears to have been written quickly and may have been inserted at a later date. Three blank pages follow the end of the decree.

Decree 10 (page 49)

5 Oct. 1677.   Baron Littleton; Justice Jones;[35] Thomas Barker, Esq.
                     (s); James Reading, Esq. (s); Peter Rich, Esq. (s); John
                     Freeman, Esq. (s); John Applebee, Esq.

Thomas Cole of Southwark, Tallow Chandler, and Margaret his Wife v.
Thomas Browker, Esq.; Edward Lloyd, Esq.; Dorothy his Wife; William
Kent, Clerke; Jane his Wife; Sir Littleton Osbaldeston, Baronet; Dame
Katherine his Wife; Thomas Lowfeild, an Infant; and Mary and Martha
Browker, Infants

Mary Browker, widow and relict of Thomas Browker, Esquire,
of Upper Peover in the county of Chester, was seised in fee of the
messuage or tenement described below. She settled this messuage, as
well as others, on herself for ninety-nine years (should she live so long)
and then on family members in the manner described in Decree 8.[36]
The property settlement included a proviso (not described in Decree 8)
that the person with the present interest in the premises could enter a
lease up to forty-one years in length, as long as the tenant new built on
the land and the ancient rent was not reduced.

The premises, previously known by the sign of the Plough and
Harrow, lay on the west side of the High Street.

Upon the death of Mary and her son Thomas Browker the elder,
the interest in the reversion of the premises came to the defendant
Thomas Browker the younger for ninety-nine years (should he live so
long). Under the property settlement, Dorothy Lloyd, Jane Kent, Dame
Katherine Osbaldeston, Thomas Lowfeild (the son of Robert Lowfeild
and Mary Browker's daughter Elizabeth, both now deceased), and Mary
and Martha Browker (the daughters of Thomas Browker the elder and
the sisters of Thomas Browker the younger) held contingent interests
upon the death of Thomas Browker the younger.

Browker the younger settled his interest in the messuage (and in other
things) on the defendant Sir Littleton Osbaldeston. The settlement,
commencing on 30 June 1674 and determinable on Browker's death,
was for eighty years. The interest was held in trust for the maintenance
and advancement of Mary and Martha Browker.[37]

---

35 This decree is the first, and one of only a few, that no common law judge
signed.

36 See pp. 120–21.

37 The will of Littleton Osbaldeston, made on 20 December 1691 and proved
on 20 January 1692, made no reference to this interest or its further disposition. See
TNA, PROB 11/408/73. Since I have been unable to determine the date of Thomas

In December 1676, Browker and Osbaldeston came to an agreement with the petitioners, under which the petitioners would new build the messuage or tenement that had burned down in the fire. This messuage had formerly been in the occupation of Richard Barron and Isabel his wife. At the time of the fire, it was in the occupation of the petitioners and their undertenants. The lease ran for forty-one years, the maximum allowable under the proviso. It commenced on 11 September 1676, at the yearly rent of £12, payable quarterly. The lease included not only the ground belonging to the premises that had burned down but also the cellar lying under the next adjoining house, which William Bennet had lately rebuilt.[38]

Browker and Osbaldeston would have been willing to grant a term longer than forty-one years had it been in their power to do so. They agreed that it would be lawful for the petitioners to have a longer term if one could be obtained from a court of judicature or other authority created to deal with losses from the fire — provided that the rent of £12 not be reduced.[39]

In pursuance of this agreement and in the hope of a further term of years that the Court would think fit and reasonable, the petitioners rebuilt the messuage at their expense.

Summonses to the defendants were issued. The petitioner Thomas Cole appeared personally, with Mr Jenner as his counsel. Among the defendants, Thomas Lowfeild, Mary Browker and Martha Browker appeared personally. The Court specially admitted Anne Cooke, widow, as guardian of Thomas Lowfeild. The Court also specially admitted Mary Leighton, wife of Charles Leighton, Gentleman, and mother of Mary and Martha Browker, as their guardian;[40] Mr Ward and Mr Pettitt were their counsel.

Browker's death (but see *Sledd v. Browker* (Decree 47)), I do not know whether this interest may have terminated before Osbaldeston's death. Osbaldeston's will made no bequests to his nieces-in-law, Mary and Martha.

38   Bennet is likely the petitioner in *Bennett v. Browker* (Decree 12), where his name is spelled 'Bennett' and his given occupation is merchant.

39   In September 1676, Parliament was prorogued, and it was uncertain whether Parliament might establish a court of judicature or other mechanism to address the Southwark fire. Nonetheless, the fire-court concept, first created to deal with the London Fire ten years earlier, had evidently seeped into the decision-making processes of sophisticated parties.

40   Even as he spiralled into debt, Thomas Browker the younger was evidently attempting to preserve some of his inheritance to maintain family members. For another sale of his interests, probably to maintain his mother, see *Sledd v. Browker* (Decree 47).

The remaining defendants (Thomas Browker, the Lloyds, the Kents and the Osbaldestons) did not appear personally or through counsel, but rather 'made default'. To be satisfied in the matter, the Court took sworn testimony from John Moth of the parish of St Saviour and Benjamin Colinbine of London, Haberdasher. Both testified as they had done in Decree 8. On 21 September 1677, Moth served a summons on the turnkey of the King's Bench prison after determining that Thomas Browker the younger was a prisoner there, and Colinbine served summonses on Katherine Osbaldeston at Woodstocke in Oxfordshire on 13 August 1677; on Edward Lloyd at his dwelling called Beth Lloyd in Montgomery shire on 15 August 1677; and on Jane Kent at Roade in Sommersetshire on 19 September 1677. The Court's registrar collected affidavits to this effect.

The petitioner's counsel informed the Court that the petitioner can have no compensation for his great charge in rebuilding other than a term longer than forty-one years, given that the agreed rent of £12 constituted a very small contribution on the landlord's behalf. He requested a term of ninety-nine years. Defendants' counsel did not oppose this request.

Without any opposition, the Court thought it very reasonable to increase the term to ninety-nine years.

The Court ordered that:

(1) In pursuance of and according to the intention of the parties' agreement, the petitioners Thomas and Margaret Cole shall have a term of ninety-nine years in the rebuilt premises and grounds, as well as in the cellar lying beneath the adjoining house of William Bennet. The term ran from the feast of St Michael the Archangel 1677.

(2) The rent of £12, payable quarterly on the usual feast days, shall be paid to the various defendants, and those to whom the payment might revert, according to their interests.

(3) To ascertain the mutual covenants to be performed, Thomas Browker, Edward and Dorothy Lloyd, William and Jane Kent, and Sir Littleton Osbaldeston and Dame Katherine his wife shall sign a lease by indenture prepared at the petitioners' expense; and when they attain the age of twenty-one, Thomas Lowfeild, Mary Browker and Martha Browker (or whoever enjoys the reversion of the premises at that time) shall also sign the lease for as many years as are unexpired and yet to come. The lease should contain reasonable covenants usual in leases made of houses in and about London. The petitioners must accept the

signed lease and return the counterpart.

(4) The petitioners may enjoy the premises, with all yards, ways, passages, lights, easements, watercourses and appurtenances, for the term of ninety-nine years, notwithstanding the coverture of the feme coverts, the infancy of the infants or any other interest.

Decree 11 (page 54)

5 Oct. 1677.   Baron Littleton; Justice Jones; Thomas Barker, Esq. (s); James Reading, Esq. (s); Peter Rich, Esq. (s); John Freeman, Esq. (s); John Applebee, Esq.[41]

Elizabeth Roberts of Southwark, Widow, v. Thomas Browker, Esq.; Edward Lloyd, Esq.; Dorothy his Wife; William Kent, Clerke; Jane his Wife; Sir Littleton Osbaldeston, Baronet; Dame Katherine his Wife; Thomas Lowfeild, an Infant; Mary and Martha Browker, Infants; and John Snell, Citizen and Merchant Taylor of London

Mary Browker, widow relict of Thomas Browker, Esquire, of Upper Peover in the County of Chester, was seised in fee of the messuage or tenement described below. She settled the premises on herself for ninety-nine years (should she live so long) and then on various family members in the manner described in Decree 8.[42] Notwithstanding her limited interest, the settlement permitted Mary Browker to make a lease for new building of forty-one years. Together with Thomas Browker the elder, her son, she made a lease by indenture on 9 December 1663 with John Shakell of the parish of St Mary Newington in the county of Surrey, Carpenter. The lease ran from the feast of St Michael the Archangel 1663 at an annual rent of £5, payable quarterly.

The lease demised a messuage then in the possession of John Wakefeild and some outbuildings behind the messuage that Shakell had new built. The messuage and outbuildings were sometimes used as a bakehouse. The lease was given in consideration of the surrender of two leases and Shakell's agreement to new build three messuages where the outbuildings stood. The premises were situated on the south side of the way or passage in St Saviour's Churchyard, and still lay in ruins.

---

41 No common-law judge signed this decree. In addition, in the decrees that he signed, Peter Rich's signature is often very faint due to fading ink. In this decree, all that exists in the portion of the decree where Rich usually signed is a single swirl that looks like a part of the 'R' that Rich made. Because Rich invariably signed the decrees when he sat as judge, I am crediting this swirl as evidence that he signed this decree.

42 See pp. 120–21.

The lease also demised the messuage or tenement containing a cellar and three rooms, one above the other, then in the occupation of Mathew Bates, Glover, with a little yard lying behind the tenement. The yard was situated in Angel Yard in or near the front lane. The lease granted free ingress, egress and regress to and from the premises through Angel Yard with or without horses, carts and carriages — except the eavesdroppings, waterfalls, lights and watercourses belonging to any other tenements of the lessors next to or near the premises, which were also to have full current light and prospect into and from the premises during the term of the lease.[43]

Shakell's interest in the lease was now legally vested in the petitioner.

Mary Browker and Thomas Browker the elder had both since died, and the landlord's interest came to Thomas Browker the younger, Thomas Browker the elder's son, for ninety-nine years (should he live so long). Under Mary Browker's property settlement, Dorothy Lloyd, Jane Kent, Dame Katherine Osbaldeston, Thomas Lowfeild (the son of Robert Lowfeild and Mary Browker's daughter Elizabeth, both now deceased) and Mary and Martha Browker (the daughters of Thomas Browker the elder and the sisters of Thomas Browker the younger) held contingent interests upon the death of Thomas Browker the younger.

For the yearly rent of one peppercorn, Browker the younger had demised his interest in the premises and the £5 rent to John Snell[44] for some long term of years determinable on Browker's life.

The premises burned down in the fire. The petitioner was willing to rebuild on reasonable encouragement: an increase in the term of years and an abatement of the rent. But she could not obtain terms without the aid of the Court.

Summonses to all the defendants were issued. The petitioner Elizabeth Roberts appeared personally, with Mr Jenner as her counsel. Among the defendants, Thomas Lowfeild, Mary Browker and Martha Browker

---

43 The parenthetical clause describing this exception defies easy grammatical parsing; this is the best sense that I can make of it, although there are alternate constructions. The parenthetical reads: '(except all Evesdroppings Waterfalls Lights and watercourses of or belonging to any other of the Tenements of the said Lessors next or neere adjoyning to the premises to have full Currant light and prospect into and from the same demised premises during the continuance of the said Lease)'.

44 Snell was a defendant in *Ely v. Mence* (Decree 1); *Williams v. Browker* (Decree 50); and *Williams v. Browker* (Decree 51). He was the petitioner in *Snell v. Browker* (Decree 13); *Snell v. Browker* (Decree 14); and *Snell v. Browker* (Decree 15). He also purchased and then sold an interest in the property at issue in *Hudson v. Browker* (Decree 49).

appeared personally. The Court specially admitted Anne Cooke, widow, as guardian of Thomas Lowfeild. The Court also specially admitted Mary Leighton, wife of Charles Leighton, Gentleman, and mother of Mary and Martha Browker, as their guardian; Mr Ward and Mr Pettitt were their counsel. Snell appeared personally, with Sir George Jeffreys as his counsel.

The remaining defendants (Thomas Browker, the Lloyds, the Kents and the Osbaldestons) did not appear personally or through counsel. To be satisfied in the matter, the Court took sworn testimony from John Moth of the parish of St Saviour and Benjamin Colinbine of London, Haberdasher. Both testified as they had done in Decree 8. On 21 September 1677, Moth served a summons on the turnkey of the King's Bench prison after determining that Thomas Browker the younger was a prisoner there, and Colinbine served summonses on Katherine Osbaldeston at Woodstocke in Oxfordshire on 13 August 1677; on Edward Lloyd at his dwelling called Beth Lloyd in Montgomery shire on 15 August 1677; and on Jane Kent at Road in Somersetshire on 19 September 1677. The Court's registrar collected affidavits in writing to this effect.

The petitioner's counsel prayed for her twenty-seven-year lease to be considerably extended with some abatement of rent. Snell's counsel opposed an abatement of rent, stating that the rent was already very small and could not reasonably be sunk lower. Petitioner's counsel responded that the houses when standing were small. Being in a bad place far from the street and out of the way of trade, they were of very little value, and small advantage was likely to arise from rebuilding. Counsel therefore insisted on an abatement of rent and an additional term of years.

Having heard the allegations of counsel and being well advised, the Court declared it just and reasonable that the petitioner's term be increased to seventy years and the rent be abated to £3 6s. 8d.

The Court ordered that:

(1)   On demand, the petitioner Elizabeth Roberts must pay to John Snell two-thirds of the reserved rent for Midsummer quarter 1676, during which the petitioner enjoyed the use of the premises. The petitioner was discharged of the remaining one-third of the quarterly rent.

(2)   The petitioner was also discharged of all rent from the feast of the Nativity of St John the Baptist 1676 until the feast of the Annunciation of the Blessed Virgin Mary 1678. Thereafter the yearly rent of £5 was sunk, abated and reduced to £3 6s. 8d.

per annum for the remainder of the lease. The petitioner was discharged of paying the remaining £1 13s. 4d.

(3)   The petitioner was to receive an additional term of forty-three years in the premises, to take effect immediately on the expiration of the present lease on the feast of St Michael the Archangel 1704, which would make a total lease of seventy years from the feast of St Michael the Archangel 1677. The yearly rent for the new lease was to be £3 6s. 8d., payable to the various defendants according to their interests.

(4)   The rent was to be paid quarterly at the times and in the manner provided in the present lease. The first quarterly payment would be due on the feast of the Nativity of St John the Baptist 1678.

(5)   With all convenient speed and at her own cost, the petitioner must erect and rebuild the premises with good and substantial messuages and buildings of brick and other good and sufficient materials and must finish the building in good workmanlike manner.

(6)   To avoid difficulties in recovering the yearly rent and for ascertaining the covenants to be performed, the defendants (now or when they came of age at twenty-one) must, on the petitioner's reasonable request, sign a good and sufficient lease by indenture prepared at petitioner's expense for the unexpired term of the extended lease. The petitioner must accept the lease and deliver up the counterparts.

(7)   The petitioner might enjoy the premises according to the tenor and purport of this decree, notwithstanding the coverture of the feme coverts, the infancy of the infants or any other interest.

Decree 12 (page 60)

5 Oct. 1677.   Baron Littleton; Justice Jones; Thomas Barker, Esq. (s);[45] James Reading, Esq.; Peter Rich, Esq.; John Freeman, Esq.; John Appellbe, Esq.

                   and

17 Oct. 1677.   Baron Littleton; Justice Jones (s); James Reading, Esq. (s); John Freeman, Esq. (s); John Applebee, Esq.

William Bennett of London, Merchant, v. Thomas Browker, Esq.; Edward Lloyd, Esq.; Dorothy his Wife; William Kent, Clerke; Jane his Wife;

---

45   Baker signed the decree even though he was not listed as being present at the 17 October hearing, when the petitions were finally determined.

Sir Littleton Osbaldeston, Baronet; Dame Katherine his Wife; Thomas Lowfeild, an Infant; and Mary and Martha Browker, Infants

and

Audry Bayley, Widow, and Lydia Bayley of Southwark v. Thomas Browker, William Bennet, and John Whiteingslowe

Mary Browker, widow relict of Thomas Browker, Esquire, of Upper Peover in the County of Chester, was seised in fee of three messuages or tenements. She settled them to her own use for ninety-nine years (if she should live so long) and then on various family members in the manner described in Decree 8.[46] The settlement contained a proviso that the person with the present interest in the premises might make leases in case of new building for forty-one years, reserving the ancient rent. Mary Browker has since died, as had her son Thomas Browker the elder. The landlord's interest in the property came to Thomas Browker the younger, Thomas Browker the elder's son, for ninety-nine years (should he live so long). Under Mary Browker's property settlement, Dorothy Lloyd, Jane Kent, Dame Katherine Osbaldeston, Thomas Lowfeild (the son of Robert Lowfeild and Mary Browker's daughter Elizabeth, both now deceased) and Mary and Martha Browker (the daughters of Thomas Browker the elder and the sisters of Thomas Browker the younger) held contingent interests upon the death of Thomas Browker the younger.

After the interest came into the possession of Thomas Browker the younger, he made a settlement of the three messuages (together with other things) for a term of eighty years on Sir Littleton Osbaldeston, determinable on Browker's death. The settlement was in trust for and toward the maintenance and advancement of his sisters, Mary and Martha Browker. The settlement commenced on 30 June 1674.

In September 1676, Browker and Osbaldeston came to an agreement with the petitioner to build the three messuages, which were located in the High Street. All had burned down in the fire. At the time of the fire, the messuages were in the possession or tenure of Valentine Sawyer, David Burrell and William Cowper the younger.

In pursuance of the power granted him, Thomas Browker the younger granted the petitioner a term of forty-one years in the tofts and grounds of the three messuages, with the exception of one low room.[47] The lease

---

46 See pp. 120–21.

47 This 'lowe Roome' is likely the cellar mentioned in *Cole v. Browker* (Decree 10), in which the decree stated that the lease given to the petitioners in that case included a cellar under the adjoining premises of William Bennet (spelled with one 't').

commenced on 11 September 1676 at the annual rent of £42, payable quarterly. The parties were willing to grant the petitioner a longer term if it had been in their power to do so, and agreed that the petitioner could have a longer term if he could obtain one by order or decree of a judicature or other authority that might be established — provided that the rent of £42 was not diminished.

In pursuance of the agreement, the petitioner had rebuilt three brick messuages at his cost and in hope of a further term of years that the Court thought reasonable.

Summonses to all the defendants were issued. The petitioner William Bennett appeared personally, with Mr Bowes and Mr Jenner as his counsel. Among the defendants, Thomas Lowfeild, Mary Browker and Martha Browker appeared personally. The Court specially admitted Anne Cooke, widow, as guardian of Thomas Lowfeild. The Court also specially admitted Mary Leighton, wife of Charles Leighton, Gentleman, and mother of Mary and Martha Browker, as their guardian; Mr Ward and Mr Pettitt were their counsel.

The remaining defendants (Thomas Browker, the Lloyds, the Kents and the Osbaldestons) did not appear personally or through counsel. To be satisfied in the matter, the Court took sworn testimony from John Moth of the parish of St Saviour and Benjamin Colinbine of London, Haberdasher. Both testified as they had done in Decree 8. On 21 September 1677, Moth served a summons on the turnkey of the King's Bench prison after determining that Thomas Browker the younger was a prisoner there, and Colinbine served summonses on Katherine Osbaldeston at Woodstocke in Oxfordshire on 13 August 1677; on Edward Lloyd at his dwelling called Beth Lloyd in Montgomery shire on 15 August 1677; and on Jane Kent at Road in Somersetshire on 19 September 1677. The Court's registrar collected affidavits in writing to this effect.

The petitioner's counsel stated that, since the petitioner could have no other encouragement under the rebuilding agreement than a longer term, the term should be increased to seventy-one years. The defendants' counsel did not object.

At that point, Mr Ward declared that he was counsel for Awdry Bayley and Lydia Bayley. He presented a petition in their names against Thomas Browker, William Bennett and John Whiteingslowe. The Bayleys claimed an interest in the premises by virtue of an original lease made by Thomas Browker,[48] now deceased, to Awdrey Nicholls,

48 The petition does not make clear whether the 'aforesaid Thomas Browker' is Thomas Browker of Upper Peover (Mary Browker's husband) or Thomas Browker the elder (son of Thomas and Mary Browker). Given that Thomas Browker the

widow, now also deceased. Nicholls's lease devised the rents and profits of the lease on Awdry and Lydia Bayley in trust. Whiteingslowe was the surviving executor of the will. Mr Ward asked that the matter of Bennett's lease not be determined by the Court until the Bayleys' interests were resolved.

Having heard the matter, the Court declared it most just and reasonable that the petitioner Bennett have his lease increased to seventy-one years from the feast of St Michael the Archangel 1677 at the rent of £42 — unless Awdry and Lydia Bayley could show sufficient cause to the contrary at the Court's next sitting.

At the next sitting, on 17 October 1677, the parties and their counsel returned to court. John Whiteingslowe was also present.

The Bayleys' counsel showed for cause that the Bayleys had an interest of £25 per annum, which was the rent received over and above the rent payable to the head landlord. That amount should not be taken from them without some recompense, for they would have been willing to rebuild.

Counsel for Bennett then informed the Court that this interest in the lease had only a short time left and was so inconsiderable that John Whiteingslowe was willing to surrender the interest in return for being discharged from performance of the lease's covenants. In fact, Whiteingslowe had already surrendered the lease, and one of the petitioners had consented.

Counsel for the Bayleys denied this claim.

At this point, the Court took the sworn testimony of Whiteingslowe. Whiteingslowe testified that he regarded the Bayleys' interest to be of little value, that he had surrendered the lease and that Awdry Bayley had consented to his doing so.

After full debate, the Court declared that it was not reasonable for the Bayleys to obtain any relief on their petition. With respect to Bennett's original petition, it reiterated its decision to give Bennett a term of 'threescore and eleven yeares' in the premises.

The Court ordered that:

(1)   The petition of Awdry and Lydia Bayley was dismissed without any relief.

(2)   Except for the low room described above, the petitioner William Bennett was to have a lease of the premises for seventy-one

---

elder's interest was a limited life interest and (except for new building) he was unable to agree to any lease beyond that interest, it seems likely that the lease had been made by Thomas Browker of Upper Peover, who held the property in fee until his death.

years, at an annual rent of £42, payable quarterly on the usual feasts to the defendant or defendants who held the interest in the rent at that time. The lease began on the feast of St Michael the Archangel 1677.

(3) To avoid difficulties in recovering the yearly rent and for ascertaining the covenants to be performed, the defendants (now or when they came of age at twenty-one) must, on the petitioner's reasonable request, sign a good and sufficient new lease by indenture prepared at the petitioner's expense. The lease should contain reasonable covenants usual of leases made in and about London. Bennett must accept the lease and deliver up the counterparts.

(4) The petitioner might enjoy the premises according to the tenor and purport of this decree, notwithstanding the coverture of the feme coverts, the infancy of the infants or any other interest.

Decree 13 (page 66)

5 Oct. 1677.   Baron Littleton; Justice Jones (s); Thomas Barker, Esq. (s); James Reading, Esq. (s); Peter Rich, Esq. (s); John Freeman, Esq. (s); John Appellbe, Esq.

John Snell of London, Citizen and Merchant Taylor, v. Thomas Browker, Esq.; Edward Lloyd, Esq.; Dorothy his Wife; William Kent, Clerke; Jane his Wife; Sir Littleton Osbaldeston, Baronet; Dame Katherine his Wife; Thomas Lowfeild, an Infant; Mary and Martha Browker, Infants; and Jonadab Ballam, Citizen and Grocer of London[49]

Thomas Browker, Esquire,[50] was seised in fee of a messuage or tenement. By his will he devised this interest to Mary, his wife. She settled this interest to her own use for ninety-nine years (if she should live so long) and then on various family members in the manner described in Decree 8.[51] The settlement contained a proviso that the person with the present interest in the premises might, in the case of new building, make leases for forty-one years at the ancient rents. Mary Browker had since died,

---

49   Snell was a defendant in *Ely v. Mence* (Decree 1); *Williams v. Browker* (Decree 50); and *Williams v. Browker* (Decree 51). He was the petitioner in *Snell v. Browker* (Decree 11); *Snell v. Browker* (Decree 14); and *Snell v. Browker* (Decree 15). He also purchased and then sold an interest in the property at issue in *Hudson v. Browker* (Decree 49).

50   Unlike most of the *Browker* decrees, this decree did not mention Browker's residence in Upper Peover.

51   See pp. 120–21.

as had her son Thomas Browker the elder. The landlord's interest in the property came to Thomas Browker the younger, Thomas Browker the elder's son, for ninety-nine years (should he live so long). Under Mary Browker's property settlement, Dorothy Lloyd, Jane Kent, Dame Katherine Osbaldeston, Thomas Lowfeild (the son of Robert Lowfeild and Mary Browker's daughter Elizabeth, both now deceased) and Mary and Martha Browker (the daughters of Thomas Browker the elder and the sisters of Thomas Browker the younger) held contingent interests upon the death of Thomas Browker the younger.

By indenture of lease on 27 July 1674, Thomas Browker the younger demised the premises to John Surman of Christ Church in the County of Surrey. The lease ran for forty-one years at the yearly rent of forty-five shillings, payable quarterly.

The premises were two tenements or dwelling houses that had formerly been one messuage but had been severed and divided. The premises had been in the occupation of Anne Rowland, widow, and her undertenants. The premises lay on the north side of Fowl Lane, 'sometime being parcell' of the messuage called the sign of the Angel. The premises included free liberty of ingress, egress and regress to and from the tenements of Angel Yard, with or without horses, carts and carriages.

The premises burned down in the fire and were still in ruins.

By good and lawful assignment, Surman's interest came into the possession of the petitioner John Snell. Meanwhile, Thomas Browker bargained and sold his interest in the property to Jonadab Ballam for 'fourescore' years, if Browker should live so long. The agreement commenced on 29 September 1676 at an annual rent of one peppercorn.

The petitioner was willing to rebuild on encouragement from the interested parties, but needed the assistance of the Court.

Summonses to all the defendants were issued. The petitioner John Snell appeared personally, with Sir George Jeffreys, Mr Bowes and Mr Jenner as his counsel. Among the defendants, Thomas Lowfeild, Mary Browker and Martha Browker appeared personally. The Court specially admitted Anne Cooke, widow, as guardian of Thomas Lowfeild. The Court also specially admitted Mary Leighton, wife of Charles Leighton, Gentleman, and mother of Mary and Martha Browker, as their guardian; Mr Ward and Mr Pettitt were their counsel.

The Lloyds, the Kents and the Osbaldestons did not appear personally or through counsel. To be satisfied in the matter the Court took sworn testimony from John Moth of the parish of St Saviour and Benjamin Colinbine of London, Haberdasher. Both testified as they had done in Decree 8. On 21 September 1677, Moth served a summons on the turnkey of the King's Bench prison after determining that Thomas Browker the younger was a prisoner there, and Colinbine served summonses on Katherine Osbaldeston at Woodstocke in Oxfordshire on 13 August 1677; on Edward Lloyd at his dwelling called Beth Lloyd in Montgomery shire on 15 August 1677; and on Jane Kent at Road in Somersetshire on 19 September 1677. The Court's registrar collected affidavits in writing to this effect.[52]

The petitioner's counsel stated that he and John Surman had spent nearly £100 on the tenements before they were burned down. The ground was also small and far from the High Street, so it was of very small value. Therefore, counsel prayed for a term increased to seventy years and an abatement of rent to thirty shillings per annum.

The defendants' counsel objected to sinking the rent so low because the ground was of better value than alleged. The petitioner's counsel responded that, unless the rent was shrunk to thirty shillings, he could not undertake the rebuilding.

Having heard the matter, the Court declared it just and reasonable for the lease to be increased to seventy years from the feast of St Michael the Archangel 1677 at an annual rent of thirty shillings, with accrued rent payments from the fire until the feast of the birth of our Lord 1677 discharged and the first quarterly payment due on the feast of the Annunciation of the Blessed Virgin Mary 1678.

The Court ordered that:

(1) Because the rent for the quarter in which the fire occurred had already been paid, the petitioner John Snell was discharged from paying all rent from the time of the fire until the feast of the birth of our Lord 1677.

(2) From that point forward, the yearly rent of forty-five shillings was sunk, abated and reduced to thirty shillings for the unexpired remainder of the lease. The petitioner was discharged from payment of the remaining fifteen shillings, notwithstanding the reservation of the rent of forty-five shillings. The rent, payable quarterly on the usual feast days as provided in the prior lease, was to be paid to the defendants or other persons according to their interests.

---

52 The decree makes no mention of an attempt to serve Jonadab Ballam with a summons. The decree does not note his appearance (personally or through counsel).

(3)   The term of years in the premises and buildings to be built was increased to seventy years by adding years onto the present lease after its expiration. The seventy-year term commenced on the feast of St Michael the Archangel 1677.

(4)   In consideration of the increase in years and abatement of rent, the petitioner, at his cost and with all convenient speed, must new build other good and substantial messuages or tenements of brick and finish them in good workmanlike manner.

(5)   To avoid difficulties in recovering the yearly rent and for ascertaining the covenants to be performed, the defendants presently of age (Ballam, Thomas Browker, the Lloyds, the Kents and the Osbaldestons), as well as the infant defendants (Lowfeild and Mary and Martha Browker) when they came of age at twenty-one, must, on the petitioner's reasonable request and at his expense, sign a good and sufficient new lease by indenture. The lease should contain reasonable covenants as found in the existing lease. The petitioner must accept the lease and deliver up the counterparts.

(6)   The petitioner might enjoy the premises according to the tenor and purport of this decree, notwithstanding the coverture of the feme coverts, the infancy of the infants or any other interest.

Decree 14 (page 71)

5 Oct. 1677.   Baron Littleton; Justice Jones (s); Thomas Barker, Esq. (s); James Reading, Esq. (s); Peter Rich, Esq. (s); John Freeman, Esq. (s); John Appellbe, Esq.

John Snell of London, Citizen and Merchant Taylor, v. Thomas Browker, Esq.; Edward Lloyd, Esq.; Dorothy his Wife; William Kent, Clerke; Jane his Wife; Sir Littleton Osbaldeston, Baronet; Dame Katherine his Wife; Thomas Lowfeild, an Infant; and Mary and Martha Browker, Infants[53]

By indenture of lease on 1 December 1651, Thomas Browker, Esquire,[54] demised to Arthur Slipper, Citizen and Merchant Taylor of London, two adjoining messuages or tenements in Fowl Lane. Each contained

---

53   Snell was a defendant in *Ely v. Mence* (Decree 1); *Williams v. Browker* (Decree 50); and *Williams v. Browker* (Decree 51). He was the petitioner in *Snell v. Browker* (Decree 11); *Snell v. Browker* (Decree 13); and *Snell v. Browker* (Decree 15). He also purchased and then sold an interest in the property at issue in *Hudson v. Browker* (Decree 49).

54   As in Decree 13, this decree omits Thomas Browker's residence in Upper Peover.

three rooms lying one above the other. The rooms were then in the occupation of Slipper. The lease ran from the feast of the birth of our Lord 1651 for thirty-one years at the annual rent of £6, payable quarterly.

By another indenture of lease dated 20 June 1655, Browker demised to Lambert Daggett, Cordwainer of Southwark, and Sarah his wife a house or tenement of brickwork with outhouses and a little adjoining yard or backside. The premises were then in the possession of Daggett, and were situated near the West Chain Gate over against the stables of the house sometimes called Winchester House. It lay between another of Browker's messuages then in the tenure of Cornwallis Pigeon on the north and a brick tenement then in the tenure of Gomer Williams on the south. The lease ran from the feast of the Nativity of St John the Baptist 1655 for forty-one years at the annual rent of £4, payable quarterly.

By his will, Thomas Browker devised this interest, along with divers others, to Mary, his wife. She settled this interest to her own use for ninety-nine years (if she should live so long) and then on various family members in the manner described in Decree 8.[55] Mary Browker had died, as had her son Thomas Browker the elder. The landlord's interest in the property came to Thomas Browker the younger, Thomas Browker the elder's son, for ninety-nine years (should he live so long). Under Mary Browker's property settlement, Dorothy Lloyd, Jane Kent, Dame Katherine Osbaldeston, Thomas Lowfeild (the son of Robert Lowfeild and Mary Browker's daughter Elizabeth, both now deceased) and Mary and Martha Browker (the daughters of Thomas Browker the elder and the sisters of Thomas Browker the younger) held contingent interests upon the death of Thomas Browker the younger.

The leases and interests of Slipper and the Daggetts came by good and sufficient assignments into the petitioner's hands. Both premises burned down in the fire. The petitioner was willing to rebuild on reasonable encouragement by means of an increased term of years and an abatement of rent, but he could not obtain this encouragement without the assistance of the Court.

Summonses to all the defendants were issued. The petitioner John Snell appeared personally, with Sir George Jeffreys, Mr Bowes and Mr Jenner as his counsel. Among the defendants, Thomas Lowfeild, Mary Browker and Martha Browker appeared personally. The Court specially admitted Anne Cooke, widow, as guardian of Thomas Lowfeild. The

---

55 See pp. 120–21.

Court also specially admitted Mary Leighton, wife of Charles Leighton, Gentleman, and mother of Mary and Martha Browker, as their guardian; Mr Ward and Mr Pettitt were their counsel.

The Lloyds, the Kents and the Osbaldestons did not appear personally or through counsel. To be satisfied in the matter, the Court took sworn testimony from John Moth of the parish of St Saviour and Benjamin Colinbine of London, Haberdasher. Both testified as they had done in Decree 8. On 21 September 1677, Moth served a summons on the turnkey of the King's Bench prison after determining that Thomas Browker the younger was a prisoner there, and Colinbine served summonses on Katherine Osbaldeston at Woodstocke in Oxfordshire on 13 August 1677; on Edward Lloyd at his dwelling called Beth Lloyd in Montgomery shire on 15 August 1677; and on Jane Kent at Road in Sommersetshire on 19 September 1677. The Court's registrar collected affidavits in writing to this effect.

The petitioner's counsel stated that the premises demised by the Daggett lease were not burned down, but had been considerably defaced and damnified. The petitioner had been put to great expense to repair the damage, and the premises were as yet not rented. Nonetheless, he sought only an increase in the term of years, not an abatement of rent. On the other hand, the premises demised to Slipper had burned down, and the petitioner had enjoyed their use for only a short time before the fire. He had since laid out a considerable sum in repair, but the ground was so small and lay in so bad a place that it was not worth building on. To undertake the rebuilding, the rent of £6 must be abated to thirty shillings.

Counsel for the defendants acknowledged that the ground lay in a bad place and was of small value, but nonetheless opposed so great a rent reduction.

The petitioner then advised the Court that he had a much better piece of ground held of the same defendants under another lease for which he paid just forty-five shillings per annum when the houses were still standing.[56] No other person would give as much as thirty shillings for the present ground if they were obliged to build on it.

Having heard the matter fully debated, the Court declared it just and reasonable for the Slipper lease to be increased to seventy years from the feast of St Michael the Archangel 1677 at an annual rent of thirty shillings, with all accrued rent payments from the fire until Christmas

56   It is likely that Snell's counsel was referring to the property described in *Snell v. Browker* (Decree 13).

1677 discharged, with the first quarterly payment next due on the feast of the Annunciation of the Blessed Virgin Mary 1678. As for the Daggett lease, the term should be increased to seventy years at the old rent of £4 per annum.

The Court ordered that:

(1) With respect to the Slipper lease,

    (a) Because the rent for the quarter in which the fire occurred had already been paid, the petitioner John Snell was discharged from paying all rent from the time of the fire until the feast of the birth of our Lord 1677.

    (b) From that point forward, the yearly rent of £6 was to be sunk, abated and reduced to thirty shillings for the unexpired remainder of the lease. The petitioner was discharged from payment of the remaining £4 10s., notwithstanding the reservation of the rent of £6. The rent was to be paid to the defendants or other persons according to their interests. The rent was to be paid at the days and times provided in the prior lease.

    (c) The petitioner would receive an additional term of sixty-four and three-quarter years at the expiration of the lease. The additional term would commence on the feast of the birth of our Lord 1682, for a total term of seventy years from the feast of St Michael the Archangel 1677.

    (d) In consideration of the increase in years and abatement of rent, the petitioner, at his cost and with all convenient speed, must new build other good and substantial messuages or tenements of brick and finish them in good workmanlike manner.

(2) With respect to the Daggett lease,

    (a) The petitioner would have an additional term of fifty-one and a quarter years added to the lease. The additional term would commence on the feast of the Nativity of St John the Baptist 1696, for a total term of seventy years from the feast of St Michael the Archangel 1677.

    (b) The rent remained £4. The rent was to be paid to the defendants or other persons according to their interests. The rent was to be paid at the days and times provided in the prior lease.

(3) To avoid difficulties in recovering the yearly rents and for ascertaining the covenants to be performed for the two leases, the defendants presently of age (Thomas Browker, the Lloyds,

the Kents and the Osbaldestons), as well as the infant defendants (Thomas Lowfeild and Mary and Martha Browker) when they become of age at twenty-one, must, on the petitioner's reasonable request, sign a good and sufficient new lease (or two new leases) by indenture. The lease or leases were to be prepared at the petitioner's expense. The lease or leases should contain reasonable covenants as found in the existing leases. The petitioner must accept the lease or leases and deliver up the counterparts.

(4) The petitioner might lawfully, peaceably and quietly enjoy the premises according to the tenor and purport of this decree, notwithstanding the coverture of the feme coverts, the infancy of the infants or any other interest.

Decree 15 (page 77)

5 Oct. 1677. Baron Littleton; Justice Jones (s); Thomas Barker, Esq. (s); James Reading, Esq. (s); Peter Rich, Esq. (s); John Freeman, Esq. (s); John Appellbe, Esq.

John Snell of London, Citizen and Merchant Taylor, v. Thomas Browker, Esq.; Edward Lloyd, Esq.; Dorothy his Wife; William Kent, Clerke; Jane his Wife; Sir Littleton Osbaldeston, Baronet; Dame Katherine his Wife; Thomas Lowfeild, an Infant; and Mary and Martha Browker, Infants[57]

By indenture of lease on 23 July 1652, Thomas Browker, Esquire,[58] demised to Margaret Buckland, widow, five properties. First was a messuage or tenement late in the possession of Robert Buckland, deceased husband of Margaret, and then in the possession of Margaret.[59] The messuage adjoined the gateway or passage leading into Angel Yard on the west side. Second was a tenement or house lately erected and new built over the gateway or passage on the west side of Angel Yard; this house was then in the possession of Anne Pennington, widow. Third was a tenement or house within Angel Yard then in the tenure of Francis Banbury, Silkweaver. Robert Buckland had recently built this house, along with another tenement. Fourth was another tenement recently built by Buckland that lay on the east side of the

---

57 Snell was a defendant in *Ely v. Mence* (Decree 1); *Williams v. Browker* (Decree 50); and *Williams v. Browker* (Decree 51). He was the petitioner in *Snell v. Browker* (Decree 11); *Snell v. Browker* (Decree 13); and *Snell v. Browker* (Decree 14). He also purchased and then sold an interest in the property at issue in *Hudson v. Browker* (Decree 49).

58 This petition omits Thomas Browker's residence in Upper Peover.

59 The registrar sometimes gives the Christian name as 'Margaret' and sometimes as 'Margarett'. I use 'Margaret' throughout.

last-mentioned tenement; it was then in the tenure of Richard Moore, Bodicemaker. Fifth was a tenement then in the occupation of Thomas Symms, Porter, which was situated in Angel Yard. All of the premises were situated in or near Fowl Lane.

The lease for these premises ran from the Nativity of St John the Baptist 1652 for forty-one years at the yearly rent of £8 6s. 8d., payable quarterly.

Browker subsequently made a will devising these premises, along with divers others, on his wife Mary. After Thomas died, Mary settled this interest to her own use for ninety-nine years (if she should live so long) and then on various family members in the manner described in Decree 8.[60] Mary Browker since died, as had her son Thomas Browker the elder. The landlord's interest in the property came to Thomas Browker the younger, Thomas Browker the elder's son, for ninety-nine years (should he live so long). Under Mary Browker's property settlement, Dorothy Lloyd, Jane Kent, Dame Katherine Osbaldeston, Thomas Lowfeild (the son of Robert Lowfeild and Mary Browker's daughter Elizabeth, both now deceased) and Mary and Martha Browker (the daughters of Thomas Browker the elder and the sisters of Thomas Browker the younger) held contingent interests upon the death of Thomas Browker the younger.

After making this settlement, Mary Browker and her son Thomas the elder, by indenture of lease on 20 May 1664, demised to William Medley, Citizen and Skinner of London, a corner messuage or tenement containing several rooms, which was lately in the tenure of Anne Bowney, widow, or her assigns. The property was located at or near Fowl Lane. The lease ran from the Nativity of St John the Baptist 1664 for twenty-nine years at the yearly rent of £4, payable quarterly.

Mary Browker and Thomas Browker the elder were now dead, leaving the interest of the landlord in Thomas Browker the younger.

All of the above-recited leases came by good and sufficient assignments into the hands of the petitioner. All of the premises were burned down in the fire, but the petitioner was willing to rebuild on reasonable encouragement: an increase in term and abatement of rent.

Summonses to all the defendants were issued. The petitioner John Snell appeared personally, with Sir George Jeffreys, Mr Bowes and Mr Jenner as his counsel. Among the defendants, Thomas Lowfeild, Mary Browker and Martha Browker appeared personally. The Court specially admitted Anne Cooke, widow, as guardian of Thomas Lowfeild. The

---

60 See pp. 120–21.

Court also specially admitted Mary Leighton, wife of Charles Leighton, Gentleman, and mother of Mary and Martha Browker, as their guardian; Mr Ward and Mr Pettitt were their counsel.

The Lloyds, the Kents and the Osbaldestons did not appear personally or through counsel. To be satisfied in the matter, the Court took sworn testimony from John Moth of the parish of St Saviour and Benjamin Colinbine of London, Haberdasher. Both testified as they had done in Decree 8. On 21 September 1677, Moth served a summons on the turnkey of the King's Bench prison after determining that Thomas Browker the younger was a prisoner there, and Colinbine served summonses on Katherine Osbaldeston at Woodstocke in Oxfordshire on 13 October last past;[61] on Edward Lloyd at his dwelling called Beth Lloyd in Montgomery shire on 15 August 1677; and on Jane Kent at Roade in Sommersetshire on 19 September 1677. The Court's registrar collected affidavits in writing to this effect.

The petitioner's counsel prayed for a considerable addition of years and abatement of rent. The counsel for the defendants opposed an abatement of rent. They also informed the Court that the premises originally leased to Medley had not burned down in the fire, but had been only partially defaced.

The petitioner's counsel responded that the premises were so defaced and shattered that, although the tenant in possession had laid out a considerable sum in repair, they would not stand long before they would need to be pulled down and new built. In addition, the premises stood in a very bad place for trade, as did the premises described in the other leases. Without a considerable abatement of rent and increase in years, he could never rebuild the premises described in the first set of leases.

Having heard the matter fully, the Court declared it most just and reasonable that the terms in the two sets of leases be extended to seventy years from the feast of St Michael the Archangel 1677. For the first lease, the rent would be £5, with the first payment due on the feast of the Annunciation of the Blessed Virgin Mary 1678. For the premises only defaced, the rent would be £4 annually, to be paid without ceasing.

---

61   This date is a mistake — likely an error in transcription or perhaps in the witness's testimony. Because the Court heard this case on 5 October 1677, the court was not yet in existence on 13 October 'last past' (i.e. 13 October 1676). The word 'August' should be substituted for the word 'October'. That date — 13 August 1677 — would accord with the other *Browker* decrees, in which Colinbine gave the date of service on Dame Katherine as 13 August 'last past' (i.e. 13 August 1677). The mistaken substitution of 'October' for 'August' is confirmed one sentence later, when the registrar described Colinbine as testifying that service on the Lloyds occurred 'upon the fifteenth day of the *said* month of August' (italics added).

The Court ordered that:

(1)   With respect to the Buckland lease,

    (a)   Because the rent for the quarter in which the fire occurred had already been paid, the petitioner John Snell was discharged from paying all rent from the time of the fire until the feast of the birth of our Lord 1677.

    (b)   From that point forward, the yearly rent of £8 6s. 8d. was sunk, abated, and reduced to £5 for the unexpired remainder of the lease. The petitioner was discharged from payment of the remaining £3 6s. 8d., notwithstanding the reservation of the rent of £8 6s. 8d. The rent was to be paid to the defendants or other persons according to their interests. The rent was to be paid at the days and times provided in the prior lease, with the first payment due on the feast of the Annunciation of the Blessed Virgin Mary 1678.

    (c)   The petitioner would receive an additional term of fifty-four and a quarter years at the expiration of the lease at the annual rent of £5. The additional term would commence on the feast of the Nativity of St John the Baptist 1693, for a total term of seventy years from the feast of St Michael the Archangel 1677.

    (d)   In consideration of the increase in years and abatement of rent, the petitioner, at his cost and with all convenient speed, must new build other good and substantial messuages or tenements of brick and finish them in good workmanlike manner.

(2)   With respect to the Medley lease,

    (a)   The petitioner was to have an additional term of fifty-four and a quarter years added to the lease. The additional term would commence on the feast of the Nativity of St John the Baptists 1693, for a total term of seventy years.

    (b)   The rent was £4, to be paid without ceasing. The rent was to be paid to the defendants or other persons according to their interests. The rent was to be paid at the days and times provided in the prior lease.

(3)   To avoid difficulties in recovering the yearly rents and for ascertaining the covenants to be performed for the two leases, the defendants presently of age (Thomas Browker, the Lloyds, the Kents and the Osbaldestons), as well as the infant defendants (Thomas Lowfeild and Mary and Martha Browker) when they become of age at twenty-one, must, on the petitioner's reasonable

request, sign a good and sufficient new lease (or two new leases) by indenture. The lease or leases were to be prepared at the petitioner's expense. The lease or leases should contain reasonable covenants as found in the existing leases. The petitioner must accept the lease or leases and deliver up the counterparts.

(4)   The petitioner might lawfully, peaceably and quietly enjoy the premises according to the tenor and purport of this decree, notwithstanding the coverture of the feme coverts, the infancy of the infants or any other interest.

Decree 16 (page 83)

5 Oct. 1677.   The Lord Mayor of London [Thomas Davies]; Baron Littleton; Justice Jones (s); Sir Thomas Allen (s); Sir John Fredericke (s); Thomas Barker, Esq. (s); James Reading, Esq. (s); Peter Rich, Esq.; John Freeman, Esq. (s); John Appellbe, Esq.[62]

Samuel Peck of London, Citizen and Painter Stainer, v. Thomas Waggorne of Southwark, Haberdasher, and William French[63]

Thomas Waggorne leased from William French certain premises. By indenture of lease dated 29 April 1676, Waggorne then leased a messuage or tenement and a shop to the petitioner in consideration of a sum of £28, which the petitioner then paid Waggorne. The premises had recently been in the possession of [...] Boulter.[64] Also included in the lease were a certain passage or counting house with a back kitchen and a small yard lately in the possession of Elizabeth Ascue, widow; this property lay in the parish of St Saviour and St Thomas in Southwark.[65]

---

62   In this decree, the registrar rendered Frederick's name as 'Fredericke'. Moreover, similar to Decree 4, at least one signature is cut off at the bottom of the page. Although most signatures appear in full, only the very top of one signature is observable at the bottom edge of the page. This signature seems to be that of Reading, so I have marked him as signing the decree. As mentioned in Decree 4, Rich habitually signed the decrees when he sat on the Court, but his signature does not appear on this decree. He typically signed near the bottom, below the signatures of Barker, Freeman and Reading. It is likely that his signature was cut off when the decree was fitted to the book.

63   The decree provides no occupation or residence for French.

64   A blank space, likely to insert Boulter's first name at a later point, was left in the decree.

65   It might be inferred from this description that the property lay on the east side of the High Street near St Thomas's Hospital, but the decree provides no additional information regarding location.

The petitioner's lease ran from the feast of the Nativity of St John the Baptist 1676 for four and a half years plus eleven weeks. The rent was £28 for the first three and three-quarter years and a peppercorn for the last three-quarters of a year plus eleven weeks.[66]

The petitioner then entered the premises and spent £20 fitting them to his use. Before the renovations were finished, on 26 May 1676, the fire partially demolished the forepart of the messuage and much defaced it. The petitioner was willing to repair the messuage, but soon after the fire, the defendants Waggorne and French entered the premises and kept the petitioner from acquiring possession. French had since repaired the premises and let it out to another tenant notwithstanding the petitioner's lease. The petitioner therefore requested either that he be given possession of the premises or that his £28 be returned to him.

Summonses were issued. The petitioner appeared personally, with Sir George Jeffreys as his counsel. Waggorne appeared, with Mr Jenner as his counsel. French also appeared personally.

The petitioner's counsel began by stating that, because the defendants together agreed to repair the premises and let them to a new tenant, the petitioner should get back the £28 that he paid for a term he never enjoyed, given that the term did not commence until after the fire.

Waggorne's counsel much opposed this request, saying that he paid a much greater fine to French upon his taking the lease, which he had now lost. Moreover, the petitioner was in possession of the house before the fire, since he took the lease in April. The petitioner might have repaired the messuage and enjoyed it if he pleased, but after several people, acting on behalf of Waggorne, applied to him to do so, the petitioner absolutely refused to concern himself with the house or to repair it. As a result, Waggorne was 'forced to Pale in the same'[67] to preserve the materials from being stolen and was forced to surrender the lease to French in order to prevent French from suing him — which French much threatened to do after refusing to give Waggorne any terms for rebuilding.[68]

Several witnesses gave sworn testimony to this effect, but the petitioner's counsel insisted that the petitioner was under no covenant to repair the premises (given that his obligation arose only on

---

66 In effect, Peck's initial payment of £28 prepaid the rent for the final fifty-week term covered by the peppercorn.

67 To 'pale' an area is to fence it in, typically with 'pales' (or stakes).

68 The sense of the decree is that French was the head landlord, Waggorne his tenant, and Peck was Waggorne's undertenant. But French's relationship to the premises or to Waggorne is never specified.

commencement of the lease). Moreover, he had been in possession no more than to spend £20 to fit the house and shop for his trade. It was then much controverted whether the petitioner, being in possession of the house before the fire, was liable under the covenants to repair it.

Having heard the arguments on both sides, the Court declared that, because the petitioner was in actual possession of the messuage at the time of the fire, he was liable to repair it. Having refused to repair the house or to intermeddle with it in any way, he ought not[69] to have his fine repaid and his petition should be dismissed without relief.

The petitioner's counsel then prayed that the petitioner might be discharged from the rent, covenants and all obligations to repair. The court thought this request reasonable.

The Court ordered that:

(1) The petitioner Samuel Peck was to have no relief on his petition against Thomas Waggorne.
(2) The petitioner was acquitted and discharged from any rent incurred on the lease since its commencement and from any covenants under it.
(3) The petitioner must deliver up his lease to Waggorne, who must accept it and deliver up the counterpart to be cancelled.
(4) French, who has repaired the premises, might lawfully enjoy the premises free of any claims of the petitioner or any other person claiming an interest under his lease.

Decree 17 (page 86)

5 Oct. 1677.   The Lord Mayor of London [Thomas Davies]; Baron Littleton; Justice Jones (s); Sir Thomas Allen (s); Sir John Fredericke (s); Thomas Barker, Esq. (s); James Reading, Esq. (s); Peter Rich, Esq. (s); John Freeman, Esq. (s); John Appellbe, Esq.

Christopher Marshall the Elder of London, Citizen and Dyer, v. Edith Peryn of London, Widow; Margaret Lone, Widow; John Medford, Gentleman; Mary, his wife; and Charles Hutchest of Southwark, Butcher

---

69 I have inserted a 'not' here because I believe that there may be a missing word or at least a misspelled word in the decree at this point. The decree reads as follows: 'he having alsoe since the said fire refused to repaire the house or to intermeddle anyway with the same ought now to have his fine repaid'. The 'now' likely should be a 'not', or at least a 'not' should have been inserted before 'now', given the court's refusal to give the petitioner relief on his petition.

By indenture of lease dated 30 April 1660, Edith Peryn[70] and Tobell Aylmer, Citizen and Draper of London, demised to George Gilfren of Southwark a messuage or tenement that was then in Gilfren's occupation. The lease ran from the feast of the Annunciation of the Blessed Virgin Mary 1660 for twenty-one years. The annual rent was £12, payable quarterly to Edith Peryn while she lived and then to Tobell Aylmer. The premises were located near the Meal Market.

Gilfren willed his interest in the lease to his wife Mary, who was executrix of his will. Gilfren died, and Mary then married the defendant, Charles Hutchest.

Tobell Aylmer died. By indenture of lease on 10 November 1670, Edith Peryn — together with Arthur Lone, Gentleman (since deceased), Margaret, his then wife,[71] and Mary Gregg (daughter of Margaret, first married to Abraham Gregg, now deceased, and then remarried to John Medford)[72] — demised the premises described above to Charles Hutchest in consideration of £90 to be laid out in new building and repair. The lease ran for eighteen years after the expiration of the prior lease at the annual rent of £12, payable quarterly.

Hutchest then decided to sell his interest in the premises. He treated with the petitioner to purchase his interest. Hutchest asserted that the premises were worth at least £26 per annum and demanded £126 for the sale of his interest. To induce the petitioner to buy his interest, Hutchest offered to lease the property back from the petitioner at a rent of £26 per annum. Therefore, by indenture of assignment dated 4 June 1673, in consideration of petitioner's payment of £126, Hutchest assigned his two verified leases to the petitioner. Then, by indenture of lease on 20 June 1673, the petitioner demised the premises to Hutchest. The lease ran from the feast of the Annunciation of the Blessed Virgin Mary 1673 for twenty-five years at the annual rent of £26, payable quarterly. The lease contained the usual covenants on the tenant's part to pay the rent and to repair and uphold the messuage. Hutchest also entered into a bond of £100 for performance of the covenants.[73]

70 The caption had rendered Peryn's name as 'Edyth', but the body of the decree rendered it as 'Edith'. I use 'Edith' throughout.

71 In the body of the decree, the registrar sometimes renders Margaret Lone's name as 'Margarett'. I use 'Margaret' throughout.

72 At one point, the decree refers to Margaret Lone and the Medfords as the 'reversioners', suggesting that the Lones and Mary Gregg inherited Aylmer's reversionary interest in the lease on Peryn's death. Thus, they would be required to be parties to a lease that might extend beyond Peryn's life interest.

73 Of all the property transactions described in the decrees, this one is the most puzzling: why would Hutchest take back a £26 sublease on a property that he

The premises burned down in the fire and were still in ruins. The petitioner was willing to rebuild on reasonable encouragement from Edith Peryn, Margaret Lone and the Medfords to increase the term and abate the rent. He also hoped to obtain a contribution from Hutchest in view of his covenants.

Summonses were issued. The petitioner appeared personally, with Mr Jenner and Mr Ward as his counsel. All the defendants also appeared. Peryn, Lone and the Medfords were represented by Mr Bowes, and Hutchest by Sir George Jeffreys.

The petitioner's counsel prayed to have a term of years from Peryn, Lone and the Medfords, and further stated that Hutchest, as undertenant, might either rebuild the premises on reasonable terms or surrender his lease and pay some contribution to the petitioner in view of the covenants. Mr Bowes then informed the Court that, after Hutchest contacted them, Peryn, Lone and the Medfords agreed that he should have a new lease of sixty-one years at the rent of £12 in return for new building. In pursuance of that agreement, they had entered a new lease. They were also informed that the petitioner consented to this arrangement, so the petitioner should be barred from obtaining any other relief from the Court.

Counsel for Hutchest then alleged that, because Hutchest was acquainted with the other defendants, the petitioner gave him directions to come to an agreement with them on a new lease on as good terms as he could get; the petitioner would then abide by those terms. Hutchest delivered the above-negotiated lease to the petitioner, who kept it for some time before returning it and refusing to accept it.

The petitioner's counsel denied that the lease Hutchest negotiated was taken at the request of or with the consent of the petitioner.

The Court therefore took the testimony of the parties. Under oath, the petitioner acknowledged that he directed Hutchest to treat with the other defendants on his behalf, but the petitioner never gave Hutchest

---

was leasing for £12? The decree provides no answers. Obviously, Marshall's £126 up-front payment gave Hutchest enough ready money to occupy the premises for nearly five years rent-free; perhaps he was in poor health and not expecting to live so long. Perhaps he needed cash immediately to pay creditors or to invest in another opportunity. Or perhaps he expected to sub-sublease the property for £26 and pocket a handsome £126 in the process. Whatever the answer, Hutchest's retention of Sir George Jeffreys, Common Serjeant of London, as well as his other behaviour in the case, suggests that he was far from unsophisticated. Another puzzling feature of this decree is that, at one place, the registrar states that Hutchest assigned two verified leases to the petitioner. Elsewhere, the decree refers to only one lease.

authority to take the lease in Hutchest's own name. Hutchest then testified under oath that the petitioner gave him directions to agree upon as good terms as he could get, so long as the old rent was not increased. He took the new lease in his own name because he thought that he could get better terms in doing so. When he took the lease to the petitioner, he offered to assign it to the petitioner; and he was still ready to do so.

At this point, Hutchest's counsel prayed that the petitioner accept the assignment and that Hutchest be otherwise discharged from rebuilding or the other covenants. Hutchest had suffered a great loss in the fire, and he had been paying the ground rent on the new lease to the other defendants — which should all be regarded as sufficient contribution. But the petitioner's counsel insisted on more contribution from Hutchest in return for discharging him.

Hutchest's counsel then argued that Hutchest's taking of a new lease with the petitioner's consent amounted to a surrender in law of the under-lease, so that he need not contribute further.

Having fully heard the allegations, the Court declared it just and reasonable that the petitioner accept the new lease without further contribution from Hutchest. The petitioner's counsel then prayed that, because the new lease was not made in the petitioner's name and because one defendant was a feme covert, the Court decree to him a sixty-year lease and order the defendants to execute it. The Court thought this very reasonable.

The Court ordered that:

(1) The petitioner Christopher Marshall was to have a term of sixty years in the premises that had been demised for sixty-one years to Hutchest, this being the residue of the term to which the defendants and Hutchest had agreed. The lease ran from the feast of the Nativity of St John the Baptist 1677.

(2) The annual rent was £12, payable quarterly to Peryn, Lone and the Medfords according to their respective interests.

(3) The petitioner was to build at his own cost with all convenient speed another good and substantial messuage of brick and finish it in the good workmanlike manner in which other new-built front houses in the High Street are usually built.

(4) To avoid difficulties in recovering the yearly rents and for ascertaining the covenants to be performed, Peryn, Lone and the Medfords must, on the petitioner's reasonable request, surrender the sixty-one-year lease made to Hutchest and then make a good and sufficient new lease by indenture. The lease or leases were

to be prepared at the petitioner's expense. The lease or leases should contain reasonable covenants usual in leases of new-built houses in and about London, as found in the existing leases. The petitioner must accept the lease and deliver up the counterparts.

(5) The petitioner might lawfully, peaceably and quietly enjoy the premises according to the tenor and purport of this decree, notwithstanding the coverture of Mary Medford or any other interest.

(6) On reasonable request from the petitioner, Hutchest must deliver up his sublease with the petitioner and the petitioner must accept it and deliver up the counterpart.

(7) The petitioner must surrender and deliver up Hutchest's performance bond to be cancelled.

(8) On delivery and surrender, Hutchest was discharged from all arrears of rent, from all covenants and from the performance bond.

Decree 18 (page 91)

5 Oct. 1677.   Baron Littleton; Justice Jones; Thomas Barker, Esq. (s); James Reading, Esq. (s); Peter Rich, Esq. (s); John Freeman, Esq. (s); John Appellbe, Esq.[74]

Thomas Lane of Southwark, Turner, v. Daniell Sledd of London, Linen Draper[75]

By indenture of lease dated 20 May 1671, Daniell Sledd, who possessed a messuage for some long term of years, demised the messuage, along with a yard and back house consisting of two rooms one above the other, to the petitioner. The lease was given in consideration of a £100 fine, with an annual rent of £34, payable quarterly. The lease ran from the feast of the Nativity of St John the Baptist 1671 for twenty-one years. The lease contained a covenant on the petitioner's part to repair, as well as other usual covenants.

The messuage had been in the tenure of William Frith and then lately of Thomas Mathewes. It lay on the east side of the High Street, and was known by the sign of the Antelope and then the sign of the Three Horseshoes.

The premises burned down in the fire. The petitioner was willing to rebuild on reasonable encouragement (an abatement of rent and increase in term), but the landlord refused to grant it.

74 No common-law judge signed this decree.
75 *Sledd v. Browker* (Decree 47), determined the relationship between Sledd and his head landlord regarding this property.

A summons was issued. The petitioner appeared personally, with Sir George Jeffreys as his counsel. The defendant also appeared personally. Mr Bowes and Mr Jenner were his counsel.

The petitioner's counsel expressed the petitioner's desire to rebuild and prayed for an increase in term and an abatement of the rent to £15 per annum. He claimed that this amount was as much as the ground was worth if it were let for new building.

The defendant's counsel opposed building on these terms. He claimed that the £100 fine paid on taking the lease in effect made the rent of the house £44 per annum and that the ground lay in one of the best places in Southwark. Therefore, the defendant required £26 per annum if the petitioner was to be the rebuilder.

After the petitioner's counsel much insisted on a greater abatement, Sledd's counsel proposed that Sledd rebuild at his own charge and then allow the petitioner enjoy the building for the remainder of his term (which was fifteen years from Midsummer last). The petitioner would not need to pay rent until the building was finished. Thus, the petitioner would be at no loss from the fire.

The petitioner refused the offer, but the Court declared the offer to be very fair and fit for the petitioner to accept. The Court then propounded it as most just and reasonable for the petitioner to have one of two options: (1) either to be the builder and pay £22 per annum in rent to Sledd, or (2) to have Sledd as rebuilder and to enjoy the messuage during the remainder of his lease at the former rent. Under the second option, Sledd must finish the building by the feast of the Annunciation of the Blessed Virgin Mary 1678, and the petitioner must be discharged of the whole rent until that time, with his first rent payment due on the feast of the Nativity of St John the Baptist 1678.

The Court gave the petitioner liberty to make an election between these possibilities. The petitioner chose to have Sledd rebuild the house rather than to be the rebuilder, at an annual rent of £22. The Court pronounced the same decreed.

The Court ordered that:

(1) The petitioner Thomas Lane must pay to Daniell Sledd two-thirds of the former rent of £34 for Midsummer quarter 1676. He was discharged of paying the remaining third, as well as the whole rent of £34 from the feast of the Nativity of St John the Baptist 1676 until the feast of the Annunciation of the Blessed Virgin Mary 1678.

(2) At his own charge, Sledd must well and substantially rebuild the messuage with brick and finish it in good workmanlike manner.

He must be finished before the feast of the Annunciation of the Blessed Virgin Mary 1678, so that the petitioner might inhabit the messuage by that time.

(3) Sledd must suffer the petitioner to enter the premises by the feast of the Annunciation of the Blessed Virgin Mary 1678. The petitioner might lawfully, peaceably and quietly hold the same at the annual rent of £22 for the remaining term of years in the original lease, without hindrance from Sledd or anyone claiming Sledd's interest.

(4) The first quarter's payment for the premises was to be due on the feast of the Nativity of St John the Baptist 1678.

Decree 19 (page 93)

17 Oct. 1677.   Baron Littleton; Justice Jones (s); James Reading, Esq. (s); John Freeman, Esq. (s); John Applebee, Esq.

Samuel Hyland of Southwark, Distiller, v. Richard How the Elder of the parish of Christ Church in the County of Surrey and Richard How the Younger, his Son

By indenture of lease dated 10 May 1656, Thomas Browker, Esquire,[76] demised to the petitioner two messuages or tenements then in the occupation or tenure of the petitioner and Miles Bayley. The lease ran from the feast of the Annunciation of the Blessed Virgin Mary 1656 for sixty-one years. The annual rent was £22, payable quarterly.

The property was on St Margaret's Hill, and lay between tenement then in the occupation of John Rushley, Baker, towards the south and a tenement adjoining the Talbot Inn then in the tenure or occupation of Hugh Blundell, Grocer, towards the north. It included two gardens or garden plots lying on the back side of the messuages.

The reversion or inheritance of this property was subsequently purchased by Richard How the elder. How had settled his interest on himself for life, with the reversion in tail to his son Richard How the younger, an infant.

The messuages burned down, and the petitioner rebuilt the premises at his own cost. In consideration of the rebuilding, How the elder agreed to extend the lease to ninety-nine years, accounted from the feast of the Annunciation of the Blessed Virgin Mary 1677, at the annual rent of

---

76 I assume that this Thomas Browker is Thomas Browker of Upper Peover, rather than his son (Thomas the elder) or grandson (Thomas the younger), the last of whom featured in the various *Browker* decrees (Decrees 8, 10–15 and 47–51).

£22. Because How the elder had only a life estate and How the younger was yet an infant, the petitioner could not have a secure estate without a decree from the Court.

Summonses were issued. The petitioner appeared personally. So did How the elder and How the younger. The elder How was specially admitted as the younger How's guardian.

In view of his great expense in rebuilding, the petitioner prayed the court to extend his lease to ninety-nine years in accordance with the promise of How the elder. How the elder then informed the court that he had agreed to add forty years to the petitioner's term at a rent of £22, but he was under no obligation to make up the lease to ninety-nine years. He stated that, in discourse with a third person not concerned in the matter, he had said that he would be willing to make up the lease to ninety-nine years if the Court thought it reasonable to do so.

The Court declared that it was not reasonable to decree the petitioner a longer term than the forty years which How had absolutely agreed to grant and the petitioner to accept. But if How was willing to consent to the additional years, the Court would not hinder his kindness to his tenant, especially because there was no abatement of rent. At this point, How the elder consented that the term in being should be increased to ninety-nine years from the feast of the Annunciation of the Blessed Virgin Mary 1677 at the annual rent of £22.

The Court ordered that:

(1) The petitioner Samuel Hyland was to have the term of years in the premises extended to ninety-nine years, accounted from the feast of the Annunciation of the Blessed Virgin Mary 1677, by adding fifty-nine years to the end of the present lease, which was set to expire on the feast of the Annunciation of the Blessed Virgin Mary 1717.

(2) The annual rent was £22, payable to Richard How the elder for his life and then, for the rest of the term, to Richard How the younger or such other persons to whom the reversion and inheritance belonged. Payment was to be made at the time and manner as provided in the present lease.

(3) To avoid difficulties in recovering the yearly rents and for ascertaining the covenants to be performed for the lease, on the petitioner's reasonable request and at his expense, How the elder (and How the younger when he reached the age of twenty-one) must execute a good and sufficient lease by indenture for the additional term of fifty-nine years at the annual rent of £22. The lease should contain reasonable covenants as found in the

present lease. The petitioner must accept the lease and deliver up the counterpart.

(4) The petitioner might lawfully, peaceably and quietly hold the messuages and gardens for the remaining term of years in the original lease and for the fifty-nine years hereby added, notwithstanding the infancy of How the younger or any other interest.

Decree 20 (page 96)

17 Oct. 1677. Baron Littleton; Justice Jones (s); James Reading, Esq. (s); John Freeman, Esq. (s); John Appellbe, Esq.

Henry Hawkes, Citizen and Tallow Chandler of London, v. Richard How the Elder of the parish of Christchurch[77] in the County of Surrey and Richard How the Younger, his Son, an Infant

By indenture of lease dated 13 February 1649, Thomas Browker, Esquire,[78] demised to Henry Hawkes, the petitioner's father, a messuage or tenement once in the occupation of Nicholas Newton or his assigns and then in occupation of the petitioner's father. The lease ran from the feast of the Annunciation of the Blessed Virgin Mary 1649 for forty-one years. The annual rent was £13 6s. 8d., payable quarterly.

By another indenture of lease dated 20 January 1656, Browker demised to Henry Hawkes, the petitioner's father, the same premises, to hold from the end of the present lease (on the feast of the Annunciation of the Blessed Virgin Mary 1690) for eighteen years at the same rent of £13 6s. 8d.

The property was located on the High Street. It had been lately known by the sign of the Black Boy. The premises also included a garden.

The interest of Henry Hawkes, the petitioner's father, was legally vested in Henry Hawkes, the petitioner. Browker's reversion or inheritance of the property was subsequently purchased by Richard How the elder. How settled this interest on himself for life, with the reversion in tail to his son Richard How the younger, an infant.

The messuage burned down, and the petitioner rebuilt the premises at his own cost. In consideration of the rebuilding, How the elder agreed

---

77 Unlike the caption in the prior decree, 'Christchurch' was rendered as a single word.

78 As in the prior decree, and given the date of the lease described, the reference here is almost certainly to Thomas Browker of Upper Peover, not to his son (Thomas the elder) or grandson (Thomas the younger).

to extend the lease to ninety-nine years, accounted from the feast of the Annunciation of the Blessed Virgin Mary 1677, at the annual rent of £13 6s. 8d. Because How the elder had only a life estate and How the younger was yet an infant, the petitioner could not have a secure estate without a decree from the Court.

Summonses were issued. The petitioner appeared personally. So did How the elder and How the younger. The elder How was specially admitted as the younger How's guardian.

In view of his rebuilding, the petitioner prayed the court to extend his lease to ninety-nine years in accordance with the promise of How the elder. How the elder then informed the court that he had agreed to add forty years to the petitioner's term at a rent of £13 6s. 8d., but he was under no obligation to make up the lease to ninety-nine years. He stated that, in discourse with a third person not concerned in the matter, he had said he would be willing to make up the lease to ninety-nine years if the Court thought it reasonable to do so.

The Court declared that it was not reasonable to decree the petitioner a longer term than the forty years which How had absolutely agreed to grant and the petitioner to accept. But if How was willing to consent to the additional years, the Court would not hinder his kindness to his tenant, especially because there was no abatement of rent. At this point, How the elder consented that the term in being should be increased to ninety-nine years from the feast of the Annunciation of the Blessed Virgin Mary 1677 at the annual rent of £13 6s. 8d.

The Court ordered that:

(1)   The petitioner Henry Hawkes was to have the term of years in the premises extended to ninety-nine years, accounted from the feast of the Annunciation of the Blessed Virgin Mary 1677, by adding sixty-eight years to the end of the present leases, the last of which was set to expire on the feast of the Annunciation of the Blessed Virgin Mary 1708.

(2)   The annual rent was £13 6s. 8d., payable to Richard How the elder for his life and then, for the rest of the term, to Richard How the younger or such other persons to whom the reversion and inheritance belonged. Payment should be made at the time and manner as provided in the present lease.

(3)   To avoid difficulties in recovering the yearly rents and for ascertaining the covenants to be performed for the lease, on the petitioner's reasonable request and at his expense, How the elder (and How the younger when he reached the age of twenty-one) must execute a good and sufficient lease by indenture for

the additional term of sixty-eight years at the annual rent of £13 6s. 8d. The lease should contain reasonable covenants as found in the present lease. The petitioner must accept the lease and deliver up the counterpart.

(4) The petitioner might lawfully, peaceably and quietly hold the messuages and gardens for the remaining term of years in the original lease and for the sixty-eight years hereby added, notwithstanding the infancy of How the younger or any other interest.

Decree 21 (page 100)

17 Oct. 1677.   Baron Littleton; Justice Jones (s); James Reading, Esq. (s); John Freeman, Esq. (s); John Appellbe, Esq.

Jeremiah Rushley, Citizen and Salter of London, v. Richard How the Elder of the parish of Christchurch[79] in the County of Surrey and Richard How the Younger, his Son, an Infant

By indenture of lease dated 22 November 1655, Thomas Browker, Esquire,[80] demised to John Rushley, Baker, a messuage or tenement once in the tenure or occupation of Rowland March and then in tenure or occupation of John Rushley. The lease ran from the feast of St Michael the Archangel 1655 for fifty-one years. The annual rent was £10, payable quarterly.

The property was located between a tenement then in the occupation of Andrew Kembe towards the south and a tenement in the tenure or occupation of Samuell Hyland toward the north.[81] It also included a garden belonging to the premises, then in the tenure or occupation of John Rushley.

The interest of John Rushley was now vested in the petitioner. Browker's reversion or inheritance of the property was subsequently purchased by Richard How the elder. How settled this interest on himself for life, with the reversion in tail to his son Richard How the younger, an infant.

79 'Christchurch' was again rendered as a single word.

80 As in the other *How* decrees, the reference here is likely to Thomas Browker of Upper Peover, not to his son (Thomas the elder) or grandson (Thomas the younger).

81 Although the spelling of 'Samuell' is different, this is likely the Samuel Hyland who was the petitioner in *Hyland v. How* (Decree 19). If so, the present property was located on St Margaret's Hill, which is where Hyland's property was situated.

The messuage was burned down and demolished. The petitioner rebuilt the premises at his own cost. In consideration of the rebuilding, How the elder agreed to extend the lease to ninety-nine years, accounted from the feast of the Annunciation of the Blessed Virgin Mary 1677, at the annual rent of £10. Because How the elder had only a life estate and How the younger was yet an infant, the petitioner could not have a secure estate without a decree from the Court.

Summonses were issued. The petitioner appeared personally. So did How the elder and How the younger. The elder How was specially admitted as the younger How's guardian.

In view of the great charge of his rebuilding, the petitioner prayed the court to extend his lease to ninety-nine years in accordance with the promise of How the elder. How the elder then informed the court that he had agreed to add forty years to the petitioner's term at a rent of £10, but he was under no obligation to make up the lease to ninety-nine years. He stated that, in discourse with a third person not concerned in the matter, he said that he would be willing to make up the lease to ninety-nine years if the Court thought it reasonable to do so.

The Court declared that it was not reasonable to decree the petitioner a longer term than the forty years which How had absolutely agreed to grant and the petitioner to accept. But if How was willing to consent to the additional years, the Court would not hinder his kindness to his tenant, especially because there was no abatement of rent. At this point, How the elder consented that the term in being should be increased to ninety-nine years from the feast of the Annunciation of the Blessed Virgin Mary 1677 at the annual rent of £10.

The Court ordered that:

(1) The petitioner Jeremiah Rushley was to have the term of years in the premises extended to ninety-nine years, accounted from the feast of the Annunciation of the Blessed Virgin Mary 1677, by adding sixty-nine and a half years to the end of the present lease, which was set to expire on the feast of St Michael the Archangel 1706.

(2) The annual rent was £10, payable to Richard How the elder for his life and then, for the rest of the term, to Richard How the younger or such other persons to whom the reversion and inheritance belonged. Payment should be made at the time and manner as provided in the present lease.

(3) To avoid difficulties in recovering the yearly rents and for ascertaining the covenants to be performed for the lease, on the petitioner's reasonable request and at his expense, How the elder

(and How the younger when he reached the age of twenty-one) must execute a good and sufficient lease by indenture for the additional term of sixty-nine and a half years at the annual rent of £10. The lease should contain reasonable covenants as found in the present lease. The petitioner must accept the lease and deliver up the counterpart.

(4) The petitioner might lawfully, peaceably and quietly hold the messuage and garden for the remaining term of years in the original lease and for the sixty-nine and a half years hereby added, notwithstanding the infancy of How the younger or any other interest.

Decree 22 (page 103)

17 Oct. 1677.   Baron Littleton; Justice Jones (s); James Reading, Esq. (s); John Freeman, Esq. (s); John Appellbe, Esq.

Marke Weyland of Southwark, Innkeeper, and Mary his Wife v. John Sayer of Battersey in the County of Surrey, Gentleman

The petitioners were in possession of a messuage or inn commonly called the George Inn. The landlord was Nicholas Andrewes. The lease was due to expire on the feast of St Michael the Archangel 1678. The annual rent was £150.

In a prior 'violent fire', the inn in great part was burned down and demolished. The petitioners petitioned the fire court established to deal with the Great Fire of London and also certain fires in Southwark. That court decreed that the rent be reduced to £80 for the remaining term of the lease, with forty years added to the lease.[82] The annual rent

---

[82] The London fire court issued its decree on 18 July 1671. According to that decree, Andrewes, who was possessed of a long lease on the inn, demised the George to Thomas Underwood, Innkeeper, on 16 November 1668. The term ran from the feast of St Michael the Archangel 1668, for ten years. The decree recited that Andrewes held the lease as a tenant of John Sawyer (likely the 'John Sayer' of this decree). Underwood died, and his interest was devised to Mary, his wife, who subsequently married Marke Weyland. The fire at the George occurred on 25 July 1670, and burned down most of the George, as well the barns, stables and goods of the petitioners. Andrewes also filed a cross-petition against Sawyer to force him to contribute to the lowered rent. The cross-petition recited that the annual rent on Andrewes's lease was £50 and one sugar loaf; Andrewes was therefore pocketing a handsome £100 on the sublease to Underwood. The real dispute in the case was between Andrewes and Sawyer, with Andrewes asking that Sawyer contribute to the rebuilding through a reduction in the £50 rent Andrewes paid Sawyer. Among Sawyer's arguments was the negligence of one of the George's tenants in operating a forge. While the court did not accept that argument, it declined to reduce the rent

of £80 and one sugar loaf was to be paid to Nicholas Andrewes for the remaining term of the lease plus the first year of the additional forty-year term (which was all of Andrewes's remaining interest in the property); thereafter, for the remaining thirty-nine years of the new lease, the annual £80 rent was to be paid to the defendant John Sayer, who had the inheritance of the premises.[83] Sayer executed a new lease for the added thirty-nine-year term, commencing on the feast of St Michael the Archangel 1679. In accordance with that decree, the petitioners rebuilt the inn and enjoyed its use until it was entirely burned down and demolished in the 1676 Southwark fire.

The petitioners treated with Sayer for encouragement to rebuild a second time. They came to an agreement: in consideration of the petitioners' great loss which they again incurred, Sayer would reduce the rent to £50 per annum and a sugar loaf.[84] An additional nineteen years would also be added to the term of the lease, which made the lease fifty-eight years commencing on the feast of St Michael the Archangel 1679. Sayer executed the lease and the petitioners had rebuilt the inn (Fig. 14).

To better secure the petitioners their enjoyment of the premises, the petitioners asked for a decree. A summons was issued. The petitioner Marke Weyland appeared personally, as did the defendant John Sayer.[85]

In view of their great expense, the petitioner prayed the Court to corroborate the parties' agreement by decreeing the agreed term of years and sinking the rent as agreed. Sayer consented.

due to Sawyer, since Sawyer contributed by virtue of the forty-year extension of the lease. See Weyland v. Andrewes, *Fire of London Court of Judicature Decrees*, vol. G, fols 265–69ᵛ (18 July 1671).

The present petition imprecisely stated the terms of the 1671 decree. In fact, the rent was reduced to £50 plus one sugar loaf for the first year of the new lease, and then increased to £80 plus one sugar loaf for the last seven years. The decree correctly recited the payment of a sugar loaf in the next sentence.

83   The decree of the London fire court did not require the Weylands to pay Sawyer a sugar loaf for the final thirty-nine years of the lease.

84   In effect, Sayer was no worse off, save for the nineteen-year extension of the lease, since he was already receiving only £50 plus one sugar loaf under his lease with Andrewes.

85   Although the parties were unrepresented in this case, the more contentious case before the London fire court involved counsel for all parties: Messrs. Sturges, Bowes, Jenner and King represented the Weylands. Mr Unicum was counsel to Andrewes, and Messrs Ofley and Barry were counsel to Sawyer. Jenner and Bowes, of course, were frequently counsel in the Southwark fire court. As for Ofley's possible role in shaping the Southwark fire-court legislation, see Introduction, pp. 55 and 64.

Fig. 14.   The George Inn, the only building to survive, if only in part, from reconstruction after the fire of 1676.

Photograph Sheila O'Connell

The Court ordered that:

(1) The rent of fourscore pounds decreed in the prior Court of Judicature for the term of thirty-nine years, commencing from the feast of St Michael the Archangel 1679, was to be sunk and abated to £50 and a sugar loaf for the entire term of thirty-nine years.

(2) The petitioners Marke and Mary Weyland were discharged from paying £30 of the yearly rent during the term of thirty-nine years, notwithstanding the prior decree or any reservation, clause or covenant contained in the decree or the lease made pursuant to it.

(3) The petitioners were to have an additional term of nineteen years in the inn now in their occupation, to take effect immediately at the end of the thirty-nine-year lease (which was to occur on the feast of St Michael the Archangel 1718). The annual rent would be £50 and a sugar loaf, payable quarterly on the usual feasts.

(4) Under the covenants contained in the last executed lease and on payment of the annual rent, the petitioners should lawfully, peaceably and quietly enjoy the premises, notwithstanding the prior decree and lease made pursuant to it or any other interest.

Decree 23 (page 106)

5 Dec. 1677.　　　Baron Littleton; Baron Thurland (s); Justice Jones (s); Adam Browne, Baronet; Sir Thomas Allen (s); Sir Thomas Bludworth (s); Edward Smith, Esq. (s); Thomas Barker, Esq. (s); James Reading, Esq. (s); Richard How, Esq. (s); Peter Rich Esq. (s); John Appellbe, Esq.

Robert Gale of Southwark, Victualler, v. Daniell Wight of Southwark, Distiller[86]

---

86 This decree completes the story begun in *Bankes v. Wight* (Decree 2). In this petition, Wight's name is rendered as 'Daniell'; in Decree 2, it has been 'Daniel'. A bit of additional colour about Robert Gale: the *Calendar of State Papers Domestic* includes an examination of James Gardiner, apprentice to Robert Gale of Southwark, conducted on 17 June 1676, less than a month after the Southwark fire. Gardiner admitted that, on the prior Tuesday (16 June), he had set fire to wood and lath in Gale's cellar in order to burn down Gale's house. Gardiner's aim was to free himself of Gale's service. Examination of James Gardiner, TNA, SP 29/382/129 (17 June 1676).

In 1674, the petitioner was in possession of a messuage in Compter Lane. The lease was nearing its end. The property was used in the calling of a victualler. Daniell Wight had recently purchased the inheritance of the messuage and others adjoining. In consideration of his new building of a messuage, the petitioner treated with Wight for a long lease. They agreed a term of forty-four years at the annual rent of £9. For the petitioner's further encouragement, Wight agreed to enter a covenant that, when he let his next or near-adjoining houses or lands, he would obtain a covenant from those tenants that none should 'send or vend publiquely any Beere or Ale'.[87]

Afterwards, the petitioner pulled down the messuage and rebuilt a brick messuage on the same ground. The building cost more than £200. Thereafter, Wight executed a forty-four-year lease to the petitioner commencing on the feast of St John the Baptist 1675 at the aforesaid rent. The lease contained a covenant to restrain other tenants of the defendant from selling beer and ale.

The petitioner enjoyed the messuage for less than a year when the fire partially burned and much defaced and damnified it. The petitioner had many goods lost and spoiled. Soon after the fire, in order to better preserve his trade, the petitioner at his own charge repaired the messuage, which cost at least threescore pounds. Wight contributed nothing toward the petitioner's great loss and charges. Then he leased his adjoining ground to one Bankes[88] to build on without taking a covenant of restraint. In view of the petitioner's great losses already sustained, he might be utterly ruined unless the Court relieved him.

A summons was issued. The petitioner appeared personally, with Sir George Jeffreys, Mr Bowes and Mr Jenner as counsel. The defendant appeared personally. Mr Ward was his counsel.

The petitioner's counsel prayed the Court to increase the petitioner's term and abate the rent in light of the petitioner's great charge in rebuilding the house and Wight's refusal to restrain Bankes from selling beer or ale.

Wight's counsel opposed this request. With respect to the repairs, aside from beautifying repairs, all necessary repairs could have been done for £20, and the landlord's contribution should be so limited.

The petitioner then examined under oath the carpenter who made the repairs and several witnesses. It was fully proved that the petitioner

---

87 I have quoted the language of the decree. Perhaps 'send' was intended to be 'sell'.

88 Presumably John Bankes, Carpenter, who, according to Decree 2, agreed to develop the property.

laid out about £40 in necessary repairs, in addition to the money he spent at the time of the fire to preserve his messuage.

With respect to the covenant, Wight's counsel informed the Court that Wight did not voluntarily lease the land to Bankes without a restraining covenant and that he refused to execute the lease to Bankes until this Court ordered him to do so. By that order, Wight was protected and indemnified, and the petitioner should get no allowance. Moreover, the covenant was a collateral covenant only, and none of the houses built by Bankes presently sold beer or ale.

The petitioner's counsel stated that, since the petitioner was not party to the Court's prior decree, he was not heard at that time. If the decree hindered the petitioner's remedy, he should receive some recompense, again insisting on an increase in term and an abatement of rent — or else a confirmation of the lease and covenant already in existence.

Having heard the matter fully, the Court stated that it would not meddle with the covenant or unsettle the prior decree. Nor would it abate the petitioner's rent or increase the term of his lease. Rather, Wight should be ordered to pay the petitioner 20 marks [£13 6s. 8d.] toward his charges in repairing the messuage and on no other account. Wight assented.

The court ordered that, on the demand of the petitioner Robert Gale, Samuell Wight must pay the petitioner £13 6s. 8d. The petitioner must accept the same in full satisfaction and recompense for his charges in repairing the damage to his messuage.[89]

Decree 24 (page 109)

5 Dec. 1677.   Baron Littleton; Baron Thurland (s); Adam Browne, Baronet; Sir Thomas Allen (s); Sir Thomas Bludworth (s); Edward Smith, Esq. (s); Thomas Barker, Esq. (s); James Reading, Esq. (s); Richard How, Esq. (s); Peter Rich Esq. (s); John Appellbe, Esq.

William Cooper of Southwark, Butcher, v. Urian Arnold, Citizen and Poulterer of London; Daniell Williamson, Citizen and Haberdasher of

---

89   According to a notation found at the bottom of a draft folio of this decree, Wight paid Gale this amount on 15 March 1678. See TNA, C 108/129/29. Perhaps still aggrieved, Gale refused to sign the receipt acknowledging the payment. Two witnesses — Thomas Rous, who himself had other matters before the Court (see Decrees 43 and 45), and William Hooke — signed the bottom of the draft folio to reflect that payment had been made.

London; Thomas Mathew, also Citizen and Haberdasher of London; and William Dorrell of Southwark, Victualler

By indenture of lease dated 6 December 1666, Adria Nicholls of Southwark, widow, demised to Richard Davies of Southwark, Salter, a messuage or tenement that was then in Davies's possession. The lease ran from the feast of the Annunciation of the Blessed Virgin Mary 1667 for twenty-one years at the annual rent of £18, payable quarterly. The premises were on the west side of the High Street.

Thereafter, Davies assigned the lease and all his interest in the messuage to Urian Arnold. Arnold in turn assigned the lease to Daniell Williamson. Williamson (so the petitioner is informed) entered into a covenant with Arnold to pay Arnold £4 annually during the term of the lease, as well as the £18 rent due to the lessor. Then Williamson assigned the lease and all his interest in the messuage to Thomas Mathew. Mathew covenanted to pay Williamson the yearly rent of £4 during the remaining term of the lease.[90] In addition, Mathew and William Dorrell became bound to Williamson through a bond of a considerable penalty for the payment of the £4.

Nicholls had since died, and her executor obtained possession of the premises due to non-payment of the £18 reserved rent. The executor then made a new lease with the petitioner. At that time, the petitioner was drawn in by Mathew to give him a bond with a £200 penalty to save Mathew and Dorrell harmless against Williamson under their prior bond and against any actions, suits and damages concerning the bond.

The messuage burned down in the fire. The petitioner had since surrendered the lease and the head landlords had rebuilt the messuage. Nonetheless, Arnold brought an action at law against Williamson for the arrears of £4 per annum incurred since the fire. In turn, Williamson brought two actions against Mathew and Dorrell on their bond. And then Dorrell brought an action against the petitioner on his bond, which was to save Mathew and Dorrell harmless.

Summonses to appear were issued. The petitioner was personally present, with Mr Jenner as his counsel. Mr Wynn appeared on behalf of Williamson. Mr Ward appeared on behalf of Mathew and Dorrell. Arnold did not appear personally or through counsel. To satisfy itself regarding the service of a summons on Arnold, the Court heard the

---

90 Presumably Mathew was also required to pay the underlying rent of £18. But the decree does not so say, given that the case was concerned only with the fate of the £4 profit that Arnold took on subleasing the property.

sworn testimony of the petitioner that he personally served Arnold with a summons. At that point, Mr Richardson owned himself to be of counsel for Arnold.

The petitioner's counsel prayed that the £4 per annum additional lease, being only a rent that a tenant created on assigning the lease, be discharged and that the bond given by petitioner to Mathew and Dorrell be delivered up. Arnold's counsel opposed this relief, alleging that Arnold had paid a considerable fine to Davies on taking the assignment; further, that the £4 per annum was reserved and made payable to him when he assigned the lease to Williamson as recompense for this fine.

Williamson's counsel then stated that the petitioner had not paid the £4 since the time of the fire, but Arnold had brought an action at law to recover £5, which was the amount incurred since the fire. Williamson had paid this amount. If the Court thought fit to discharge the £4 annual rent, counsel asked that the petitioner be required to pay Williamson back the £5 already paid. The petitioner's counsel agreed to pay this amount, but wished to be discharged for the future; given that the rent was charged for a house that burned down in the fire, a discharge seemed equitable. Counsel also argued for discharge because the £4 per annum charge was only for the continuance of the lease, which was subsequently made void by re-entry and a new lease made to petitioner.

Having heard the matter fully debated, the Court declared that the grant of the £4 rent appeared void after the re-entry and the voiding of the old lease. If the petitioner wanted to have the £4 rent discharged to avoid trouble, however, it was fit to be done. The petitioner's counsel then prayed that the decree's discharge also order the petitioner to pay the £5 in arrears, that the bonds and securities to hold harmless be given up and that all suits commenced on the matter cease, with all parties bearing their own costs. The Court declared all this to be just and reasonable.

The Court ordered that:

(1)   The petitioner William Cooper must pay Daniell Williamson £5, and Williamson must accept it in full payment of all arrears.

(2)   The £4 per annum payable under the lease was discharged, and neither the petitioner nor other parties need pay it.

(3)   The covenant of payment from Williamson to Arnold, all bonds and securities given by parties for performance of the covenant to pay the £4 per annum, and the petitioner's bond to save Mathew and Dorrell harmless were discharged. All bonds must be delivered up on request.

(4) All actions and suits between the present parties concerning this matter must cease, with each party to bear his own costs of the actions.

Decree 25 (page 113)

5 Dec. 1677.   Baron Littleton; Baron Thurland (s); Justice Jones (s); Adam Browne, Baronet; Sir Thomas Allen (s); Sir Thomas Bludworth (s); Edward Smith, Esq. (s); Thomas Barker, Esq. (s); James Reading, Esq. (s); Richard How, Esq. (s); Peter Rich Esq. (s); John Appellbe, Esq.

Jonathan Whaley and Joane his Wife v. Robert Mercy, Richard Blake, and Thomas Wells[91]

Robert Mercy had leased to Richard Blake one messuage or tenement with the back side for divers years, of which (the petitioner was informed) about one year was still to come. The annual rent was £23. Blake assigned the lease to James Elficke. By this assignment, Elficke became bound to Blake in a bond with a £40 penalty, conditioned on Elficke paying the rent and performing the lease's covenants. Elficke also agreed to save Blake harmless and indemnify Blake against payment of the rent and the covenants contained in Blake's lease with Mercy.

Elficke died, leaving his wife Joane as his relict executrix. In due form, she proved his will and became possessed of the title and term to come in the premises. About three years ago, Joane took to husband the petitioner Jonathan Whaley, who then also became interested in the lease.

The premises burned down in the fire. Blake assigned his bond to Thomas Wells and made out to Wells a letter of attorney to sue — facts that Blake, in his answer in Chancery to the petitioners' bill for relief, confessed. There was only half of a year's rent due before the fire, which the petitioners had offered to pay to settle with Blake and Wells. But Blake, or Wells in the name of Blake, had obtained judgment against the petitioners on the bond and had demanded from the petitioners not only the rent due before the fire but also the rent incurred since. Blake (or Wells in his name) had threatened to levy the same and the costs of suit on the petitioners to their great vexation and damage — notwithstanding that the petitioners were willing to rebuild if the head landlord [Mercy] had not re-entered and rebuilt the premises.

---

91 Unlike most other decrees, this decree recites neither the place where the parties resided nor their occupations.

Summonses to the defendants were issued. The petitioner Jonathan Whaley appeared personally, with Mr Richardson and Mr Dowling as counsel. Mercy and Wells also appeared personally, with Mr Jenner as counsel. To satisfy itself regarding the service of a summons on Blake, the Court heard the sworn testimony of Elias Swan, Porter, who testified that he personally served Blake with a summons to appear in court on a former day appointed for hearing the case. Because the Court did not sit that day, Swan served Blake with another summons on last Thursday.[92]

The petitioners' counsel stated that the petitioners were willing to pay all rent due at the time of the fire and the costs that the defendants incurred in obtaining their judgment. He prayed the Court to set aside the judgment.

Counsel for Mercy informed the Court that the judgment was obtained on an action commenced before the fire. The judgment was for rent then due. Therefore, the matter was not properly within this Court's jurisdiction. The petitioners' counsel responded that, because the lease from Mercy to Blake was not quite expired, the petitioners should be discharged from paying the rent since the time of the fire and from the covenants contained in the lease.

Mercy's counsel opposed this request. He informed the Court that Mercy gave the head landlord 30 guineas [£31 10s.] to accept a surrender of his lease in the messuage and other adjoining properties. He therefore demanded payment of the rent for two months in the Midsummer quarter 1676, plus some contribution toward the sum paid to the head landlord.

Having heard the matter fully debated, the Court declared that it was not proper for it to order anything concerning rent due before the fire. But it was just and reasonable to order the petitioners to pay two-thirds of the rent for Midsummer quarter 1676 and to be discharged from all other rent incurred and from all covenants.

The Court ordered that:

(1) The petitioners Jonathan and Joane Whaley must, on demand, pay Thomas Wells two-thirds of the quarterly rent that was due on the feast of the Nativity of St John the Baptist 1676.

(2) The petitioners were discharged from paying the other one-third of the quarterly rent and from any other reserved rent due since

---

92 The day on which the Court heard this case, 5 December 1677, was a Wednesday, thus affording Blake six days' notice.

the feast of the Nativity of St John the Baptist 1676, as well as from the covenants in the lease.

(3)   The residue of the term of years in the lease would cease and be hereby determined.

Decree 26 (page 116)

19 Dec. 1677.   Baron Littleton; Justice Windham (s);[93] Justice Jones (s); Sir Thomas Bludworth (s); Thomas Barker, Esq. (s); John Freeman, Esq. (s); John Appellbe, Esq.

Anne Lane of Southwark, Widow, v. Mayor, Aldermen, and Burgesses of the Town of Shrewsbury in the County of Salop and Marke Houghton of Southwark, Vintner[94]

The petitioner was in possession of a messuage whose inheritance lay in the Town of Shrewsbury. The messuage was located in Three Crown Court, and it burned down in the fire. Having obtained encouragement from the Town, the petitioner was proceeding with rebuilding the messuage. But the defendant Mark Houghton, who obtained the inheritance of the next adjoining ground backwards, laid claim to a small parcel of ground. Before the fire, the parcel had been a hole under the staircase of the petitioner's house, about six feet in length and about three feet in breadth. At the entrance it was about four feet high. The hole slanted downwards to a point.

Rather than be hindered in her building, the petitioner was content to give Houghton some consideration for the hole. She treated with Houghton, and he agreed that she should have the hole and proceed with her building. He said that he would not differ with her on price. Afterwards he offered to let two indifferent persons set the value for what the petitioner should pay, and he encouraged her to continue with her building. In pursuance of that agreement, the petitioner took in the said hole and rebuilt the messuage, placing a stack of chimneys where the hole had been.

Houghton, however, reneged on his agreement and would no longer accept any recompense for the ground. Instead, he now required the land, even though the petitioner built on it with his consent.

---

93   In the cases in which Justice Hugh Wyndham sat on the Court, the registrar rendered his name as either 'Windham' or 'Wyndham'. He signed the decrees as 'Wyndham'. Per my convention, I render the spelling as the registrar did.

94   Houghton was the petitioner in *Houghton v. Mayor of Shrewsbury* (Decree 4).

Summons to the defendants were issued. The petitioner appeared personally and was represented by Mr Jenner and Mr Ward. The Town of Shrewsbury was represented by its agent, Mr Gibbons.[95] Houghton also appeared personally. He was represented by Sir George Jeffreys and Mr Bowes.[96]

The petitioner's counsel prayed for a considerable term of years in the hole at a reasonable rent. Counsel for Houghton alleged that the matter was not properly within the jurisdiction of the Court because the parties were not in privity at the time of the fire. The petitioner's counsel responded that, by the general words of the Act of Parliament creating the Court, such differences were within the power of the Court. Moreover, Houghton had agreed a lease on reasonable terms (although it was not then concluded what the terms should be) and the petitioner had rebuilt and placed a stack of chimneys in the hole.

For further satisfaction of the Court, William Surflett, Scrivener, testified under oath that Houghton agreed in his presence to let the petitioner have the hole and bid the petitioner to go on with her building. Houghton also said that he would not differ with her about the terms. Surflett further testified that Houghton once asked the petitioner for twenty shillings per annum for the rent, but in Surflett's opinion, the hole was not worth above fifteen shillings per annum. Then Thomas Kentish, Carpenter, testified under oath that the ground would not be worth more than fifteen shillings per annum to a builder.

At this point, Houghton's counsel insisted that the hole was larger than stated and of better value than fifteen shillings. In fact, the next neighbour had offered Houghton £3 per annum for the hole. Walter Browne testified under oath that he had been employed by one Mrs Overman, who then had the interest in the hole.[97] Overman sold the

---

95 The decree contains a blank space before 'Gibbons', likely to insert a first name that was never filled in. Gibbons is undoubtedly the same person who acted as the Town's agent in Decree 4, where his name was rendered as 'Gibbon' — again with no first name given.

96 In Decree 4, Houghton had been represented by Jenner and Bowes. Under modern ethics principles, Jenner could not have so easily sued his former client on a matter related to his prior representation.

97 No first name was given, but it is likely that Mrs Overman was Elizabeth Overman, the widow of Thomas Overman. The Overmans appeared in *Nicolson v. Cressett* (Decree 9), and feature prominently in *Ferris v. Cressett* (Decree 36), and *Marshall v. Overman* (Decree 38). According to Decree 36, after Thomas Overman died, Elizabeth remarried John Cressett. In Decree 36, Browne testified that he was in Elizabeth Cressett's employment. Decree 36 involved property leased to James Lane (perhaps the petitioner's deceased husband) in Three Crown Court.

interest to Houghton to make a claim for her. Browne was informed that the hole was eight feet long and four feet wide. Then John Vanbenden testified under oath that he lived in the adjoining house and that he would give £3 for the hole in order to make a stove.

Having heard the allegations and evidence, the Court decreed it was most just and reasonable that, having the inheritance of the petitioner's house, it was to the great convenience of the Town of Shrewsbury to have this piece of ground. It should therefore pay Houghton £20 for the whole 500-year residue of the term that he had in the hole. The Town should then make a sixty-year lease to petitioner of the hole at the annual rent of fifteen shillings.

The Court ordered that:

(1) By the feast of the Annunciation of the Blessed Virgin Mary 1678, the Town of Shrewsbury was to pay £20 to Mark Houghton for Houghton's full interest in the hole. Houghton must accept the same and by good conveyances in law must convey and assure to the Town his interest. The Town must bear the cost of the conveyance.

(2) On payment of the £20, the Town should lawfully, peaceably and quietly enjoy the hole for the residue of the term of 500 years, notwithstanding any other interests.

(3) As between the Town and the petitioner Anne Lane, after the conveyance of the land, the Town must execute a good and sufficient lease of the hole for a term of sixty years, commencing on the feast of the Nativity of St John the Baptist 1677 at the yearly rent of fifteen shillings, payable quarterly. The lease should contain reasonable and usual covenants. The petitioner must accept the lease and deliver up the counterpart.

(4) The petitioner should lawfully, peaceably and quietly enjoy the hole for the term of sixty years, notwithstanding any other interest.

Decree 27 (page 119)

19 Dec. 1677. Baron Littleton; Justice Windham (s); Justice Jones (s); Sir Thomas Bludworth; Thomas Barker, Esq.; Richard How, Esq.; John Freeman, Esq. (s); John Appellbe, Esq.

Robert Taynton, Executor of Edmond Geary late of Southwark, Innholder, v. John Collett of the Middle Temple London, Esq.

In about 1667, Edmond Geary took an assignment of a lease from Thomas Collett and his wife to Joseph Rotheram. The leased property was a messuage or inn called the White Hart. By accident, the back part of the inn burned down in 1669. The petitioner was informed that Thomas Collett and his wife made no allowance for the rebuilding and repair. The rebuilding cost Geary about £700, to Geary's almost utter undoing. On 21 October 1670, Geary took a new lease of the inn from Thomas Collett (father of John Collett, who now claimed the premises) and his wife. The lease ran from the feast of St Michael the Archangel 1670 for twenty-one years at an annual rent of £55.

The premises burned down in the fire in 1676, at which point Geary had about fifteen years left in his lease. With the help of his friends, Geary erected and built a large messuage or inn and tenements on the ground of the old inn, expending more than £2,400. After Geary died, the petitioner made several applications to John Collett for reasonable encouragement and recompense. Collett refused, pretending that Geary had made an agreement concerning the rebuilding yet refused to disclose it. Rather, Collett insisted that the petitioner take a lease according to a draft that Collett sent to the petitioner. This draft contained many hard and unreasonable conditions, as well as no recompense for rebuilding. It did, however, provide an addition to the term in being. The petitioner conceived that he ought not be obliged to honour this agreement.

A summons to the defendant was issued. Both the petitioner and the defendant appeared personally. Mr Jenner and Mr Ward appeared for the petitioner, and Sir George Jeffreys and Mr Bowes for the defendant.

The petitioner's counsel prayed reasonable terms in view of the great expense in rebuilding the inn. The defendant's counsel told the Court that the defendant had treated with Geary regarding terms for encouragement. They had come to an absolute agreement in the presence of John Oliver, one of the three surveyors of the City of London appointed after the Great Fire. Geary rebuilt the inn pursuant to this agreement.

At that point, John Oliver testified under oath that he was present when the agreement was made. Oliver reduced the agreement to writing, subscribed his name and gave copies to both parties. The defendant produced a copy in court, and Oliver agreed that that it was the parties' agreement.

The agreement, dated 29 May 1676, was between Collett and Geary for the rebuilding of the White Hart Inn. Geary's term was be made up to sixty-one years at the old yearly rent of £55 — save for the first year, when the rent was a peppercorn. The rent was due quarterly, with the first payment for the Midsummer quarter to be paid on the feast of St Michael the Archangel 1677. The rebuilding was to be accomplished according to a ground draft drawn by Oliver and the inn to be rebuilt at the second rate as described in the Act of Parliament for building in London.[98] Geary was to pay nothing for the rent due at Midsummer 1676.

The petitioner's counsel alleged that this agreement was very hard on the builder, as it provided only an increase in term of years for an expenditure of £2,400.

Nonetheless, Collett insisted that the petitioner take this lease with its very hard covenants. Collett informed the Court that he had insisted on no covenants other than those to which Geary had agreed, even though the covenants were not expressed in writing. He asked Oliver, on his oath, whether this was not true. Oliver said that he could not testify on his oath whether the parties agreed what covenants the lease should contain: it had been a long time since the agreement was made and he did not mention any covenants in his writing.

The petitioner's counsel then prayed that, for the petitioner's security, the Court decree a new term according to the agreement but that the most unreasonable covenants be discharged. In particular, the covenant that the inn could not be turned or converted into tenements should be voided, because a considerable part of the inn was now built into tenements. Next, the covenant that the inn should not stand void or be shut up should be removed because it might not be in the petitioner's power to hinder. Finally, the petitioner wanted a term permitting the petitioner, at the end of the lease, to remove items mentioned in a schedule attached to the lease.

After debate, and in order further to corroborate the agreement, the Court thought it fit that as much of the inn as was new built as tenements should continue in that use and that the covenant against tenements should be construed to apply only to the part of the rebuilt premises now used as an inn. In addition, the covenant that the inn not stand void or be shut up should be wholly discharged. At the end of the sixty-one-year term, the petitioner should also have liberty to remove items listed on the schedule. Collett should execute a new lease to commence at the expiration of the present lease with the present lease's covenants, except as the Court's decree provided.

The Court ordered that:

---

98 After the Great Fire of London, Parliament not only passed legislation to create the London fire court, but it also enacted specifications for new building in London. 18 and 19 Car. 2, c. 8 (1667) (Eng.), reprinted in *Statutes of the Realm*, v, p. 603. There were four types, or rates, of building permitted, with regulations for the number of storeys, trim and so on applicable to buildings of each rate. William

(1)   The lease to the petitioner Robert Taynton was to be made up to sixty-one years from the feast of the Nativity of St John the Baptist 1676 by adding forty-five and three-quarter years to the present lease, with the term to commence immediately after the expiration of the present lease on the feast of St Michael the Archangel 1691.

(2)   The rent was to be one peppercorn for the first year of the sixty-one-year term and £55 for the next sixty years, payable at the days and times as the present lease required.

(3)   So much of the inn as then built into tenements might continue to be so employed. The covenant restraining the inn from being converted into tenements should be construed to apply only to the part of the new building that was used as an inn.

(4)   The covenant that the inn should not stand void was discharged.

(5)   At the end of the sixty-one-year term, the petitioner might remove the things contained on the schedule annexed to the present lease.

(6)   To avoid difficulties in recovering the rent and for ascertaining the covenants to be performed, Collett, on the petitioner's reasonable request and at his expense, must execute a good and sufficient lease by indenture. The lease should contain the covenants of the present lease, except as those covenants were altered by this decree. A schedule of the items contained in the present lease should be annexed to the new lease. The petitioner must accept the lease and deliver up the counterpart.

(7)   The petitioner might lawfully, peaceably and quietly enjoy the premises notwithstanding any other interest — except that Collett had free leave to make use of so much of the walls belonging to the inn and tenements lying on the north side of Three Crane Court as needed to make a party wall. Collett had leave and licence to build against and stop up the lights and windows in the wall, except for the two stairways' lights and the gable end lights already made. Collett also had leave to make use of a watercourse at the east end of Three Crane Court, which ran through the inn, according to the agreement by indenture between Geary and Collett, dated 28 April 1677.[99]

Morgan's map (see Frontispiece) shows the White Hart, numbered 112, on the east side of the High Street.

99   The portion of the decree that includes these exceptions is written in a slightly smaller hand that squeezes the text into the space above the judge's signatures. Given that there was no discussion of these matters in the body of the

Decree 28 (page 124)

19 Dec. 1677.   Baron Littleton; Justice Windham (s); Sir Thomas
                  Bludworth (s); Thomas Barker, Esq. (s); James Reading,
                  Esq. (s); John Freeman, Esq. (s); John Appellbe, Esq.

*Edmund Debnam, Citizen and Ironmonger of London, v. Mary Body of
the parish of St Mary Magdalen in Bermonsey,*[100] *Widow; Harry Casson
of London, Gentleman;*[101] *Richard Lloyd, Gentleman;*[102] *William Bright,
Citizen and Goldsmith of London; and Thomas Chander*[103] *and John
Stevens of the City of Westminster, Carpenters*

The petitioner is informed that the following parties were 'copartners'
in the inheritance of a premises: William Romney and Mary his wife;
Thomas Cason, Esquire, as father and guardian of the bodies, lands,
goods and chattels of Harry Cason and Thomas Cason; and Thomas
Thicknes, Gentleman. By indenture of lease dated 11 January 1661,
these parties demised to Roger Askew, Citizen and Merchant Taylor
of London, all the messuage or tenement, containing several rooms,
that was then in the tenure and possession of Askew. The lease ran for
twenty-three years from the feast of the Annunciation of the Blessed
Virgin Mary 1661 at the yearly rent of £18, payable in thirds to the three
lessors named above. Located on the west side of the High Street near
the Market, the messuage was a corner house on Fowl Lane.[104]

By lawful ways and means, Askew's interest came to be vested in Elianor
Stockholme, widow. By indenture of assignment dated 7 February
1668, in consideration of a payment of £40, Stockholme assigned her
interest in the lease to the petitioner. The lessors' inheritance of the
premises was now claimed by Mary Body, Mary Cason, Richard Lloyd
and William Bright.[105]

---

decree, the reservations seem to be a later addition that may have reflected other
terms to which Geary had agreed and which Collett was keen to memorialize in the
agreement.

100 'Bermonsey' is the rendering in the decree.

101 The body of the decree refers to this defendant as 'Cason', as does the next
decree. I use 'Cason' hereafter.

102 The decree does not list the place of Lloyd's residence.

103 The body of the decree refers to this defendant as 'Chandler', as does the
next decree. I use 'Chandler' hereafter.

104 Although usually rendering it as 'Fowle Lane', the registrar spelled the street
as 'Foule Lane' in this decree. I have used the modern 'Fowl Lane' throughout.

105 The decree refers to these four individuals as 'abovenamed'. Other than
Mary Cason, they were all named as defendants in the caption. But neither the
caption nor the decree had previously mentioned Mary Cason. Her relationship to

The messuage burned down. Soon afterwards, to better preserve his trade, the petitioner built a shed on the premises. He paid a rent of £9 per annum to the 'aforesaid persons interested' [i.e. Body, Cason, Lloyd and Bright]. The petitioner was very desirous to rebuild the messuage and keep his trade in the same place, and he wished reasonable encouragement through an increase of years and abatement of rent. But the interested persons refused. The petitioner was lately informed that they instead made an agreement with Chandler and Stevens to rebuild on the petitioner's property and some adjoining ground, notwithstanding the six years remaining on the petitioner's term and his willingness to rebuild.

Summonses to the defendants were issued. The petitioner appeared personally, as did all of the defendants except Richard Lloyd; Bright appeared on his behalf. The petitioner's counsel was Sir George Jeffreys. Mr Jenner was the defendants' counsel.

The petitioner's counsel informed the Court that the petitioner was very willing to rebuild so he might continue in his place of trade. He asked for an increase of years and an abatement of rent.

The defendants' counsel informed the Court that, soon after the fire, the petitioner came to an agreement with the defendants, under which he had the liberty to build a shed at the annual rent of £9. But the petitioner was to give possession to the landlords on six-months' notice, so that the defendants could either rebuild themselves or let the ground to rebuild. The defendants treated with several persons to take their entire ground lying at Fowl Lane end, which is a large piece (of which the petitioner's piece is the corner part next to the High Street). At length they agreed with Chandler and Stevens[106] on a term of fifty-one years at a rent of £54 per annum. It is not reasonable for the petitioner to rebuild because it would spoil the design of letting all the ground together. The defendants' counsel prayed for a determination of the petitioner's interest.

The petitioner then denied that he had ever agreed to quit possession on six-months' notice, affirming that he always intended to rebuild. Several witnesses were examined under oath on both sides of the matter, as well as Bright, Body and the petitioner.

others in the case is unclear. I suspect a scrivener's error: the registrar had intended to write 'Harry Cason' but, having just written 'Mary Body', repeated 'Mary' before 'Cason' by mistake.

106 Here the decree rendered the name as 'Stephens', not 'Stevens'. I used 'Stevens' throughout.

The Court was not fully satisfied, but pronounced it expedient that the landlords pay the petitioner £20 for his interest. The petitioner was also allowed to keep his shed on the premises until the feast of the Annunciation of the Blessed Virgin Mary 1678, paying the annual rent of £9 until then. On the payment of £20 by that date, he must remove the shed and quit possession.

The Court ordered that:

(1) On or before the feast of the Annunciation of the Blessed Virgin Mary 1678, the petitioner Edmund Debnam was to remove his shed and quit possession to Body, Cason, Lloyd and Bright (or their tenants or assigns).

(2) Until he quit possession, the petitioner must pay the rent of £9 per annum according to the agreement.

(3) On removal of the shed, Body, Cason, Lloyd and Bright must immediately pay the petitioner £20. The petitioner must accept this amount and surrender the lease to be cancelled, with the defendants delivering up the counterpart for cancellation.

(4) On this payment, the petitioner's interest in the premises would cease and be absolutely discharged. Body, Cason, Lloyd and Bright, and their tenants and assigns, may then enter the ground and quietly and peaceably enjoy it, and may rebuild at their pleasures without any hindrance from the petitioner or those claiming an interest under the petitioner's lease.

Decree 29 (page 127)

19 Dec. 1677.   Baron Littleton; Justice Windham (s); Justice Jones (s); Sir Thomas Bludworth (s); Thomas Barker, Esq. (s); James Reading, Esq. (s); Richard How, Esq. (s); Peter Rich, Esq. (s); John Freeman, Esq. (s); John Appellbe, Esq.

Thomas Chandler and John Stevens of the City of Westminster, Carpenters, v. Mary Body of the parish of St Mary Magdalen in Bermondsey, Widow; Harry Casson of London, Gentleman;[107] *William Bright, Citizen and Goldsmith; and Richard Lloyd, Gentleman*[108]

---

107 The body of the decree referred to this defendant as 'Cason', as had the prior decree. I use 'Cason' hereafter.

108 As in the prior decree, this decree did not list the place of Lloyd's residence. It also did not list Bright's residence, which the prior decree had given as London. This decree did, however, correctly spell Bermondsey.

The defendants Body, Cason, Bright and Lloyd were seised of an inheritance in divers messuages or tenements in or near the south side of Fowl Lane. These premises were in the several tenures or occupations of Edmund Debnam, Thomas Radford, Richard Wells, […] Ingram, Thomas Berry, Widow Coffey, Charles Austin and several others.[109] Two fronted the High Street and others extended westward about 192 feet. All burned down in the fire.

The tenants in possession of the messuages refused to rebuild and surrendered their leases. Not being willing to rebuild themselves but minded to dispose of the ground for rebuilding, Body, Cason, Bright and Lloyd came to agreement with the petitioners. The agreement provided that the petitioner should have a term of fifty-one years in the tofts and grounds, commencing on the feast of the birth of our Lord 1677. The rent was one peppercorn for the first three-quarters of a year and £54 for the residue of the term. The petitioners were to rebuild the premises in brick after the rate and manner of houses thereabouts before the feast of the birth of our Lord 1679. The front houses were to be of the height and number of storeys of houses of the second rate in London.[110] The agreement also required the parties to appear in court and consent to any decree made by this Court.

Summonses to the defendants were issued. The petitioners were present in court; Mr Jenner was their counsel. Body, Cason and Bright personally appeared, with Bright also appearing on behalf of Lloyd.

The petitioners' counsel prayed for a decree to corroborate the parties' agreement. The defendants consented.

The Court ordered that:

(1) The petitioners Thomas Chandler and John Stevens[111] were to have a term of fifty-one years in the tofts and grounds of the various burned messuages or tenements, commencing on the feast of the birth of our Lord 1677.

(2) The rent to be paid to Body, Cason, Bright and Lloyd was one peppercorn for the first three-quarters of a year and £54, payable quarterly in equal portions, for the residue of fifty and one quarter years.

109 A blank was left before the name 'Ingram' (presumably to insert a first name at a later date), and no first name was given for Widow Coffey.

110 On the meaning of 'second rate', see p. 179, note 98.

111 The name 'Stevens' was rendered here as 'Stephens', although it is rendered as 'Stevens' elsewhere in the decree (as well as in the caption). I used 'Stevens' throughout.

(3) By the feast of the birth of our Lord 1679, and at their cost, the petitioners must erect and rebuild messuages or tenements with brick and other good and sufficient materials after the rate and manner of houses thereabouts, with the front houses to be the height and number of storeys as houses of the second rate of building in London.

(4) To avoid difficulties in recovering the rent and for ascertaining the covenants mutually to be performed, on the petitioners' reasonable request and at their expense, Body, Cason, Bright and Lloyd must execute a good and sufficient lease by indenture. The petitioners must accept the lease and deliver up the counterpart.

(5) The petitioners may lawfully, peaceably and quietly enjoy the premises notwithstanding any other interest.

Decree 30 (page 131)

9 Jan. 1678. Baron Littleton; Justice Wyndham (s); Sir William Hayward (s);[112] Sir Thomas Allen (s); Thomas Barker, Esq. (s); James Reading, Esq. (s); Richard How, Esq. (s); Peter Rich, Esq. (s); John Freeman, Esq. (s); John Appellbe, Esq.

Mary Sledd of Southwark, Widow Relict of William Sledd her Husband, v. Oliver Gregory, Gentleman

Oliver Gregory v. Mary Sledd (Cross-Petition)

Michael Hart of Southwark, Citizen and Goldsmith of London, was interested and possessed for a long term of years in the Talbot Inn and other buildings adjoining. By indenture of lease dated 13 December 1654, in consideration of £40, Hart demised to William Sledd the shed or stable lying at the back side of the Talbot Inn and adjoining the Inn's stable. The lease also included a piece of ground lying behind the kitchen of the Talbot Inn; this ground ran from the corner of the shed where the pump then stood to the corner of the little chamber in the back yard. Under the lease, Sledd had free liberty of ingress, egress and regress for horses and carts through the gates and foreyards of the Talbot during lawful and seasonable hours. The lease ran from the feast of the birth of our Lord 1654 for twenty-eight and a half years at the annual rent of one peppercorn for eight years and £5 per annum for the residue of twenty and a half years. The rent was payable semi-annually,

---

112 Histories sometimes render this name as 'Hawarde'. He signed the decrees as 'Haward'. Per my usual convention, I render the name as the registrar did.

on the feast of the Annunciation of the Blessed Virgin Mary and the feast of St Michael the Archangel.

After taking the lease, William Sledd erected a messuage which cost £300. In view of Sledd's great cost of repairing and building his premises, Hart covenanted with Sledd by an indenture dated 4 November 1658. At that time, Hart was considering whether to renew his lease of the Talbot or to purchase the inheritance. Hart and Sledd agreed that, if Hart should either renew the Talbot lease for at least twenty-one years or purchase the inheritance of the Talbot, Hart would grant Sledd a further term of twenty-one years at the existing rent. If Hart did not renew the lease or purchase the inheritance, then Sledd could take the lease himself or purchase the inheritance.[113]

Oliver Gregory recently purchased the inheritance of the Talbot Inn and of the premises demised to Sledd.

The messuage and buildings erected by Sledd burned down in the fire. The stable did not. William Sledd and Michael Hart were both recently deceased, and Sledd's interest in the premises was now vested in the petitioner, Sledd's widow. The petitioner was very desirous to rebuild the messuage through the addition of a considerable term of years, but Gregory absolutely refused to grant any encouragement.

A summons to the defendant was issued. Both the petitioner and the defendant appeared personally. Sir George Jeffreys and Mr Jenner represented the petitioner, and Mr Bowes, Mr Ward and Mr Reading represented the defendant.

The defendant's counsel opened the proceedings by asking that the defendant's cross-petition be read at this point. The petitioner's counsel opposed this request, stating that the defendant had not summoned the petitioner. The Court nonetheless ordered the cross-petition to be read. The cross-petition stated, in effect, that Gregory had received a summons in July from William Sledd. Given his intention to rebuild, Gregory, represented by counsel, attended the Court and delivered his

---

113   The decree's language is ambiguous: whether, in the event that Hart did not renew the lease or purchase the inheritance of the Talbot, Sledd could then take over the lease (or purchase the inheritance) of the entire Talbot, or rather take over the lease (or purchase the inheritance) only of Sledd's sublet premises. It is also unclear how this agreement between Hart and Sledd could give Sledd enforceable rights against Hart's landlord, who held the reversion in both the Talbot and the sublet premises. My best understanding is that, if Hart did not extend his lease or purchase the Talbot, Sledd was free to pursue with Hart's landlord either a new lease of the sublet premises or a purchase of the landlord's interest in the premises. In any event, the agreement between Hart and Sledd never came to fruition, although it coloured Mary Sledd's claim to be the rebuilder of her premises.

petition to the Court. The petition showed that Gregory was willing to give Sledd whatever satisfaction the Court thought fit in return for Sledd's surrender of the lease. The Court then adjourned until October with the cause not being heard. Given the necessity of rebuilding a stable for the inn, Gregory treated with Mrs Susan Palmer, who was the relict of John Palmer, the subtenant of William Sledd. Mrs Palmer agreed to surrender her lease in order to allow for the better enlargement of Gregory's new building. Relying on the justice of this Court, Gregory then built one stable for the use of the inn and another for Mrs Palmer. William Sledd now being dead, the cross-petition requested that a summons be issued to Mrs Sledd.

At this point, Sledd's counsel informed the Court of her earnest desire to rebuild the messuage and other buildings. The use of these buildings was necessary to carry on of her late husband's trade as an ironmonger, a trade that she was now following. She was unable to manage the trade without the buildings. Counsel therefore prayed the Court to provide reasonable encouragement.

Gregory's counsel much opposed any terms for Sledd, alleging that Gregory had agreed with Mrs Palmer, an undertenant, to take her interest; and Gregory had already built on this ground. Sledd's building on other parts of the ground would be very inconvenient to the inn in many respects — chiefly because William Sledd's former building was prejudicial to the lights of the inn. Gregory's rebuilding of the inn is much 'streightned'[114] for want of ground. Therefore, counsel insisted that the Court determine Sledd's interest, so that Gregory, who had the inheritance of the premises and also of the inn, might improve the whole to his best advantage. This result was especially warranted because Mary Sledd had but a short term yet to come in the lease. In fact, because William Sledd had subleased part of the premises to Mrs Palmer for £6 10s. per annum — while having paid only £5 per annum for the entire premises — he was already a sufficient gainer; if she surrendered the lease now, Mary Sledd would have no loss.

Sledd's counsel responded that, after William Sledd took the lease, he built chiefly for the accommodation of his trade with warehouse rooms. Mary Sledd could not now part with this ground because she had not sufficient convenience without it. The inn could be accommodated without the addition of the new ground, as it had been before Gregory

---

114 In modern English, the inventively spelling 'streightned' could be 'straightened', 'straitened' or 'strained'. In context, the best fit is 'straitened' (in the sense of '[c]ontracted, narrowed; insufficiently spacious', see *Oxford English Dictionary* (2009), definition 1.a).

purchased it. William Sledd was burned out in the fire and suffered a great loss, and the present lease still had five and a half years to run. Therefore, Sledd should have the benefit of the Act of Parliament in having the privilege of rebuilding, as other tenants had. Because Gregory obtained the interest in the Palmer lease and had rebuilt on it, Mary Sledd would be content for him to enjoy that parcel if she could have a considerable term in the residue of the demised premises at a proportional part of the rent.

Having heard the matter fully debated as well and hearing the allegations of counsel on the value of the land that had been let to John Palmer, the Court thought it just and reasonable that Gregory hold the part of the premises demised to John Palmer and that Gregory should be discharged of the rent of £6 10s., as well as all arrears. Mary Sledd should then be the rebuilder of the residue of the premises, with a sixty-year term, commencing on the feast of the birth of our Lord 1677, at the yearly rent of £3 10s. The first payment would be due on the feast of the Nativity of St John the Baptist 1678. Sledd should also be discharged of any arrears of rent from the fire until the feast of the Annunciation of the Blessed Virgin Mary 1678. Gregory should execute a new lease that contained covenants for passage as in the former lease and other usual covenants.

After the Court pronounced this order, Gregory and his counsel informed the Court that it should order Mary Sledd to build in a way that would not be prejudicial to the inn, as long as it did not prejudice her own building. In fact, the petitioner might conveniently exchange some of the ground she had for some of the ground of the inn and thus accommodate both parties. Gregory's counsel prayed the Court to order the same and also to restrain Sledd from building a common brewhouse.

Being willing to further any accommodation between the parties, the Court declared it reasonable to refer the matter to Thomas Barker and John Freeman, esquires — two of the Court's commissioners now present — to see if the parties could do so. They might direct how the building could be done for the convenience of both parties and might make an exchange of ground that accommodated both parties, with neither being prejudiced thereby.

The Court also thought it reasonable to restrain Mary Sledd from building a public brewhouse.

The Court ordered that:

(1)   On the reasonable request of Oliver Gregory and at his expense, the petitioner Mary Sledd must assign her right and interest in the premises demised to John Palmer, now in the possession of

Gregory and Susan Palmer. Gregory may lawfully, peaceably and quietly hold these premises free from any claims by the petitioner or any person claiming under her or William Sledd.

(2) Gregory was discharged from paying the annual rent of £6 10s. for these premises, and from all arrears and covenants.

(3) The petitioner was discharged from paying any rent incurred since the fire for the premises leased by William Sledd. She was also discharged from any covenants under the lease.

(4) The petitioner was to have a total term of sixty years in the premises leased by William Sledd (except for the parcel with stables demised to John Palmer). The term was to commence on the feast of the birth of our Lord 1677.

(5) The petitioner must pay Gregory one peppercorn for the first quarter of a year (if it be demanded); £3 10s. per annum, payable quarterly, for the ensuing fifty-nine years of the lease; and proportionally according to the same rate for the last three-quarters of a year. The first quarterly payment of the £3 10s. annual rent would be due on the feast of the Nativity of St John the Baptist 1678.

(6) At her cost and with all convenient speed — or at least within the space of two years — the petitioner must erect a good and substantial messuage on some part of the ground for her best accommodation and convenience, so long as the building does not stop up or prejudice any windows, lights, easements or watercourses that belonged to the Talbot Inn before the fire. The messuage was to be built with brick and other good and sufficient materials and finished in good workmanlike manner. At least £250 must be spent in rebuilding.

(7) The petitioner must not convert the messuage into a common brewhouse during the lease, and must repair, maintain and support the messuage.

(8) To avoid difficulties in recovering the rent and for ascertaining the covenants mutually to be performed, on the petitioners' reasonable request and at her expense, Gregory must execute a good and sufficient lease by indenture decreed to the petitioner. The lease should contain a covenant for passage through the inn like the covenant in the lease made to William Sledd, as well as covenants to repair and support and not to convert any of the premises into a common brewhouse. It should also contain other reasonable and usual covenants. The petitioner must accept the lease and deliver up its counterpart.

(9)   The petitioner might lawfully, peaceably and quietly enjoy the premises notwithstanding any other interest.

Decree 31 (page 137)

9 Jan. 1678.   Baron Littleton; Justice Wyndham (s); Sir William Hayward (s); Thomas Barker, Esq. (s); James Reading, Esq. (s); Peter Rich, Esq. (s); John Freeman, Esq. (s); John Appellbe, Esq.

Mary Duffeild of Southwark, Widow, v. Robert Smith of Staple Inn, London, Gentleman; Richard How, Esquire; and Thomas Lowfeild of London, Mercer[115]

Edward Bushell of London, Merchant, and John Maddox, Citizen and Goldsmith of London, were interested and possessed of a messuage or inn for a term of years unknown to the petitioner. This interest had been granted them by the right Honourable Lord Ward,[116] who was seised in fee. The premises were known by the sign of the King's Head and were located on the east side of the High Street.

By indenture of lease dated 16 April 1659, Bushell and Maddox demised to Miles Fleetwood, Citizen and Haberdasher of London, the messuage or inn, together with all cellars and other chambers, rooms, lights, easements, gardens, stables, buildings, commodities and appurtenances. The lease was for twenty years from the feast of the Annunciation of the Blessed Virgin Mary 1659 at an annual rent of £60, payable quarterly. The lease contained a covenant, among others, obligating the tenant to repair the premises.

By good and sufficient assignment in the law, Fleetwood's interest came to John Duffeild, the petitioner's late husband. On his death, the petitioner, as sole executrix of the will, became interested in the property.

115   It is possible that this Thomas Lowfeild is the same person described as an infant with a contingent reversionary interest in the various Browker suits (Decrees 8, 10–15, 47–49 and 50–51). But they are likely different individuals. After Richard How's death, an assignment from How's widow and administratrix recited that Thomas Lowfeild, Mercer, had married How's daughter, Elizabeth. See West Sussex Record Office WISTON/4880. It seems unlikely that the *Browker* decrees would list Thomas Lowfeild as an infant if he were of age and already admitted to membership in the Worshipful Company of Mercers. For this reason, I list the Thomas Lowfeild mentioned in this decree separately in the Index of Persons.

116   Presumably Humble Ward, the 1st Baron Ward (*c.* 1614–70). Ward, the son of William Ward, jeweller to Queen Henrietta Maria, married Frances Sutton, 6th Baroness Dudley, and was created Lord Ward in 1644.

The Great Fire of London had raised the value of the premises. A few years after the Fire, Robert Smith, who had become interested in the premises from and under the lessors Bushell and Maddox,[117] demised the premises to the petitioner by indenture of lease dated 22 February 1672. The lease ran from the feast of the Annunciation of the Blessed Virgin Mary 1679 (the expiration of the original lease) for ten and a half years at the annual rent of £66, payable quarterly. As additional consideration, the petitioner paid Smith £144 10s., as well as £6 per annum paid yearly, commencing on the feast of the birth of our Lord 1671, for seven years.

The premises burned down. Since then, Smith, with the assistance of the petitioner's son and upon Smith's promise to the son that the petitioner should have an equal share of the benefit, purchased the fee simple of the tofts and grounds from Lord Ward on advantageous terms. Smith mortgaged the property or made some other estate to Richard How and Thomas Lowfeild (or one of them).

The petitioner treated several times with Smith for terms to encourage rebuilding the inn, and Smith made several fair promises that the petitioner should have good terms from him and reap part of the advantage of the purchase. As a result, the petitioner began rebuilding and laid out a considerable sum. Now Smith utterly refused to grant the petitioner any encouragement, but would exact the full rent and cast the whole loss on the petitioner.

Summonses to the defendants were issued. John Duffeild, son of the petitioner, appeared for her. Mr Jenner was her counsel. All the defendants appeared personally. Sir George Jeffreys and Mr Reading were counsel for Smith and Lowfeild.

The petitioner's counsel stated that the parties had continued to treat with each other about rebuilding and finishing the inn and had come to an agreement. Counsel produced the written agreement. Smith and Lowfeild agreed to demise to the petitioner the toft of ground on which the King's Head had formerly stood, as well as all buildings built or to be built on that ground. The lease ran for sixty-one years from the feast of the Annunciation of the Blessed Virgin Mary 1677. The annual rent was to be £38, payable quarterly, from the feast of the Annunciation of the Blessed Virgin Mary 1678, with the first quarterly payment due on the feast of the Nativity of St John the Baptist 1678.

---

117 The decree does not say whether Smith obtained all of the Bushell's and Maddox's interest as landlord or merely a portion sufficient to grant petitioner the subsequently described ten-year extension on the lease.

The lease contained the usual covenants. The hostelry[118] and warehouse were excepted from the demise, and the petitioner was to demise her interest in the warehouse to Smith and allow him to receive all rent due from Henry Bartlett[119] for the warehouse. The agreement was dated 1 January 1678, and was signed by Smith, Lowfeild and the petitioner.

The writing was left with the registrar of the Court, and the petitioner's counsel prayed the Court to decree terms according to the agreement. The defendants' counsel consented.

The Court ordered that:

(1) The petitioner Mary Duffeild was acquitted and discharged of the annual rent of £60, as well as the additional annual £6 rent due to Smith, from the feast of the Annunciation of the Blessed Virgin Mary 1676 until the feast of the Annunciation of the Blessed Virgin Mary 1678.

(2) At that point, the rents of £6 and £60 were reduced to a yearly rent of £38 for the residue of the lease, notwithstanding any reservations, considerations, or covenants in the prior leases.

(3) The lease was to be made up to sixty-one years from the feast of the Annunciation of the Blessed Virgin Mary 1677 by adding a term of forty-eight and a half years to commence immediately after the end of the present lease, which is due to expire on the feast of St Michael the Archangel 1689.

(4) The annual rent was to be £38, payable to whoever held the right to the rent, payable from the feast of the Annunciation of the Blessed Virgin Mary 1678 for the residue of the present lease and the forty-eight and a half years of the extended lease. Payment was due quarterly, at the times described in the lease.

(5) Excepted from this lease were (a) a parcel of ground on which stood a building called the Ostry, which was granted to Thomas Kentish[120] and (b) a parcel of ground where there lately stood

118 This word is rendered as both 'hostry' and 'ostry' at various points in the decree. In modern parlance, a 'hostelry' refers to an inn, but in this context the word appears to refer just to the stables where the hostler cared for the horses of the inn's guests. It would make little sense for the petitioner to cede the right to operate the King's Head Inn in view of the transactions described in the decree.

119 A man named Henry Bartlett is mentioned as one of the multitude of defendants in the principal encroachment case (Decree 45), and a Henry Bartlett, Grocer, is also mentioned in *Sledd v. Browker* (Decree 47). It is likely that the references are all to the same person, so I grouped all the references to Bartlett under a single heading in the Index of Persons.

120 Kentish, a Carpenter, testified in *Lane v. Mayor of Shrewsbury* (Decree 26), and in *Hudson v. Mayor of London* (Decree 33).

a building called Darbyes' Warehouse, which was granted to Henry Bartlett.

(6) In consideration of the abatement of rent and increased term, the petitioner must at her cost new build and finish a good and substantial messuage or inn and all other buildings necessarily belonging to it, with good and sufficient materials and in a workmanlike manner. The portions of ground excluded from the lease were excepted from this order.

(7) To avoid difficulties in recovering the rent and for ascertaining the covenants mutually to be performed, on the petitioners' reasonable request and at her expense, Smith and Lowfeild must execute a good and sufficient lease for the forty-eight and a half years by indenture decreed to the petitioner. The lease should contain reasonable covenants as are contained in the present lease. The petitioner must accept the lease and deliver up its counterpart.

(8) Except as noted, the petitioner might lawfully, peaceably and quietly enjoy the premises notwithstanding any other interest.

(9) On the reasonable request of Smith and at his cost, the petitioner must by deed in writing assign to Smith the right, title and interest in the parcel of ground where Darbyes' Warehouse stood and must permit Smith to receive all rent due from Robert Bartlett[121] for these premises.

Decree 32 (page 142)

9 Jan. 1678.   Baron Littleton; Justice Wyndham (s); Sir Thomas Allen (s); Sir William Hayward (s); Thomas Barker, Esq. (s); James Reading, Esq. (s); Richard How, Esq. (s);[122] Peter Rich, Esq. (s); John Freeman, Esq. (s); John Appellbe, Esq.

William Eyre of London, Gentleman, v. Mayor, Commonalty, and Citizens of the City of London

By indenture of lease dated 25 October 1664, the City of London, under its seal, demised to the petitioner all the messuage or tenement

---

121 'Robert' is likely an error. Earlier the possessor of this parcel had been identified as 'Henry' Bartlett. The registrar likely confused the defendant Robert Smith, whose name he had just written, with Henry Bartlett.

122 How had sat on the Court for *Sledd v. Gregory* (Decree 30), stepped aside for *Duffeild v. Smith* (Decree 31), where he was a named defendant but otherwise seemed disinterested in the case. He returned to the Court here and for later cases the same day — except for *May v. How* (Decree 34), and *Kendall v. Penn* (Decree 35), where he was again a defendant.

known as the Compter in Southwark, as well as one other adjoining tenement in the occupation of John Gawton. The lease ran for ninety-nine years, if the petitioner should live so long and continue as Bailiff of the Liberties and Manors of Southwark and the keeper of the gaol and prison called the Compter. The yearly rent was £50, payable half-yearly. In addition to other covenants, the lease contained the usual covenants for the petitioner to repair and uphold the premises.

Also included was a proviso that, if the rent of £50 (or any part of it) should remain unpaid for twenty-eight days, or if the petitioner should not keep all and singular the covenants, then the lease — as well as the deed of grant of the same date granting the petitioner the offices of Bailiff and Keeper — was void.

The premises burned down in the fire and had not been rebuilt. The petitioner had applied to the Lord Mayor and the Court of Aldermen: since the premises were their public prison belonging to their Liberties in Southwark, the petitioner had requested that the City rebuild the premises and relieve him of the rent and covenants. But the petitioner could not obtain any relief.

A summons was issued. The petitioner appeared personally, with Mr Jenner and Mr Bowes as counsel. Sir George Jeffreys, the City's common serjeant, and Mr Lane,[123] its comptroller, appeared for the City.

The petitioner's counsel stated that the petitioner was not in a position to undertake the rebuilding of the houses, as they were large buildings. He was, however, willing to surrender the lease so the City would be at liberty to rebuild. This task was most properly undertaken by the City, as the building was its public prison, and it would be convenient to have it rebuilt as one.

Counsel for the City stated that the City did not desire a surrender of the lease. The City did not intend to rebuild a prison at this location. It was, however, willing to grant the petitioner reasonable terms for building and would not oblige him to build a new prison. Rather, the petitioner would be at liberty to build as he saw fit for his best advantage.

The petitioner's counsel stated that the petitioner could not undertake the building. In addition, the petitioner had given the City £50, which was one full year of rent, since the fire, notwithstanding

123 No first name is given for Lane, and I have been unable to identify the comptrollers of the City in the 1600s. Thomas Lane, Clothworker, was later alderman (in 1688) and Lord Mayor of London (in 1694), but it is not likely that the Lane mentioned in this case was the same person.

the fact that the premises were lying in ashes. Moreover, the City had enclosed part of the premises and carried away materials. These were sufficient contributions from the petitioner to bear, and he prayed to be discharged from the lease.

Counsel for the City offered to accept surrender of the lease if the petitioner also surrendered the office of bailiff of Southwark, but would not take a surrender of the lease alone. Moreover, counsel for the City did not acknowledge the receipt of the £50 in rent for the past year, suggesting that this payment might have been for arrears from a prior year.

The petitioner then made an oath in court (the City's counsel being desirous that he do so) that he paid the £50 for rent due since the fire and that all rent from the time before the fire was also paid.

Having heard the matter fully debated, the Court thought it most equitable and reasonable for the petitioner to surrender his lease without further contribution, and the petitioner was then discharged of the lease and its covenants. The City could dispose of the ground as it saw fit.

The Court ordered that:

(1) In consideration of £50 paid by the petitioner William Eyre, the petitioner must surrender his lease. The City must accept the surrender without further contribution.

(2) The City must deliver up the counterpart to the lease and also a bond conditioned on the performance of the lease's covenants.

(3) The petitioner was discharged of all arrears, other than what he had paid.

(4) The petitioner's interest was to cease and be absolutely void. The City might enter the premises and rebuild, and might hold and enjoy the premises without interference, molestation or denial by petitioner or any person claiming under him.

Decree 33 (page 145)

9 Jan. 1678.   Baron Littleton; Justice Wyndham (s); Sir Thomas Allen (s); Sir William Hayward (s); Thomas Barker, Esq. (s); James Reading, Esq. (s); Richard How, Esq. (s); Peter Rich, Esq. (s); John Freeman, Esq. (s); John Appellbe, Esq.

Thomas Hudson of Southwark, Scrivener,[124] *v. Mayor, Commonalty, and Citizens of the City of London*

124 Hudson appeared as a witness in *Bankes v. Wight* (Decree 2), and *Nicolson v. Browker* (Decree 8). He was again a petitioner in *Hudson v. Browker* (Decree 48).

Mary Cartwright, widow, and Thomas Cartwright, Grocer, were seised of an estate or inheritance in a messuage. By indenture of lease dated 10 April 1654, they demised the premises to George Gill, who already dwelt there. The lease ran from the feast of the Annunciation of the Blessed Virgin Mary 1654 for twenty-one years. The rent was £10 per annum. The premises, known by the sign of the Castle, were located at or near St Margaret's Hill.

George Gill subsequently died, and Lucy Gill, relict and administratrix of Gill's estate, became interested in the premises for the residue of the lease. Lucy Gill then assigned her interest in the premises to the petitioner.

Mary Cartwright was now dead, and Thomas Cartwright became fully seised in the inheritance. Cartwright had lately conveyed the lessors' interest in the premises (so the petitioner is informed) to the City of London.

The messuage burned down in the fire and still lay in ruins. The petitioner was willing to rebuild on encouragement by means of an abatement of rent and increase in term of years.

A summons was issued. The petitioner appeared personally; Mr Jenner was his counsel. Sir George Jeffreys, the City's common serjeant, and Mr Lane, its comptroller, appeared for the City.

The petitioner's counsel informed the Court that the petitioner had agreed with the undertenant who was in possession of the premises at the time of the fire and therefore wished to rebuild. Counsel prayed for reasonable encouragement.

The City's counsel much opposed any abatement of rent. Counsel alleged that the City had recently purchased the ground, along with adjoining ground. It gave twenty-years purchase as the value of the premises as they had been rented before the fire.[125] The ground of the petitioner's lease alone was worth £10 per annum if it were let to a new contractor.

---

125 'Blank years purchase' was a common way to determine the worth of land at the time of sale or, conversely, to set the rental value of a property. To determine the value of land, the parties would determine the rent presently received and then multiply it by a number of years (often twenty, but more or less valuable land might be based on a lower or higher multiplier) to determine the land's value. Conversely, a landlord who knew the value of the land would set the rate of return (often 5%) desired and multiply the value of the land by this percentage to set the rental price. For a guide to this method of valuation, see Stephen Primatt, *The City and Country Purchaser and Builder* (London, 1667). In part, Primatt wrote the book to assist the judges of the London fire court in setting rental values.

To further satisfy the Court about the value of the ground, John Oliver, one of the surveyors of new buildings for the City of London, made oath that he well knew the ground in question. He believed that the petitioner might receive £10 per cent for his money laid out in building in that place and pay the full rent of £10 per annum for the ground.[126]

The petitioner's counsel alleged that the ground was not as deep as the City's other adjoining ground and was therefore not as good a value in proportion. Thomas Kentish, Carpenter and inhabitant of Southwark, made oath. He was well acquainted with the value of most of the ground and houses in the area. He stated that this ground was shorter than other adjoining parcels that the City held.[127] He did not esteem the ground to be worth above £7 per annum, and he would not give more for it himself.

Having heard the allegations and well considering the evidence, the Court propounded as most just and reasonable that the petitioner should have a term of sixty years from the feast of the birth of our Lord 1677 at the annual rent of £8, to commence on the feast of the Nativity of St John the Baptist 1678, with the first quarter's payment due on the feast of St Michael the Archangel 1678. The petitioner should be discharged of all rent from the fire until that time.

The Court ordered that:

(1) The petitioner Thomas Hudson was discharged of all rent from the time of the fire and any covenants in the existing lease.

(2) The petitioner was to have a term of sixty years in the premises, commencing on the feast of the birth of our Lord 1677.

(3) The rent was to be one peppercorn, if it be demanded, for the first half year and then £8 per annum, payable quarterly in equal portions, for the ensuing fifty-nine years. A proportional amount of rent would be due for the final half year.

(4) The petitioner must, at his cost and with all convenient speed, build another good and substantial messuage of brick and other good and sufficient materials and must finish it in a good and workmanlike manner such as other new-built front houses in Southwark are generally built.

---

126 If I understand Oliver's testimony, a landlord who spent £100 in rebuilding would be justified in charging an annual rent of £20, calculated as 10 per cent of the amount spent rebuilding (or £10) plus £10 for ground rent.

127 The references to this parcel being 'not as deep' and 'shorter' presumably mean that, as measured from the street, the parcel did not extend back as far as adjoining parcels. As a smaller piece of ground, its value would therefore be less than the larger adjacent parcels.

(5)   To avoid difficulties in recovering the rent and for ascertaining
      the covenants mutually to be performed, on the petitioners'
      reasonable request and at his expense, and on surrender of the
      present lease, the City must execute a good and sufficient lease
      by indenture for sixty years. The lease should contain reasonable
      covenants as the City made for newly built houses in and about
      London. The petitioner must accept the lease and deliver up its
      counterpart.

(6)   The petitioner might enjoy the premises notwithstanding any
      other interest.

Decree 34 (page 149)

9 Jan. 1678.   Baron Littleton; Justice Wyndham (s); Sir William
                      Hayward (s); Thomas Barker, Esq. (s); James Reading,
                      Esq. (s); Peter Rich, Esq. (s); John Freeman, Esq. (s);
                      John Appellbe, Esq.

*Richard May of Canterbury, Gentleman, v. Richard How the Elder of
Christ Church and Richard How the Younger, his Son an Infant*

At the time of the fire, Sarah Johnson, widow, was interested in a
messuage and garden on the east side of the High Street. The premises
had formerly been in the occupation of Andrew Kembe, and then
of Thomas Kendall and Stephen Adams, by virtue of a lease made
by Thomas Browker, Esquire,[128] who was seised in fee. Browker was
since deceased. Johnson's interest ran for a long term of years,[129] and it
expired on the feast of St Michael the Archangel 1706. The annual rent
was £10, payable quarterly.

Browker's reversionary interest had been purchased by Richard How
the elder, who later made a settlement of the property on himself for
life and the remainder in tail to Richard How the younger, his infant
son.

The premises burned down. Johnson was willing to undertake the
rebuilding and treated with How for encouragement. They agreed to

---

128 I assume that this is the Thomas Browker who had been described in several
of the *Browker* decrees as residing in Upper Peover — and not his son (Thomas
Browker the elder) or grandson (Thomas Browker the younger). As seen in *Hyland
v. How* (Decree 19), *Hawkes v. How* (Decree 19), *Rushley v. How* (Decree 19), and
Kendall v. Penn (Decree 35), How had purchased Browker's reversionary interest as
landlord in a number of Southwark properties.

129 The decree did not indicate the date of the lease or the exact length of its
term.

increase Johnson's term to ninety-nine years, commencing on the feast of the Annunciation of the Blessed Virgin Mary 1677 at the annual rent of £10.[130]

Subsequently, Johnson's interest became vested by assignment in the petitioner. Because How the elder had only a life estate and How the younger was yet an infant, the petitioner needed a decree of this Court to have a secure estate.

Summonses to the defendants were issued. Mr Jenner appeared as counsel on behalf of the petitioner. How the elder appeared personally, without counsel, on behalf of himself and his son. He was specially admitted as guardian for his son.

The petitioner's counsel prayed that, in consideration of the considerable expense in rebuilding, the Court increase the petitioner's term to ninety-nine years according to the prior agreement. How consented to the new term, commencing on the feast of the Annunciation of the Blessed Virgin Mary 1677, but he also desired that the petitioner hold the lease under the covenants and conditions as were in the existing lease. The petitioner's counsel consented to this request.

The Court ordered that:

(1)   The petitioner Richard May was to have the term of years in the lease made by Thomas Browker increased and made up to ninety-nine years, accounted from the feast of the Annunciation of the Blessed Virgin Mary 1677, by adding sixty-nine and a half years to the present lease. The new term would commence immediately at the end of the present lease, which was to expire on the feast of St Michael the Archangel 1706.

(2)   The yearly rent was £10, payable to How the elder for his life and then to How the younger and his heirs or others to whom the reversion of right belongs. Payment was to be made at such days and times as provided in the present lease.

(3)   To avoid difficulties in recovering the rent and for ascertaining the covenants mutually to be performed, on the petitioners' reasonable request and at her expense, How the elder, as well as How the younger when he reached the age of twenty-one (or such other persons at that point entitled to the reversion) must execute a good and sufficient lease by indenture for the

---

130   This arrangement may be the source of the misunderstanding referred to in Decrees 19–21, where some of How's other tenants believed that he had promised them ninety-nine-year leases.

sixty-nine and a half years decreed to the petitioner. The lease should contain reasonable covenants as were contained in the present lease. The petitioner must accept the lease and deliver up its counterpart.

(4) The petitioner might lawfully, peaceably and quietly enjoy the premises notwithstanding the infancy of How the younger or any other interest.

Decree 35 (page 152)

9 Jan. 1678.   Baron Littleton; Justice Wyndham (s); Sir William Hayward (s); Thomas Barker, Esq. (s); James Reading, Esq. (s); Peter Rich, Esq. (s); John Freeman, Esq. (s); John Appellbe, Esq.

Thomas Kendall, Citizen and Skinner of London, v. John Penn; Sarah his Wife; Richard May, Gentleman; Richard How the Elder, Esquire; and Richard How the Younger, his Son an Infant[131]

Thomas Johnson, Gentleman, and Sarah his wife[132] were possessed and interested for a long term of years in a messuage that they had leased from Thomas Browker, Esquire.[133] The messuage had formerly been in the occupation of Andrew Kembe, and then of the petitioner and John Forster. It was located on the east side of the High Street.

By indenture of lease dated 22 September 1668, Thomas Johnson and Sarah his wife, together with George Ewer (now deceased), demised part of the messuage then in the petitioner's possession to the petitioner. The lease ran from the feast of St Michael the Archangel 1668 for twenty-one years. The annual rent was £20, payable quarterly. The remainder of the messuage was in the possession of John Forster, at the annual rent of £16.

Richard How the elder had since purchased the inheritance of the premises. How later made a settlement of the property on himself for life and the remainder in tail to Richard How the younger, his infant son.

---

131 The caption of this petition did not provide the residences of the defendants or the occupation of John Penn.

132 Likely the same Sarah Johnson, widow, mentioned in the prior decree, *May v. How* (Decree 34). The property in this case may have adjoined the property in Decree 34: both decrees mentioned that Andrew Kembe was at one point the undertenant.

133 I again assume that this reference is to Thomas Browker of Upper Peover. See p. 198, note 128.

The property burned down. The petitioner, who was willing to rebuild, treated with Sarah Johnson (her husband Thomas having died) for encouragement. They came to an agreement under which the petitioner would have a term of fifty-three years, commencing on the feast of the Nativity of St John the Baptist 1676. The lease extended to the ground on which the messuage, garden and yard of the petitioner had formerly stood, as well as the part formerly in the possession of John Forster. The agreed rent for the entire premises was £22 per annum. In addition, they agreed that, if Sarah Johnson should get any further term of years from How the landlord (which How has already agreed to give her in consideration of new building), then the petitioner should get a like term of years from her at the agreed rent of £22 per annum.

Sarah Johnson then executed a lease to the petitioner, and the petitioner rebuilt the messuage. Meanwhile, Sarah Johnson made an assignment or estate of the messuage and her original lease to Richard May. She had also since married John Penn.

How was willing to grant John Penn and his wife Sarah (or Richard May) a further increase in term, as How had done with his other tenants in adjoining houses in pursuance of a promise that he had made. The petitioner would like the agreement corroborated according to the Act of Parliament establishing the Court and also have such further term of years as How was willing to grant.

Summonses to the defendants were issued. The petitioner appeared personally, with Mr Jenner as his counsel. John Johnson of London, Goldsmith, appeared on behalf of John and Sarah Penn; he also produced a letter of attorney authorizing him to act on behalf of Richard May. How the elder appeared personally, without counsel, on behalf of himself and his son. How was specially admitted as guardian for his son.

The petitioner's counsel prayed that, in consideration of the petitioner's great expense in rebuilding, the Court should corroborate the agreement — with the addition of years to which How had consented in court. John Johnson, however, informed the Court that Sarah Penn did not agree to give the petitioner the full term of years that she received from How, but only some part of the term. He was willing to consent to a new term for petitioner of sixty-seven years from the feast of St Michael the Archangel 1677 at the annual rent of £22, payable quarterly.

The petitioner consented to this proposal.

The Court ordered that:

(1)   The petitioner Thomas Kendall was to have a term of sixty-seven years in the grounds and messuage formerly in his occupation

and the occupation of John Forster, together with the garden
and yard. The term was to commence on the feast of St Michael
the Archangel 1677

(2)   The rent was to be £22 payable quarterly on the most usual feast
days.

(3)   To avoid difficulties in recovering the rent and for ascertaining
the covenants mutually to be performed, on the petitioners'
reasonable request and at his expense, May must execute a good
and sufficient lease by indenture for the sixty-seven years. The
lease should contain reasonable covenants usual in leases of
new-built houses in and about London. The petitioner must
accept the lease and deliver up its counterpart.

(4)   The petitioner might lawfully, peaceably and quietly enjoy the
premises notwithstanding any other interest.

Decree 36 (page 156)

9 Jan. 1678.   Baron Littleton; Justice Wyndham (s); Sir William
Hayward (s); Thomas Barker, Esq. (s); James Reading,
Esq. (s); Richard How, Esq. (s); Peter Rich, Esq. (s);
John Freeman, Esq. (s); John Appellbe, Esq.

*John Ferris of Southwark, Cordwayner, v. John Cressett, Gentleman;
Elizabeth his Wife; and Edward Keyling, Gentleman*[134]

By indenture of lease dated 19 December 1667, Thomas Overman of
Southwark, Gentleman, demised a premises to James Lane, Citizen and
Leatherseller of London. The premises had previously been in Lane's
possession. The lease ran from the feast of the Nativity of St John
the Baptist 1668 for twenty-one years. The annual rent was £8, payable
quarterly.

   The premises contained the following: a back kitchen and coal
hole; the 'house of Office', which was part of the messuage in which
Overman had lately dwelt; a part of a paved yard as it was then severed
and divided, about six feet in breadth and twelve feet in length; and one
low room, lying on the north side of the passage out of the High Street
into Three Crowne Court, which had previously been used as a buttery
or larder.

---

134 The caption did not provide the residences of the defendants. The Cressetts
and Keyling had been defendants in *Nicolson v. Cressett* (Decree 9); and Elizabeth
Cressett (previously Overman) was mentioned in *Lane v. Mayor of Shrewsbury*
(Decree 26).

Overman had since died, and Elizabeth his relict was interested in the kitchen and other things mentioned during the term of her life. She had since married John Cressett. John Keyling claimed the reversion of Elizabeth's interest upon her death.

By good and sufficient means in the law, Lane's interest became vested in the petitioner. The rooms and building were burned down and demolished in the fire. Hoping for encouragement by means of an increase in term and abatement of rent, the petitioner had rebuilt the premises at his expense. So far, however, he had obtained no encouragement.

Summonses to the defendants were issued. The petitioner appeared personally. Sir George Jeffreys and Mr Jenner were his counsel. John Cressett appeared personally on his own behalf and that of Elizabeth his wife. Edward Keyling also appeared personally. They were not represented by counsel.

The petitioner's counsel prayed that, in consideration of his costs in rebuilding, the petitioner should receive an increased term and abatement of rent. Cressett opposed this request, alleging that the petitioner had come to an agreement after the fire and he should be bound by it. Cressett prayed liberty to prove the agreement.

At this point, Walter Browne made oath in court that he had been employed by Mrs Cressett after the fire to treat with the petitioner. They came to the following agreement: the petitioner was to have an abatement of rent for one year and liberty to build a shed.

The petitioner's counsel argued that the agreement to build a shed was for the petitioner's present occasion after the fire. Because she was interested only for her life, Mrs Cressett had no power to agree to any further terms for the petitioner to build substantially, as he had now done. He further alleged that the new building has cost the petitioner at least £60. Moreover, the Town of Shrewsbury, which is the landlord of almost all the houses in Three Crowne Court and whose ground lay much better that the petitioner's, voluntarily abated one-half of its rents, as well as giving its tenants four years rent-free. Counsel prayed for the Court to abate the rent by half and to allow some reasonable term in consideration of building.

Having heard the matter fully and having been well advised, the Court propounded it as most just and reasonable to increase the petitioner's term to sixty years from the feast of the birth of our Lord 1677 at the annual rent of £4 10s., with all rent from the time of the fire discharged.

The Court ordered that:

(1) The petitioner John Ferris was discharged from payment of all rent incurred on the lease from the time of the fire until the feast

of the birth of our Lord 1677.

(2) From that point, the annual rent of £8 was to be reduced to £4 10s. for the remainder of the lease. The petitioner was discharged from paying the £3 10s. residue of the yearly £8 rent.

(3) The lease was to be made up to a total of sixty years, accounted from the feast of the birth of our Lord 1677, by adding forty-eight and a half years to the present lease. The new lease would commence immediately at the end of the present lease, which was due to expire by effluxion of time on the feast of the Nativity of St John the Baptist 1689. The annual rent for the new lease was to be £4 10s.

(4) The rent was payable to John Cressett and Elizabeth his wife and to Edward Keyling, according to their several interests, on the days and times payable under the present lease. The first quarterly payment should be made on the feast of the Annunciation of the Blessed Virgin Mary 1678.

(5) To avoid difficulties in recovering the rent and for ascertaining the covenants mutually to be performed, on the petitioners' reasonable request and at her expense, the Cressetts and Keyling must execute a good and sufficient lease by indenture for the term of sixty years decreed to the petitioner. The lease should contain reasonable covenants as are contained in the present lease. The petitioner must accept the lease and deliver up its counterpart.

(6) The petitioner might lawfully, peaceably and quietly enjoy the premises notwithstanding the coverture of Elizabeth Cressett or any other interest.

Decree 37 (page 160)

28 May 1678.   Justice Wyndham (s); Edward Smith, Esq. (s); Thomas Barker, Esq. (s); James Reading, Esq. (s); Richard How, Esq. (s); Peter Rich, Esq. (s); John Freeman, Esq. (s)

Susanna Sicklemore of Southwark, Widow Relict of Edmund Sicklemore Deceased, v. the Right Honourable Elizabeth Lady Dowager Burgevenny; the Right Honourable George Lord Burgevenny, an Infant; and the Right Honourable Mary Lady Burgevenny, his Guardian now Wife of Sir Charles Shelley, Knight[135]

By indenture of lease dated 20 April 1664, the Right Honourable John Lord Burgevenny demised to Thomas Knight, Citizen and Stationer

of London, the following: (1) all his moiety 'part or purpart' of one
messuage or tenement, with the yard and garden adjoining, known by
the name of the Blew Bore,[136] that had sometimes been in the tenure
of Elizabeth Howard, widow, and then late in the tenure of William
Kitchin or his assigns (Fig. 15); (2) all his moiety 'part and purpart' of
one acre of land called the Duke's Acre situated in St George's Field
near or within the Borough of Southwark; (3) one acre of land called
the Toll Acre lying by the bridge in Kentish Street;[137] and (4) all his
estate, right, title, interest and demand in all manner of toll, tollages,
rents, customs or services of right due and payable within Southwark
(which had for the greater part of twenty years past been demised and
let to farm). The lease ran for twenty-one years from the feast of the
Annunciation of the Blessed Virgin Mary 1664. Knight paid a fine of
£20 for the lease. The annual rent was £5, payable half-yearly on the
feasts of St Michael the Archangel and the Annunciation of the Blessed
Virgin Mary.

By good and sufficient means in law, Knight's interest in the moiety of
the messuage became vested in the petitioner. John Lord Burgevenny
had since died, and Elizabeth Lady Dowager Burgevenny, his relict,
claimed a one-third part of the moiety for her life as her dower. George
Lord Burgevenny, the grandson of Lord John, was entitled to the other
two-thirds part of the moiety during Lady Elizabeth's life and to the
whole upon her death. Lord George was not yet twenty-one years old,
so Mary Lady Burgevenny, his mother (who had since remarried Sir
Charles Shelley) was his guardian.

The premises burned down. The petitioner received some
encouragement from the proprietor of the other moiety,[138] and rebuilt
the premises. Because the petitioner could not obtain sufficient terms
of encouragement from Lady Elizabeth or Lord George, she sought

---

135 The caption did not provide the residences of the defendants. The registrar
also rendered the Bergavenny (or Abergavenny) barony as 'Burgavenny'.

136 Perhaps an inventive spelling of 'Blue Boar'. The Blue Boar's Head was the
sign of a distiller located behind the Compter on St Margaret's Hill. See J. Holden
MacMichael, 'The London Signs and Their Associations', *The Antiquary*, 45 (1909),
305. See Figure 15.

137 Kentish Street (later Kent Street and now Tabard Street) would have been
the start of the route for Chaucer's pilgrims upon their departure from the Tabard
(Talbot). The road had a bridge that crossed over a stream or ditch. Edward
Walford, *Old and New London*, VI (London, 1878), p. 70. I thank Sheila O'Connell
for tracking down this information.

138 The decree did not mention who owned the other half of the reversion in
the message.

Fig. 15. Trade card of Jonathan Grant, Distiller, at the Blue Boar's Head, St Margaret's Hill, about 1700.

the aid of this Court.

Summonses to the defendants were issued. Mr Jenner appeared as counsel for the petitioner. Mr Woolfe appeared on behalf of all the

139 The decree contains a blank space before 'Woolfe', suggesting that the registrar intended to insert a first name at some future point.

defendants after being sufficiently authorized to do so.[139]

The petitioner's counsel informed the Court that Mr Woolfe had treated with the petitioner, and the parties had come to an agreement. Under the agreement, the petitioner obtained a lease of the other moiety of the premises from the feast of the Nativity of St John the Baptist 1676 for forty years at the yearly rent of £6. The agreement further recited that the petitioner had paid the rent on the defendants' moiety without ceasing until the feast of the Annunciation of the Blessed Virgin Mary 1678. The agreement went on to give the petitioner a term in the defendants' moiety of thirty-eight and a quarter years (which is as long as remained on the term for the other moiety), commencing from the feast of the Annunciation of the Blessed Virgin Mary 1678. Like the other moiety, the rent was £6 per annum. Furthermore, because the moiety of the parcel known as the Duke's Acre, which had been demised by the lease, was never enjoyed by the petitioner, the petitioner agreed to except this parcel to the defendants.

Woolfe declared his consent to this agreement.

The Court ordered that:

(1) Given that the petitioner Susanna Sicklemore had already paid all arrears of rent until the feast of the Annunciation of the Blessed Virgin Mary 1678, the petitioner was discharged from paying all further rent and from the lease's covenants.

(2) The petitioner was to receive a term of thirty-eight and a quarter years in the moiety of the premises demised to Thomas Knight, except for the acre of land called the Duke's Acre. The term was to run from the feast of the Annunciation of the Blessed Virgin Mary 1678.

(3) The annual rent for the first thirty-eight years was to be £6, payable quarterly on the usual feasts in equal proportions. For the final quarter year, the rent was proportional according to the same rate.

(4) To avoid difficulties in recovering the rent and for ascertaining the covenants mutually to be performed, on the petitioners' reasonable request and at her expense, George Lord Burgevenny, when he reached the age of twenty-one, and Elizabeth Lady Dowager Burgevenny, should she still be living, must execute a good and sufficient lease by indenture of the moiety for as many years of the term of thirty-eight and a quarter years as yet remained. The lease should contain reasonable covenants usual in leases made of houses in and about London. The petitioner

must accept the lease and deliver up its counterpart.

(5)   Except as noted above, the petitioner might lawfully, peaceably and quietly enjoy the premises notwithstanding the infancy of George Lord Burgevenny or any other interest.

Decree 38 (page 163)

28 May 1678.   Justice Wyndham (s); Edward Smyth, Esq. (s); Thomas Barker, Esq. (s); James Reading, Esq. (s); Richard How, Esq. (s); Peter Rich, Esq. (s); John Freeman, Esq. (s)

Christopher Marshall the Elder of Southwark, Citizen and Dyer of London, v. Thomas Overman, Gentleman[140]

Hester Overman, widow, was seised for life in a messuage or tenement, with Thomas Overman seised of the inheritance. By indenture of lease dated 17 June 1661, and in consideration of a £15 fine, they demised a messuage or tenement containing eight rooms, a yard on the foreside with a cartway toward the street to a pair of great gates, a privy with a pump and sheds or warehouses in the yard. The premises were then in the tenure and occupation of the petitioner and his undertenants or assignees. The lease ran from the feast of the Annunciation of the Blessed Virgin Mary 1661 for thirty-two and a half years. The annual rent was £14, payable quarterly. The premises were situated within the close commonly called Mountague Close.[141]

Both of the lessors were now dead, and Thomas Overman had claimed the inheritance.[142]

After taking the lease, the petitioner pulled down the old warehouses and built new ones in the rooms thereof. The cost to do so was about £150.

In the fire, the messuage was shattered and defaced when adjoining houses, which were on fire, were blown up. Great parts of the warehouses were demolished and the other parts much shattered and spoiled.

After the fire, the petitioner and his tenant repaired the messuage

---

140 The caption did not provide the residence of the defendant.

141 The modern spelling is Montague Close.

142 'Thomas' was a common Christian name in the Overman family. Hester Overman's husband had been named Thomas. After his death, she held a life interest in her husband's property holdings. Thomas and Hester had four children, one of whom was also named Thomas. This Thomas Overman, who inherited the Overman estate when Hester died in 1663, married a woman named Elizabeth. Thomas and Elizabeth had no children. When Thomas died in or around 1675, Elizabeth Overman (later Cressett) held a life interest in property estimated to

and rebuilt and repaired the warehouses. The cost was £70. Thomas Overman had refused to contribute a reasonable share, whether by abatement of rent, increase in term or contribution of money.

A summons to the defendant was issued. The petitioner appeared personally, with Mr Jenner as his counsel. Overman also appeared personally, with Mr Thompson as his counsel.

The petitioner's counsel prayed for contribution in some form. Overman's counsel stated that the damage caused by the fire was very small and the petitioner's costs were inconsiderable; the costs should therefore be borne by the petitioner given his covenant to repair. The petitioner's counsel responded that the repairs cost a very considerable sum, which he was ready to prove.

At that point, several witnesses were examined on oath. It was fully proved that the petitioner spent about £50 in rebuilding and repairing the warehouses, in addition to the costs that the tenant in possession of the dwelling house spent to repair glass windows and tiles.

Having heard the evidence and the full debate, the Court propounded as most just and reasonable that Overman either pay the petitioner two-thirds part of £50 (that being £33 6s. 8d.) on the feast of St Bartholomew the Apostle [24 August] 1678, or else increase the petitioner's term to thirty years at the old rent. Overman was given liberty to make his choice. Overman decided to pay the petitioner £33 6s. 8d.

The Court ordered that the defendant Thomas Overman pay the petitioner Christopher Marshall £33 6s. 8d in full satisfaction and recompense toward his charges in repair and rebuilding.

Decree 39 (page 166)

28 May 1678.   Justice Wyndham (s); Edward Smyth, Esq. (s); Thomas Barker, Esq. (s); James Reading, Esq. (s); Richard How, Esq. (s); Peter Rich, Esq. (s); John Freeman, Esq. (s)

Nathaniell Butcher of Southwark, Distiller, v. Robert Taynton[143]

be worth between £2,200 and £3,000. Elizabeth was the defendant in *Nicholson v. Cressett* (Decree 9) and *Ferris v. Cressett* (Decree 36); she was also mentioned in *Lane v. Town of Shrewsbury* (Decree 26).

Having no children, Thomas was generous in granting interests in his properties to his nieces and nephews. One of his nephews was Edward Keyling, son of his sister Grace, who held the reversionary interests in *Nicholson* and *Ferris*. Another nephew, the son of his brother William, was also named Thomas. It is very likely that this nephew was the Thomas Overman who was the defendant in this case. See Will of Hester Overman, TNA, PROB 11/311/316 (2 June 1663); Petition, *Leigh v. Cressett*, TNA, C 8/263/101; Petition, *Cressett v. Cressett*, TNA, C 5/149/49.

143   The caption provided neither residence nor occupation for the defendant.

By virtue of his lease with John Collett, Esquire, Edmund Geary of Southwark, Innkeeper, was interested in and possessed of the White Hart Inn, with its yards, buildings and appurtenances, for a considerable number of years.[144] By indenture of lease dated 5 December 1671, Geary demised to the petitioner a piece of ground adjoining the lowermost stable of the inn. The ground was a parcel in the great yard, measuring about thirty-eight feet north to south and twenty-five feet east to west. The parcel had free liberty of passage through the gateway or passage leading into the inn, in common with Geary. The petitioner also had free liberty to lay his ashes and soils on the common laystall of the inn, as well as liberty to lay a leaden pipe along the passage from the High Street to the premises. The lease ran from the feast of the birth of our Lord 1671 for nineteen and a half years at the annual rent of £7, payable quarterly.

The petitioner enjoyed the premises until the fire burned down both the inn and the premises. Geary had since died, and Robert Taynton had been appointed executor of his estate. In consideration of rebuilding, Taynton obtained a new lease with a long term of years either from Collett, the head landlord, or from a decree of this Court. Confident of encouragement from Geary during his lifetime and from Taynton since Geary's death, the petitioner rebuilt part of the premises. He was willing to rebuild the residue on reasonable encouragement by an increased term and abatement of rent, but Taynton refused to give encouragement.

A summons to the defendant was issued. The petitioner appeared personally. Sir George Jeffreys and Mr Jenner were his counsel. Taynton appeared personally, with Mr Tompson as counsel.[145]

The petitioner's counsel informed the Court that the petitioner was very desirous to rebuild and has laid out at least £50 to rebuild a still house. He therefore prayed the Court to give him encouragement to continue rebuilding.

Taynton's counsel opposed this request because the petitioner's building would be very inconvenient to the defendant's large adjoining inn, as well as dangerous in respect of fire. Counsel prayed that the Court

---

144 According to *Taynton v. Collett* (Decree 27), the lease was actually between Geary's assignor on the one side and Thomas Collett and his wife on the other. John Collett, Thomas's son, succeeded to his father's interests at some point after Geary took the assignment of the lease in 1667.

145 I assume that this is an alternate spelling of Thompson, who appeared as counsel in other cases that day (see *Marshall v. Overman* (Decree 38), and *Cannon v. Brace* (Decree 41)).

order the petitioner to surrender his lease, for which Taynton would give reasonable consideration. Several offers were made on both sides.

Having heard the matters debated at large, the Court propounded that Taynton pay the petitioner £140 as a gross sum for the petitioner's entire interest in the premises. Taynton refused to do so. The Court further propounded that the petitioner should be the rebuilder and have his term made up to fifty-eight and a quarter years (being the entire term that Taynton had in the premises, less one year), at the annual rent of £6. Moreover, because the petitioner had, since the fire, made some benefit of the ground by erecting a still house, he should also pay all arrears of rent at the annual rate of £7 until the feast of the Annunciation of the Blessed Virgin Mary 1678. He would then be discharged of paying rent until the feast of St Michael the Archangel 1679, with this year and one half being allowed for building.

The Court ordered that:

(1) By 24 August 1678 (this being the feast of St Bartholomew the Apostle), the petitioner Nathaniell Butcher must pay Robert Taynton[146] all arrears of the £7 rent under the present lease up to the feast of the Annunciation of the Blessed Virgin Mary 1678. The petitioner was discharged of all other rent incurred since the time of the fire or to be incurred. He was also discharged of all covenants under the lease.

(2) For his encouragement to rebuild, the petitioner was to have a term of fifty-eight and a quarter years in the premises, commencing on the feast of the Annunciation of the Blessed Virgin Mary 1678.

(3) The rent for the first year and a half was one peppercorn, if it be demanded. For the next fifty-six years, the annual rent was to be £6, payable quarterly at the most usual feasts. For the last three-quarters of a year, the rent was to be £4 10s., payable at the three feasts (the feast of the Annunciation of the Blessed Virgin Mary, the feast of the Nativity of St John the Baptist and the feast of St Michael the Archangel) by even portions.

(4) In consideration of these premises, the petitioner, at his cost, must cause to be erected and new built a good and substantial messuage of brick and other good and sufficient materials and finish it in good workmanlike manner.

(5) To avoid difficulties in recovering the rent and for ascertaining the covenants mutually to be performed, on the petitioner's

---

146 The registrar spelled Taynton's name as 'Tainton'. I use 'Taynton' throughout.

reasonable request and at his expense, Taynton must execute a good and sufficient lease by indenture for fifty-eight and a quarter years. The lease should contain reasonable covenants usual in leases of new built houses in and about London. The petitioner must accept the lease and deliver up its counterpart.

(6) The petitioner might lawfully, peaceably and quietly enjoy the premises notwithstanding any other interest.

Decree 40 (page 170)

2 March 1680. Lord Mayor of London [Sir Robert Clayton] (s); Lord Ceife Baron [William Montagu] (s);[147] Sir Thomas Bludworth (s); Sir Francis Chaplyn;[148] Sir Richard How (s);[149] James Reading, Esq. (s); John Appellbee

Grace Cannon, Widow Relict and Executrix of William Cannon Deceased,[150] *v. Mary Cannon, Spinster; and William Cannon, John Cannon, and Martha Cannon, Infants*

In his lifetime, William Cannon was seised of a messuage or tenement that he inhabited. It was known by the sign of the Starr.[151] By his will, dated 27 July 1675, Cannon devised the premises to the petitioner for her life and then to William Cannon, his eldest son. The will required, among other things, the payment of £100 each to John, Mary and Martha Cannon within twelve months after his son William or John had attained the age of twenty-one.[152] William Cannon [the father] died, leaving the petitioner as executrix of the will.

The premises burned down. The petitioner rebuilt the messuage at her own expense, even though she only had an estate for her life and could have no further estate without an order of the Court — given

147 The caption misspelled 'Cheife' as 'Ceife'. In addition, Lord Chief Baron Montagu signed the decrees for which he sat as 'Mountagu'.

148 Chaplin had been Lord Mayor in 1677–78 and, in that capacity, served as a member of the Court in one of the encroachment decrees, Decree 46. Most histories render his name as 'Chaplin'.

149 How had been knighted on 28 October 1677, but this is the first caption to elevate his name to the rank of knight.

150 Cannon was also the petitioner in *Cannon v. Brace* (Decree 41).

151 According to the will of William Cannon, which was made on 27 July 1675 and proved on 27 September 1676, Cannon was a Citizen and Apothecary of London. TNA, PROB 11/352/138.

152 The language is confusing: it did not say who was, in the language of the decree, 'forever charged' with making these payments; it also did not explain why the payments of £100 depended on either of two events (William or John attaining

that all the children except Mary were infants. In order for the petitioner to have compensation for building, she wished to have a certain term of years decreed to her, commencing on her death, at a reasonable rent. Such a decree would allow her to lease the premises to a tenant.

Summonses to the defendants were issued. The petitioner appeared personally, with Mr Jenner as counsel. All the defendants also appeared. On the choice of William, John and Martha Cannon, Gabreill Brownrigge was specially admitted as their guardian.

The petitioner's counsel informed the Court that the petitioner spent about £300 in rebuilding, with about £60 to £70 of that from money collected by the brief.[153] A tenant had now agreed to rent the house at a rack rent of £40 per annum. Counsel therefore prayed that a term of forty years be granted to the petitioner, commencing at the end of her life estate. The Court could fix a reasonable rent for the term.

The Court declared a term of twenty-one years at the yearly rent of £30.

The Court ordered that:

(1) The petitioner Grace Cannon was to have an estate and term of twenty-one years in the premises, commencing immediately on her decease.

(2) The annual rent for this interest was to be £30, payable to William Cannon and his heirs at the four most usual feasts. The first quarterly payment was to be due on the feast following the death of the petitioner.

the age of twenty-one), or why John should receive £100 in the event that he obtained the interest in the premises. On the former point, the will 'charged' the house itself with the required payments once William or John had both reached twenty-one and possessed the house, which would not occur until the death of their mother, Grace. The penalty for William's non-payment was forfeiture of his interest in the premises, which would then pass to John. The ambiguity about what would happen if William did not survive until twenty-one, but John did, was not resolved in the will, which on this point appeared to assume that William would survive and left open what might happen if he did not. The will also charged the house with the payment of £10 annually to each child until the child either turned twenty-one or married, and another £200 apiece to John, Mary and Martha when they turned twenty-one, with each child's share divided among the surviving siblings if the child did not survive to twenty-one. See ibid. Because the issues in the case did not require the Court to sort through the niceties of Cannon's will, the decree did not recite these additional details. Clearly, though, Cannon was a man of some wealth. Grace also brought money into the marriage. See Discharge of Legacy, DE/Pr/77118, Hertfordshire Archives and Local Studies (describing a discharge on 30 November 1647 by William Cannon of Southwark, Apothecary, and Grace his wife given to Thomas Reeve, executor of the estate of William Underwood, father of Grace Cannon, for £200 bequeathed by Underwood to

(3) To avoid difficulties in recovering the rent and for ascertaining the covenants mutually to be performed, on the petitioners' reasonable request and at her expense, William Cannon, when he reaches the age of twenty-one (or his heirs in case of his death), must execute a good and sufficient lease by indenture for the twenty-one years decreed to the petitioner. The lease should contain reasonable covenants. The petitioner must accept the lease and deliver up its counterpart.

(4) The petitioner, during her life and without payment of rent, may lawfully, peaceably and quietly enjoy the premises, as may her executors, administrators and assignees for twenty-one years after her death at the yearly rent of £30, notwithstanding any other interest.

Decree 41 (page 173)

28 May 1678.   Justice Wyndham; Edward Smyth, Esq.; Thomas Barker, Esq.; James Reading, Esq.; Richard How, Esq.; Peter Rich, Esq.; John Freeman, Esq.

2 March 1680.   Lord Mayor of London [Sir Robert Clayton] (s); Lord Cheife Baron [William Montagu] (s); Sir Thomas Bludworth (s); Mr Recorder of London;[154] Sir Richard How (s); Peter Rich, Esq. (s); James Reading, Esq. (s); John Freeman, Esq. (s); Thomas Barker, Esq. (s); John Appellbe

Grace Cannon,[155] *Widow Relict and Executrix of William Cannon Deceased, v. Margaret Brace, Widow;*[156] *and James Brace, her Son*[157]

Grace). A later discharge, on 24 October 1660, was for an additional dividend of £28 11s. 5d. paid to William and Grace Cannon under the terms of her father's will. Discharge of Legacy, DE/Pr/77125, Hertfordshire Archives and Local Studies.

153 After major catastrophes, the Crown would sometimes authorize the national publication of a 'brief', or solicitation for donations to aid the victims.

154 There were two Recorders of London in 1680: Sir George Jeffreys and George Treby. Treby did not become Recorder until later in 1680. Thus, Jeffreys apparently sat as a judge for the 1680 hearing. Jeffreys had also been counsel to the petitioner at the 1678 hearing. It would be an appalling breach of modern ethical rules for a judge to hear a case in which he or she had been previously engaged as a lawyer.

155 Cannon was also the petitioner in *Cannon v. Cannon* (Decree 40).

156 In the body of the decree, the registrar sometimes rendered 'Margaret' as 'Margarett'. I use 'Margaret' throughout.

157 The decree does not provide the residences of the parties.

Thomas Browker, Esquire,[158] was seised in fee of a messuage then in the occupation of William Cannon. The messuage was located on the High Street. Designing to rebuild and repair the messuage, Browker reached an agreement with Samuell Warcupp, who held the next adjoining messuage backwards. By indenture of lease dated 13 August 1652, Warcupp demised to Browker a parcel of ground and its watercourses and convenient lights to the south-east of Cannon's messuage for Browker's use. The lease ran from 13 August 1652 for 2,000 years at the yearly rent of a peppercorn. Soon thereafter, Cannon purchased the inheritance of his messuage and the said lights from Browker.

Cannon then repaired and rebuilt the messuage and made the lights commodious for his messuage. The premises were enjoyed until his death and thereafter by the petitioner, who is executrix of his will, until the fire burned the premises down.

The interests of Warcupp became vested in Edward Brace, who soon after the fire rebuilt his back messuage. This building stopped up the south-east lights, so that a large portion of the house that the petitioner had rebuilt was so damnified that it was of little use. Edward Brace was now dead, and Margaret Brace, his relict, had become interested in his premises for life, with James Brace inheriting the reversion on her death.

The petitioner wished to have the benefit of her lights, and sought relief from the Court.

Summonses to the defendants were issued. The petitioner appeared personally, with Sir George Jeffreys as counsel. The defendants also appeared personally, with Mr Thompson as their counsel.

The petitioner's counsel prayed that, for the better information and satisfaction of the Court concerning the stopping up and darkening of the lights, and of how much the house was darkened, skilful workmen should view the premises. The Court thought this reasonable. It ordered Thomas Kentish, Carpenter, on behalf of the petitioner, and John Oliver, Surveyor, on behalf of the defendants, to view the buildings and lights. They should then make a report in writing by the Court's next sitting.

On 2 March 1680, the petitioner and defendants again came to court. Mr Ward and Mr Jenner now represented the petitioner, and Mr Bowes and Mr Thompson represented the defendants.

---

158   As in other decrees, it seems likely that the Thomas Browker referred to in this decree is Thomas Browker of Upper Peover, not his son (Thomas the elder) or grandson (Thomas the younger).

A report under the hands of Kentish and Oliver was produced and submitted to the Court. The report stated that Margaret Brace and her son (or their tenant) were possessed of a house known by the name of the Red Lyon Taverne.[159] The back rooms of the petitioner's house were partly over the kitchen and partly over the entry belonging to the tavern. The petitioner's kitchen was up one pair of stairs. The kitchen had a window at the south-east corner that was four feet and eight inches in breadth and about six feet in height; this window was over the tavern's entry. Another window that adjoined this window was three feet and ten inches wide and six feet high; this window was stopped up and darkened. Another window near the chimney, which was about two feet wide and two and a half feet high, was stopped up and darkened by the building over the Red Lyon's kitchen; thus, the end of the room next to the chimney was darkened. The rooms over this kitchen were darkened in the same manner. The report also recited the petitioner's allegation that she had had clear lights all along the east side of her house before the fire.

The Court then examined several witnesses on oath on both sides and heard allegations by counsel on both sides. The Court declared itself satisfied that part of the petitioner's house over the passage leading to the defendant's back house was the most south-eastern part of the petitioner's house. The petitioner's present enjoyment of the lights which were over the passage fully satisfied the true intent and meaning of the deed granting the lights. It was unreasonable to construe the deed to hinder the defendants from building up the part of their house that adjoined the back of the petitioner's house to the height of the petitioner's house, if they saw fit — even if doing so darkened or stopped up those of the petitioner's back lights which were not over the passage. Therefore, the Court had no cause to order the defendants to pull down or alter the part of the house that stopped up the lights or to order that the petitioner receive any damage or satisfaction.

The Court ordered that:

(1) The petitioner Grace Cannon may peaceably and quietly enjoy, without any manner of impeachment, all the lights which are now placed at the back part of her house over the passage leading to the defendant's house.

---

159 'Red Lion' was a common name for taverns and public houses. *Nicolson v. Browker* (Decree 8), also involved a Red Lion, which was located on property of which Thomas Browker had been seised in fee. From the description of the tenants, however, that Red Lion appears to be a different property.

(2) The defendants need not give recompense or damage for darkening and stopping up of lights which are in the back part of the petitioner's house not over the passage.

Decree 42 (page 176)

2 March 1680.   Lord Cheife Baron [William Montagu] (s); Sir Richard How (s); Peter Rich, Esq. (s); James Reading, Esq. (s); John Freeman, Esq. (s); Thomas Barker, Esq. (s); John Appellbee

John Young, Citizen and Ironmonger of London, v. Sarah Bradway, Widow; Robert Bedford; Rebecca Inglebert, Spinster; and John Ward and Elizabeth his Wife[160]

The petitioner was seised in fee of a messuage adjoining the gateway of the Queen's Head Inn near St Margaret's Hill. The messuage was blown up and demolished in the fire. The house adjoining to the north lay in the inheritance of Abraham Bradway and Sarah Bradway his wife, Robert Bedford and Sarah his then wife, Rebecca Englebert,[161] and John Ward and Elizabeth his wife. This house had a jetty into the petitioner's house in the first storey, one pair of stairs high, that was about eighteen feet in length and four feet in breadth. The petitioner had the interest over the jetty to the top of his house.

Desirous of rebuilding his house with brick and to have party walls of brick on all sides, the petitioner offered to buy the jetty. Several treaties concerning the price were had, with the defendants demanding £10. Although this price was much more than the interest was worth, the petitioner agreed for his convenience to pay it. The petitioner then went on with his building and took in the jetty, agreeing with the defendants that the wall between the defendants' house and his should be a party wall. By agreement, one-half of the wall in length was built to the top by the petitioner and the other half by the defendants — with the defendants building upright that part of the wall where the jetty had been.

---

160 The decree provides neither the occupations for Bedford or Ward nor the residence of any of the defendants. *Young v. Bradway* (Decree 7), seems to involve largely the same group of defendants: except that Sarah Bradway was not yet widowed and Rebecca Inglebert's name was spelled 'Englebert'. In Decree 7, Bradway's then husband, Abraham, was a Citizen and Weaver of London; Bedford was a Citizen and Haberdasher of London; and John Ward was a Citizen and Dyer of London. Neither decree gives a residence for Rebecca Englebert.

161 The registrar switches the spelling of Inglebert to Englebert throughout the decree. I render the spelling as the registrar does.

In pursuance of the agreement, the petitioner gave directions to a scrivener to draft a conveyance of the jetty. The draft was shown to the interested defendants. By the direction of some of all of them, the draft was altered in some ways and engrossed accordingly. But the defendants then refused to seal the agreement and still did so — and indeed threatened to disturb the petitioner's possession of his premises. Nonetheless, the petitioner, who built according to the agreement, was willing to pay £10 upon their execution of a conveyance of the jetty.

In addition, another jetty began on the east end of the petitioner's house. It was about five feet from the ground and extended over the house of the parties about two feet, upright to the top. When the petitioner began his building, he treated with Robert Bedford, who was employed by the other defendants to take care of building their adjoining house. Bedford agreed on behalf of all the defendants that the jetty of two feet should be equally divided between the petitioner and them, with the petitioner being able to build upright and take in one foot and the defendants able to build upright the other foot, with a party wall between the houses of the petitioner and the defendants. The petitioner built accordingly. But he was then informed that the defendants would controvert this division of ground and the erecting of the party wall, in addition to the agreement for the other jetty.

Abraham Bradway and Sarah Bedford had since died. According to the petitioner's information, Sarah Bradway, as relict of Abraham, had the right to the premises during her life. Robert Bedford (in right of his deceased wife Sarah) and John Ward (in right of his wife Elizabeth) were interested in the reversion.

Summonses to the defendants were issued. All the parties appeared personally. Mr Jenner was counsel for the petitioner, while Mr Bowes and Mr Land were counsel for the defendants.

The petitioner's counsel prayed to have the jetty decreed to the petitioner on payment of £10. The defendant's counsel opposed this request, alleging that neither the defendants nor anyone having their authority made any agreement. Indeed, they had always refused to accept £10 for the jetty because it was of far greater value. The defendants' counsel alleged that the defendants had the jetty all the way to the top of the house (not just one floor). The petitioner's counsel denied this claim.

At this point, several witnesses were examined under oath on both sides.[162] After hearing the witnesses and further debate, the Court

---

162 One of the witnesses may have been Robert Hooke, one of the City surveyors. Hooke noted in his diary that, on 28 February 1680, he was 'at Mr

declared that the defendants held some small portion over the jetty up to the top, but not of the same dimensions as it was on the floor one pair of stairs high. Therefore, it was reasonable for the petitioner to pay some additional amount, but the petitioner should also enjoy the house as now built. The same was true for the jetty on the east end of the house where the exchange of ground had been made. The petitioner should therefore pay the defendants 20 marks [£13 6s. 8d.] within a fortnight in full satisfaction.

The Court ordered that:

(1) On or before this day fortnight [16 March 1680], the petitioner John Young must pay the defendants £13 6s. 8d. for their entire interest in the jetty. The payment should occur at the house of Sarah Bradway, and payment should be made to Sarah Bradway, Robert Bedford, Rebecca Englebert and John and Elizabeth Ward (or some or one of them).

(2) In consideration of this payment, the petitioner might lawfully, peaceably and quietly enjoy the jetty upright to the top of the house notwithstanding any other interest.

(3) The wall erected and built where the jetty had been was to be held and enjoyed by the parties as a party wall between the houses.

(4) In consideration of one foot of ground in the jetty at the east end of the petitioner's house and its upright building, which was to be enjoyed by the defendants, the petitioner might enjoy the other foot of the jetty and its upright building.

Decree 43 (page 180)[163]

2 March 1680. Lord Cheife Baron [William Montagu] (s); Sir Richard How (s); Peter Rich, Esq. (s); James Reading, Esq. (s); John Freeman, Esq. (s); Thomas Barker, Esq. (s); John Appellbee

---

Bradways, Southerick'; see *The Diary of Robert Hooke*, ed. by Henry W. Robinson and Walter Adams (London, 1935), p. 441 (entry for 28 February 1680). On 2 March 1680, the date of this decree, Hooke went '[t]o Guildhall for Bradway till 12' (ibid., p. 442, entry for 2 March 1680). Given that Bradway had died before this case was heard, Hooke must have used 'Mr. Bradways' as an indicator of location rather than as an indicator that he met with Abraham Bradway.

163 This decree is written in a different hand than the prior decrees. A few words at the bottoms of some pages are illegible due to faded ink, but the meaning of the affected sentences can easily be determined from the words that remain.

Thomas Rous, Gentleman,[164] *v. Francis Kellett of New Inn, London, Gentleman, and Margarett Pateman alias Packeman, Widdow*[165]

The defendant Francis Kellett was seised in fee of an estate or inheritance in several small tenements lying on the back part of and adjoining a messuage in the occupation of the petitioner. The tenements were in the several tenures or occupations of Henry Browne, John Williams and Nicholas West. These premises were blown up, burned or otherwise demolished in the fire. They were located in Three Crowne Court.

The petitioner intended to rebuild the messuage and hoped to use the tofts and grounds of the tenements lying convenient to make some additional buildings and conveniences. Therefore, the petitioner treated with the defendant Francis Kellett. They agreed that the petitioner should have a term of sixty years, commencing on the feast of the Nativity of St John the Baptist 1677, at the rent of one peppercorn for the first year and £8 10s. per annum for the remaining fifty-nine years, payable quarterly at the most usual feasts. They also agreed that, for the petitioner's security, this Court should decree terms.

Thereafter, the petitioner built on part of the ground and made use of the rest for his convenience. But Kellett now refused to seal the lease. The petitioner was also informed that Margaret Pateman, Kellett's mother-in law, claimed an annuity or yearly rent charge of £40, payable out of the premises and divers other messuages and tenements in Southwark. The petitioner needed a decree from the Court to be secure against the annuity payable to Pateman.

Summonses to the defendants were issued. The petitioner appeared personally, with Mr Ward as his counsel. Kellett also appeared, with Mr Jenner as his counsel. Pateman did not appear personally, nor did anyone appear on her behalf.

The petitioner's counsel stated that Kellett had agreed to the lease and had actually sealed and delivered the same. Soon afterwards, however, a dispute arose about the time for the payment of the first quarterly rent. Kellett picked up the lease and carried it away. Since then, he had

164 Thomas Rous was one of the defendants in the principal encroachment decree (Decree 45). He was likely the same person as the petitioner in this case.

165 I follow the registrar's spelling of 'widow'. In the decree, the registrar sometimes rendered the second defendant's name as 'Pateman als Packeman' and other times simply as 'Packeman'. Once she is referred to as 'Packman'. To reduce confusion, I use 'Pateman' throughout. In addition, although generally sticking to the spelling 'Margarett', on one occasion the registrar spelled the first name as 'Margaret'. I use the modern 'Margaret'.

detained the agreement under the pretence that the petitioner was to pay rent from the feast of the Annunciation of the Blessed Virgin Mary 1678. In fact, the lease stated that rent was to be paid from the feast of the Nativity of St John the Baptist 1678.

The defendant's counsel insisted that the defendant's other tenants had all paid rent from the feast of the Annunciation of the Blessed Virgin Mary, and the defendant made agreements with them for the rents to commence all from the same time. Moreover, it was expressly agreed that the petitioner should have only the defendant's covenant against the annuity claimed by Pateman. It was not reasonable that her interest should be bound by this decree when it was not the intent of the agreement.

John Harrison, one of the defendant's other tenants, was then examined under oath about the commencement of the first rent payment.

After hearing what was further alleged on both sides, the Court declared it most just and reasonable that the rent should commence on the feast of the Nativity of St John the Baptist 1678 but that the petitioner should have only the defendant's covenant against the annuity. A new lease should be executed in pursuance of this decree, with a covenant from Kellett to save the petitioner harmless against the annuity payable to Pateman. The petition against Pateman was dismissed.

The Court ordered that:

(1) The petitioner Thomas Rous was to have a term of sixty years in the small tenements agreed to be let, commencing on the feast of the Nativity of St John the Baptist 1677.

(2) The rent was to be one peppercorn for the first year, payable on the last day of the first year (if the same should be demanded), and £8 10s. for the remaining fifty-nine years, at the four most usual feast days in even and equal portions. The first quarterly rent was payable on the feast of St Michael the Archangel 1678.

(3) To avoid difficulties in recovering the rent and for ascertaining the covenants mutually to be performed, on the petitioners' reasonable request and at his expense, the defendant Francis Kellett must execute a good and sufficient lease by indenture for the sixty years decreed to the petitioner. The lease should contain reasonable and usual covenants. In addition, the lease should contain a covenant well and sufficiently saving harmless and indemnifying the petitioner against the annuity of Margaret Pateman. The petitioner must accept the lease and deliver up its counterpart.

(4) The petitioner might lawfully, peaceably and quietly enjoy the small tenements notwithstanding any other interest.

Decree 44 (page 185)

17 July 1677.   Lord Mayor of London [Thomas Davies]; Baron
                   Littleton; Justice Jones (s); Adam Browne, Baronet; Sir
                   William Hooker (s); Edward Smith, Esq. (s); Thomas
                   Barker, Esq. (s); James Reading, Esq. (s); Richard
                   Howe, Esq. (s);[166] Peter Rich, Esq. (s); John Freeman,
                   Esq. (s); John Appellbe, Esq.

Together with divers other persons in possession of encroachments and
purprestures on the High Street between the Bridge Foot and Compter
Lane, John Gerrard was summoned to appear in court on 8 June 1677.
He appeared at that time, and the Court, entering into consideration
of and fully debating the matter, ordered that the surveyors of new
buildings in the City of London, as well as William Gray and such of
the commissioners of the Court as wished to join them, should on
Friday 13 July 1677 meet and view the encroachments and purprestures.
They were then to consider in what manner and how far these
encroachments were fit to be regulated and reformed according to the
Act of Parliament. They should then make a report under their hands
at the Court's next sitting.

   In addition, the parties were to be given convenient notice of the
viewing time, so they might be present. The order provided that all
affected parties should be present on this day. Finally, the Court ordered
the tenants of the several houses to which the encroachments belong
to give notice to their landlords, so that the landlords might also appear
if they saw fit.

   After 8 June 1677, Gerrard and others in possession of encroachments
were given notice, and on 13 July Robert Hooke and John Oliver, the
surveyors of new buildings in London, William Gray, Thomas Barker,
Esquire, and Peter Rich, Esquire, met and viewed the encroachments.
They then made a report in writing and presented it to the Court.

   In effect, the report stated that the examiners found, at the very corner
of the street at the Bridge Foot, on the east side of the way, a post that
stood without the ancient post of the house nearly two feet. The stall
of the house and all the other stalls and posts belonging to the persons
mentioned in the order on the east side of the street had encroached on
the street beyond the foundations of the houses by, in general, two to
three feet — and in some instances more. These encroachments were
obstructions to his Majesty's subjects in their passage through the street
and to the Market held there. The report stated that the stalls and other

---

166 In this decree How's name is rendered 'Howe'. He signed as 'How'.

encroachments should be taken away to the ancient foundations and upright peers, with liberty granted to hang a stall board to turn over and extend into the street one foot and no more. This recommendation was according to the Act of Parliament.

The report, along with other things, was filed with the registrar of the Court.

The Court then demanded from Gerrard whether he had anything to offer concerning the encroachment. Gerrard stated that he was a tenant in the house for only a few years yet to come. He gave notice to Richard Edlinson, his landlord, of the order to appear. The Court called on Edlinson, but he did not appear.

The Court then required Hooke, Oliver and Gray to make an oath about the dimensions of the encroachment. They testified that the property's post extended twenty inches beyond the ancient foundation and that the stall extended about two feet at the north end and about two and a half feet at the south end beyond the ancient foundation.

The Court ordered that:

(1) At his own expense, John Gerrard must pull down the encroaching post and the stall back to the ancient foundation and upright piers ['peeres'] of the house.

(2) He must also lay the ground underneath the encroachment even with the street, and well and sufficiently pave it so that it would be fit for commodious passage.

(3) The work must be accomplished within the next two months.[167]

Decree 45 (page 187)

17 Oct. 1677.　　Baron Littleton; Justice Jones (s); James Reading, Esq. (s); John Freeman, Esq. (s); John Appellbe, Esq.

The following persons were in possession of encroachments and purprestures on the High Street between the Bridge Foot and Compter Lane: John Gerrard; John Page; Dorothy Norris, widow; Sarah

---

167 In the following year, the *Repertories of the Court of Aldermen* described a Bridge Foot property that the Southwark fire court had 'declared to be a Common Nuisance'. Rep., LXXXIII, fol. 147ᵛ (19 March 1678). Because the 'Proprietors' had not yet removed the obstruction, the Court of Aldermen instructed the City Solicitor, William Lightfoote, to prefer and prosecute a bill of indictment at Southwark's next Quarter Session. The records of the Borough Quarter Session indicate that John Gerrard, Hosier of Bridge Foot, was brought before the court on 26 June 1678. See LMA CLA/046/01/003. For further discussion of the proceedings and Gerrard's fate, see p. 71.

Phillipps, widow;[168] William Boyes; Samuell Shipton;[169] Richard Pope; Francis Walker; Joseph Boyes; Robert Greene; James Lambe; Daniell Williamson;[170] Benjamin Newington; George Vandike; John Russell; William Head; John Bankes;[171] Edmund Yalden; Joseph Edwards; Joane Merrey;[172] William Paxton; James Cumber; Walter Bushnell; Thomas Clarke; Thomas Champneyes;[173] John Rockett;[174] Thomas Morgan; Richard Allen; Robert Titchborne; William Bromsall; Nicholas Uridge; Jeremy Colloway; Thomas Smith; John Fowler; William Chapman; Richard Stannard;[175] Nathaniell Collier; Samuell Thornebury; Samuell Graves; Robert Martin; Nathaniell Joyner;[176] Francis Johnson; Martha Sanders; John Arnold; Henry Bartlett;[177] The President Treasurer and Governors of St Thomas's Hospital; Jonadab Ballam;[178] […] Phillips, widow;[179] Thomas Lane;[180] Philip Kimpland; William

168 The decree rendered her last name as 'Phillips' when ordering her to remedy the encroachment.

169 The decree rendered his given name as 'Samuell' when ordering him to remediate his encroachment.

170 Daniell Williamson had been a defendant in *Cooper v. Arnold* (Decree 24). This defendant is likely the same person.

171 It is likely that this defendant is the same John Bankes who had been the petitioner in *Bankes v. Wight* (Decree 2), and whose name appeared again in *Gale v. Wight* (Decree 23).

172 The subsequent order rendered her name as 'Merry'.

173 In stating that he had been summoned, the decree rendered his last name as 'Champneys' but again as 'Champneyes' in the order requiring defendants to remediate their encroachments.

174 The registrar rendered his name as 'Rocket' when stating that he had been summoned, but again as 'Rockett' when ordering him to remediate his encroachment.

175 The decree did not again mention Stannard, either when reciting the individuals summoned or when ordering defendants to remediate their encroachments.

176 The decree did not again mention Joyner, either when reciting the individuals summoned or when ordering defendants to remediate their encroachments.

177 It is likely that this defendant is the same Henry Bartlett, Grocer, who was mentioned as a subtenant in *Duffeild v. Smith* (Decree 31), and was mentioned again in *Sledd v. Browker* (Decree 47).

178 Ballam had been a defendant in *Snell v. Browker* (Decree 13), and was again mentioned in *Hudson v. Browker* (Decree 49).

179 The decree left a blank space at this point for Philips's first name. The decree did not again mention her. She was neither issued a summons nor ordered to remediate any encroachment — unless she is the Sarah Phillipps, widow, mentioned p. 224, note 168.

180 It is likely that this defendant is the Thomas Lane, Turner, who had been the petitioner in *Lane v. Sledd* (Decree 18). The decree did not again mention Lane, either when reciting the individuals summoned or when ordering defendants to

Cooper;[181] Thomas Radford;[182] Charles Hutchest;[183] William Ellis; Joseph Peck; Edward Lole; William Frewin; John Smith; John Bacon; John Middleton; James Bend; Andrew Harrison; John Bodle; Edmund Rous; William Wilson; John Webb; Roger Harris; Roger Dixy;[184] Christopher Farrington; Thomas Harris; Joseph Nicholls; Richard Mansfeild; James Chitty;[185] Elizabeth Miller; Richard Smith; George Crips; Thomas Williams; [...] Clarke, widow;[186] Thomas Hawes; William Nelson; James Woollball;[187] William Dingley;[188] John Johnson; William Weston; Joseph Brockett; Peter Morris; and John Badmoring.

All these individuals were summoned to appear in court on 8 June 1677. The greatest number of them appeared, but a few did not. Tristram Lucas, Gentleman, made oath in court that he had summoned these persons to appear in court.

At this time, the Court came to the decision, described in Decree 44, to order the surveyors of new buildings in London — together with William Gray, Carpenter, and such commissioners of the Court as wished to join them — to survey the encroachments on 13 July.[189] As stated in Decree 44, they were then to make a report to the Court at its next sitting. The parties were to be given convenient notice of this inspection, and tenants were to give notice to their landlords of the inspection. The parties were then to appear on 17 July.

The persons in possession of the encroachments were given notice of the inspection on 13 July.

remediate their encroachments. The outcome of Decree 18, which was rendered on 5 October 1677 (or twelve days before this decree) may have rendered Lane's participation in this decree moot.

181 It is likely that this defendant is the William Cooper who was the petitioner in *Cooper v. Arnold* (Decree 24).

182 This defendant may be the Thomas Radford who had been had been mentioned as a tenant in *Chandler v. Body* (Decree 29).

183 It is like that this defendant is the Charles Hutchest who had been a defendant in *Marshall v. Peryn* (Decree 17).

184 The registrar spelled the name as 'Dixey' when reciting the individuals summoned.

185 The registrar spelled the name as 'Chittey' in the order requiring him to remediate his encroachment.

186 The decree left a blank space at this point for Clarke's first name.

187 The registrar spelled the name 'Woolball' when reciting the individuals summoned but again as 'Woollball' when ordering defendants to remediate their encroachments.

188 The registrar rendered the name as 'Dingly' in the order requiring him to remove his encroachment.

189 Unlike Decree 44, this decree provided Gray's trade.

As described in Decree 44, Robert Hooke and John Oliver, the surveyors of new buildings in London, Gray, Barker and Rich viewed the encroachments. They subsequently made a report which stated that they began their viewing at the corner of the east side of the High Street at Bridge Foot. At the corner of Bridge Foot on the east side of the High Street, the post of the house was nearly two feet beyond the ancient post. Beyond that, the stalls and the posts of the houses of the defendants on the east side of the High Street generally encroached on the street beyond the foundations by two to three feet, with some of them more. Moreover, some of the houses encroached in their upper parts. On the west side of the High Street from Compter Lane to Bridge Foot, the stalls, posts and penthouses of the defendants generally encroached on the street by three feet — and some of them considerably more.

The report conceived that these encroachments obstructed the passage of his Majesty's subjects through the street and to the market. The report recommended that the stalls and other encroachments be taken away to the ancient foundations and upright piers ['peeres']. Moreover, the penthouses should not extend beyond the projection of the jetty windows on the head of the first storey. The exception was houses built of brick, which should have the liberty to have a penthouse not exceeding four feet. Liberty should also be granted to persons to hang stall boards to turn over and extend into the street one foot and no more. This was in accord with the Act of Parliament.

The report also conceived that the gully hole at the Bridge Foot was a great obstruction to passage into Southwark, and it should be amended and reformed by moving it about forty feet further to the south and then making an arched 'Shoare' (or sewer) with flat grates for the conveyance of water.[190]

The report was submitted to the Court on 13 July 1677. At that time, after debate, the Court decreed that Gerrard must pull down the corner post and stall of his shop. But the cases involving all other persons were adjourned to this day.

All persons in present possession of an encroachment were summoned to appear. At this point, the decree again recited the parties listed at the beginning of the decree. Nonetheless, a few alterations occurred:

- As stated in footnotes above, several parties (Stannard, Joyner and Phillips) were not mentioned in the list of parties summoned. His

190 Mould has obscured parts of this sentence of the decree. Letters in the middle of the phrase that I rendered as 'gully hole' are partially illegible. Likewise, letters in the middle of the phrase that appears to be 'Arched Shoares' are partially

case having been determined in Decree 44, Gerrard was also left off the list.

- Several new parties or relationships were mentioned:
  - Christopher Cope was summoned because he was now in possession of the encroachment lately possessed by William Paxton (Paxton is not again mentioned in the decree);
  - Robert Titchborne was summoned 'by the aforesaid Thomas Clarke';
  - Jeremy Colloway was summoned 'by Mr Thomas Rous';[191]
  - Francis Johnson was summoned 'by his wife';
  - Mr. Lock and Mr Jekyll were summoned on behalf of St Thomas's Hospital;
  - William Ellis was summoned for himself and on behalf of Joseph Peck;
  - William Frewin was summoned for himself and on behalf of Edward Lole;
  - William Baker, whose name was not previously mentioned, was summoned by his landlord John Smith, who was mentioned;
  - James Bend was summoned for himself and on behalf of John Middleton;
  - Thomas Rous was summoned on behalf of John Bodle and Edmund Rous;
  - William Wilson was summoned for himself and on behalf of John Goldsmith;[192]
  - Elizabeth Miller was summoned by Andrew Godin;
  - George Crips was summoned for himself and on behalf of James Chitty; and
  - William Oxley was summoned because he was recently married to widow Clarke;
  - William Smith was summoned, although his name did not appear among the parties listed at the outset of the decree, nor did the decree state on whose behalf he was summoned.

---

illegible. I am fairly (but not entirely) confident that my rendering of both phrases is correct.

191 Rous was the petitioner in *Rous v. Kellett* (Decree 43).

192 Goldsmith was not among the parties listed at the outset of the decree.

The following defendants did not appear: George Vandike, Joane Merry, Richard Allen, William Boyes (who was now in possession of the encroachment lately in the possession of William Chapman), William Owen,[193] John Arnold, Richard Dingle (who was now in possession of the stall lately in the possession of Henry Bartlett), Jonadab Ballam, William Cooper, John Cooper,[194] Charles Hutchest and John Badmoring. Tristram Lucas made an oath that he had served these parties.

The Court heard what the parties had to offer concerning the encroachments. John Oliver and William Gray then testified under oath about the dimensions of each of the following encroachments. After the testimony, the Court formulaically declared each 'encroachment and purpresture' — whether a stall, a 'shoppe' or posts — a nuisance. The Court ordered removal of the encroachments by 17 November 1677 (unless otherwise noted). It also ordered the laying and paving of the ground where the encroachments had been to make it level with the High Street and commodious for passage. The extent of each encroachment, as given by Oliver's and Gray's testimony, was as follows:

- The stall of the shop in the occupation of John Page encroached into the street beyond the ancient foundation and upright piers two feet across the whole front.

- The stall of the shop in the occupation of Dorothy Norris encroached two feet and three inches across the whole front.

- The stall of the shop in the occupation of Sarah Philips encroached two feet across the whole front.

- The stall of the shop in the occupation of Samuell Shipton encroached two feet and nine inches across the whole front.

- The stall of the shop in the occupation of Richard Pope encroached two feet and nine inches across the whole front.

- The stall of the shop in the possession[195] of Francis Walker encroached two feet and nine inches across the whole front.

- The stall of the shop in the possession of Joseph Boyes encroached two feet and nine inches across the whole front.

193 Owen was not among the parties listed at the outset of the decree, and the decree does not mention his relationship to any of the listed parties.

194 John Cooper was not among the parties listed at the outset of the decree, although William Cooper was listed.

195 In reciting the testimony of Oliver and Gray, most properties were described as being 'in the occupation' of a defendant, but some properties were described as being 'in the possession' of a defendant. It is not clear that this

- The stall of the shop in the occupation of Robert Greene encroached two feet and six inches at the north end and two feet and nine inches at south end.

- The stall of the shop in the possession of James Lambe encroached two feet and four inches at the north end and five feet and eight inches at south end.

- The stall of the shop in the possession of Daniell Williamson encroached two feet and eight inches across the whole front.

- The stall of the shop in the occupation of Benjamin Newington encroached two feet and ten inches across the whole front.

- The stall of the shop in the occupation of George Vandike encroached two feet and nine inches across the whole front.

- The stall of the shop in the occupation of John Russell encroached two feet and six inches across the whole front.

- The shop[196] in the occupation of William Head encroached two feet and six inches across the whole front.

- The stall of the shop in the occupation of John Bankes encroached three feet across the entire front.

- The stall of the shop in the occupation of Edmund Yalden encroached three feet at the north end and two feet and nine inches at south end.

- The stall of the shop in the occupation of Joseph Edwards encroached two feet and seven inches across the whole front.

- The stall of the shop in the occupation of Joane Merry encroached two feet and nine inches across the whole front.

- The stall of the shop in the occupation of Christopher Cope encroached two feet and six inches across the whole front.

- The stall of the shop in the possession of James Cumber encroached three feet across the whole front.

- The stall of the shop in the occupation of Edmund Yalden encroached three feet at the north end and two feet and nine inches at south end.

difference is meaningful; in the order requiring remediation for the properties 'in the occupation' of a defendant, the Court usually referred to the property as being in that defendant's 'possession'. I replicate the witnesses' description (whether 'occupation' or 'possession') in this list of orders.

196 This property is the first one in which the shop (and not merely the stall of the shop) extended into the High Street. The number of affected 'shoppes' or 'stalls of shoppes' demonstrated the commercial nature of the High Street.

- The stall of the shop in the possession of Walter Bushnell encroached three feet across the whole front.
- The stall of the shop in the possession of Thomas Clarke encroached two feet and six inches across the whole front.
- The stall of the shop in the occupation of Thomas Champneyes encroached three feet across the whole front.
- The stall of the shop in the occupation of John Rockett encroached three feet across the whole front.
- The stall of the shop in the occupation of Thomas Morgan encroached two feet and nine inches at the north end and two feet and nine inches at south end.
- The posts before the doors of the house in the possession of Richard Allen encroached two feet.
- The stall of the shop in the occupation of Robert Titchborne encroached two feet and nine inches across the whole front.
- The stall of the shop in the occupation of William Bromsall encroached two feet and nine inches at the north end and two feet and six inches at the south end.
- The stall of the shop in the occupation of Nicholas Uridge encroached two feet and six inches at the north end and two feet and nine inches at the south end.
- The stall of the shop in the occupation of Jeremy Colloway encroached two feet and nine inches at the north end and three feet and six inches at the south end.
- The stall of the shop in the occupation of Thomas Smith encroached three feet and three inches across the whole front.
- The stall of the shop in the occupation of John Fowler encroached three feet and two inches across the whole front.
- The stall of the shop in the occupation of William Boyes encroached three feet across the whole front.
- The posts before the door of the house in the possession of William Owen encroached two feet and six inches.
- The posts before the door of the house in the occupation of Nathaniell Collier encroached two feet and six inches.
- The stall of the shop in the occupation of Samuell Thornebury encroached two feet and six inches across the whole front.
- The shop in the occupation of Samuel Graves, who was one of the tenants of St Thomas's Hospital, encroached two feet and six inches

across the whole front. Graves was given until the feast of the birth of our Lord 1677 to abate and take away the encroachment.

- The shop in the occupation of Robert Martin, who was also one of the tenants of St Thomas's Hospital, encroached four feet and nine inches across the whole front. Martin was given until the feast of the birth of our Lord 1677 to abate and take away the encroachment.

- The shop in the occupation of Francis Johnson, who was also one of the tenants of St Thomas's Hospital, encroached four feet across the whole front. Johnson was given until the feast of the birth of our Lord 1677 to abate and take away the encroachment.

- The shop in the occupation of Martha Sanders, who was also one of the tenants of St Thomas's Hospital, encroached four feet across the whole front. Sanders was given until the feast of the birth of our Lord 1677 to abate and take away the encroachment.

- The shop in the occupation of John Arnold, who was also one of the tenants of St Thomas's Hospital, encroached four feet across the whole front. Arnold was given until the feast of the birth of our Lord 1677 to abate and take away the encroachment.

- The shop in the occupation of Richard Dingle, who was also one of the tenants of St Thomas's Hospital, encroached four feet across the whole front. Dingle was given until the feast of the birth of our Lord 1677 to abate and take away the encroachment.

- The posts before the door of St Thomas's Hospital encroached three feet. The President, Treasurer, and Governors of the Hospital were given until the feast of the birth of our Lord 1677 to abate and take away the encroachment. The Hospital was, however, given liberty, if it thought fit, to bring the wall of the hospital forward toward the street, so as to make it even with the shops on each side (once those shops were regulated and reformed according to this decree).

- The stall of the shop in the occupation of Jonadab Ballam encroached two feet and nine inches across the whole front.

- The stall of the shop in the occupation of William Cooper encroached two feet and six inches across the whole front.

- The stall of the shop in the occupation of Philip Kimpland encroached two feet across the whole front.

- The stall of the shed[197] in the occupation of Thomas Radford encroached two feet and six inches across the whole front.

197 The decree described a 'shed', not a 'shoppe'.

- The stall of the shop in the occupation of John Cooper encroached two feet and nine inches across the whole front.
- The stall of the shop in the occupation of Charles Hutchest encroached two feet and nine inches at the south end and two feet and six inches at the north end.[198]
- The stall of the shop in the occupation of William Ellis encroached two feet and ten inches across the whole front.
- The stall of the shop in the occupation of Joseph Peck encroached two feet and nine inches across the whole front.
- The stall of the shop in the occupation of Edward Lole encroached two feet across the whole front.
- The stall of the shop in the occupation of William Frewin encroached two feet and six inches across the whole front.
- The stall of the shop in the occupation of William Baker encroached two feet and nine inches across the whole front.
- The stall of the shop in the occupation of John Smith encroached three feet across the whole front.
- The stall of the shop in the occupation of John Bacon encroached three feet across the whole front.
- The stall of the shop in the occupation of John Middleton encroached three feet across the whole front.
- The stall of the shop in the possession of James Bend encroached three feet across the whole front.
- The stall of the shop in the occupation of Andrew Harrison encroached three feet and three inches across the whole front.
- The stall of the shop in the occupation of John Bodle encroached three feet and six inches across the whole front.
- The stall of the shop in the occupation of Edmund Rous encroached three feet and six inches across the whole front.
- The stall of the shop in the occupation of John Goldsmith encroached three feet and six inches across the whole front.
- The stall of the shop in the occupation of William Wilson encroached three feet and six inches across the whole front.

198 This order is the first to reverse directions from south to north; until now, the orders had given the encroaching dimension on the north end first. My surmise is that, somewhere between the properties occupied by Ballam and Hutchest, the Court finished dealing with the properties on the east side of the High Street and began dealing with properties on the west side of the High Street (starting from St Margaret's Hill and moving north to the Bridge).

- The stall of the shop in the occupation of John Webb encroached three feet and six inches across the whole front.
- The stall of the shop in the occupation of Roger Harris encroached four feet across the whole front.
- The stall of the shop in the occupation of Roger Dixey encroached three feet and six inches across the whole front.
- The stall of the shop in the occupation of Christopher Farrington encroached three feet and nine inches across the whole front.
- The stall of the shop in the occupation of Thomas Harris encroached three feet and three inches at the south end and three feet and six inches at the north end.
- The stall of the shop in the occupation of Joseph Nicholls encroached three feet and six inches across the whole front.
- The stall of the shop in the occupation of Richard Mansfeild encroached three feet across the whole front.
- The stall of the shop in the occupation of James Chitty encroached three feet across the whole front.
- The stall of the shop in the occupation of Elizabeth Miller encroached three feet and three inches across the whole front.
- The stall of the shop in the occupation of Richard Smith encroached three feet and three inches at the south end and three feet and six inches at the north end.
- The stall of the shop in the occupation of George Crips encroached three feet and six inches at the south end and three feet and three inches at the north end.
- The stall of the shop in the occupation of Thomas Williams encroached three feet and three inches at the south end and three feet and six inches at the north end.
- The stall of the shop in the occupation of William Oxley encroached three feet and six inches across the whole front.
- The stall of the shop in the occupation of Thomas Hawes encroached two feet and six inches at the south end and two feet and nine inches at the north end.
- The stall of the shop in the occupation of William Nelson encroached three feet and three inches across the whole front.
- The stall of the shop in the occupation of James Woollball encroached two feet and six inches across the whole front.

- The stall of the shop in the occupation of William Dingly encroached three feet across the whole front.
- The stall of the shop in the occupation of John Johnson encroached two feet and six inches across the whole front.
- The stall of the shop in the occupation of William Weston encroached two feet and nine inches at the south end and three feet at the north end.
- The stall of the shop in the occupation of Joseph Brockett encroached three feet across the whole front.
- The stall belonging to the shop[199] in the occupation of Peter Morris encroached three feet across the whole front.
- The stall of the shop in the occupation of John Badmoring encroached three feet at the south end and two feet and six inches at the north end.
- The post standing by the door of the messuage in the occupation of William Smith encroached three feet.

In addition, the decree provided that, where any penthouses belonging to the aforesaid persons exceeded the measurements mentioned in the surveyors' report, the persons pull down and reduce their penthouses to the measurements stated in the report. The order gave those affected until 17 November 1677 to comply.

Finally, the Court stated that, notwithstanding the prior orders, the persons ordered to reform their encroachment had liberty and power to maintain a stallboard that could be turned over and extended into the street one foot when the shops or shop windows were open.

Decree 46 (page 211)

8 May 1678.   Lord Mayor of London [Francis Chaplin]; Justice Wyndham (s); Sir George Waterman; Sir William Hooker (s); Edward Smith (s); Thomas Barker (s); Richard Howe (s);[200] Peter Rich, Esq. (s); John Freeman, Esq. (s)

Several persons in possession of encroachments and purprestures had been summoned by the Court on 8 June 1677 and appeared accordingly.

---

199 It is not clear whether a difference exists between 'the stall of the shoppe', which is how the registrar characterized previous encroachments, and 'the stall belonging to the shoppe', which is how this encroachment was described.

200 Although the registrar usually spelled the name as 'How', this decree varied the spelling. How signed the decree as 'How'.

The Court ordered the surveyors of new buildings in London, as well as William Gray and such commissioners of this Court as wished to join them, to meet and view the encroachments on 13 July 1677. They were then to submit a report. On 13 July, Robert Hooke and John Oliver (the City Surveyors), William Gray, Thomas Barker and Peter Rich viewed the properties and submitted a report.

Among other matters, the report found that the house in the occupation of Evan Evans on the north end of the High Street at Bridge Foot encroached into the street on its south end. The encroachment, a stall and post, jutted into the street about two feet. In addition, Evans's house on the east side encroached two feet, to the great obstruction of the passage in the street.

Evans appeared personally in court. Mr Jenner was his counsel. Counsel informed the Court that the house was not located within the borough of Southwark, but rather was located in Bridge Ward within London. The house was rated to all duties in London. The Act of Parliament establishing this Court gave it power only over encroachments in the borough of Southwark.

Upon debate, it appeared plainly to the Court that the south end of the house encroached into the High Street in the Borough, even though the ancient foundations of the house were admitted to be within London. Therefore, the Court required an account under oath of the dimensions of the encroachment. Robert Hooke and John Oliver made oath that the stall and post at the corner of the house extended toward the south end into the High Street two feet beyond the ancient foundations.[201]

The Court declared this encroachment to be a nuisance.

The Court ordered that:

(1) By 29 September 1678, Evan Evans was to abate and take away the encroachment of a stall and post at the corner of his house, extending toward the High Street.

(2) Evans must also lay the ground even with the street and pave it to be fit and commodious for passage.

(3) Given that it was alleged that a considerable part of the encroachment on the east side of the house was also regulated by this Court, but that this allegation was not fully proven, Robert Hooke, John Oliver and William Gray, together with such commissioners of the Court as wished to join them, should meet and review the encroachment on the east side. They should

---

201 Hooke's diary entry for 8 May 1678 made no mention of an appearance before the Court.

examine and discover as they think most proper whether this portion of the house, or any part of it, lies within the High Street of the Borough of Southwark. They were to make a report under their hands as soon as convenient, after which the Court would further proceed.[202]

Decree 47 (page 213)

5 Oct. 1677.   Baron Littleton; Justice Jones; James Reading, Esq. (s); Peter Rich, Esq. (s); John Freeman, Esq. (s); John Applebee[203]

Daniell Sledd, Citizen and Ironmonger of London,[204] v. Thomas Browker, Esq.; Edward Lloyd, Esq.; Dorothy his Wife; William Kent, Clerke; Jane his Wife; Sir Littleton Osbaldeston, Baronet; Dame Katherine his Wife; Thomas Lowfeild, an Infant; Mary Browker, an Infant; Martha Browker, an Infant; Nicholas Hare, Citizen and Grocer of London; and Joseph Gibbon, Citizen and Tallow Chandler of London[205]

Thomas Browker, Esquire, was seised in fee of a messuage. By an indenture of lease dated 30 June 1656, Browker demised the premises to the petitioner's father, Daniell Sledd, Citizen and Ironmonger of London, for a term of forty-two years commencing on 26 December 1663. The annual rent was £17, payable quarterly. The premises, on the east side of the High Street, were known by the sign of the Antelope and then by the sign of the Three Horseshoes. The premises included a yard and backhouse. It had been in the tenure or occupation of William Frith.[206]

The petitioner's father had since died and by his will devised the premises to the petitioner.

By his will, Thomas Browker, the lessor, devised his reversionary interest in the messuage, and in divers others, to Mary Browker, his wife.

---

202 The decrees do not contain any further report or describe any actions that the Court took regarding this alleged encroachment.

203 No common-law judge signed this decree.

204 This decree involves the same property as *Lane v. Sledd* (Decree 18), which was also rendered on 5 October 1677. In that decree, Daniell Sledd, the defendant, was described as a Linen Draper. It may be that the registrar erroneously assigned Sledd the trade of his father who, according to this decree, was an Ironmonger.

205 It seems unlikely that Joseph Gibbon is the same 'Gibbon' (or 'Gibbons') described as the agent for Shrewsbury in *Houghton v. Mayor of Shrewsbury* (Decree 4), and *Lane v. Mayor of Shrewsbury* (Decree 26). In the Index of Persons, I list them separately.

206 See Decree 18.

She then settled this messuage, as well as others, on herself for ninety-nine years (should she live so long) and then on various family members in the manner described in Decree 8.[207] Upon the death of Mary and her son Thomas Browker the elder, the interest in the reversion of the premises came into the hands of the defendant Thomas Browker the younger for ninety-nine years (should he live so long). Under Mary Browker's property settlement, Dorothy Lloyd, Jane Kent, Dame Katherine Osbaldeston, Thomas Lowfeild (the son of Robert Lowfeild and Mary Browker's daughter Elizabeth, both now deceased) and Mary and Martha Browker (the daughters of Thomas Browker the elder and the sisters of Thomas Browker the younger) held contingent interests upon the death of Thomas the younger.

Thomas Browker the younger then demised, bargained and sold his interest and the yearly rent of £17 to Henry Bartlett, Grocer, for a term of eighty years, if Browker should live so long, commencing on the feast of St Michael the Archangel 1675. Bartlett was to pay an annual rent of one peppercorn for this interest.[208] By good and sufficient ways and means, Bartlett's interest came to be vested in the defendants, Hare and Gibbon.

The messuage and back tenement burned down and still lay in ruins. The petitioner was willing to rebuild on encouragement.

Summonses to the defendants were issued. The petitioner Daniell Sledd appeared personally, with Mr Bowes and Mr Jenner as his counsel. Among the defendants, Thomas Lowfeild, Mary Browker and Martha Browker appeared personally. The Court specially admitted Anne Cooke, widow, as guardian of Thomas Lowfeild. The Court also specially admitted Mary Leighton, wife of Charles Leighton, Gentleman, and mother of Mary and Martha Browker, as their guardian; Mr Ward and Mr Pettit were their counsel. Hare and Gibbon appeared personally without counsel.

The remaining defendants (Thomas Browker, the Lloyds, the Kents and the Osbaldestons) did not appear personally or through counsel,

---

207 See pp. 120–21.

208 As *Cole v. Browker* (Decree 10), and *Bennett v. Browker* (Decree 12), have shown, Thomas Browker the younger used some of his inheritance to maintain family members — in those cases his sisters — even as he spiralled into bankruptcy. Although none of the fire court's decrees mentioned any dispositions to his mother, the will of Mary Leighton (Thomas the younger's mother), which was made on 24 March 1685 and proved on 27 February 1686, stated that Thomas Browker had sold his interest in certain assets to Henry Bartlett, Salter of Southwark, in return for Bartlett agreeing to provide an annuity to Mary Leighton for her maintenance during Browker's life. The will recited that Mary Leighton, in turn, sold her interest

but rather 'made default'. To be satisfied in the matter, the Court took sworn testimony from John Moth of the parish of St Saviour and Benjamin Colinbine of London, Haberdasher. Both testified as they had done in Decree 8. On 21 September 1677, Moth served a summons on the turnkey of the King's Bench prison after determining that Thomas Browker the younger was a prisoner there, and Colinbine served summonses on Katherine Osbaldeston at Woodstock[209] in Oxfordshire on 13 August 1677; on Edward Lloyd at his dwelling called Beth Lloyd in Montgomery shire on 15 August 1677; and on Jane Kent at Roade in Sommersetshire on 19 September 1677. The Court's registrar collected affidavits in writing to this effect.

The petitioner's counsel informed the Court that the petitioner had twenty-eight years to come on his lease, and he was willing to rebuild if he had encouragement through an increased term and abated rent. The defendants' counsel much opposed abatement, alleging that the messuage was a front house to the High Street and on the best side of the way. The rent of £17 was but a ground rent, so the petitioner should be required to build and pay the rent without abatement.

The petitioner's counsel responded that an increase in the term was of very small value; moreover, as the messuage was a front house, it would need to be rebuilt with brick. This was more expensive, and the charge should not fall wholly on the petitioner but should be borne in part by the landlords.

Having heard the matter fully, the Court pronounced it just and reasonable that the petitioner's term be increased to seventy years from the feast of St Michael the Archangel 1677, with the rent reduced to 20 marks [£13 6s. 8d.]. All rent was discharged until the feast of St Michael the Archangel 1677, and the first quarterly payment was due on the feast of the birth of our Lord 1677.

in the annuity. One portion of the proceeds, £100, was the only asset mentioned in Leighton's will. Leighton bequeathed this £100 to several individuals. Among the bequests were £10 apiece to her daughters, Mary (Monck) and Martha (Browker). See TNA, PROB 11/382/275. No bequest was made to her son, Thomas, suggesting that he may have been dead by 1685.

The annuity described in Leighton's will may involve the transaction to which this decree refers. In Leighton's will, Henry 'Bartelett' of Southwark was described as a Salter, and here Henry 'Bartlett', also of Southwark, was described as a Grocer. If it is the same transaction, that fact helps to make sense of Thomas the younger's disposition of his life interest in various rents in return for a peppercorn or other trivial value.

209 In prior decrees involving the Osbaldestons, the registrar had rendered the location as 'Woodstocke'.

The Court ordered that:

(1) The petitioner Daniell Sledd was discharged of paying all rent incurred on the premises from the time of the fire until the feast of St Michael the Archangel 1677.

(2) Thereafter, the yearly rent was sunk to £13 6s. 8d for the duration of the lease. The petitioner was discharged of paying the remaining £3 13s. 4d. of the original £17 annual rent.

(3) The petitioner was to receive an additional term of forty-one and three-quarter years, commencing and taking effect immediately at the end of the present lease on the feast of the birth of our Lord 1705. The petitioner's whole term was to be seventy years from the feast of St Michael the Archangel 1677. The annual rent for this term was to be £13 6s. 8d., payable to the defendants according to their interests. Payment would be made at the days and times specified in the present lease.

(4) The petitioner's first rent payment was due on the feast of the birth of our Lord 1677.

(5) The petitioner must, with all convenient speed and at his charge, build one or more good and substantial messuages and buildings of brick and other good and sufficient materials. The messuage must be finished in good workmanlike manner as other newly-built messuages in Southwark were built.

(6) To avoid difficulties in recovering the rent and for ascertaining the covenants mutually to be performed, on the petitioners' reasonable request and at his expense, the defendants Hare, Gibbon, Browker, the Lloyds, the Kents and the Osbaldestons — together with Thomas Lowfeild and Mary and Martha Browker when they reached the age of twenty-one — must execute a good and sufficient lease by indenture for the additional forty-one and three-quarter years decreed to the petitioner. The lease should contain such reasonable covenants as contained in the present lease. The petitioner must accept the lease and deliver up its counterpart.

(7) The petitioner might lawfully, peaceably and quietly enjoy the small tenements notwithstanding the coverture of the feme coverts, the infancy of the infants or any other interest.

Decree 48 (page 220)

5 Oct. 1677. Baron Littleton; Justice Jones (s); Thomas Barker, Esq. (s); James Reading, Esq. (s); Peter Rich, Esq. (s); John Freeman, Esq. (s); John Applebee

Thomas Hudson of Southwark, Scrivener,[210] *v. Thomas Browker, Esq.;*
Edward Lloyd, Esq.; Dorothy his Wife; William Kent, Clerke; Jane his
Wife; Sir Littleton Osbaldeston, Baronet; Dame Katherine his Wife;
Thomas Lowfeild, an Infant; Mary Browker, an Infant; Martha Browker,
an Infant; and Joseph Day of Southwark, Brewer

Thomas Browker, Esquire, was seised in fee of a messuage or tenement.
By an indenture of lease dated 24 July 1651, Browker demised the
premises to Robert Knightley of St Saviour's Parish in in Southwark,
clerk. The premises were then in the tenure of Knightley. The lease ran
from the feast of the Nativity of St John the Baptist 1651 for forty-one
years. The annual rent was £3 10s., payable quarterly.

The messuage contained a hall with a chimney. The hall was sixteen
feet and ten inches in length and fourteen feet in breadth. Beneath the
hall was a coal hole ['colehole'] measuring eleven feet and eight inches
in length and nine feet and three inches in breadth. The premises were
located within and abutting the Chaingate.

By good assignment in the law, Knightley's interest in the premises
came to be vested in the petitioner.

By his will, Thomas Browker devised his interest in the messuage,
and in divers others, to Mary Browker, his wife. She then settled this
messuage, as well as others, on herself for ninety-nine years (should
she live so long) and then on various family members in the manner
described in Decree 8.[211] Upon the death of Mary and her son Thomas
Browker the elder, the interest in the reversion of the premises came into
the hands of the defendant Thomas Browker the younger for ninety-
nine years (should he live so long). Under Mary Browker's property
settlement, Dorothy Lloyd, Jane Kent, Dame Katherine Osbaldeston,
Thomas Lowfeild (the son of Robert Lowfeild and Mary Browker's
daughter Elizabeth, both now deceased) and Mary and Martha Browker
(the daughters of Thomas Browker the elder and the sisters of Thomas
Browker the younger) held contingent interests upon the death of
Thomas the younger.

210 Hudson appears as a witness in *Bankes v. Wight* (Decree 2), and *Nicolson v.*
Browker (Decree 8), and as the petitioner in *Hudson v. Mayor of London* (Decree 33),
and *Hudson v. Browker* (Decree 49).

211 See pp. 120–21. Due to the poor condition of this decree, a handful of the
words describing the Browker family members and their interests are illegible, but
the legible words are identical to the formulaic descriptions in all the previous
decrees involving the Browkers. In my summary of this decree, I assumed that
the illegible words were likewise identical. This petition omits Thomas Browker's
residence in Upper Peover.

At the yearly rent of one peppercorn, Thomas Browker the younger then demised, bargained and sold his interest in the premises and the yearly rent of £3 10s. for a long term of years determinable on Browker's death. That interest was now vested in the defendant Joseph Day.

The messuage burned down. The petitioner was willing to rebuild the premises on encouragement (by an increase in the term of years and abatement of the rent) from the interested defendants. But the petitioner needed the aid of the Court to get this encouragement.

Summonses to the defendants were issued. The petitioner Thomas Hudson appeared personally, with Sir George Jeffreys, Mr Bowes and Mr Jenner as his counsel. Among the defendants, Thomas Lowfeild, Mary Browker and Martha Browker appeared personally. The Court specially admitted Anne Cooke, widow, as guardian of Thomas Lowfeild. The Court also specially admitted Mary Leighton, wife of Charles Leighton, Gentleman, and mother of Mary and Martha Browker, as their guardian; Mr Ward and Mr Pettitt were their counsel. Day also appeared personally without counsel.

The remaining defendants (Thomas Browker, the Lloyds, the Kents and the Osbaldestons) did not appear personally or through counsel. To be satisfied in the matter, the Court took sworn testimony from John Moth of the parish of St Saviour and Benjamin Colinbine of London, Haberdasher. Both testified as they had done in Decree 8. On 21 September 1677, Moth served a summons on the turnkey of the King's Bench prison after determining that Thomas Browker the younger was a prisoner there, and Colinbine served summonses on Katherine Osbaldeston at Woodstocke in Oxfordshire on 13 August 1677; on Edward Lloyd at his dwelling called Beth Lloyd in Montgomery shire on 15 August 1677; and on Jane Kent at Road in Sommersetshire on 19 September 1677.[212] The Court's registrar collected affidavits in writing to this effect.

The petitioner's counsel prayed the Court to provide encouragement for his rebuilding. Given that he had only fifteen years (from the feast of the Nativity of St John 1677) remaining on the lease, a considerable addition of years was warranted, as was an abatement of rent. The defendants' counsel opposed abatement of any rent because the present rent was very small; an increase in term of years was therefore a sufficient contribution to the petitioner.

---

212 A few words at a corner of a page, describing service on Jane Kent, are no longer legible, but the legible words, when combined with the context provided by other decrees reciting the same event, indicate that service on Jane Kent occurred on 19 September 1677.

The petitioner's counsel then alleged that the piece of ground on which the messuage stood was very small, scarcely big enough to rebuild a single house. The ground was so small that the petitioner would never have meddled with it had he not built a part of the chimney for his adjoining house, where he lived, on this ground. Nonetheless, the petitioner was content to give one-half of the former rent if accompanied by a considerable increase in the term of years.

Having heard the matter fully, the Court pronounced it just and reasonable that the petitioner's term be increased to seventy years from the feast of St Michael the Archangel 1677, at the yearly rent of forty shillings, with all rent from the time of the fire discharged until the feast of the birth of our Lord 1677. The first quarterly payment would be due on the feast of the Annunciation of the Blessed Virgin Maty December 1678.

The Court ordered that:

(1)   The petitioner Thomas Hudson was discharged of paying all rent incurred on the premises from the time of the fire until the feast of the birth of our Lord 1677.[213]

(2)   Thereafter, the yearly rent was to be sunk to forty shillings for the duration of the lease. The petitioner was discharged of paying the remaining thirty shillings of the original £3 10s. annual rent.

(3)   The petitioner was to receive an additional term of fifty-five and a quarter years, commencing and taking effect immediately at the end of the present lease on the feast of the Nativity of St John the Baptist 1692. The petitioner's whole term was to be seventy years from the feast of St Michael the Archangel 1677. The annual rent for this term was to be forty shillings, payable to the defendants according to their interests. Payment would be made at the days and times specified in the present lease.

(4)   The petitioner's first quarterly payment was due on the feast of the birth of our Lord 1677.

(5)   The petitioner must, with all convenient speed and at his charge, build a good and substantial messuage and building of brick and must finish the same in a good workmanlike manner.

(6)   To avoid difficulties in recovering the rent and for ascertaining the covenants mutually to be performed, on the petitioners' reasonable request and at his expense, the defendants Day, Browker, the Lloyds, the Kents and the Osbaldestons — together

---

213   Again, despite a few missing words in the corner, the purport of the formulaic recitation of this portion of the decree is not in doubt.

with Thomas Lowfeild and Mary and Martha Browker when they reached the age of twenty-one — must execute a good and sufficient lease by indenture for the additional fifty-five and a quarter years decreed to the petitioner. The lease should contain such reasonable covenants as contained in the present lease. The petitioner must accept the lease and deliver up its counterpart.

(7) The petitioner might lawfully, peaceably and quietly enjoy the small tenements notwithstanding the coverture of the feme coverts, the infancy of the infants or any other interest.

Decree 49 (page 227)

5 Oct. 1677.   Baron Littleton; Justice Jones (s); Thomas Barker, Esq. (s); James Reading, Esq. (s); Peter Rich, Esq. (s); John Freeman, Esq. (s); John Appellbe

Thomas Hudson of Southwark, Scrivener,[214] *v. Thomas Browker, Esq.; Edward Lloyd, Esq.; Dorothy his Wife; William Kent, Clerke; Jane his Wife; Sir Littleton Osbaldeston, Baronet; Dame Katherine his Wife; Thomas Lowfeild, an Infant; Mary Browker, an Infant; Martha Browker, an Infant; and Joseph Day of Southwark, Brewer*

Thomas Browker, Esquire, of Upper Peover in the County of Chester, was seised in fee of a messuage or tenement. By an indenture of lease dated 29 June 1658, Browker demised the premises to the petitioner and Sarah his wife. The premises had lately been in the tenure of Cornwallis Pigeon[215] and then of the petitioner. The premises included a messuage and two yards, and other things belonging to the messuage. The lease ran from the feast of the Nativity of St John the Baptist 1668 for forty-one years. The annual rent was £4, payable quarterly.

By his will, Thomas Browker devised his interest in the messuage, and in divers others, to Mary Browker, his wife. She then settled this messuage, as well as others, on herself for ninety-nine years (should she live so long) and then on various family members in the manner described in Decree 8.[216] Upon the death of Mary and her son Thomas

214 Hudson appears as a witness in *Bankes v. Wight* (Decree 2), and *Nicolson v. Browker* (Decree 8), and as the petitioner in *Hudson v. Mayor of London* (Decree 33), and *Hudson v. Browker* (Decree 48).

215 Although this decree does not mention the location of the property, *Snell v. Browker* (Decree 14), involved another Browker property near the West Chain Gate. It mentioned a messuage in the tenure of Cornwallis Pigeon that was located next to the property at issue there.

216 See pp. 120–21.

Browker the elder, the interest in the reversion of the premises came into the hands of the defendant Thomas Browker the younger for ninety-nine years (should he live so long). Under Mary Browker's property settlement, Dorothy Lloyd, Jane Kent, Dame Katherine Osbaldeston, Thomas Lowfeild (the son of Robert Lowfeild and Mary Browker's daughter Elizabeth, both now deceased) and Mary and Martha Browker (the daughters of Thomas Browker the elder and the sisters of Thomas Browker the younger) held contingent interests upon the death of Thomas the younger.

When she settled the premises on herself and others in the family, Mary Browker retained the power to make leases for forty-one years in case of new building, as long as the ancient rent was maintained. By indenture of lease dated 10 April 1668, Mary Browker devised on the petitioner and Sarah his wife a messuage lately new built by the petitioner, as well as a cellar under the dwelling house of Mary Gilbert, widow; these premises had lately been in the occupation of Lazarus Annis and were then in the occupation of the petitioner and his undertenant or undertenants. The lease ran for forty-one years at the ancient yearly rent of fifty shillings, payable quarterly. The premises were located near the West Chain Gate in the Churchyard of St Saviour.

After his ninety-nine-year interest in various properties became vested, Thomas Browker the younger, by indenture of lease dated 27 December 1675, demised to Jonadab Ballam, Citizen and Grocer of London,[217] a corner tenement or dwelling house next to the West Chain Gate of the churchyard. These premises were then in the tenure of Richard Organ, Shoemaker. The lease ran for twenty-one years at the ancient yearly rent of £6 10s., payable quarterly. By lawful assignment, this lease and all of Ballam's interest came to be vested in the petitioner.

Thomas the younger had since demised, bargained and sold his interest in the above-mentioned two messuages (carrying the annual rents of £4 and fifty shillings) to Joseph Day for seventy-nine years (if Browker should live so long), commencing on 13 August 1676. The yearly rent for this interest was one peppercorn. Thomas the younger also demised, bargained and sold the third messuage (carrying the annual rents of £6 10s.) to John Snell, Citizen and Merchant Taylor,[218]

217 Ballam was a defendant in *Snell v. Browker* (Decree 13), where he bought an eighty-year interest in a different property from Thomas the younger. He was also a party in the principal encroachment decree, Decree 45.

218 Snell was a defendant in *Ely v. Mence* (Decree 1); *Roberts v. Browker* (Decree 11); *Williams v. Browker* (Decree 50); and *Williams v. Browker* (Decree 51). He was the petitioner in *Snell v. Browker* (Decree 13); *Snell v. Browker* (Decree 14); and *Snell v. Browker* (Decree 15).

for eighty years (if Browker should live so long), commencing on the feast of the birth of our Lord 1675. By lawful assignment, Snell's interest became vested in Day.

All three messuages or tenements burned down. In expectation of encouragement from the various interested persons, the petitioner had at his own expense rebuilt the premises into one 'intire' messuage. But he could not obtain any terms or consideration without the assistance of this Court.

Summonses to the defendants were issued. The petitioner Thomas Hudson appeared personally, with Sir George Jeffreys, Mr Bowes and Mr Jenner as his counsel. Among the defendants, Thomas Lowfeild, Mary Browker and Martha Browker appeared personally. The Court specially admitted Anne Cooke, widow, as guardian of Thomas Lowfeild. The Court also specially admitted Mary Leighton, wife of Charles Leighton, Gentleman, and mother of Mary and Martha Browker, as their guardian; Mr Ward and Mr Pettitt were their counsel. Day also appeared personally without counsel.

The remaining defendants (Thomas Browker, the Lloyds, the Kents and the Osbaldestons) did not appear personally or through counsel. To be satisfied in the matter, the Court took sworn testimony from John Moth of the parish of St Saviour and Benjamin Colinbine of London, Haberdasher. Both testified as they had done in Decree 8. On 21 September 1677, Moth served a summons on the turnkey of the King's Bench prison after determining that Thomas Browker the younger was a prisoner there, and Colinbine served summonses on Katherine Osbaldeston at Woodstocke in Oxfordshire on 13 August 1677; on Edward Lloyd at his dwelling called Beth Lloyd in Montgomery Shire on 15 August 1677; and on Jane Kent at Road in Sommersettshire on 19 September 1677. The Court's registrar collected affidavits in writing to this effect.

The petitioner's counsel informed the Court that the tofts of the tenements that burned down were so small that they were not sufficient to have more than one good house rebuilt; and the petitioner had rebuilt the house for his own habitation. Because it was a corner house and was very substantially and well built, the house cost the petitioner at least £600. Therefore, counsel prayed for a considerable addition of years to the various terms and an abatement of the several rents (which amounted to a total of £13) to £5 — which was as much as the ground was worth.

Counsel for the defendants opposed such a great abatement of rent. Counsel alleged that the petitioner had not made the best improvement of the land by building a house. Rather, it would have been better to build offices and low buildings on the best part of the land, which formerly went for the greatest rent.

The petitioner's counsel alleged that, having a long term to come on his leases, the petitioner was sure to build to his best advantage, and this building was not to the disadvantage of the reversioners. The ground itself lay in so bad a place, far from all trade, that it could not be better improved than the petitioner's building.

Having heard the allegations of counsel and having well considered the matter, the Court pronounced it most just and reasonable that the several terms of years be increased to seventy years from the feast of St Michael the Archangel 1677, at the yearly rent of twenty nobles [£6 13s. 4d.], with all rent from the time of the fire discharged until the feast of the birth of our Lord 1677. The first quarterly payment would be due on the feast of the Annunciation of the Blessed Virgin Mary 1678.

The Court ordered that:

(1)　Because all rent up to the time of the fire was paid, the petitioner Thomas Hudson was discharged of paying all rent incurred on the premises from the time of the fire until the feast of the birth of our Lord 1677.[219]

(2)　Thereafter, the yearly rent was sunk to £6 13s. 4d. for the duration of the three leases. The petitioner was discharged of paying the residue of the yearly rents.

(3)　The petitioner was to receive additional terms of years on the three leases, so that the total term for each lease was to be seventy years. The seventy-year period commenced on the feast of St Michael the Archangel 1677.

(4)　The annual rent for these terms was to be £6 13s. 4d., payable to the defendants according to their interests. Payment was to be made on the four most usual feast days.

(5)　The petitioner's first quarterly payment was due on the feast of the Annunciation of the Blessed Virgin Mary 1678.

(6)　To avoid difficulties in recovering the rent and for ascertaining the covenants mutually to be performed, on the petitioners' reasonable request and at his expense, the defendants Snell,

---

219 As part of the formulaic recitation of this provision in the decrees, the registrar would repeat again the original yearly rent before stating the amount to which the rent was reduced. I have generally edited out this recitation. In this decree, however, the registrar recited the prior rents as being 'foure pounds and tenne shillings and six pounds and tenne shillings' (or £11 in total). Assuming that the prior recitation of the terms of the leases was correct, the second lease was for

Browker, the Lloyds, the Kents and the Osbaldestons — together with Thomas Lowfeild and Mary and Martha Browker when they reached the age of twenty-one — must execute a good and sufficient lease by indenture for the grounds demised to the petitioner. The lease should contain such reasonable covenants as contained in the present lease. The petitioner must accept the lease and deliver up its counterpart.

(7) The petitioner might lawfully, peaceably and quietly enjoy the small tenements notwithstanding the coverture of the feme coverts, the infancy of the infants or any other interest.

Decree 50 (page 235)

5 Oct. 1677.   Baron Littleton; Justice Jones (s); Thomas Barker, Esq. (s); James Reading, Esq. (s); Peter Rich, Esq. (s); John Freeman, Esq. (s); John Appellbe

Joseph Williams of Southwark, Gentleman, v. Thomas Browker, Esq.; Edward Lloyd, Esq.; Dorothy his Wife; William Kent, Clerke; Jane his Wife; Sir Littleton Osbaldeston, Baronet; Dame Katherine his Wife; Thomas Lowfeild, an Infant; Mary Browker, an Infant; Martha Browker, an Infant; and John Snell, Citizen and Merchant Taylor[220]

Thomas Browker, Esquire, of Upper Peover, in the County of Chester, was seised in fee of a messuage or tenement. By his will, Thomas Browker devised his interest in the messuage, and in divers others, to Mary Browker, his wife. She then settled this messuage, as well as others, on herself for ninety-nine years (should she live so long) and then on various family members in the manner described in Decree 8.[221] Upon the death of Mary and her son Thomas Browker the elder, the interest in the reversion of the premises came into the hands of the defendant Thomas Browker the younger for ninety-nine years (should he live so long). Under Mary Browker's property settlement, Dorothy Lloyd, Jane Kent, Dame Katherine Osbaldeston, Thomas Lowfeild (the son of

---

50s., not 10s.; the prior rents were therefore £4, 50s. and £6 10s. (or £13 in total). I assume that the registrar incorrectly recited the second rent at this point, and not earlier in the decree.

220 Snell was a defendant in *Ely v. Mence* (Decree 1); *Roberts v. Browker* (Decree 11); and *Williams v. Browker* (Decree 51). He was the petitioner in *Snell v. Browker* (Decree 13); *Snell v. Browker* (Decree 14); and *Snell v. Browker* (Decree 15). He also purchased and then sold an interest in the property at issue in *Hudson v. Browker* (Decree 49).

221 See pp. 120–21.

Robert Lowfeild and Mary Browker's daughter Elizabeth, both now deceased) and Mary and Martha Browker (the daughters of Thomas Browker the elder and the sisters of Thomas Browker the younger) held contingent interests upon the death of Thomas the younger.

After settling the estate on herself, by indenture of lease dated 24 June 1668, Mary Browker and her son Thomas Browker the elder demised the premises to John Carter of St Saviour's Parish, Starchmaker. The consideration for the lease was Carter's cost in new building one tenement and repairing other tenements on the ground. The lease ran for twenty-one years at the yearly rent of £10 10s., payable quarterly. The lease encompassed ten properties: (1) a tenement or house containing two rooms, new-built by Carter and in the occupation of Thomas Martin; (2) one tenement containing three rooms then in the occupation of Mary Evans and others; (3) one stable underneath this tenement then in the occupation of Richard Loft; (4) one tenement or house containing three rooms and a cellar, then in the occupation of Richard Loft; (5) one tenement house or edifice containing three rooms, one above the other, then in the occupation of Robert Nicholls and others; (6) one tenement containing three rooms one above the other, then in the occupation of John Whiteingslowe[222] and others; (7) one tenement or house containing a cellar and four other rooms, then in the occupation of Luke Meadowes; (8) a tenement containing a cellar with three rooms above, then in the occupation of Isaac Castle; (9) a tenement containing a cellar and three rooms each above the other, together with a little yard and back side, then in the occupation of Thomas Cooke and others; (10) a tenement or house containing a kitchen and three other rooms, then in the occupation of Cooke. These premises were located in Angel Yard, near Fowl Lane.

By lawful assignment, Carter's interest came to be vested in the petitioner.

Mary Browker and Thomas Browker the elder were both now dead. After he became interested in the property, Thomas Browker the younger demised to John Snell his interest in the properties and in the reserved rent of £10 10s. for some long term of years determinable on Browker's death. The yearly rent for this interest was one peppercorn.

The messuages or tenements burned down. The petitioner was willing to rebuild them on reasonable encouragement (through an increase in term and abatement of rent) from the various interested parties. But he

222 This is likely the same John Whiteingslowe who was a defendant in the cross-petition in *Bennett v. Browker* (Decree 12).

was unable to obtain any terms or consideration without the assistance of this Court.

Summonses to the defendants were issued. The petitioner Joseph Williams appeared personally, with Mr Bowes and Mr Jenner as his counsel. Among the defendants, Thomas Lowfeild, Mary Browker and Martha Browker appeared personally. The Court specially admitted Anne Cooke, widow, as guardian of Thomas Lowfeild. The Court also specially admitted Mary Leighton, wife of Charles Leighton, Gentleman, and mother of Mary and Martha Browker, as their guardian; Mr Ward and Mr Petitt were their counsel. Snell also appeared personally, with Sir George Jeffreys as his counsel.

The remaining defendants (Thomas Browker, the Lloyds, the Kents and the Osbaldestons) did not appear personally or through counsel. To be satisfied in the matter, the Court took sworn testimony from John Moth of the parish of St Saviour and Benjamin Colinbine of London, Haberdasher. Both testified as they had done in Decree 8. On 21 September 1677, Moth served a summons on the turnkey of the King's Bench prison after determining that Thomas Browker the younger was a prisoner there, and Colinbine served summonses on Katherine Osbaldeston at Woodstocke in Oxfordshire on 13 August 1677; on Edward Lloyd at his dwelling called Berth Lloyd[223] in Montgomery Shire on 15 August 1677; and on Jane Kent at Road in Sommersetshire on 19 September 1677. The Court's registrar collected affidavits in writing to this effect.

The petitioner's counsel prayed the Court to grant a considerable addition to his term, as he had only twelve years remaining as of Midsummer last, and an abatement of rent. Counsel for the reversioners, as well as for Snell, opposed an abatement, alleging that there were a great many tenements to raise the rent and the quantity of ground on which to build was large. The petitioner's counsel alleged that the tenements were very small and of inconsiderable value; the ground was also in a very bad place far backward from the street and out of the way of all trade. The front, which led to a back alley, was no more than fifteen feet across. Without an increase in term and abatement of rent, the petitioner would not undertake rebuilding.

Having heard the allegations of counsel and being well advised, the Court pronounced it most just and reasonable that the petitioner's term be increased to seventy years from the feast of St Michael the Archangel 1677 and that the yearly rent should be abated to twenty

---

223 In all prior decrees reciting service on Edward Lloyd, his home was given as 'Beth Lloyd'.

nobles [£6 13s. 4d.], to commence on the feast of the Annunciation of the Blessed Virgin Mary 1678. All rent from the time of the fire was discharged until that time.

The Court ordered that:

(1) The petitioner Joseph Williams was required to pay John Snell two-thirds part of the annual rent of £10 10s. that was due for Midsummer quarter 1676, as the petitioner enjoyed the premises for this time. The petitioner was discharged from paying the other one-third part of the quarterly rent.

(2) The petitioner was also discharged from paying the annual rent of £10 10s. from the feast of the Nativity of St John the Baptist 1676 until the feast of the Annunciation of the Blessed Virgin Mary 1678. At that point, the annual rent was to be sunk to £6 13s. 4d. for the duration of the lease, with the petitioner discharged of paying the residue of £3 16s. 8d. per year.

(3) The term of the petitioner was to be increased by fifty-eight and a quarter years, commencing immediately at the end of the present lease on the feast of the Nativity of St John the Baptist 1689, for a total term of seventy years from the feast of St Michael the Archangel 1677.

(4) The rent for the additional term was to be to £6 13s. 4d., payable to the defendants according to their interests.

(5) The first payment was due on the feast of the Nativity of St John the Baptist 1678. Payment thereafter was to be made at the days and times specified in the present lease.

(6) The petitioner must, with all convenient speed and at his own charge, build good and substantial messuages and buildings and shall finish them in good workmanlike manner.

(7) To avoid difficulties in recovering the rent and for ascertaining the covenants mutually to be performed, on the petitioners' reasonable request and at his expense, the defendants Day, Browker, the Lloyds, the Kents and the Osbaldestons — together with Thomas Lowfeild and Mary and Martha Browker when they reached the age of twenty-one — must execute a good and sufficient lease by indenture for the grounds demised to the petitioner. The lease should contain such reasonable covenants as contained in the present lease. The petitioner must accept the lease and deliver up its counterpart.

(8) The petitioner might lawfully, peaceably and quietly enjoy the small tenements notwithstanding the coverture of the feme coverts, the infancy of the infants or any other interest.

Decree 51 (page 243)

5 Oct. 1677.   Baron Littleton; Justice Jones (s); Thomas Barker, Esq.
                 (s); James Reading, Esq. (s); Peter Rich, Esq. (s); John
                 Freeman, Esq. (s); John Appellbe

*Joseph Williams of Southwark, Gentleman v. Thomas Browker, Esq.;
Edward Lloyd, Esq.; Dorothy his wife; William Kent, Clerke; Jane his
Wife; Sir Littleton Osbaldeston, Baronet; Dame Katherine his Wife;
Thomas Lowfeild, an Infant; Mary Browker, an Infant; Martha Browker,
an Infant; and John Snell, Citizen and Merchant Taylor*[224]

Thomas Browker, Esquire, of Upper Peover, in the County of Chester,
was seised in fee of a messuage or tenement. By indenture of lease
dated 20 November 1656, for the consideration mentioned in the lease,
Browker demised to John Carter of Southwark, Starchmaker, the
premises previously in the tenure or occupation of William Burroughs,
deceased. Also included were three tenements or dwelling houses newly
erected, which stood in the yard or back side of the premises. These
tenements were late in the tenure or occupation of John Darling and
his undertenants and then of John Carter and his undertenants. The
lease ran from the feast of St Michael the Archangel 1656 for fifty-one
years. The yearly rent was £4, payable quarterly.

By lawful assignment, Carter's interest came to be vested in the
petitioner.

By his will, Thomas Browker devised his interest in the messuage,
and in divers others, to Mary Browker, his wife. She then settled this
messuage, as well as others, on herself for ninety-nine years (should
she live so long) and then on various family members in the manner
described in Decree 8.[225] Upon the death of Mary and her son Thomas
Browker the elder, the interest in the reversion of the premises came into
the hands of the defendant Thomas Browker the younger for ninety-
nine years (should he live so long). Under Mary Browker's property
settlement, Dorothy Lloyd, Jane Kent, Dame Katherine Osbaldeston,
Thomas Lowfeild (the son of Robert Lowfeild and Mary Browker's
daughter Elizabeth, both now deceased) and Mary and Martha Browker
(the daughters of Thomas Browker the elder and the sisters of Thomas

---

224 Snell was a defendant in *Ely v. Mence* (Decree 1); *Roberts v. Browker* (Decree
11); and *Williams v. Browker* (Decree 50). He was the petitioner in *Snell v. Browker*
(Decree 13); *Snell v. Browker* (Decree 14); and *Snell v. Browker* (Decree 15). He also
purchased and then sold an interest in the property at issue in *Hudson v. Browker*
(Decree 49).

225 See pp. 120–21.

Browker the younger) held contingent interests upon the death of Thomas the younger.

Mary Browker and Thomas Browker the elder were both now dead. After he became interested in the property, Thomas Browker the younger demised and sold to John Snell his interest in the properties and in the reserved rent of £4 for a term of eighty years (if Browker should live so long), commencing from the feast of the Nativity of St John the Baptist 1675. The yearly rent for this interest was one peppercorn.

The messuages or tenements burned down. In expectation of encouragement, the petitioner, at his own cost, rebuilt the property into one entire messuage. But the petitioner had been unable to obtain any terms or consideration without the assistance of this Court.

Summonses to the defendants were issued. The petitioner Joseph Williams appeared personally, with Mr Bowes and Mr Jenner as his counsel. Among the defendants, Thomas Lowfeild, Mary Browker and Martha Browker appeared personally. The Court specially admitted Anne Cooke, widow, as guardian of Thomas Lowfeild. The Court also specially admitted Mary Leighton, wife of Charles Leighton, Gentleman, and mother of Mary and Martha Browker, as their guardian; Mr Ward and Mr Petitt were their counsel. Snell also appeared personally, with Sir George Jeffreys as his counsel.

The remaining defendants (Thomas Browker, the Lloyds, the Kents and the Osbaldestons) did not appear personally or through counsel. To be satisfied in the matter, the Court took sworn testimony from John Moth of the parish of St Saviour and Benjamin Colinbine of London, Haberdasher. Both testified as they had done in Decree 8. On 21 September 1677, Moth served a summons on the turnkey of the King's Bench prison after determining that Thomas Browker the younger was a prisoner there, and Colinbine served summonses on Katherine Osbaldeston at Woodstocke in Oxfordshire on 13 August 1677; on Edward Lloyd at his dwelling called Berth Lloyd[226] in Montgomery Shire on 15 August 1677; and on Jane Kent at Road in Sommersetshire on 19 September 1677. The Court's registrar collected affidavits in writing to this effect.

The petitioner's counsel began by noting that the petitioner had rebuilt the messuage at his own charge; therefore, he should have a considerable term added to the remaining thirty years (from the feast of St Michael the Archangel 1677) on his lease, as well as an abatement of rent. Counsel for the defendants much opposed an abatement,

---

226 As in Decree 50, the registrar referred to the Lloyds' dwelling as 'Berth Lloyd' rather than 'Beth Lloyd', as it had been rendered in prior decrees.

alleging that the rent was a very low ground rent and ought not to be abated further.

The petitioner's counsel then further alleged that the house had cost at least £600 to rebuild. Being far from the street in a 'Bye Alley', the house would not yield above £30 per annum, so the petitioner would not have above £6 per cent for his money if there were no ground rent to be paid. Therefore, counsel insisted that some abatement was necessary.

The defendants' counsel then alleged that, although the petitioner may have laid out such a considerable sum, the house could have been built to the reversioners' advantage for only £300. The greatest part of the petitioner's expense had been laid out for ornament and 'extraordinary beautifying the said house, which the Landlords ought not to contribute towards'.

At this point, Mrs Leighton made oath that, when the petitioner treated with her for encouragement, he did not desire to have any abatement of rent — only an increase in term of years.

Having heard the allegations of counsel and being well advised, the Court declared that it was not reasonable in this case to abate the rent, but that the petitioner should have his term made up to eighty years from the feast of St Michael the Archangel 1677.

The Court ordered that:

(1) The petitioner Joseph Williams was to receive an additional term of fifty years in the premises, commencing immediately at the expiration of the present lease on the feast of St Michael the Archangel 1707. This extension made the petitioner's whole term eighty years.[227]

(2) The annual rent remained £4 per annum, to be paid to the defendants according to their respective interests. Payment was to be made at the days and times specified in the present lease.

---

227 In his will, dated 8 September 1681, John Snell bequeathed to his son John the leases of the tenements in St Saviour's parish that had once been Thomas Browker's. He excepted from this bequest the messuage in the occupation of Joseph Williams, described as a gentleman, in St Saviour's Churchyard. That property was bequeathed to Snell's daughter Susanna. Assuming that Snell had not sold his interest in them (as he had with the leasehold described in *Hudson v. Browker* (Decree 49)), his son John inherited the leaseholds of the properties described in Decrees 11, 13, 14, 15 and 50. But the property involved in this decree was likely the one bequeathed to Susanna.

In a postscript to his will, Snell bequeathed to the wardens of St Saviour's Church £1 6s. 8d. per annum for a sermon. He also made a £5 bequest to his maid servant if she continued in his wife's service for seven years. Both bequests were to be paid out of the rents and profits of the Browker leases.

(3) To avoid difficulties in recovering the rent and for ascertaining the covenants mutually to be performed, on the petitioners' reasonable request and at his expense, the defendants Snell, Browker, the Lloyds, the Kents and the Osbaldestons — together with Thomas Lowfeild and Mary and Martha Browker when they reached the age of twenty-one — must execute a good and sufficient lease by indenture for the grounds demised to the petitioner. The lease should contain such reasonable covenants as contained in the present lease. The petitioner must accept the lease and deliver up its counterpart.

(4) The petitioner might lawfully, peaceably and quietly enjoy the small tenements notwithstanding the coverture of the feme coverts, the infancy of the infants or any other interest.

Decree 52 (page 249)

17 Oct. 1677.   Baron Littleton; Justice Jones;[228] Sir Adam Browne, Baronet; Sir William Hooker, Knight (s); Thomas Barker, Esq. (s); James Reading, Esq. (s); Richard Howe (s);[229] Peter Rich, Esq.; Jon Freeman, Esq. (s);[230] John Appellbe

Richard Taylor of London, Esquire v. John Smith, Poulterer[231]

Snell's will raised some issues. While on his deathbed, Snell gave instructions for his will to Thomas Hudson, Scrivener, who has appeared in various capacities in Decrees 2, 8, 33, 48 and 49. According to the testimony of Hudson and Thomas Cooke, Baker of Southwark who may be the tenant referred to in Decree 49, Hudson began dictating the will to Richard Joyce in the next room. After hearing the will read back, Snell added the postscript. Upon hearing the revised will read to him, Snell assented orally, but he lapsed into 'a slumbering condition'. Snell died eight hours later without signing or sealing the will. Both Hudson and Baker also testified that the will was dated in error, and Snell had died on 7 September. After this testimony on 12 October 1681, the will was proved on 14 October 1681. See TNA, PROB 11/368/91.

228 This decree was one of the handful not signed by at least one common-law judge.

229 Although the registrar usually spelled the name as 'How', this decree varied the spelling. How signed the decree as 'How'.

230 For the only time, the registrar rendered Freeman's first name as 'Jon'. Freeman was the only member of the Court to sit on every case, and in all other decrees, his name had been given as 'John'.

231 It is likely that the John Smith in this decree was the defendant in the principal encroachment decree, Decree 45, in which John Smith was ordered to move back the stall of his shop on the west side of the High Street by three feet. Decree 45 noted that John Smith appeared on behalf of his tenant John Middleton, who occupied the encroaching property.

The petitioner was seised in fee of two tofts of ground on which two messuages had stood. One was a tavern known by the sign of the Bull's Head. The other lay on the north side of the tavern and was in the occupation of John Middleton. The messuages fronted on the High Street. Both burned down in the fire. Smith also became seised in fee of another toft on the north side of these properties, where a messuage in his own occupation had also burned down.

Before they burned down, the messuages had been intermixed. In the messuage occupied by Middleton were two pairs of stairs with a jetty over part of the messuage occupied by Smith. The jetty ran to the top, and measured about six feet in the front and about twenty-six feet in depth. The jetty had the use of [illegible][232] in common with Smith for a house of easement, which lay under [illegible] the watercourse belonging both to the Bull's Head [illegible]. [Illegible] in the occupation of Middleton anciently and until the fire lay under Smith's messuage and was carried into the street 'through the same by Smith and the former tenant of the Messuage'.

Soon after the fire, the petitioner and Smith, who were both rebuilding, came to an agreement that the party wall between their properties should be set equally between them: nine inches on petitioner's ground and nine inches on Smith's ground. One of the City's surveyors then set out the party wall accordingly. As the first builder, the petitioner began by carrying the wall up about one storey when Smith came and forcibly threw down the wall and arrested the petitioner and his workmen for coming onto Smith's ground.

The petitioner began building his foundation again, this time setting the party wall entirely on his own ground. This wall was set on a ground plate over a vault, which Smith caused to be removed so far that Smith gained three and a half inches of the petitioner's interest without giving any compensation.

Smith also built a timber wall upright against the petitioner's wall and cut off the petitioner's timber, which he had laid over for the jetty. As

232 The bottom of the first page of the decree is decomposed in places and the ink has become too faint in others. Unfortunately, unlike some other decrees, the rest of this decree does not supply enough context for me to fill in the missing words.

233 Unlike other decrees that carried over from one sitting to another, the decree ended here. It did not describe the findings of the report (if one was even written) or the Court's ultimate determination of the matter. The timing listed in the decree was also odd. Given that the decree was dated 17 October 1677, the upcoming feast of St Michael the Archangel lay more than eleven months in the future. If this dating was correct, the Court sat on only one day — 2 March 1680 — that met the requirement.

a result, Smith has excluded the petitioner from the jetty and the use of the vault.

Finally, the petitioner made his watercourse in the same place and in the same manner as before, but Smith refused to carry the water away through his house as it had been carried before. Therefore, the petitioner had no passage for his water to his great annoyance and prejudice.

The petitioner appeared personally, with Mr Jenner and Mr Lane, the comptroller of the Chamber of London, as his counsel. Smith appeared personally, with Mr Bowes as his counsel.

The first point debated was the watercourse. The petitioner's counsel proved by sufficient testimony upon oath that the ancient watercourse belonging to the petitioner's houses before the fire carried under the house of Smith into the street.

Having heard the matter fully debated, the Court was satisfied of the petitioner's right to carry his water as he had done previously.

On the other matters, after several witnesses were examined on both sides, the Court referred the matter to the surveyors of new buildings in London. The surveyors were to report to the Court, so that the matter might then be determined.

The Court ordered that:

(1) The defendant John Smith must permit and suffer the petitioner Richard Taylor, at convenient and seasonable times, to enter onto Smith's property with workmen. The petitioner might make and lay a watercourse under Smith's house and shop for the petitioner's convenience. The watercourse must be laid as near as possible to its former placement. Smith must not molest or hinder this construction.

(2) After the watercourse's completion, the petitioner would have the liberty to amend and cleanse the watercourse from time to time as needed, again without molestation, hindrance or denial from Smith.

(3) On request from the petitioner Richard Taylor, the surveyors of new buildings in the City of London were to view the premises. The viewing should be in the presence of both parties (if, on notice, Smith decided to be present).

(4) The watercourse was excepted from the viewing.

(5) The surveyors should examine and consider what the petitioner laid claim to and then discover as far as they could the truth of the matter.

(6) The surveyors should make a report in writing under their hands

to the Court. The Court would hear and determine the matter at the next sitting after the feast of St Michael the Archangel next coming.[233]

APPENDIX:
THE LEASES OF ST THOMAS'S HOSPITAL

Located just east of the High Street, St Thomas's Hospital owned property along the east side of the High Street and in St Thomas's parish, whose western boundary stopped just short of the High Street (see Frontispiece). The churchyard of St Thomas's parish lay to the east of the High Street and to the south of the Hospital. The Hospital and churchyard were connected to the High Street by a gateway.

Many of Hospital's tenants and undertenants along the High Street or in the churchyard suffered damage from the fire — either because the houses and shops burned down, were blown up or were defaced in the explosions. Immediately after the fire, the Hospital received petitions from tenants and undertenants asking the Hospital to provide them with encouragement to rebuild their properties or compensation for the cost of repairs.

At the first post-fire meeting of the Hospital's Board of Governors, on 16 June 1676, the Governors created a committee to recommend a course of action.[1]

At this point, Parliament was prorogued, and there was no guarantee that Parliament would establish, as it had done for the Great Fire of London in 1666 and the Northampton fire of 1675, a fire court. In emulation of the prior fire courts, however, the committee viewed the affected properties and negotiated new leases that gave the tenants (or another willing developer) incentives to rebuild. The establishment of the committee and the committee's recommendations reflect how much the fire-court model for achieving speedy rebuilding had seeped into Londoners' consciousness.

---

1 *Minute Books of General Court of Governors of St Thomas's Hospital, 1619–77*, LMA H01/ST/A/001/005, fol. 172ᵛ (16 June 1676). The Governors appointed twelve persons to serve on the committee, any five of whom constituted a quorum. Among the appointed members were two people who later served as judges on the Southwark fire court: James Reading (who sat for all fifty-two decrees of the fire court) and Richard How (who sat for twenty-six). Unfortunately, the committee's report was unsigned, so it cannot be determined whether Reading or How participated in the committee or whether the report influenced their thinking as judges on the fire court.

At the next meeting of the Governors, on 20 September 1676, the committee reported back with its recommendations.[2] The Governors adopted the report in full.

The report is brief, and it contains few of the details found in the decrees of the Southwark fire court. Nonetheless, the report, which is digested below, is useful for several reasons. First, it helps to mark the extent of the Southwark fire and the nature of the firefighting effort. The report reflects that, along the High Street, houses to the south of the gateway that led into St Thomas's Hospital were generally burned down or blown up, while houses to the north of the gateway were not burned down but did receive damage from nearby explosions. The report stated that the gateway was roughly ten-and-one-half feet wide — a distance that, in view of the prevailing winds and other firefighting efforts (which included blowing up houses to the south of the gate), appeared to create a sufficient fire break to arrest the spread of the fire up the east side of the High Street. In addition, the records reflect that some properties in St Thomas's parish, and particularly in St Thomas's churchyard, also burned down. Here, however, more damage came from blowing up houses or from the shock waves of the explosions. This fact suggests that the eastern extent of the fire did not penetrate very far beyond the High Street.

Second, the results that the Hospital achieved in its negotiations reflect the extent to which the Southwark fire court — and fire courts more generally — tilted the playing field toward tenants. Without the prospect of a fire court looming over them, the Governors extracted quite favourable terms from their tenants. With only a couple of exceptions, the Hospital did not reduce the rents that tenants paid; the sole encouragement that it gave tenants was an extension of the lease. Even here, the extensions were shorter than those later granted by the fire court, and the Hospital sometimes demanded a significant fine with the extension. Indeed, in a report to the Aldermen of the City of London several years later, the Governors reported that the new fines raised £405 for the Hospital, an amount that was roughly as much as the Hospital had received in rents for the properties over the previous forty years.[3]

Third, while it showed modest generosity toward those whose properties were destroyed, the Governors exhibited a certain tough-

---

2 Ibid., fols 173ᵛ–75ᵛ (20 September 1676).

3 *Minute Books of General Court of Governors of St Thomas's Hospital, 1678–1735*, LMA H01/ST/A/001/006, fol. 22 (11 November 1681).

mindedness toward those whose properties were damaged. Unless the damage to a property rose above a £50 threshold, the Governors refused to provide relief — although it was willing to take the tenant's costs of repair into account when the lease was eventually renewed.

Fourth, the report showed considerable concern for preserving the Hospital, which had narrowly escaped destruction, from future fires. A number of leases required tenants to build brick walls between their houses and the Hospital. The report also forbade the construction of any chimney or structure that blocked out the lights the Hospital presently enjoyed. It required all tenants whose rooms, watercourses or lights were intermixed with their neighbours to settle their differences before they were entitled to a new lease. Settling these differences was a prerequisite to erecting party walls, which were a critical fire-prevention measure that developed during the rebuilding of the City of London. In an attempt to head off disputes that had sometimes retarded rebuilding in the City, tenants were also required to agree among themselves about sharing the costs for party walls.

Finally, the report showed that the Hospital held some of the most desirable parcels of land in Southwark. For a number of the leases, the committee required the tenant to rebuild the house according to the 'second rate' for new buildings in London. After the Great Fire, Parliament's Act for the Rebuilding of the City of London established four levels of construction, with regulations about the heights, styles, construction materials and ornamentations required for each level. Aside from the few buildings of the first rate (mansions occupied by persons of extraordinary quality), the most substantial level of construction — and hence the most desirable places to live in London — were buildings of the second rate.

One clear constraint on the jurisdiction of the Southwark fire court was its inability to alter the terms of any post-fire lease that a lessor and a tenant had previously agreed.[4] The renegotiation of its leases with tenants thus kept St Thomas's Hospital — perhaps the largest landlord in Southwark — out of the Southwark fire court and reduced the number of petitions that the Southwark fire court heard.

The following information on the St Thomas's Hospital leases is derived principally from the committee report of 20 September 1676. For four leases (Grove, Pittman, Bartlett and Phillips), later committee reports and minutes of the Governors' meetings provide additional details.

---

4 29 Car II, c. 4, § 15 (1677), reprinted in *Statutes of the Realm*, V, p. 845.

Lease 1: Edward Farding. Farding's tenement in St Thomas's parish was destroyed and needed to be new built. The annual rent for the present lease was £3 6s., and the lease expired on the feast of the Annunciation of the Blessed Virgin Mary 1691. Farding received a new lease for the ground and for a garden plot. The annual rent remained £3 6s., with a term of thirty-five years from Midsummer 1676 (i.e., until 24 June 1711, or an extension of twenty years and three months).

Lease 2: Dennis Herbert. Herbert's tenement in St Thomas's parish was demolished in the fire. The annual rent for the present lease was 40s. plus 4s. for tithe, and the lease expired on the feast of the Annunciation of the Blessed Virgin Mary 1701. In exchange for rebuilding the tenement with brick walls, Herbert received a new lease at the same annual rent of 40s. plus 4s. for tithe, with a term of fifty-one years from Midsummer 1676 (i.e., until 24 June 1727, or an extension of twenty-six years and three months). In addition, the present lease excluded a passage in the lower storey for Mr French to access his house to the rear (see *Lease 15*); this reservation ran for six years. Herbert had paid French 50s. to purchase this right of access; hence, the new lease also included the passageway.

Lease 3: Garteret Southwood. Southwood, the relict and widow of Robert Southwood, held a tenement in St Thomas's parish. The tenement was blown up. The annual rent for the present lease was 40s. plus 4s. for tithe, and the lease expired on the feast of the Annunciation of the Blessed Virgin Mary 1693. Southwood received a new lease at the same rent of 40s. plus 4s. for tithe, with a term of forty years from Midsummer 1676 (i.e., until 24 June 1716, or an extension of twenty-three years and three months).

Lease 4: John Reeve. Reeve's tenement in St Thomas's parish adjoined Farding's property (see *Lease 1*). It was blown up, leaving the property much torn and shattered. The annual rent for the present lease was 40s. plus 4s. for tithe, and the lease expired at Michaelmas 1690. In consideration of the damage done, Reeve received a new lease at the same rent of 40s. plus 4s. for tithe, with a term of twenty-four years from Michaelmas 1676 (i.e., until 29 September 1700, or an extension of ten years).

Lease 5: Thomas Launce. Launce's tenement in St Thomas's parish burned down. The annual rent for the present lease was 40s. plus 4s. for tithe, and the lease expired at Christmas 1695. In consideration of rebuilding the tenement with a brick wall on the west side within one year, Launce received a new lease at the same annual rent of 40s. plus 4s. for tithe, with a term of forty-one years from Michaelmas 1676 (i.e., until 29 September 1717, or an extension of twenty-one years and nine months).

Lease 6: James Johnson. Johnson held three or four tenements in the churchyard of St Thomas's parish. The annual rent was £4.4s., and the lease expired at Midsummer 1683. The houses suffered damage in the fire. The committee viewed the properties and found that Johnson was repairing them. Johnson was ancient and poor. Johnson's rent was remitted for three years, computed from Christmas 1675 (which is the last rent that Johnson had paid); the same would be done for the next lease when it was renewed in the usual course. In addition, Johnson would not need to pay the fine that would be ordinarily be merited on renewal.

Lease 7: Eliza Grove. Grove was a tenant in a messuage on the High Street and over the passage or gateway leading into St Thomas's parish. She also held another messuage adjoining the first. Both were demolished in the fire. The annual rent was £15 6s. 8d., and the lease expired at Michaelmas 1689. As a condition of rebuilding the messuage, Grove was required to leave the gateway eleven feet high and ten-and-one-half feet wide at the High Street. She was also required to use such scantlings and materials of timber (or better) as Parliament's act for the rebuilding of London prescribed for buildings in streets or lanes of note.[5] Finally, she was required to run a raing line [gutter] from the north side to the south-west corner of the tenement near adjoining in the tenure of [ ][6] and from the High Street on the south side of the gateway to run in a range to the south-west corner of the doorway of Mrs Sara Phillipps (see *Lease 25*). In consideration of this building, Grove received a new lease at the same annual rent of £15 6s. 8d., with a term of forty-one years from Michaelmas 1676 (i.e., until 29 September 1717, or an extension of twenty-eight years). The committee left to the Governors' decision whether to remit the £50 unpaid residue of the fine that Grove had agreed to pay at the last renewal of the lease.

On 16 November 1677, Grove petitioned the Governors for remittance of the fine. The petition recited that, eight years before the fire, she had spent a great sum to substantially rebuild the messuage. To

---

5 This phrase described the third rate of building under the Rebuilding Act.
6 At this point the name 'Dennis Herbert' (see *Lease 2*) was struck through and a blank space left after Herbert's name, likely to insert the name of a different tenant.

obtain an additional term of years in the property, Grove had agreed to pay a £150 fine in instalments, of which £100 had already been paid. The house burned down less than one year into the additional term. The Governors remitted the £50 residue of the fine. In addition, Grove held as a tenant two small tenements with gardens in St Thomas's parish, with the lease expiring at Christmas 1685. In view of her losses, the Governors ordered that Grove be granted a new lease for the tenements at the present rent (which was unspecified), with a term of twenty-one years from Christmas 1677 (i.e., until 25 December 1698, or an extension of fourteen years).[7]

Lease 8: William Bromsall. Bromsall was a tenant of a messuage in the High Street. After viewing it, the committee found that it was damaged when houses near it were blown up. The cost of repair was about £35. The committee did not think that this level of damage required the Governors to grant an additional term of years. Rather, Bromsall's petition and his expense in repairing the messuage would be noted in the court book of the Hospital, so that the expense might be considered when the lease was renewed in its ordinary course.

Lease 9: James Pittman. Pittman was a tenant of a messuage in the High Street that adjoined the west end of the hospital.[8] After viewing the premises, the committee determined that the house was damaged when houses near it were blown up. It would likely cost between £40 and £50 to repair the house. The committee did not believe that this damage served as a ground to grant an additional term of years. Rather, Pittman's petition and his expense in repairing the messuage would be noted in the court book of the Hospital, so that the expense might be considered when the lease was renewed in its ordinary course.

In a report on 8 July 1681 concerning the best way to recompense the Hospital's tenants who were affected by the encroachment decree,[9] a committee appointed by the Governors noted that Pittman held a twenty-one-year lease, due to expire on the feast of the Annunciation of the Blessed Virgin Mary 1690, at an annual rent of £8, for which Pittman had also paid a £220 fine. The committee, which included Reading and How, acknowledged that Pittman deserved compensation because some of his lower storey had been taken away as a result of

---

7 *Minute Books, 1619–77*, fol. 178 (16 November 1677).

8 Because St Thomas's Hospital was north of the gateway, this description put Pittman's house on the north side of the gateway into the Hospital.

9 Decree 45.

the encroachment decree, but it noted that Pittman could not be given any land behind the house due to the existing porter's lodge and the pillars of the Hospital. The report noted, however, that Pittman had been given some land appropriated from the wards of the Hospital as a means to enlarge his property.[10]

Pittman negotiated a new lease on 11 November 1681. In return for a fine of £100 to be paid by the feast of the Annunciation of the Blessed Virgin Mary 1682, and at the existing annual rent of £8, Pittman was granted a new lease for forty-one years from the feast of the Annunciation of the Blessed Virgin Mary 1682 (i.e., until 25 March 1723, or an extension of thirty-three years). Pittman agreed to build a new house on the plot north of Bartlett (see *Lease 10*) according to the second rate of new buildings in London. In addition, he was to build a wall two bricks thick, all the way to the top, between his house and the Hospital and to repair any damage to the Hospital due to the construction.[11] The Hospital retained the liberty to lay timbers against the wall next to the Hospital.

Lease 10: Henry Bartelett. Bartlett[12] was a tenant of a messuage in the High Street adjoining the north side of the fore yard of Hospital. After viewing the house, the committee determined that the house was much shattered and damaged when houses near it were blown up. It would likely cost around £30 to repair it. The committee did not believe that this damage served as a ground to grant an additional term of years. Rather, Bartlett's petition and his expense in repairing the messuage would be noted in the court book of the Hospital, so that the expense might be considered when the lease was renewed in its ordinary course.

The Southwark fire court's principal encroachment decree stated that Bartlett's property, which was next to the doorway into St Thomas's Hospital, was then in the possession of Richard Dingle. The property encroached four feet into the High Street.[13] The Hospital eventually agreed to compensate Bartlett for the loss. On 8 July 1681, a committee

---

10   *Minute Books, 1678–1735*, fols 18ᵛ–19 (8 July 1681).

11   Ibid, fol. 21 (11 November 1681).

12   Bartelett is likely the 'Henry Bartlett' who was described as either a Salter or a Grocer in the decrees of the Southwark fire court. He was a subtenant in *Duffeild v. Smith* (Decree 31), above and a Browker creditor in *Sledd v. Browker* (Decree 47), above. Bartlett was also among the multitude of High Street defendants in the principal encroachment case (Decree 45), although he did not make an appearance in the case. I render his name as 'Bartlett' throughout.

13   Decree 45.

report to the Governors noted that Bartlett was the tenant of a house 'next the said Gate Northward' (i.e., on the north side of the Hospital gate). At that time, Bartlett held a twenty-one-year lease that expired at Michaelmas 1689, at an annual rent of £4, for which Bartlett had paid a fine of £88. The committee reported that Bartlett's house was only nine feet wide, and that Bartlett could not be given any land to the rear because of the porter's lodge and Hospital's pillars. It proposed to add about three feet to the width of the house at the front and four feet at the rear by giving Bartlett some of the ground on the north side of the inner gate. The report thought that this transfer would be advantageous, for it would straighten the gateway and would not narrow the prospect into the Hospital's first entrance. The gateway would still be about eight feet in breadth, the tenement would be improved and the cost of adorning and rendering the gate more conspicuous (which had long been desired) would be borne by Bartlett.[14]

A subsequent report stated that Bartlett, 'our Tennant of the late house next and over the gate', had surrendered the former lease, which had eight years to run from Michaelmas 1681, and had taken a new lease on the reconfigured plot of ground, with an agreement to build a messuage according to the second rate of houses new built in London. Bartlett was to build the back wall adjoining the Hospital two bricks thick all the way to the top, to build a brick wall the thickness of a party wall between the gateway and the house, and to make any repairs to the Hospital occasioned by his construction. The new lease gave Bartlett possession of the new house and two rooms that were to be erected over the gateway at the Hospital's charge. The Hospital reserved the right to lay timbers against the wall for an intended porter's lodge. The annual rent was £6 from the feast of the Annunciation of the Blessed Virgin Mary 1682, with the present rent of £4 payable until that time. The lease ran for forty-one years from the feast of the Annunciation of the Blessed Virgin Mary 1682 (i.e., until the feast of the Annunciation of the Blessed Virgin Mary 1723, or an extension of thirty-three years and six months). Bartlett also paid a £150 fine for this lease.[15]

The same report recited that Bartlett had previously purchased the leaseholds for the two plots that lay north of Pittman's house from John Wood and Thomas Middleton, both of whose leaseholds had been severely cut back in the encroachment decree. Previously the committee had proposed extending both properties to the rear by

14 *Minute Books, 1678–1735*, fols 18–18ᵛ (8 July 1681).
15 Ibid, fol. 20 (11 November 1681).

appropriating two wards of the Hospital for the leased land. Doing so would make each property roughly eighteen feet square, and would allow construction of two tenements at a cost of £300 apiece. The committee thought that this approach would make the Hospital safer from fire, and room for the twelve beds lost from the reappropriated wards could be found elsewhere in the Hospital.[16]

On 11 November 1681, in return for surrender of these leases and an agreement to build two tenements at the second rate of building in London, with a two-brick-thick back wall and an undertaking to repair any damage to the Hospital from construction, Bartlett received forty-one-year leases for these two properties from the feast of the Annunciation of the Blessed Virgin Mary 1682. Bartlett also paid a £130 fine for the new leases.[17]

Lease 11: Thomas Hollier. Hollier held a messuage in the High Street contiguous to the south side of the gate into the Hospital. The house was blown up before the fire was near it in order to prevent its spread. The annual rent for the present lease was £5, and the lease expired on the feast of the Annunciation of the Blessed Virgin Mary 1690. Hollier was desirous to rebuild, and wished as encouragement both an extension of the lease term and the possession of a piece of the Hospital known as Jonah's Ward, which lay under Hollier's yard. The committee noted that, if Hollier were not given the land he requested, there would be no brick wall between his premises and the Hospital, and a timber wall might pose a danger to the Hospital in the event of a future fire — given that the chief danger to the Hospital from the Southwark fire was the prospect that fire would enter the Hospital grounds through Hollier's property. Hollier agreed to build a new messuage on the ground according to the third rate of buildings in London and to divide the ground in Jonah's Ward granted him from the Hospital with a substantial brick wall from the bottom to the top of the property. The wall was to be made uniform with the ward, with plastering and painting ('whiting') done on the Ward's side of the wall. In addition, the ground was not to be dug out any deeper than it presently was, on penalty of forfeiture of the lease. In return for this agreement, Hollier received a new lease at the annual rent of £4, with a term of forty-one years from Christmas 1676 (i.e., until 25 December 1717, or an extension of twenty-seven years and nine months). Hollier also agreed to pay a fine of £20 at Christmas 1676.

16   Ibid, fol. 19 (8 July 1681).
17   Ibid., fol. 21.

Lease 12: John Winnington. Winnington was a tenant in St Thomas's parish. His tenement had been consumed in the fire. The annual rent for the present lease was 40s. plus 4s. for tithe, and the lease expired on the feast of the Annunciation of the Blessed Virgin Mary 1689. The committee ordered that some of the ground at the front of Winnington's property be taken away to make the south side of the gate more uniform[18] and that Winnington be given a lease of the remaining ground. Winnington agreed to build a new messuage or tenement of brick according to the second rate of new buildings in London. Winnington received a new lease at the same annual rent of 40s. plus 4s. for tithe, with a term of fifty-one years from Michaelmas 1676 (i.e., until 29 September 1727, or an extension of thirty-eight years and six months).

Lease 13: John Gibbons. Gibbons petitioned to build a tenement in the High Street. The previous tenement burned down in the fire. The annual rent for the present lease was £6, and the lease expired on the feast of the Annunciation of the Blessed Virgin Mary 1691. In return for new building a tenement with materials and scantlings as required for new buildings of the second rate in London, Gibbons received a new lease at the same annual rent of £6, with a term of thirty-eight years from Christmas 1676 (i.e., until 25 December 1714, or an extension of twenty-three years and nine months).

Lease 14: Richard Southern. Southern was a tenant in a small tenement in the churchyard of St Thomas's parish. The tenement was blown up. The annual rent for the present lease was 40s.[19] Southern had spent £30 in repairs in the expectation of taking a longer term at the present rent. Southern also wished to lease two adjoining tenements, lately in the possession of William Westfeild and Penelope Young, each of which was rented for 50s. without any fine. Southern was willing to repair the damage that these properties had suffered. After viewing the properties, the committee estimated that these repairs would cost at least £20. Westfeild and Young were poor and in arrears for their rent. Since they could not pay their rent, they were unlikely to be able to repair their houses. Southern was given a new lease of his premises and the other two tenements. The annual rent was £3 10s., with a term of thirty-one years from Michaelmas 1676. In addition, the arrears of Westfeild and Young were discharged out of the same account for the future.

18   This is how I interpret the phrase 'taking away soe much in the front as that it may ranige with the Southside of the gate'. Winnington's tenement may have jutted into the street.

19   The report did not provide the term of the lease.

Lease 15: William French. French held leases on an unspecified number of houses in the High Street. The fire destroyed the houses. The annual rent for the present lease was £12 13s. 4d., and the lease expired at Michaelmas 1682. In return for a fine of £200 — half payable at Christmas 1676 and half at Midsummer 1677 — and an agreement to build two or more houses according to the second or third rate of building in London, French was given a new lease at the same annual rent of £12 13s. 4d., with a term of thirty-seven years from Michaelmas 1676 (i.e., until 29 September 1713, or an extension of thirty-one years). Excepted from the new lease was a portion of the present ground that French had agreed to give John Freeman (see *Lease 18*) and the passageway through the tenement lately in the tenure of Dennis Herbert that French had sold to Herbert (see *Lease 2*).

Lease 16: Elizabeth Diaper. Diaper held a small tenement in the churchyard of St Thomas's parish. The tenement was very much damaged in the fire. Diaper was poor and had recently paid the Hospital a fine of £28. The present annual rent was 40s. plus 4s. for tithe, and the lease expired in nineteen years.[20] In consideration of the expense of repairs, Diaper was granted a new lease at the same rent of 40s. plus 4s. for tithe, with a term of twenty-nine years commencing at Michaelmas 1676 (i.e., until 29 September 1705, or an extension of ten years).

Lease 17: Thomas Hatchett. Hatchett held several small tenements in St Thomas's parish as an undertenant of [ ].[21] After viewing the properties, the committee reported that some of the tenements were so far demolished by the fire that they required rebuilding, and another building, which was a brewhouse, was much damaged. The annual rent for the present lease was £21 6s., and the lease expired on the feast of the Annunciation of the Blessed Virgin Mary 1703. In consideration of the cost of repairing the brewhouse and of rebuilding the shattered tenements with brick according the second rate of new building in London, Hatchett received a new lease at the present annual rent of £21 6s., with a term of forty-one years from Michaelmas 1676 (i.e., until 29 September 1717, or an extension of fourteen years and six months).

---

20 The report did not specify the holy day on which the lease expired. Given the report's proximity to Michaelmas, I assume that the lease expired at Michaelmas 1695.

21 A blank space was left where the name would have gone.

Lease 18: John Freeman, Esquire. Freeman[22] held a tenement in the High Street. It burned down in the fire. The annual rent for the present lease was £3, and the lease expired at Midsummer 1695. In consideration of his rebuilding the tenement according to the second rate for new building in London, Freeman received a new lease at the same annual rent of £3, with a term of twenty-two years commencing at the end of the present lease (i.e., until 24 June 1717, or an extension of twenty-two years). In the alternative, Freeman could surrender his present lease and receive a new lease of forty-one years at the present rent.

Lease 19: William Gabb and Thomas Bartholomew. Gabb was the present inhabitant of a tenement in St Thomas's parish, which sat on one parcel of two tenements lately held by Widow Read. On payment of £20 fine (payable £5 in hand and then £5 at six-month intervals), Gabb received a lease of the tenement for twenty-one years from Midsummer 1676 (i.e., until 24 June 1697) at the yearly rent of 40s. plus 4s. for tithe. Thomas Bartholomew was to enjoy the other tenement as a tenant at will (i.e., subject to eviction at any time), at the annual rent of 20s. plus 2s. for tithe. Finally, because Widow Read, who was poor, was now dead and her lease was delivered up, her arrears in the accounts were remitted and discharged.

Lease 20: John Glover. Glover held a tenement at the corner of the passage out of St Thomas's parish into the High Street. The tenement was somewhat damaged in the fire. The present lease expired on the feast of the Annunciation of the Blessed Virgin Mary 1680. In consideration of Glover's repairs and a fine of £17 to be paid before sealing the lease, Glover received an additional term of twenty-one years (i.e., until 25 March 1701). The new lease was to be made in the names of John Glover and Alice his wife.

Lease 21: James Scotson and Thomas Scotson. The Scotsons were tenants of eleven tenements in St Thomas's parish. Seven of the tenements were destroyed. The annual rent (and tithe) for the present lease was £11, and the lease expired on the feast of the Annunciation of the Blessed Virgin Mary 1704. The Scotsons had disbursed at least £150 in building new brick houses where all or some of the seven tenements had stood. The Scotsons received a new lease of the tofts of the destroyed tenements at the annual rent of £10 plus 20s. tithe, with a term of fifty-one years

22 Although neither 'John' nor 'Freeman' were uncommon names, it is likely that John Freeman was the judge who gave notable service on the Southwark fire and who also served as a Justice of the Peace for Surrey.

from Michaelmas 1676 (i.e., until 29 September 1727, or an extension of twenty-three years and six months). Excepted from the lease were the ground that they had sold to other tenants and the four tenements still standing.

Lease 22: John Pond. Pond was the tenant of a house in the passage going out of St Thomas's parish into the High Street. The house suffered £14 in damage from the fire. In consideration of the cost of repairs, Pond hoped to have an additional term added to his existing lease, which had nine years to run. The committee thought it fit to defer consideration of Pond's petition until only three years remained before the expiration of the lease.

Lease 23: John Raymer. Raymer lived near Pond. He petitioned for a like consideration in view of £5 in damage he suffered. The lease was presently near its renewal in its ordinary course, and the committee recommended that consideration of Raymer's petition be deferred until renewal.

Lease 24: Thomas Rouse. Rouse[23] held a tenement in the passage going out of St Thomas's parish into the High Street. He alleged that it cost £20 to repair the damage. After viewing the property, the committee thought it fit to defer making any satisfaction until the present lease was renewed in its ordinary course.

Lease 25: Sara Phillipps. This lease was not mentioned in the committee report of 20 September 1676. Rather, at the meeting on 30 May 1677, on the recommendation of the committee, the Governors renewed the lease of Phillips.[24] She was a tenant in a messuage on the High Street, next to the south side of the gate leading into St Thomas's parish. She also held two tenements in the parish, as well as four small tenements. The messuage and two tenements were destroyed in the fire, but the four small tenements were apparently unaffected. All of the properties were held under a single lease. The annual rent for the present lease was £13 6s. 8d., and the lease expired at Midsummer 1692. Phillips agreed

23   Rouse is very likely the 'Thomas Rous, Gentleman', who was the petitioner in *Rous v. Kellett* (Decree 43), where he proposed to be the rebuilder of several properties in Three Crowne Court. Rous was also one of the defendants summoned on behalf of two tenants in the principal encroachment decree (Decree 45), and he was a witness to a payment made to Robert Gale in *Gale v. Wight* (Decree 24).

24   Phillipps is very likely the 'Sarah Phillipps, Widow' (as well as the '[…] Phillips, Widow') who was involved in the principal encroachment decree (Decree 45). I render her name as 'Phillips'.

to surrender the present lease and to build three brick messuages or tenements. She received a lease at the same annual rent of £13 6s. 8d., with a term of forty-one years from Christmas 1676 (i.e., until 25 December 1717, or an extension of twenty-five years and six months). She also paid a fine of 20 marks (£13 6s. 8d.).[25]

INDEX OF PERSONS AND INSTITUTIONS

(Reference is to Decree number)

Adams, Stephen, tenant 34

Aleyn, Thomas (see Allen)

Allen, Richard (no occupation given) 45

Allen, Sir Thomas 1, 2, 16, 17, 23, 24, 25, 30, 32, 33

Alleyn, Thomas (see Allen)

Annis, Lazarus, tenant 49

Appelbe, John (see Appleby)

Appellbe, John (see Appleby)

Appellbee, John (see Appleby)

Applebee, John (see Appleby)

Appleby, John, esquire 1, 2, 3, 4, 5, 6, 7, 8, 9, 10, 11, 12, 13, 14, 15, 16, 17, 18, 19, 20, 21, 22, 23, 24, 25, 26, 27, 28, 29, 30, 31, 32, 33, 34, 35, 36, 40, 41, 42, 43, 44, 45, 47, 48, 49, 50, 51, 52

Arnold, John (no occupation given) 45

Arnold, Urian, Citizen and Poulterer 24

Ascue, Elizabeth, widow 16

Askew, Roger, Citizen and Merchant Taylor 28

Austen, Thomas, Brewer 3

Austin, Charles, tenant 29

Aylmer, Tobell, Citizen and Draper 17

Bacon, John (no occupation given) 45

Badmoring, John (no occupation given) 45

Baggs, Ellen, widow 4

Ballam, Jonadab, Citizen and Grocer 13, 45, 49

Banbury, Francis, Silk weaver 15

Bankes, John, Carpenter 2, 23, 45

Barker, Thomas, esquire 3, 4, 5, 6, 7, 10, 11, 12, 13, 14, 15, 16, 17, 18, 23, 24, 25, 26, 27, 28, 29, 30, 31, 32, 33, 34, 35, 36, 37, 38, 39, 41, 42, 43, 44, 45, 46, 48, 49, 50, 51, 52

Barron, Isabel, wife of Richard 10

Barron, Richard, tenant 10

Barry (no first name given), counsel 22

Bartelett (see Bartlett)

Bartlett, Henry, Grocer 31, 45, 47

Bates, Mathew, Glover 11

Bayley, Awdry, widow 12

Bayley, Lydia (no occupation given) 12

Bayley, Miles, tenant 19

Beacon, Anne, wife of Thomas 3

Beacon, Thomas, Merchant 3

Bedford, Robert, Citizen and Haberdasher 7, 42

Bedford, Sarah, wife of Robert 7, 42

Bend, James (no occupation given) 45

Bennet (see Bennett)

Bennett, William, Merchant 10, 12

INDEX OF PLACES

(Reference is to Decree number)

Angel Yard   8, 11, 13, 15, 50

Bridge Foot   44, 45
Bridge Ward   46

Chain Gate (see also West Chain
   Gate)   48
Compter   32
Compter Lane   2, 23, 44, 45

Duke's Acre   37

Fowl (Fowle or Foule) Lane   8,
   13, 14, 15, 28, 29, 50

High Street (east side)   7, 16, 18,
   31, 34, 35, 39, 45, 47
High Street (unspecified)   5, 8,
   12, 17, 41, 44, 46
High Street (west side)   1, 2, 10,
   24, 28, 29, 36, 45, 52

Inns
   The George   22
   The King's Head   31
   The Queen's Head   7, 42
   The Talbot   19, 30
   The White Hart   27, 39

Kentish Street   37

London Bridge (Bridge
   Foot)   44

Market   28, 44, 45
Meal Market   17
Montague Close   38

Sign of (premises known by the
   sign of)
   The Angel   13
   The Antelope   18, 47
   The Black Boy   20
   Blew Bore   37
   The Bull's Head Tavern   52
   The Castle   33
   The Fleece Tavern   2
   The Lion and Key   1
   The Plough and Harrow   10
   The Red Lion Brewhouse   8
   The Red Lyon Tavern   41
   The Rose and Crown   3
   The Star   40
   The Three Cupps   5
   The Three Horseshoes   18, 47
   The Three Tonnes Tavern   7

St George's Fields   8, 37
St Margaret's Hill   6, 19, 21, 33,
   37, 42
St Saviour's Churchyard   11, 49,
   51

Three Crane Court   27, 28
Three Crown Court   4, 26, 36, 43
Toll Acre   37

West Chain Gate   14, 49
Winchester House   14

283